CASE CLOSED
VOLUME 29

Gosho Aoyama

Case Briefing:

Subject:
Occupation:
Special Skills:
Equipment:

Jimmy Kudo, a.k.a. Conan Edogawa
High School Student/Detective
Analytical thinking and deductive reasoning, Soccer
Bow Tie Voice Transmitter, Super Sneakers,
Homing Glasses, Stretchy Suspenders

The subject is hot on the trail of a pair of suspicious men in black when he is attacked from behind and administered a strange substance which physically transforms him into a first grader. When the subject confides in the eccentric inventor Dr. Agasa, they decide to keep the subject's true identity a secret for the safety of everyone around him. Assuming the new identity of first-grader Conan Edogawa, the subject continues to assist the police force on their most baffling cases. The only problem is that most crime-solving professionals won't take a little kid's advice!

Table of Contents

CONFIDEN

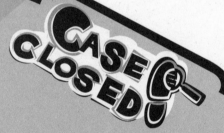

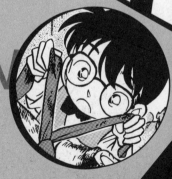

CASE CLOSED
Volume 29
Shonen Sunday Edition

Story and Art by GOSHO AOYAMA

© 1994 Gosho AOYAMA/Shogakukan
All rights reserved.
Original Japanese edition "MEITANTEI CONAN" published by SHOGAKUKAN Inc.

Translation
Tetsuichiro Miyaki

Touch-up & Lettering
Freeman Wong

Cover & Graphic Design
Andrea Rice

Editor
Shaenon K. Garrity

Printed in the U.S.A.

Published by VIZ Media, LLC
P.O. Box 77010
San Francisco, CA 94107

10 9 8 7 6 5 4 3 2
First printing, May 2009
Second printing, May 2011

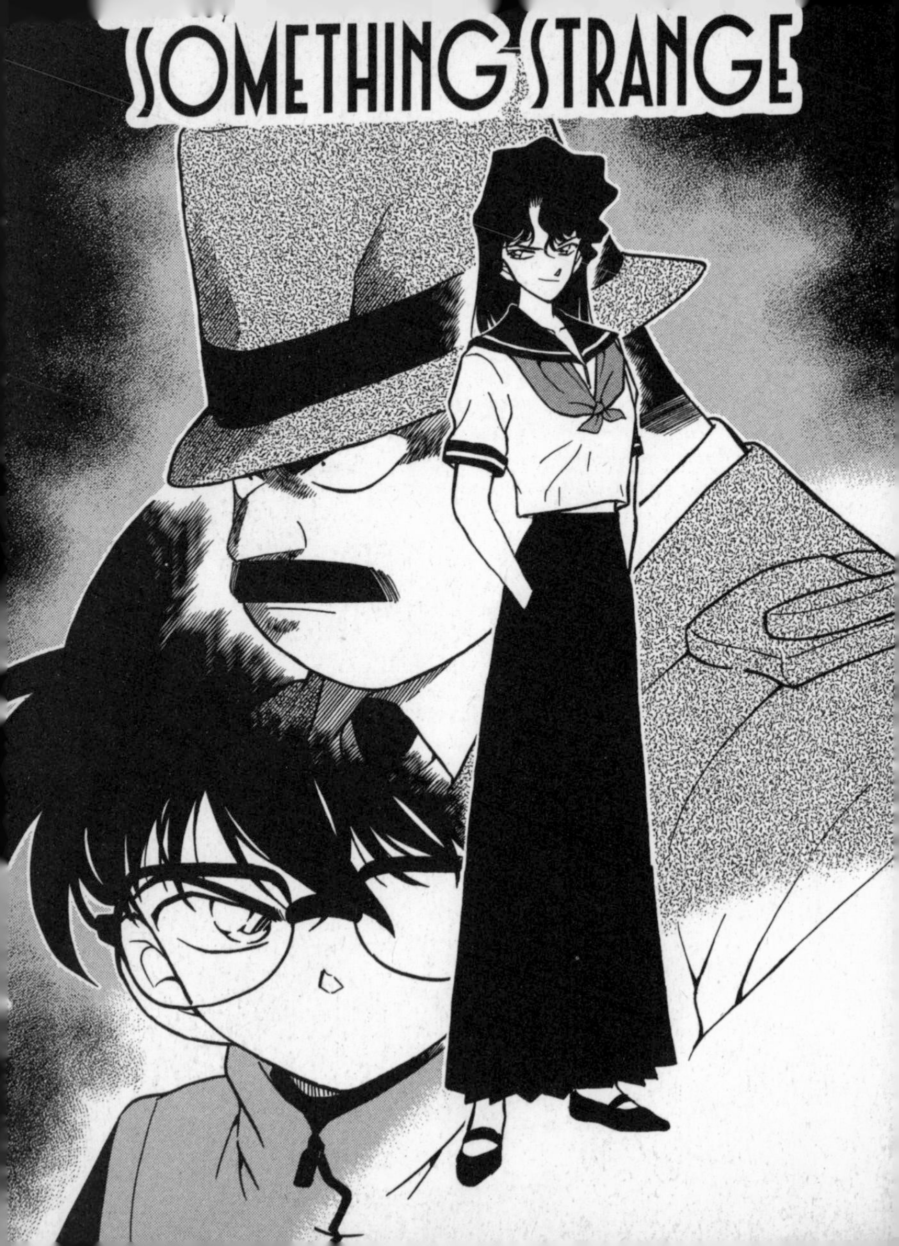
SOMETHING STRANGE

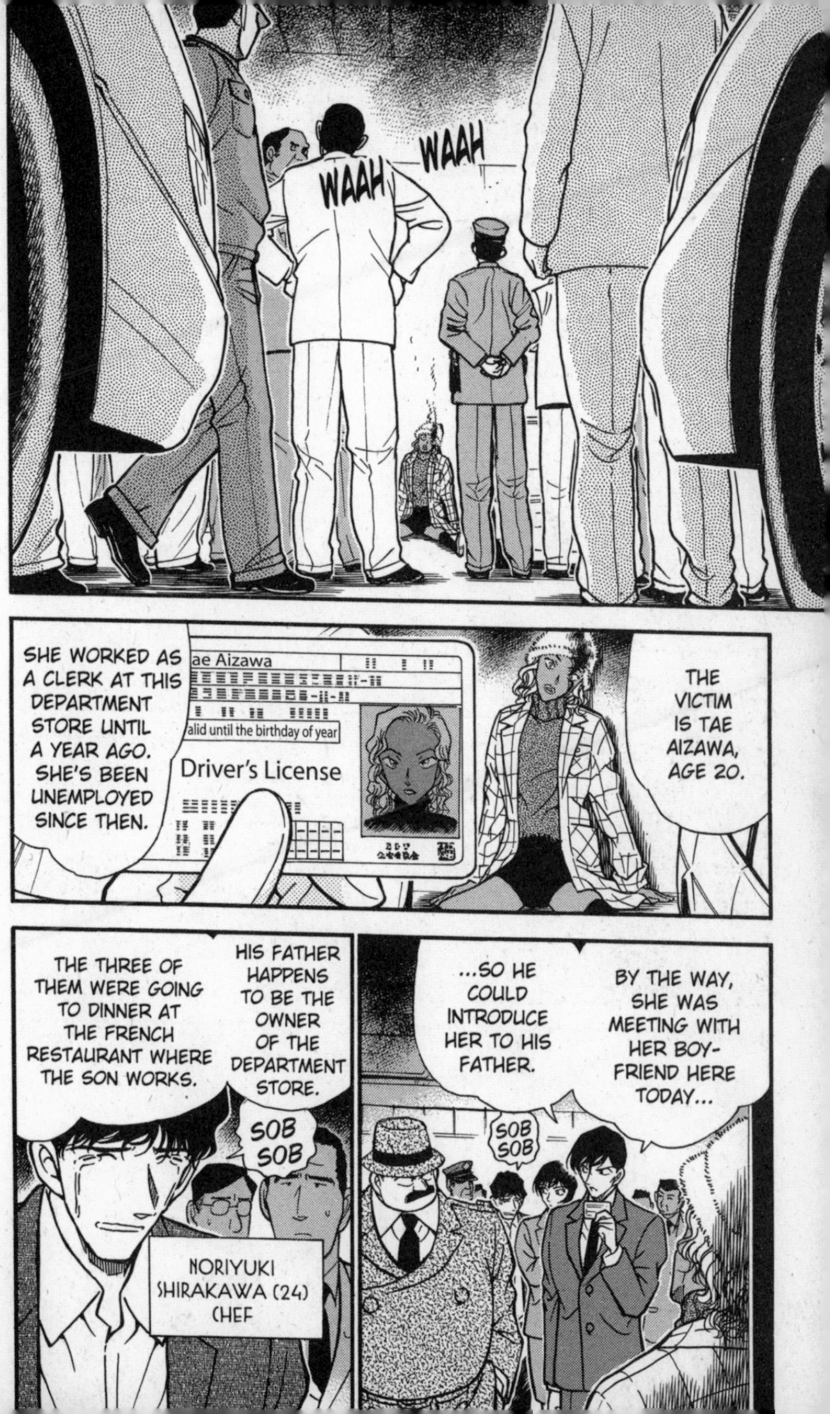
WAAH
WAAH
THE VICTIM IS TAE AIZAWA, AGE 20.
ae Aizawa
alid until the birthday of year
Driver's License
SHE WORKED AS A CLERK AT THIS DEPARTMENT STORE UNTIL A YEAR AGO. SHE'S BEEN UNEMPLOYED SINCE THEN.
BY THE WAY, SHE WAS MEETING WITH HER BOY-FRIEND HERE TODAY...
...SO HE COULD INTRODUCE HER TO HIS FATHER.
SOB SOB
HIS FATHER HAPPENS TO BE THE OWNER OF THE DEPARTMENT STORE.
THE THREE OF THEM WERE GOING TO DINNER AT THE FRENCH RESTAURANT WHERE THE SON WORKS.
SOB SOB
NORIYUKI SHIRAKAWA (24) CHEF

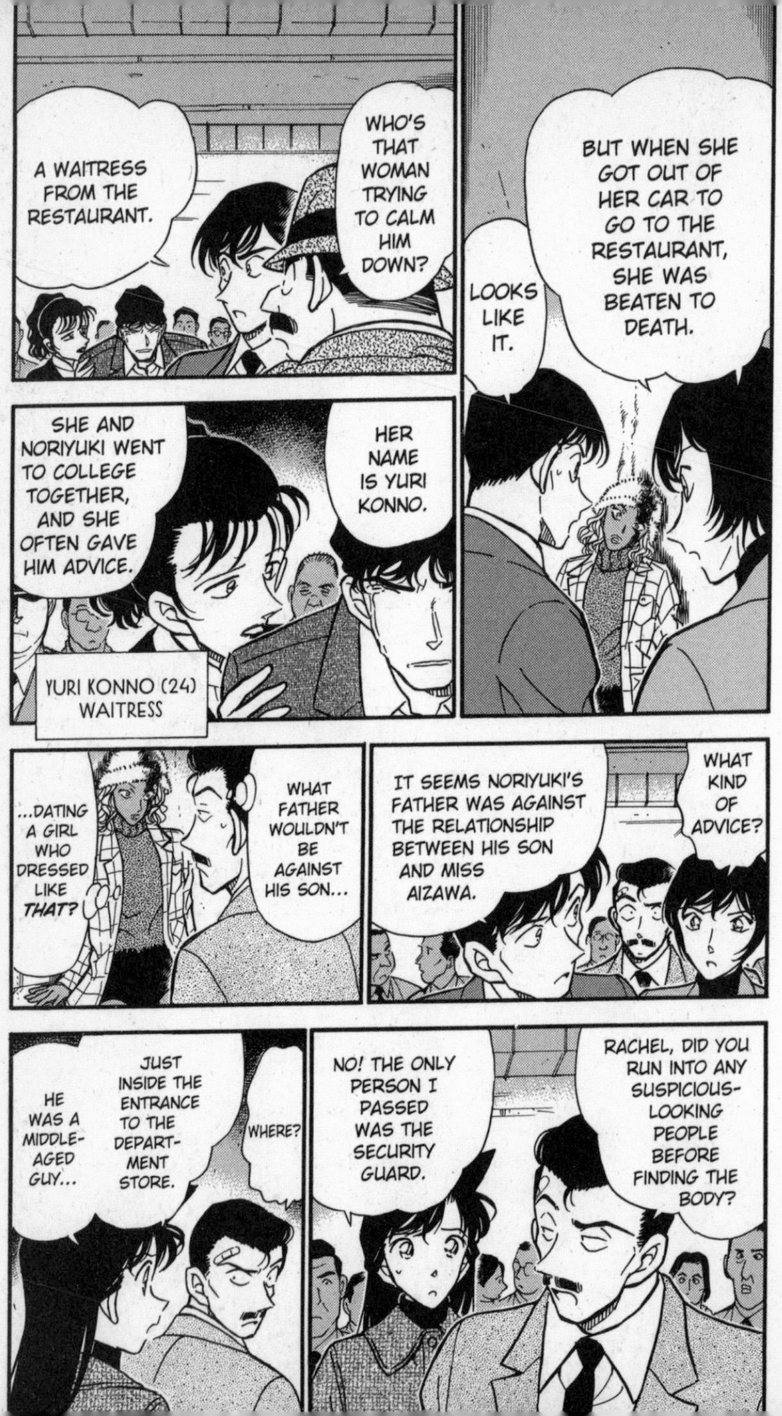
BUT WHEN SHE GOT OUT OF HER CAR TO GO TO THE RESTAURANT, SHE WAS BEATEN TO DEATH.
LOOKS LIKE IT.
WHO'S THAT WOMAN TRYING TO CALM HIM DOWN?
A WAITRESS FROM THE RESTAURANT.
HER NAME IS YURI KONNO.
SHE AND NORIYUKI WENT TO COLLEGE TOGETHER, AND SHE OFTEN GAVE HIM ADVICE.
YURI KONNO (24) WAITRESS
WHAT KIND OF ADVICE?
IT SEEMS NORIYUKI'S FATHER WAS AGAINST THE RELATIONSHIP BETWEEN HIS SON AND MISS AIZAWA.
WHAT FATHER WOULDN'T BE AGAINST HIS SON...
...DATING A GIRL WHO DRESSED LIKE *THAT?*
RACHEL, DID YOU RUN INTO ANY SUSPICIOUS-LOOKING PEOPLE BEFORE FINDING THE BODY?
NO! THE ONLY PERSON I PASSED WAS THE SECURITY GUARD.
WHERE?
JUST INSIDE THE ENTRANCE TO THE DEPART-MENT STORE.
HE WAS A MIDDLE-AGED GUY...

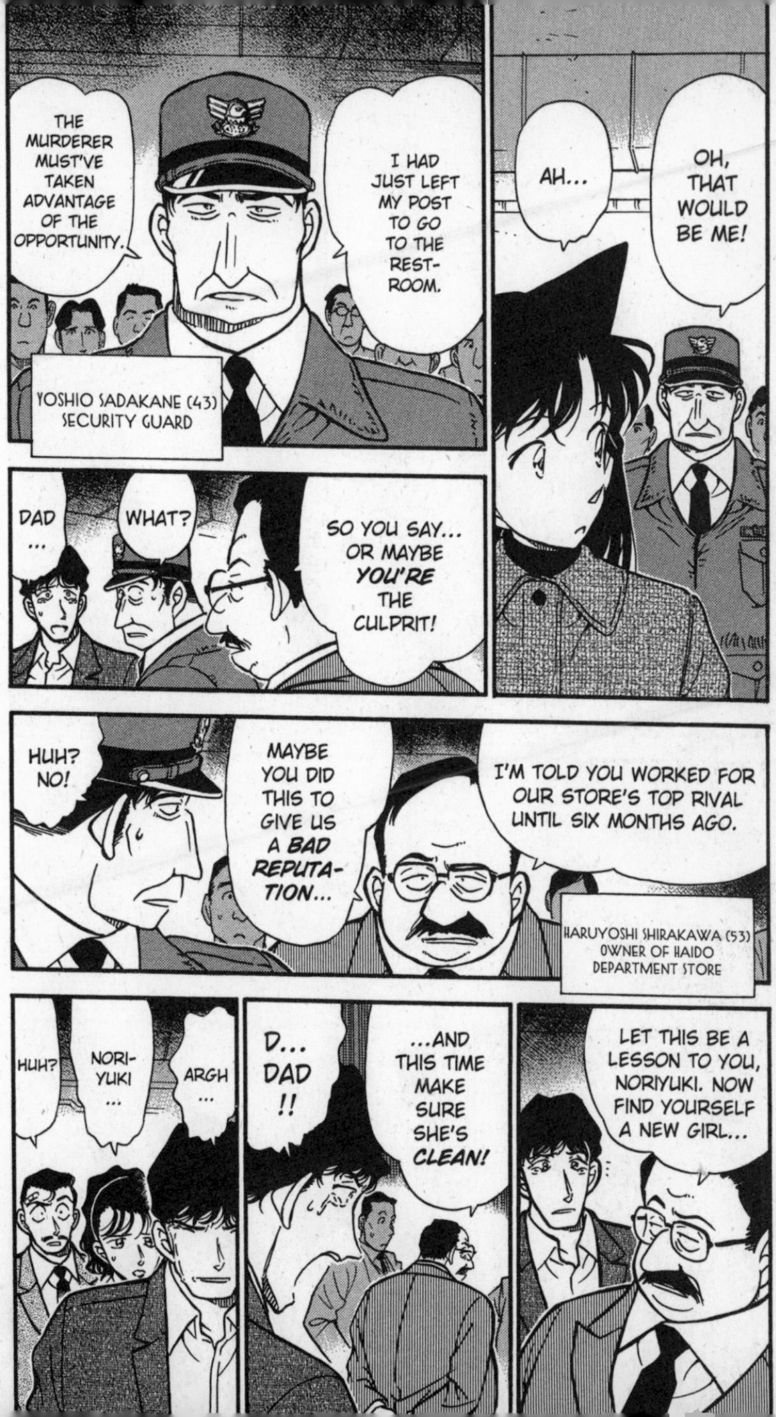
OH, THAT WOULD BE ME!
AH...
I HAD JUST LEFT MY POST TO GO TO THE REST-ROOM.
THE MURDERER MUST'VE TAKEN ADVANTAGE OF THE OPPORTUNITY.
YOSHIO SADAKANE (43) SECURITY GUARD
SO YOU SAY... OR MAYBE *YOU'RE* THE CULPRIT!
WHAT?
DAD ...
I'M TOLD YOU WORKED FOR OUR STORE'S TOP RIVAL UNTIL SIX MONTHS AGO.
HARUYOSHI SHIRAKAWA (53) OWNER OF HAIDO DEPARTMENT STORE
MAYBE YOU DID THIS TO GIVE US A *BAD REPUTATION*...
HUH? NO!
LET THIS BE A LESSON TO YOU, NORIYUKI. NOW FIND YOURSELF A NEW GIRL...
...AND THIS TIME MAKE SURE SHE'S *CLEAN!*
D... DAD !!
ARGH ...
NORI-YUKI ...
HUH?

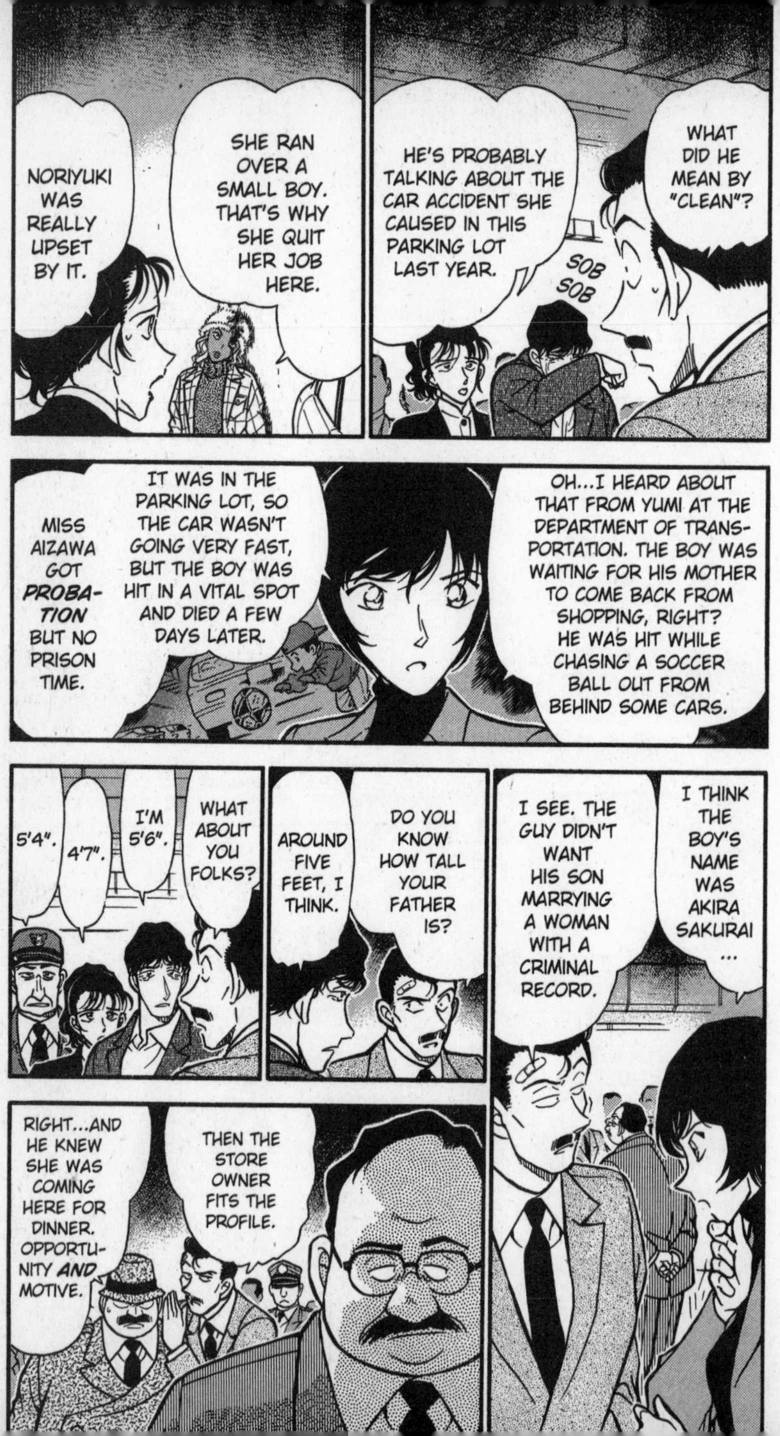
WHAT DID HE MEAN BY "CLEAN"?
HE'S PROBABLY TALKING ABOUT THE CAR ACCIDENT SHE CAUSED IN THIS PARKING LOT LAST YEAR.
SOB SOB
SHE RAN OVER A SMALL BOY. THAT'S WHY SHE QUIT HER JOB HERE.
NORIYUKI WAS REALLY UPSET BY IT.
OH...I HEARD ABOUT THAT FROM YUMI AT THE DEPARTMENT OF TRANS-PORTATION. THE BOY WAS WAITING FOR HIS MOTHER TO COME BACK FROM SHOPPING, RIGHT? HE WAS HIT WHILE CHASING A SOCCER BALL OUT FROM BEHIND SOME CARS.
IT WAS IN THE PARKING LOT, SO THE CAR WASN'T GOING VERY FAST, BUT THE BOY WAS HIT IN A VITAL SPOT AND DIED A FEW DAYS LATER.
MISS AIZAWA GOT ***PROBA-TION*** BUT NO PRISON TIME.
I THINK THE BOY'S NAME WAS AKIRA SAKURAI...
I SEE. THE GUY DIDN'T WANT HIS SON MARRYING A WOMAN WITH A CRIMINAL RECORD.
DO YOU KNOW HOW TALL YOUR FATHER IS?
AROUND FIVE FEET, I THINK.
WHAT ABOUT YOU FOLKS?
I'M 5'6".
4'7".
5'4".
THEN THE STORE OWNER FITS THE PROFILE.
RIGHT...AND HE KNEW SHE WAS COMING HERE FOR DINNER. OPPORTU-NITY ***AND*** MOTIVE.

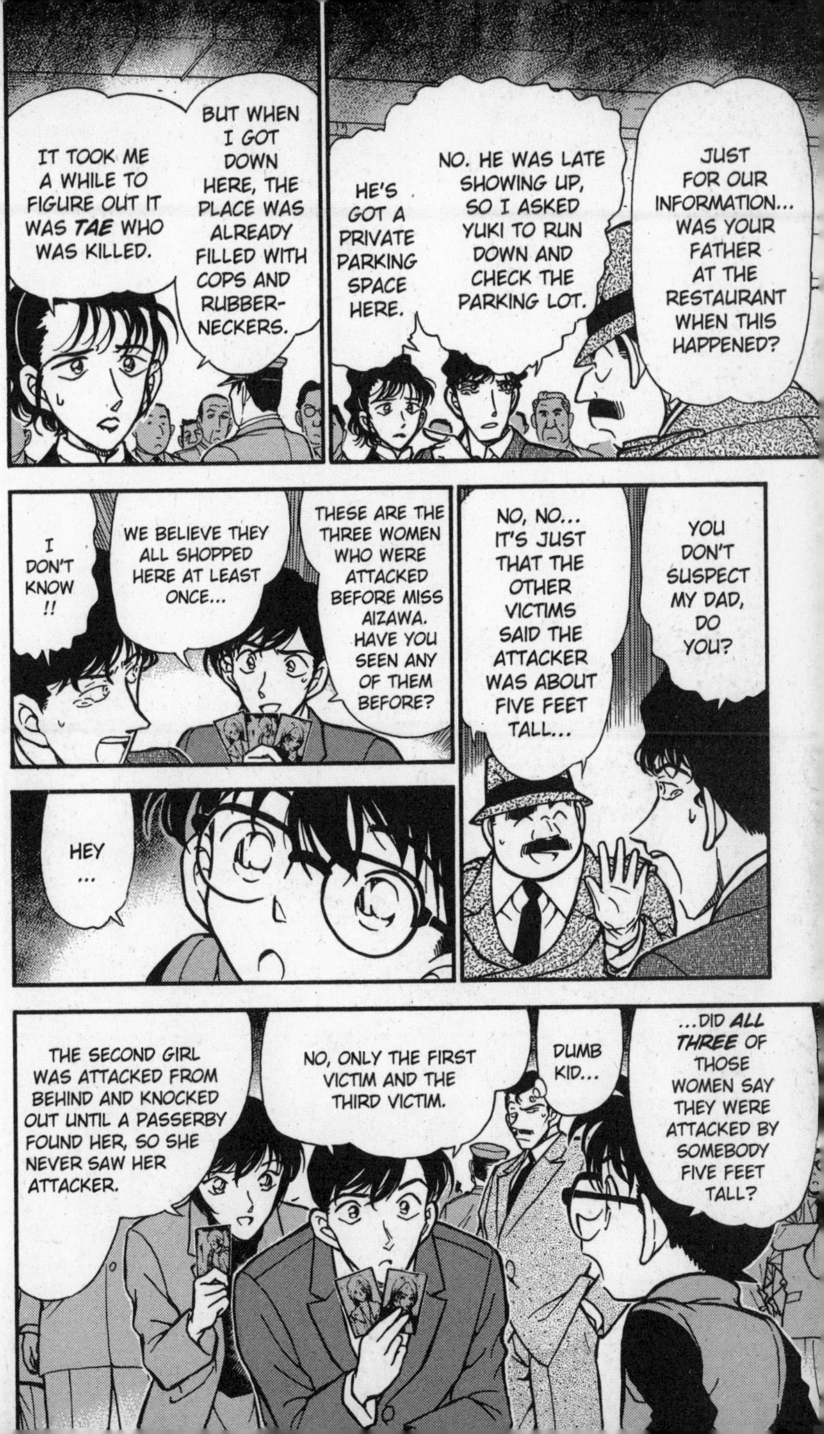
JUST FOR OUR INFORMATION... WAS YOUR FATHER AT THE RESTAURANT WHEN THIS HAPPENED?
NO. HE WAS LATE SHOWING UP, SO I ASKED YUKI TO RUN DOWN AND CHECK THE PARKING LOT.
HE'S GOT A PRIVATE PARKING SPACE HERE.
BUT WHEN I GOT DOWN HERE, THE PLACE WAS ALREADY FILLED WITH COPS AND RUBBER-NECKERS.
IT TOOK ME A WHILE TO FIGURE OUT IT WAS *TAE* WHO WAS KILLED.
YOU DON'T SUSPECT MY DAD, DO YOU?
NO, NO... IT'S JUST THAT THE OTHER VICTIMS SAID THE ATTACKER WAS ABOUT FIVE FEET TALL...
THESE ARE THE THREE WOMEN WHO WERE ATTACKED BEFORE MISS AIZAWA. HAVE YOU SEEN ANY OF THEM BEFORE?
WE BELIEVE THEY ALL SHOPPED HERE AT LEAST ONCE...
I DON'T KNOW !!
HEY ...
...DID ***ALL THREE*** OF THOSE WOMEN SAY THEY WERE ATTACKED BY SOMEBODY FIVE FEET TALL?
DUMB KID...
NO, ONLY THE FIRST VICTIM AND THE THIRD VICTIM.
THE SECOND GIRL WAS ATTACKED FROM BEHIND AND KNOCKED OUT UNTIL A PASSERBY FOUND HER, SO SHE NEVER SAW HER ATTACKER.

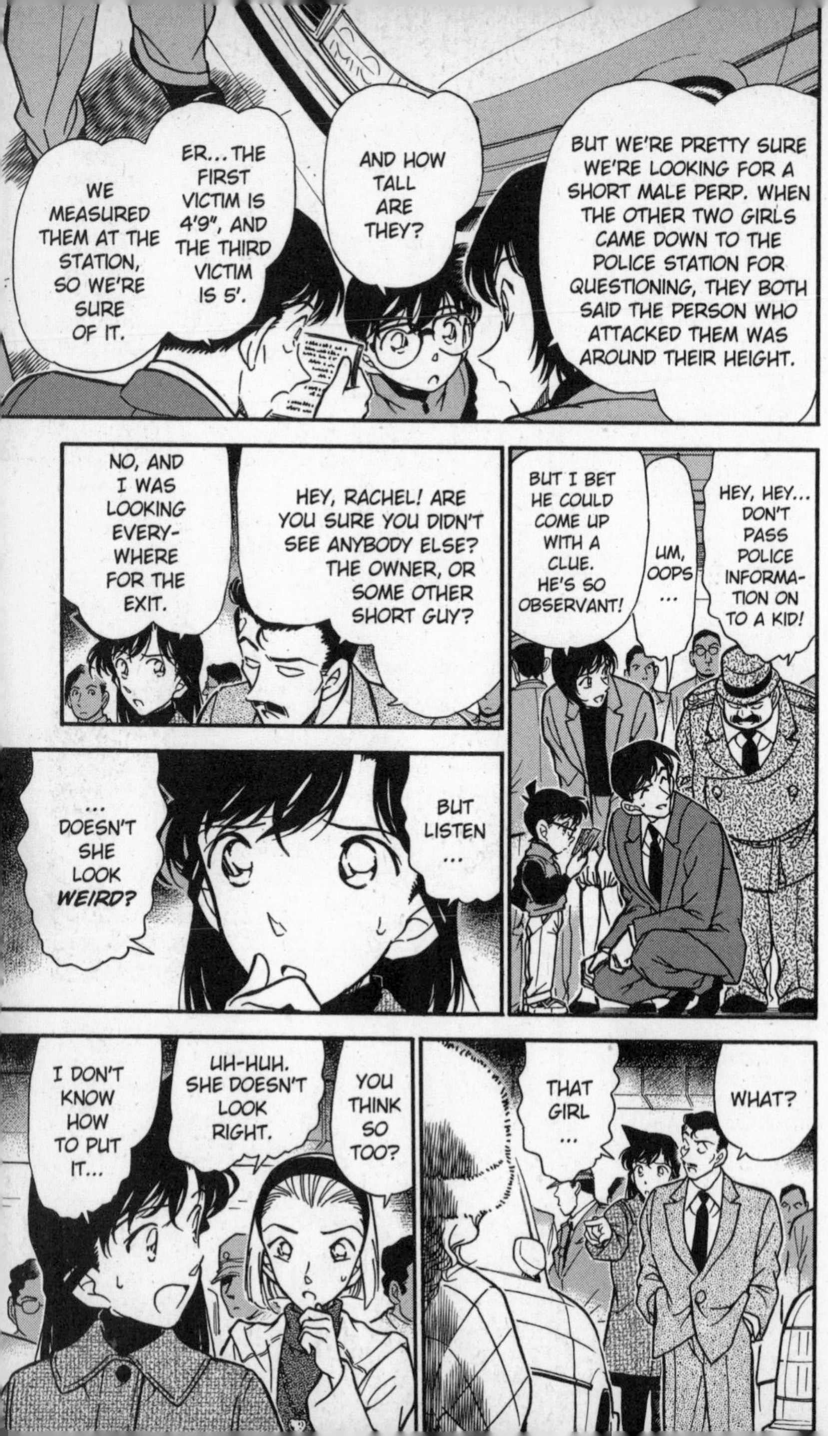
BUT WE'RE PRETTY SURE WE'RE LOOKING FOR A SHORT MALE PERP. WHEN THE OTHER TWO GIRLS CAME DOWN TO THE POLICE STATION FOR QUESTIONING, THEY BOTH SAID THE PERSON WHO ATTACKED THEM WAS AROUND THEIR HEIGHT.
AND HOW TALL ARE THEY?
ER... THE FIRST VICTIM IS 4'9", AND THE THIRD VICTIM IS 5'.
WE MEASURED THEM AT THE STATION, SO WE'RE SURE OF IT.
HEY, HEY... DON'T PASS POLICE INFORMATION ON TO A KID!
UM, OOPS...
BUT I BET HE COULD COME UP WITH A CLUE. HE'S SO OBSERVANT!
HEY, RACHEL! ARE YOU SURE YOU DIDN'T SEE ANYBODY ELSE? THE OWNER, OR SOME OTHER SHORT GUY?
NO, AND I WAS LOOKING EVERY-WHERE FOR THE EXIT.
BUT LISTEN...
...DOESN'T SHE LOOK *WEIRD?*
WHAT?
THAT GIRL...
YOU THINK SO TOO?
UH-HUH. SHE DOESN'T LOOK RIGHT.
I DON'T KNOW HOW TO PUT IT...

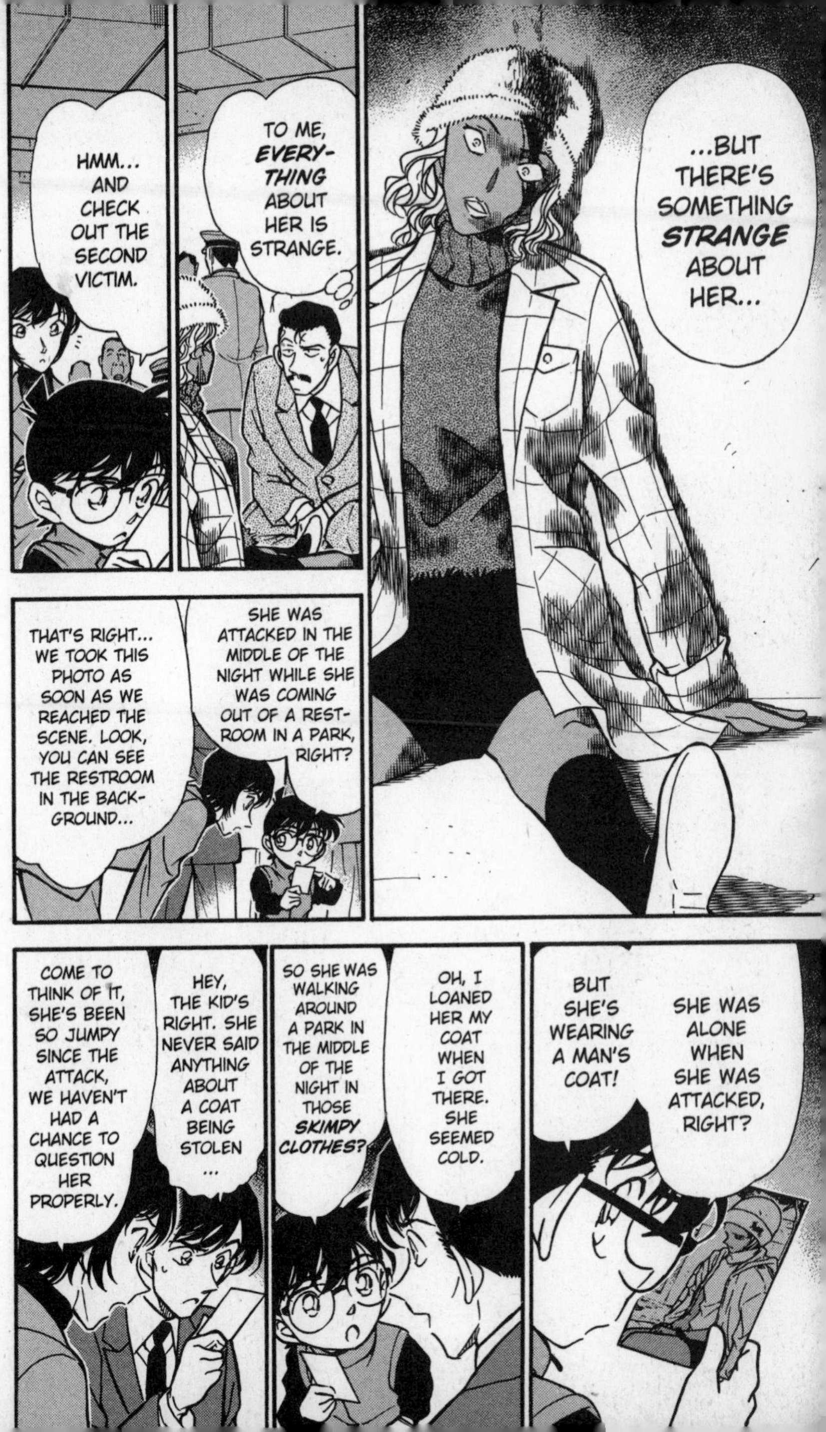
...BUT THERE'S SOMETHING STRANGE ABOUT HER...
TO ME, EVERYTHING ABOUT HER IS STRANGE.
HMM... AND CHECK OUT THE SECOND VICTIM.
SHE WAS ATTACKED IN THE MIDDLE OF THE NIGHT WHILE SHE WAS COMING OUT OF A RESTROOM IN A PARK, RIGHT?
THAT'S RIGHT... WE TOOK THIS PHOTO AS SOON AS WE REACHED THE SCENE. LOOK, YOU CAN SEE THE RESTROOM IN THE BACKGROUND...
SHE WAS ALONE WHEN SHE WAS ATTACKED, RIGHT?
BUT SHE'S WEARING A MAN'S COAT!
OH, I LOANED HER MY COAT WHEN I GOT THERE. SHE SEEMED COLD.
SO SHE WAS WALKING AROUND A PARK IN THE MIDDLE OF THE NIGHT IN THOSE SKIMPY CLOTHES?
HEY, THE KID'S RIGHT. SHE NEVER SAID ANYTHING ABOUT A COAT BEING STOLEN...
COME TO THINK OF IT, SHE'S BEEN SO JUMPY SINCE THE ATTACK, WE HAVEN'T HAD A CHANCE TO QUESTION HER PROPERLY.

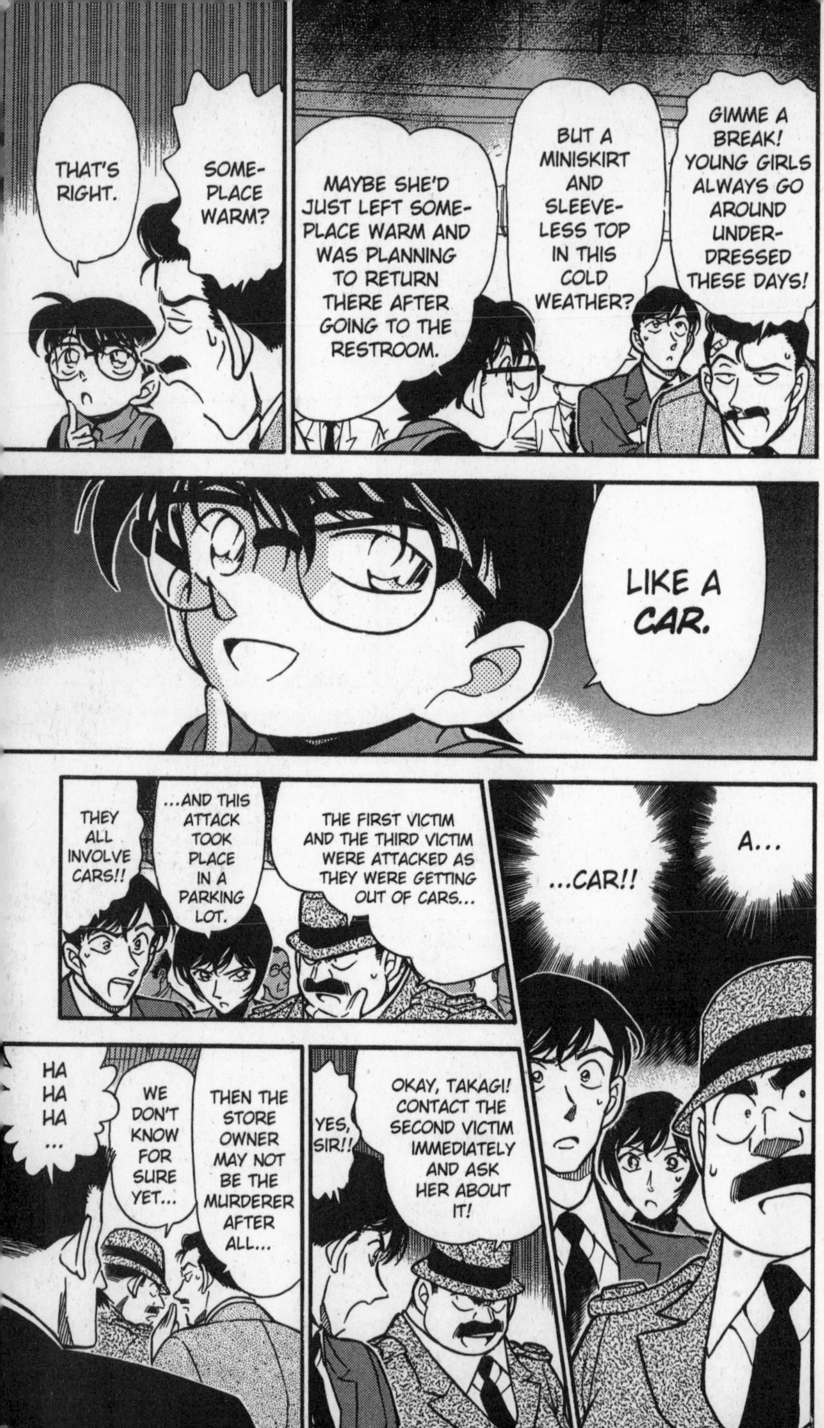
GIMME A BREAK! YOUNG GIRLS ALWAYS GO AROUND UNDER-DRESSED THESE DAYS!
BUT A MINISKIRT AND SLEEVE-LESS TOP IN THIS COLD WEATHER?
MAYBE SHE'D JUST LEFT SOME-PLACE WARM AND WAS PLANNING TO RETURN THERE AFTER GOING TO THE RESTROOM.
SOME-PLACE WARM?
THAT'S RIGHT.
LIKE A CAR.
A...
...CAR!!
THE FIRST VICTIM AND THE THIRD VICTIM WERE ATTACKED AS THEY WERE GETTING OUT OF CARS...
...AND THIS ATTACK TOOK PLACE IN A PARKING LOT.
THEY ALL INVOLVE CARS!!
OKAY, TAKAGI! CONTACT THE SECOND VICTIM IMMEDIATELY AND ASK HER ABOUT IT!
YES, SIR!!
THEN THE STORE OWNER MAY NOT BE THE MURDERER AFTER ALL...
WE DON'T KNOW FOR SURE YET...
HA HA HA ...

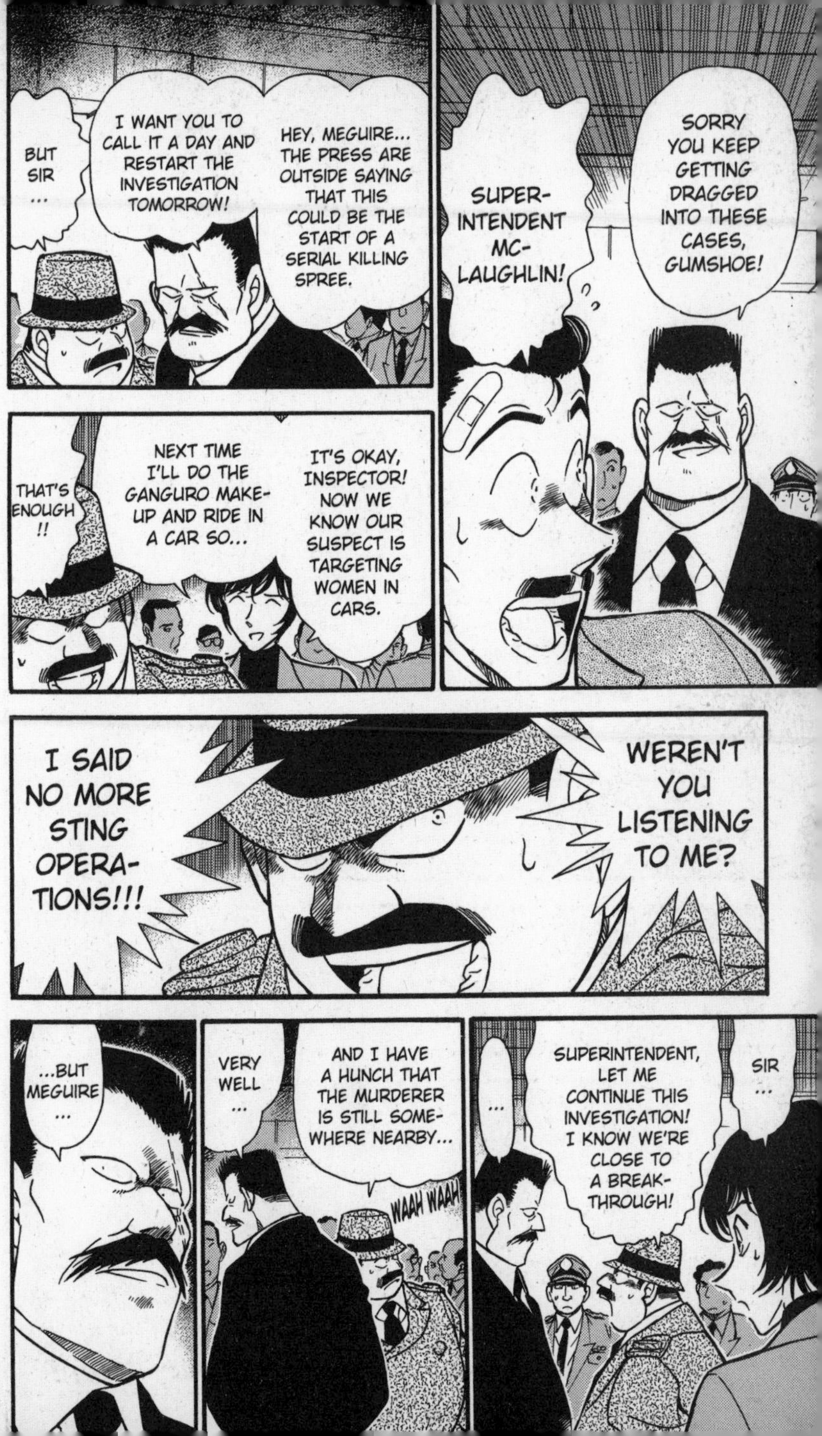
SORRY YOU KEEP GETTING DRAGGED INTO THESE CASES, GUMSHOE!
SUPER-INTENDENT MC-LAUGHLIN!
HEY, MEGUIRE... THE PRESS ARE OUTSIDE SAYING THAT THIS COULD BE THE START OF A SERIAL KILLING SPREE.
I WANT YOU TO CALL IT A DAY AND RESTART THE INVESTIGATION TOMORROW!
BUT SIR ...
IT'S OKAY, INSPECTOR! NOW WE KNOW OUR SUSPECT IS TARGETING WOMEN IN CARS.
NEXT TIME I'LL DO THE GANGURO MAKE-UP AND RIDE IN A CAR SO...
THAT'S ENOUGH !!
WEREN'T YOU LISTENING TO ME?
I SAID NO MORE STING OPERA-TIONS!!!
SIR ...
SUPERINTENDENT, LET ME CONTINUE THIS INVESTIGATION! I KNOW WE'RE CLOSE TO A BREAK-THROUGH!
...
AND I HAVE A HUNCH THAT THE MURDERER IS STILL SOME-WHERE NEARBY...
VERY WELL ...
WAAH WAAH
...BUT MEGUIRE ...

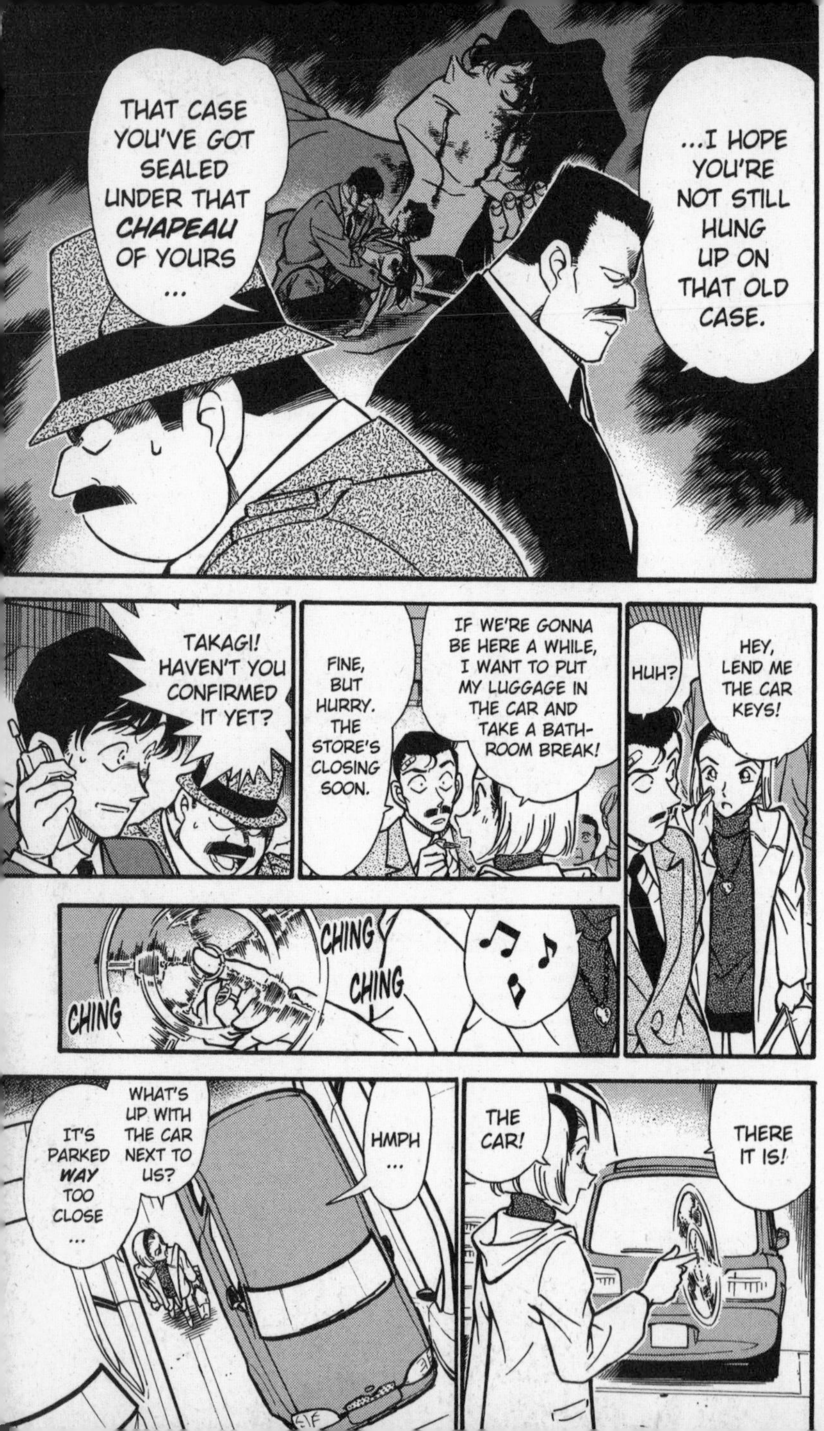
...I HOPE YOU'RE NOT STILL HUNG UP ON THAT OLD CASE.
THAT CASE YOU'VE GOT SEALED UNDER THAT *CHAPEAU* OF YOURS ...
HEY, LEND ME THE CAR KEYS!
HUH?
IF WE'RE GONNA BE HERE A WHILE, I WANT TO PUT MY LUGGAGE IN THE CAR AND TAKE A BATH-ROOM BREAK!
FINE, BUT HURRY. THE STORE'S CLOSING SOON.
TAKAGI! HAVEN'T YOU CONFIRMED IT YET?
CHING
CHING
CHING
THERE IT IS!
THE CAR!
HMPH ...
WHAT'S UP WITH THE CAR NEXT TO US?
IT'S PARKED *WAY* TOO CLOSE ...

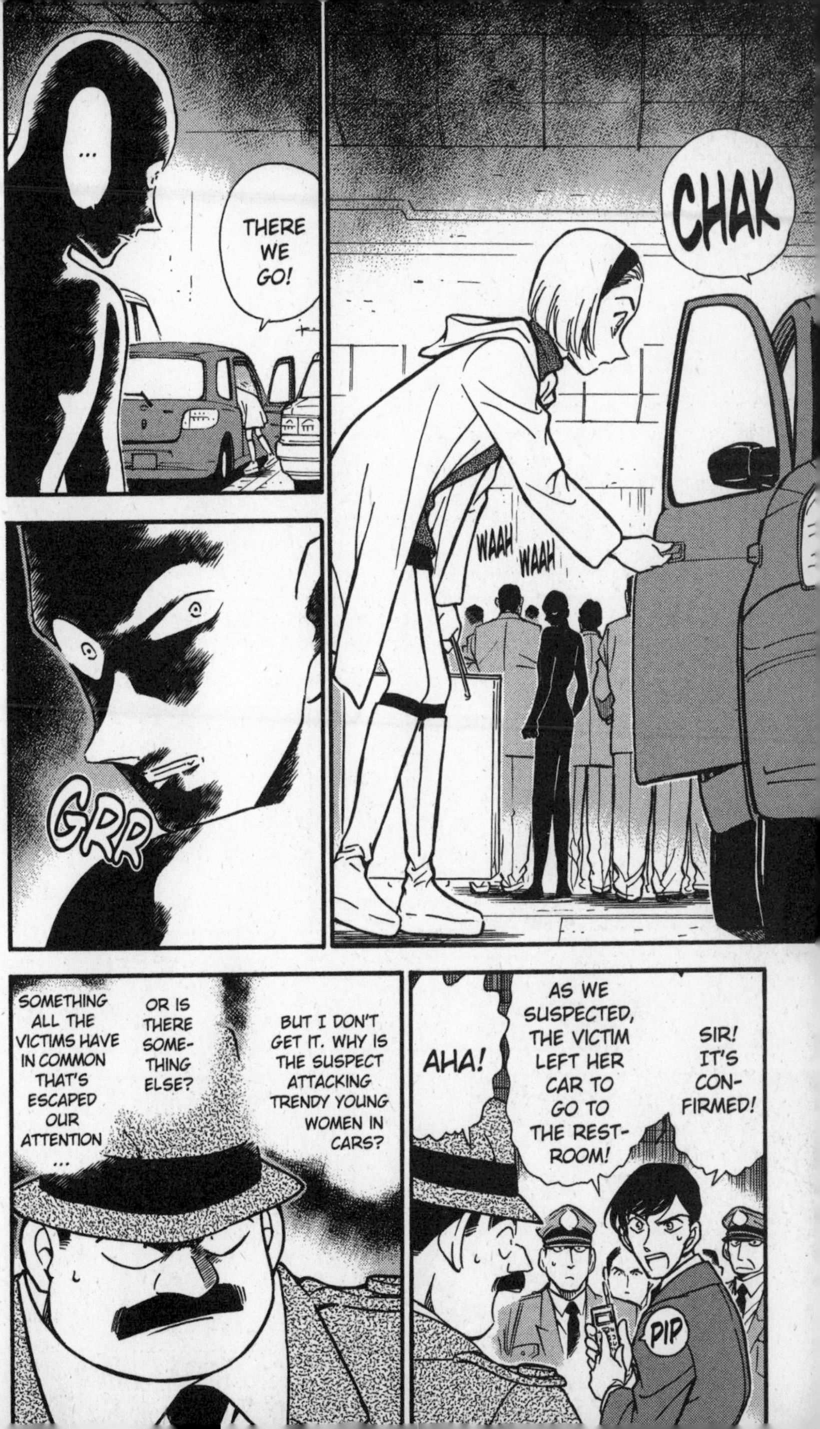
CHAK
WAAH
WAAH
THERE WE GO!
...
GRR
SIR! IT'S CON-FIRMED!
AS WE SUSPECTED, THE VICTIM LEFT HER CAR TO GO TO THE REST-ROOM!
AHA!
PIP
BUT I DON'T GET IT. WHY IS THE SUSPECT ATTACKING TRENDY YOUNG WOMEN IN CARS?
SOMETHING ALL THE VICTIMS HAVE IN COMMON THAT'S ESCAPED OUR ATTENTION ...
OR IS THERE SOME-THING ELSE?

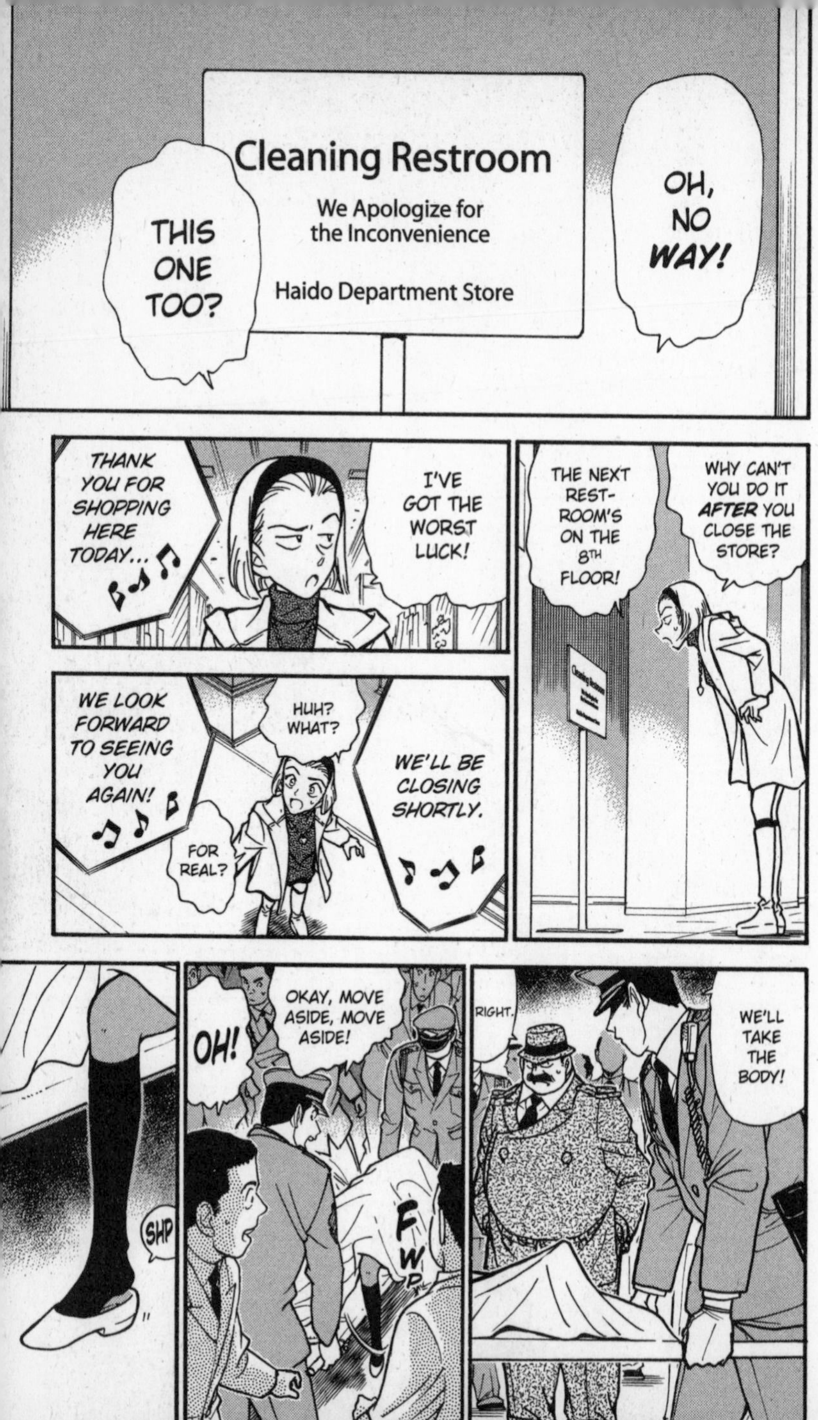

OH, NO WAY!
Cleaning Restroom
We Apologize for the Inconvenience
Haido Department Store
THIS ONE TOO?
WHY CAN'T YOU DO IT AFTER YOU CLOSE THE STORE?
THE NEXT REST-ROOM'S ON THE 8TH FLOOR!
I'VE GOT THE WORST LUCK!
THANK YOU FOR SHOPPING HERE TODAY...
HUH? WHAT?
WE'LL BE CLOSING SHORTLY.
WE LOOK FORWARD TO SEEING YOU AGAIN!
FOR REAL?
WE'LL TAKE THE BODY!
RIGHT.
OKAY, MOVE ASIDE, MOVE ASIDE!
FWP
OH!
SHP

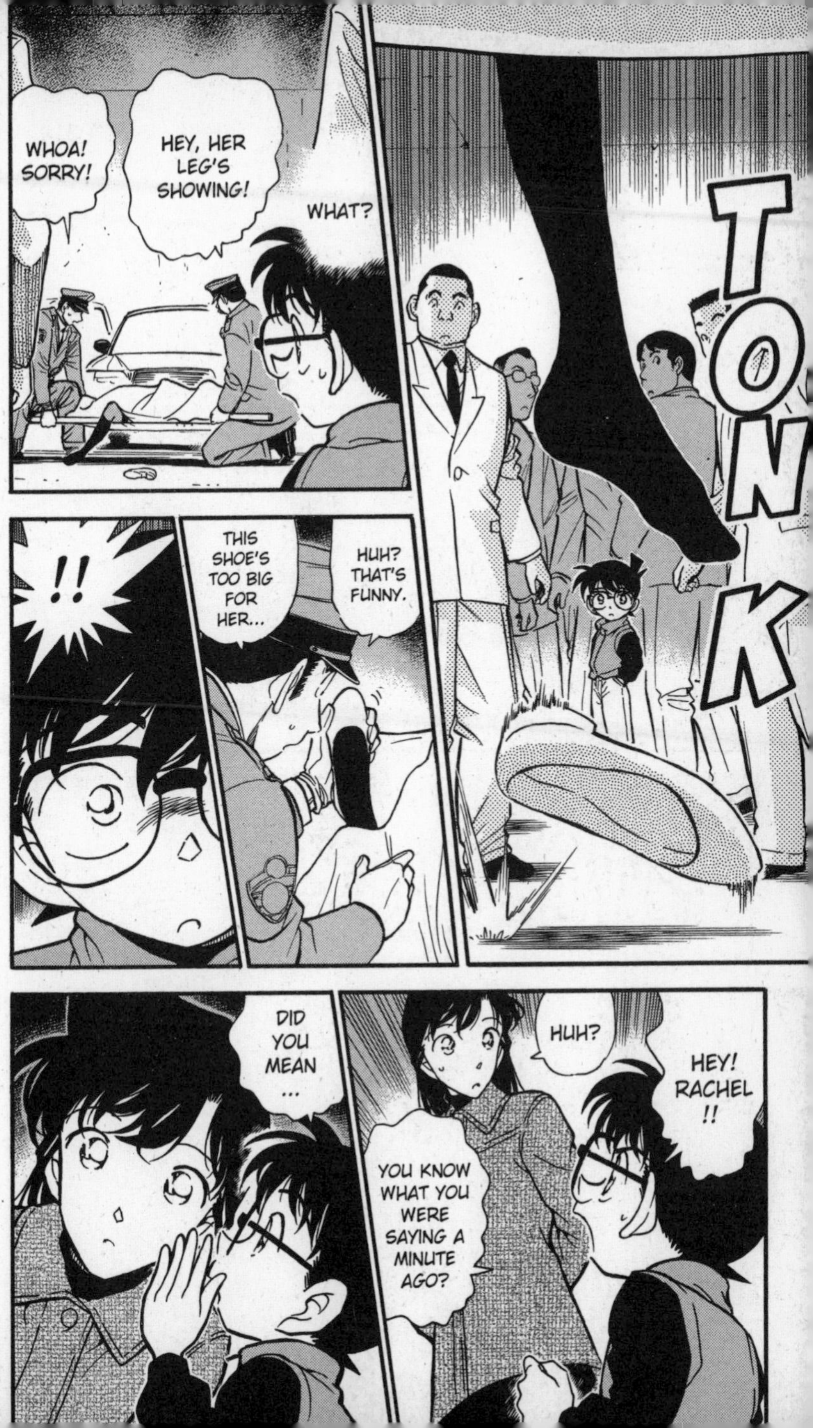
TONK
HEY, HER LEG'S SHOWING!
WHOA! SORRY!
WHAT?
HUH? THAT'S FUNNY.
THIS SHOE'S TOO BIG FOR HER...
!!
HEY! RACHEL !!
HUH?
YOU KNOW WHAT YOU WERE SAYING A MINUTE AGO?
DID YOU MEAN ...

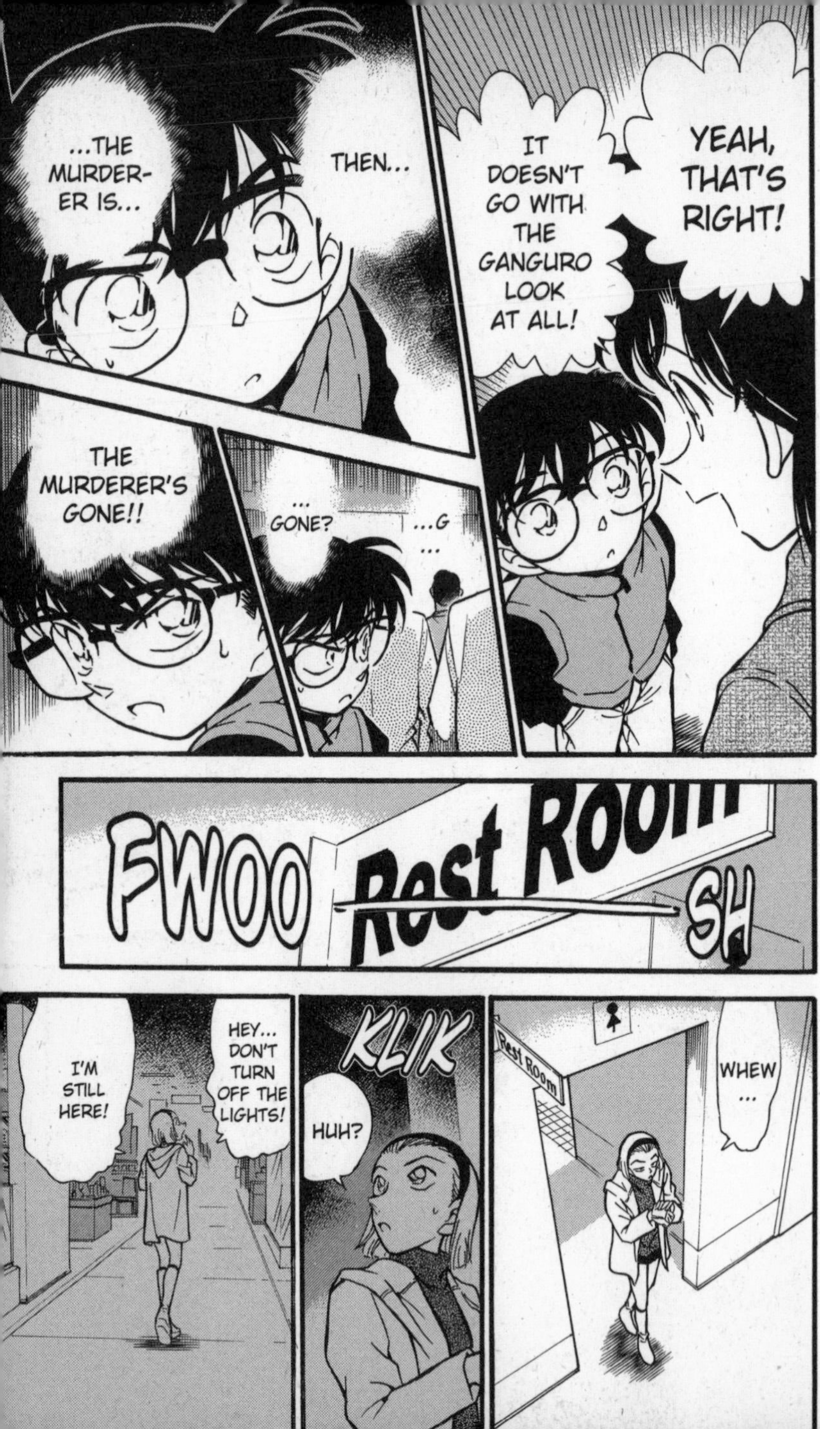
YEAH, THAT'S RIGHT!
IT DOESN'T GO WITH THE GANGURO LOOK AT ALL!
THEN...
...THE MURDERER IS...
... GONE?
...G ...
THE MURDERER'S GONE!!
FWOOSH
Rest Room
Rest Room
WHEW ...
KLIK
HUH?
HEY... DON'T TURN OFF THE LIGHTS!
I'M STILL HERE!

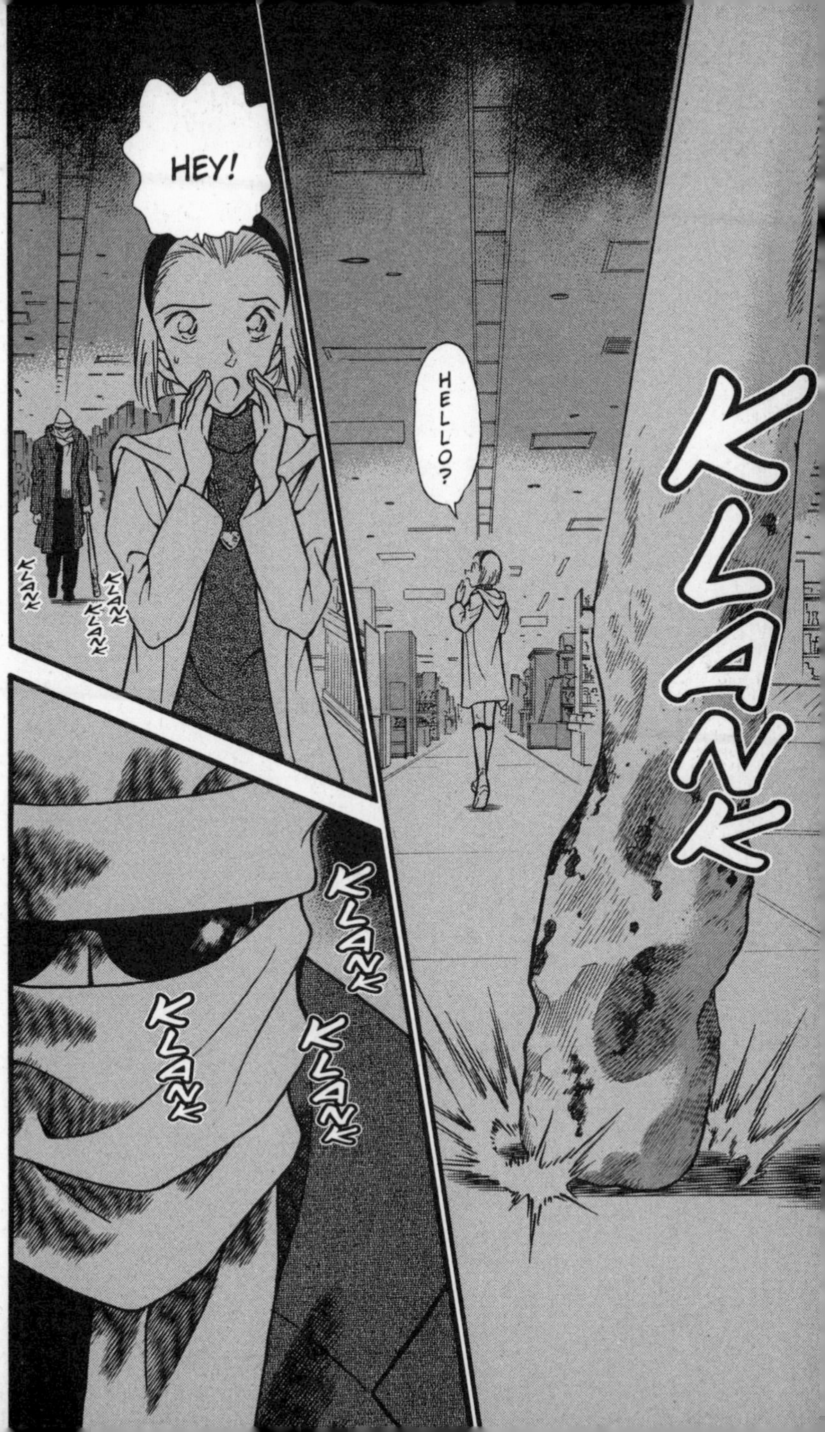
HELLO?
KLANK
HEY!
KLANK
KLANK
KLANK
KLANK
KLANK
KLANK

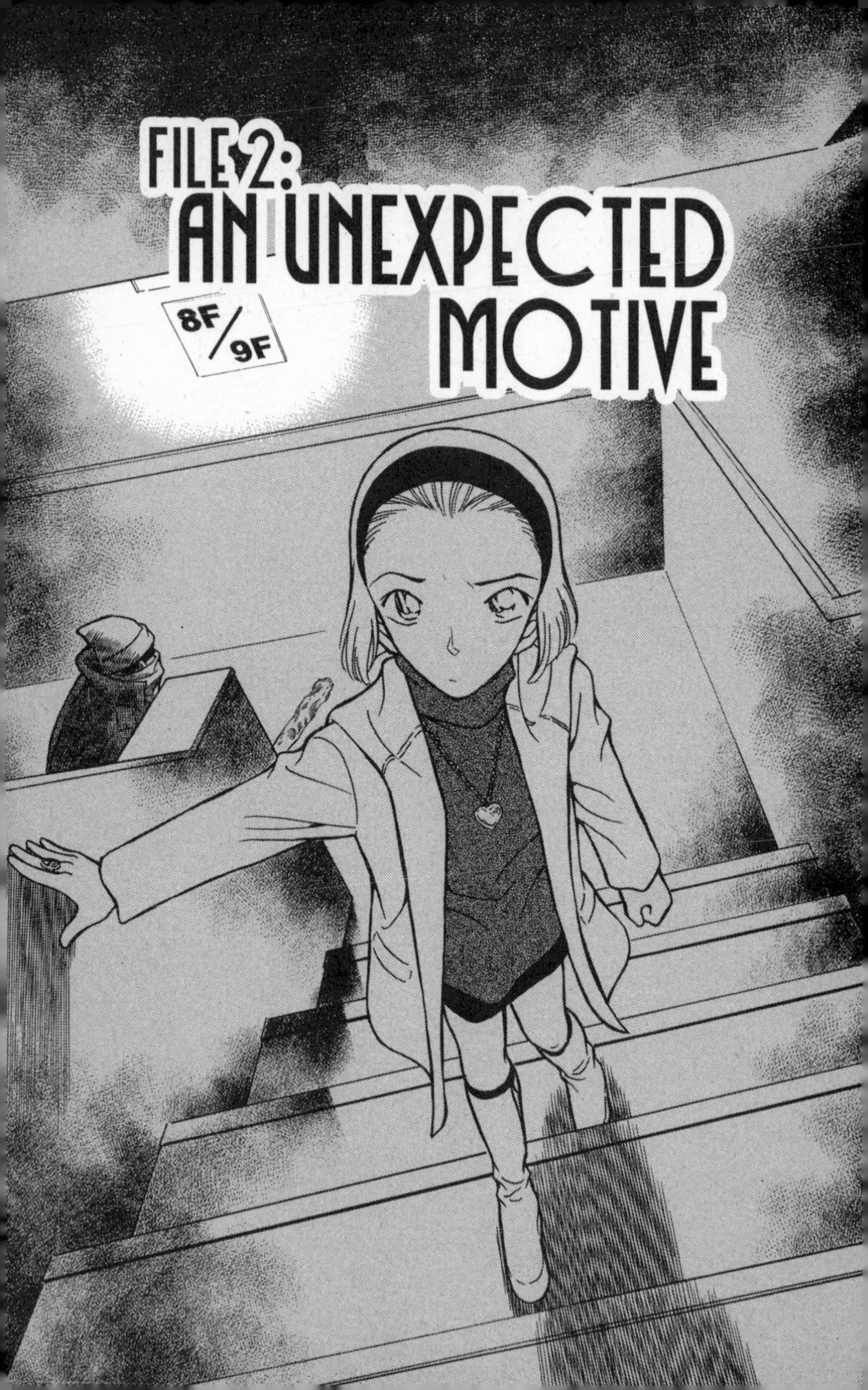
FILE 2:
AN UNEXPECTED MOTIVE
8F/9F

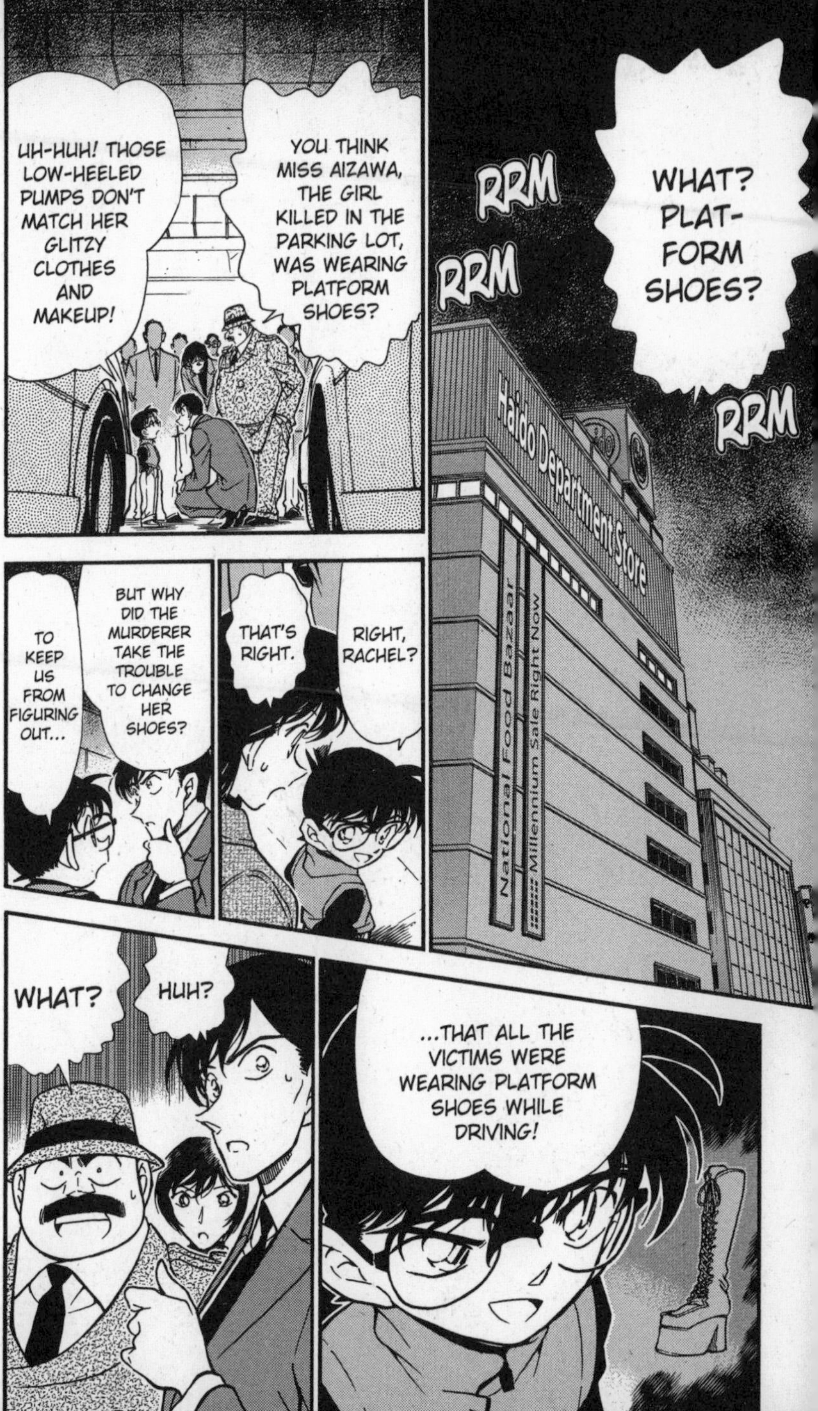

WHAT? PLAT-FORM SHOES?
RRM
RRM
RRM
Haido Department Store
Millennium Sale Right Now
National Food Bazaar
YOU THINK MISS AIZAWA, THE GIRL KILLED IN THE PARKING LOT, WAS WEARING PLATFORM SHOES?
UH-HUH! THOSE LOW-HEELED PUMPS DON'T MATCH HER GLITZY CLOTHES AND MAKEUP!
RIGHT, RACHEL?
THAT'S RIGHT.
BUT WHY DID THE MURDERER TAKE THE TROUBLE TO CHANGE HER SHOES?
TO KEEP US FROM FIGURING OUT...
...THAT ALL THE VICTIMS WERE WEARING PLATFORM SHOES WHILE DRIVING!
HUH?
WHAT?

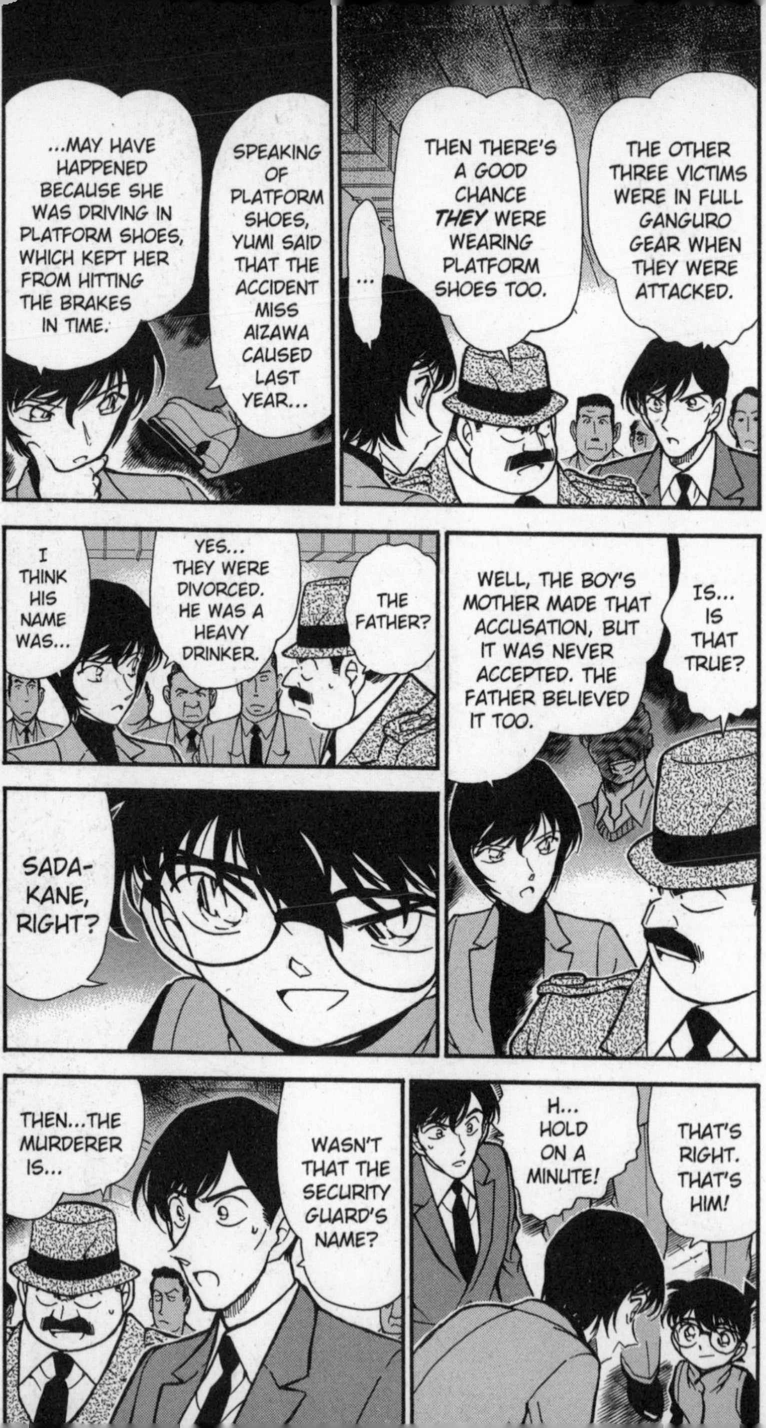
THE OTHER THREE VICTIMS WERE IN FULL GANGURO GEAR WHEN THEY WERE ATTACKED.
THEN THERE'S A GOOD CHANCE *THEY* WERE WEARING PLATFORM SHOES TOO.
...
SPEAKING OF PLATFORM SHOES, YUMI SAID THAT THE ACCIDENT MISS AIZAWA CAUSED LAST YEAR...
...MAY HAVE HAPPENED BECAUSE SHE WAS DRIVING IN PLATFORM SHOES, WHICH KEPT HER FROM HITTING THE BRAKES IN TIME.
IS... IS THAT TRUE?
WELL, THE BOY'S MOTHER MADE THAT ACCUSATION, BUT IT WAS NEVER ACCEPTED. THE FATHER BELIEVED IT TOO.
THE FATHER?
YES... THEY WERE DIVORCED. HE WAS A HEAVY DRINKER.
I THINK HIS NAME WAS...
SADA-KANE, RIGHT?
THAT'S RIGHT. THAT'S HIM!
H... HOLD ON A MINUTE!
WASN'T THAT THE SECURITY GUARD'S NAME?
THEN...THE MURDERER IS...

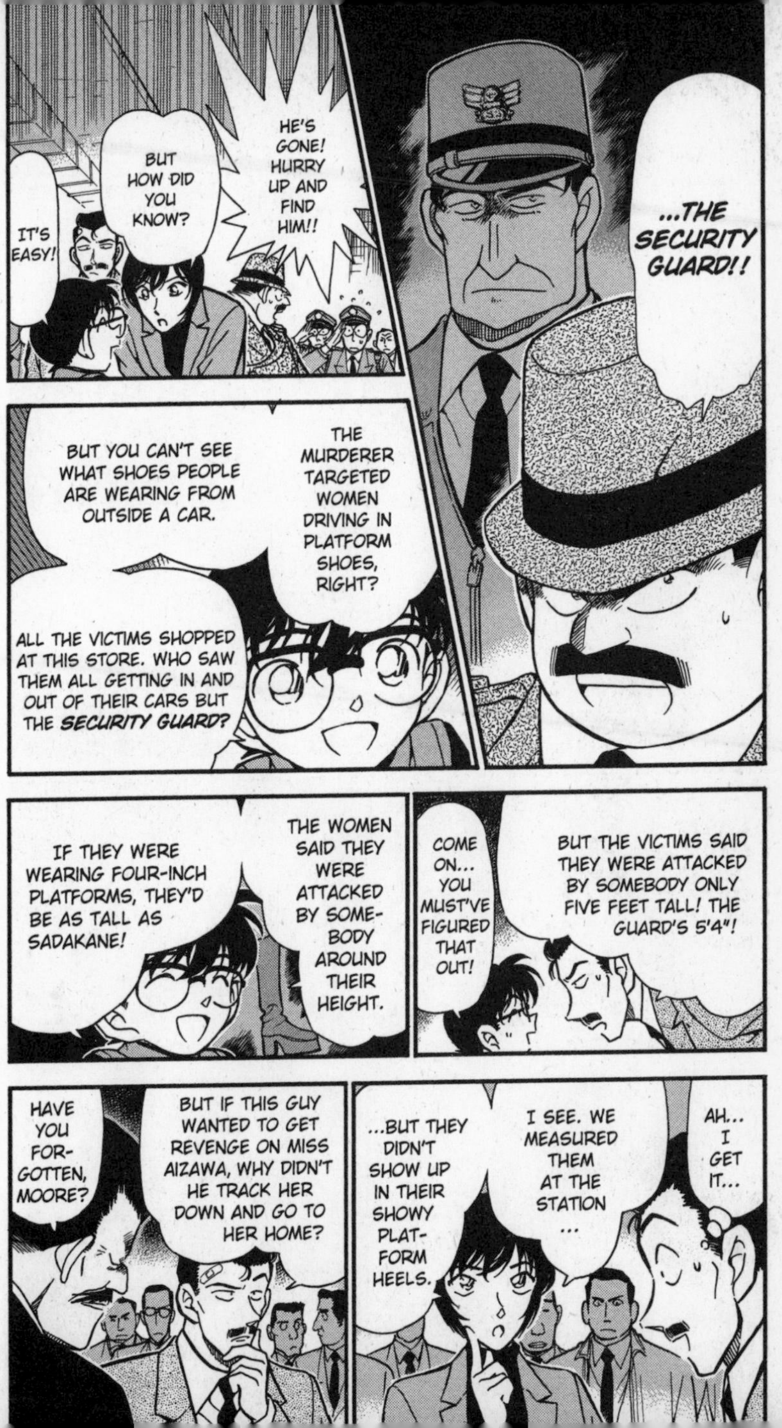
...THE SECURITY GUARD!!
HE'S GONE! HURRY UP AND FIND HIM!!
BUT HOW DID YOU KNOW?
IT'S EASY!
THE MURDERER TARGETED WOMEN DRIVING IN PLATFORM SHOES, RIGHT?
BUT YOU CAN'T SEE WHAT SHOES PEOPLE ARE WEARING FROM OUTSIDE A CAR.
ALL THE VICTIMS SHOPPED AT THIS STORE. WHO SAW THEM ALL GETTING IN AND OUT OF THEIR CARS BUT THE SECURITY GUARD?
BUT THE VICTIMS SAID THEY WERE ATTACKED BY SOMEBODY ONLY FIVE FEET TALL! THE GUARD'S 5'4"!
COME ON... YOU MUST'VE FIGURED THAT OUT!
THE WOMEN SAID THEY WERE ATTACKED BY SOME-BODY AROUND THEIR HEIGHT.
IF THEY WERE WEARING FOUR-INCH PLATFORMS, THEY'D BE AS TALL AS SADAKANE!
AH... I GET IT...
I SEE. WE MEASURED THEM AT THE STATION ...
...BUT THEY DIDN'T SHOW UP IN THEIR SHOWY PLAT-FORM HEELS.
BUT IF THIS GUY WANTED TO GET REVENGE ON MISS AIZAWA, WHY DIDN'T HE TRACK HER DOWN AND GO TO HER HOME?
HAVE YOU FOR-GOTTEN, MOORE?

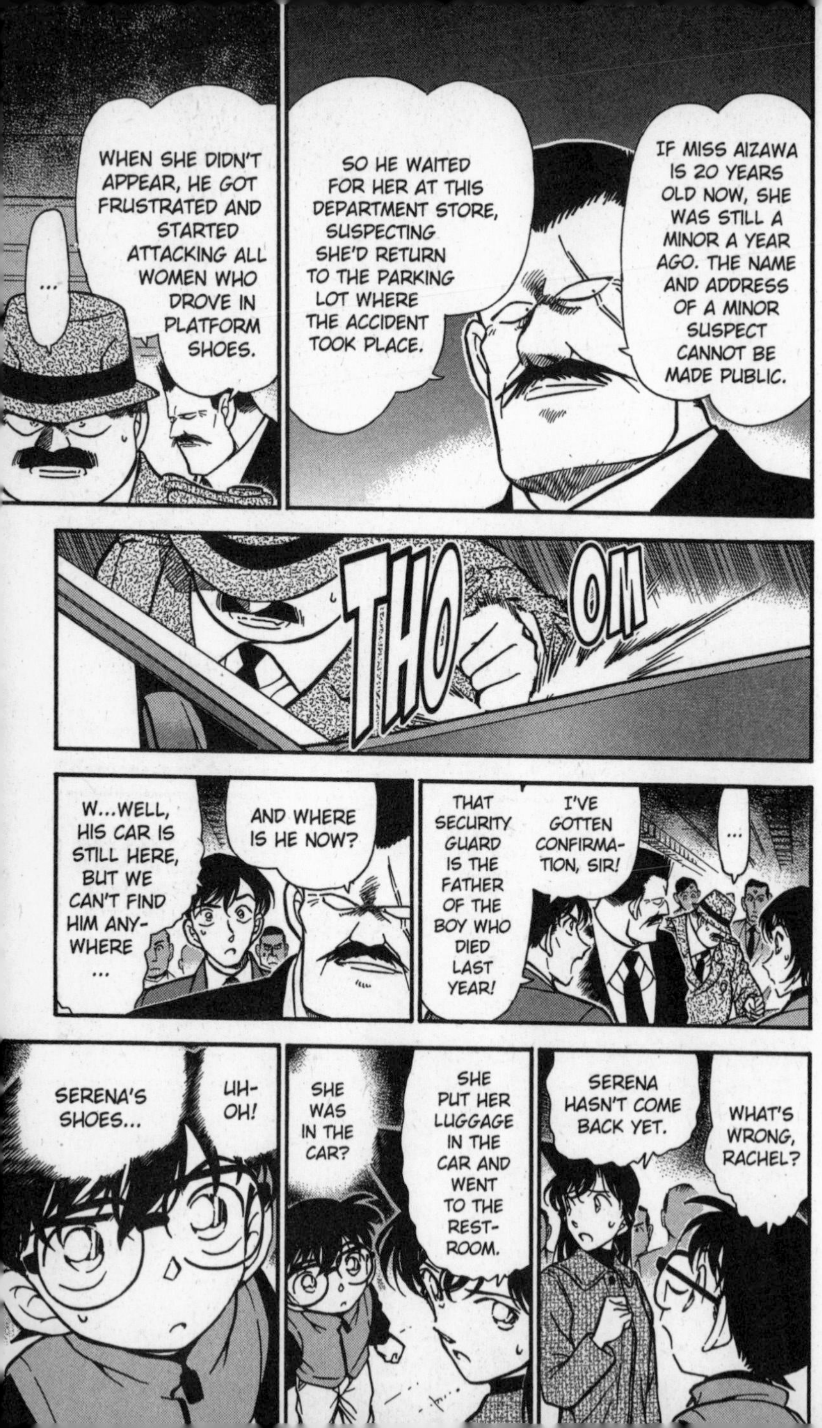
IF MISS AIZAWA IS 20 YEARS OLD NOW, SHE WAS STILL A MINOR A YEAR AGO. THE NAME AND ADDRESS OF A MINOR SUSPECT CANNOT BE MADE PUBLIC.
SO HE WAITED FOR HER AT THIS DEPARTMENT STORE, SUSPECTING SHE'D RETURN TO THE PARKING LOT WHERE THE ACCIDENT TOOK PLACE.
WHEN SHE DIDN'T APPEAR, HE GOT FRUSTRATED AND STARTED ATTACKING ALL WOMEN WHO DROVE IN PLATFORM SHOES.
...
THOOM
...
I'VE GOTTEN CONFIRMATION, SIR!
THAT SECURITY GUARD IS THE FATHER OF THE BOY WHO DIED LAST YEAR!
AND WHERE IS HE NOW?
W...WELL, HIS CAR IS STILL HERE, BUT WE CAN'T FIND HIM ANYWHERE ...
WHAT'S WRONG, RACHEL?
SERENA HASN'T COME BACK YET.
SHE PUT HER LUGGAGE IN THE CAR AND WENT TO THE REST-ROOM.
SHE WAS IN THE CAR?
UH-OH!
SERENA'S SHOES...

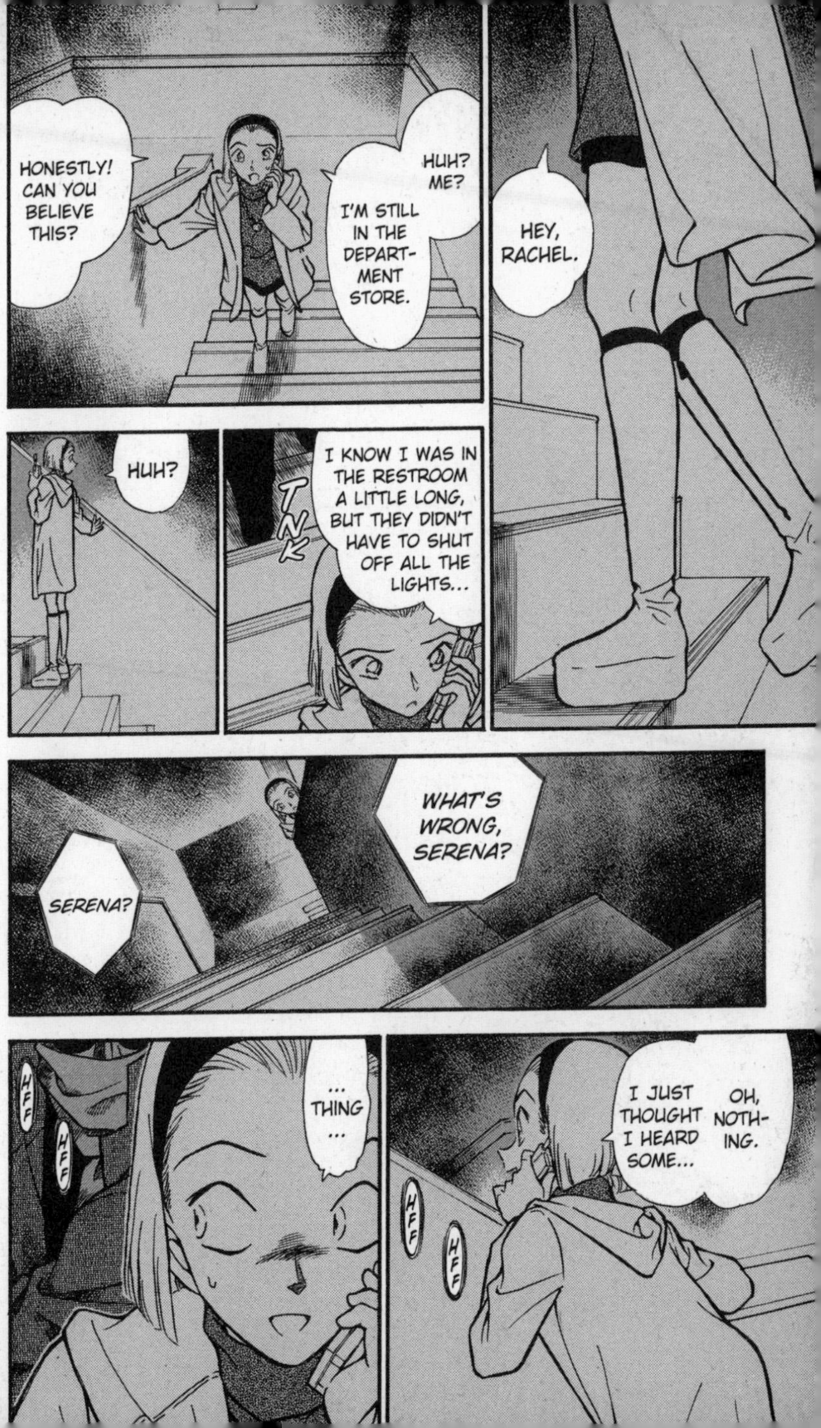
HEY, RACHEL.
HUH? ME?
I'M STILL IN THE DEPART-MENT STORE.
HONESTLY! CAN YOU BELIEVE THIS?
I KNOW I WAS IN THE RESTROOM A LITTLE LONG, BUT THEY DIDN'T HAVE TO SHUT OFF ALL THE LIGHTS...
TNK
HUH?
WHAT'S WRONG, SERENA?
SERENA?
OH, NOTH-ING.
I JUST THOUGHT I HEARD SOME...
HFF
HFF
...THING...
HFF
HFF

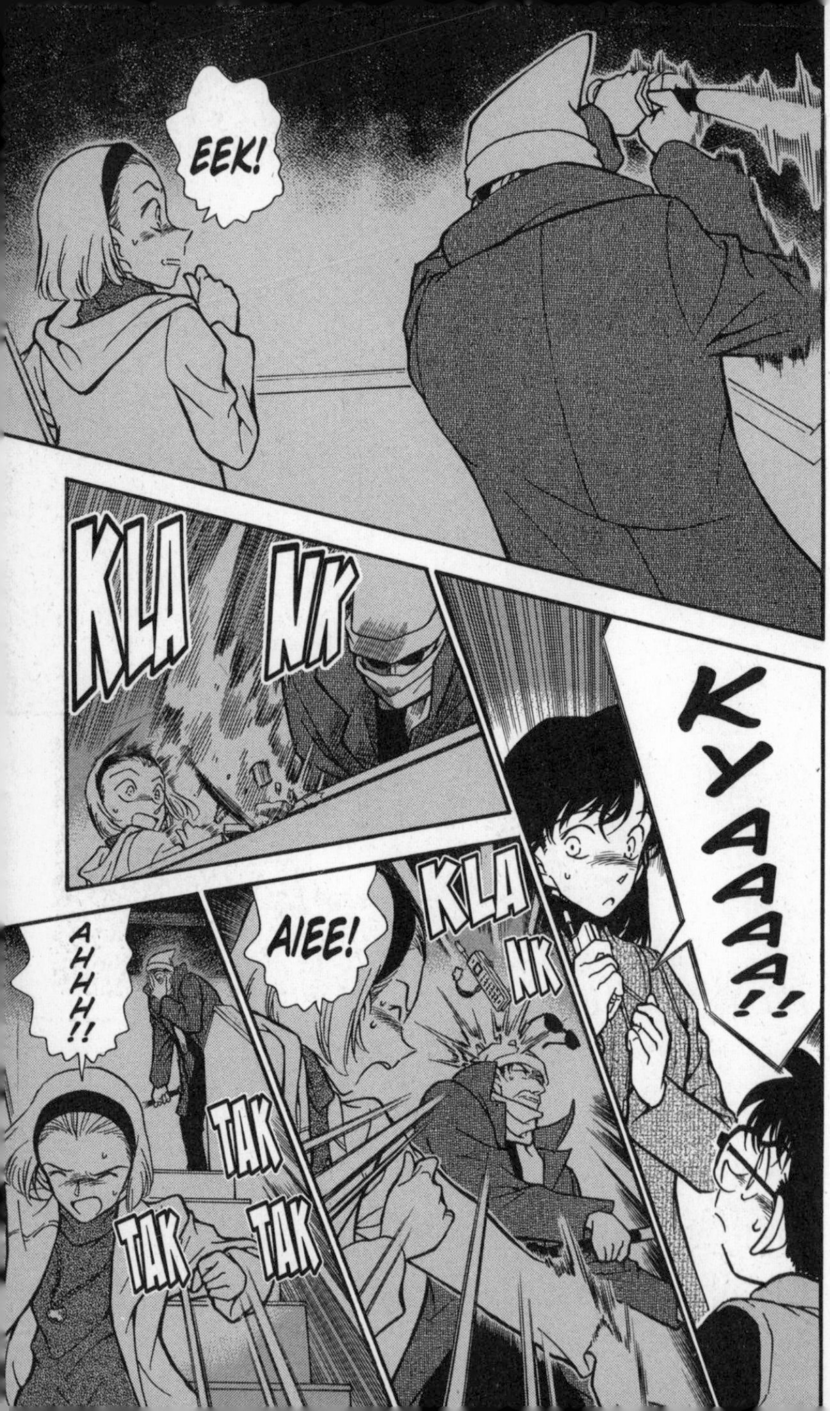
EEK!
KYAAAA!!
KLANK
KLANK
AIEE!
TAK
TAK
AHHHH!!
TAK

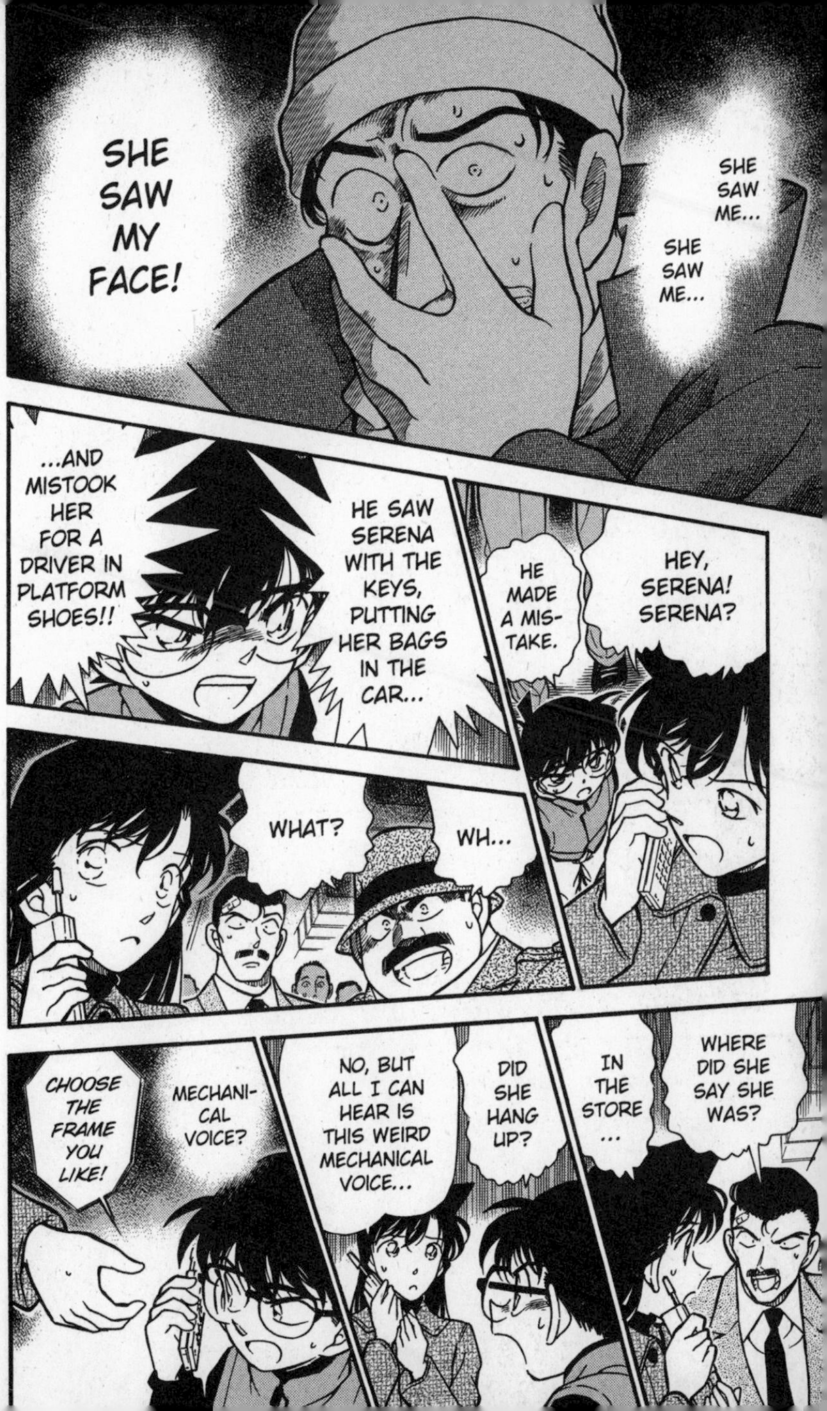
SHE SAW ME... SHE SAW ME...
SHE SAW MY FACE!
HEY, SERENA! SERENA?
HE MADE A MISTAKE.
HE SAW SERENA WITH THE KEYS, PUTTING HER BAGS IN THE CAR...
...AND MISTOOK HER FOR A DRIVER IN PLATFORM SHOES!!
WH...
WHAT?
WHERE DID SHE SAY SHE WAS?
IN THE STORE ...
DID SHE HANG UP?
NO, BUT ALL I CAN HEAR IS THIS WEIRD MECHANICAL VOICE...
MECHANICAL VOICE?
CHOOSE THE FRAME YOU LIKE!

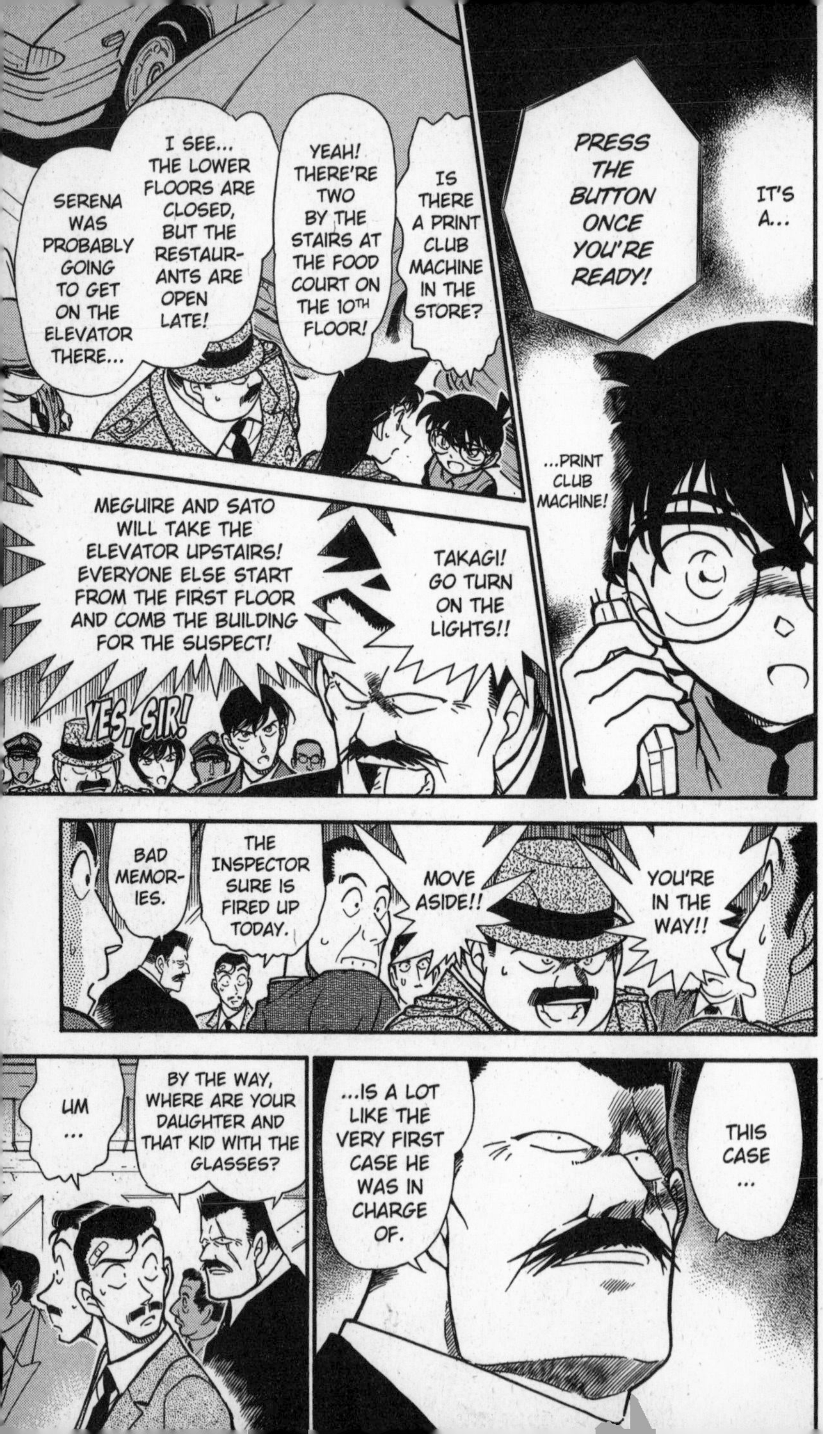
PRESS THE BUTTON ONCE YOU'RE READY!
IT'S A...
...PRINT CLUB MACHINE!
IS THERE A PRINT CLUB MACHINE IN THE STORE?
YEAH! THERE'RE TWO BY THE STAIRS AT THE FOOD COURT ON THE 10TH FLOOR!
I SEE... THE LOWER FLOORS ARE CLOSED, BUT THE RESTAUR-ANTS ARE OPEN LATE!
SERENA WAS PROBABLY GOING TO GET ON THE ELEVATOR THERE...
TAKAGI! GO TURN ON THE LIGHTS!!
MEGUIRE AND SATO WILL TAKE THE ELEVATOR UPSTAIRS! EVERYONE ELSE START FROM THE FIRST FLOOR AND COMB THE BUILDING FOR THE SUSPECT!
YES, SIR!
YOU'RE IN THE WAY!!
MOVE ASIDE!!
THE INSPECTOR SURE IS FIRED UP TODAY.
BAD MEMOR-IES.
THIS CASE ...
...IS A LOT LIKE THE VERY FIRST CASE HE WAS IN CHARGE OF.
BY THE WAY, WHERE ARE YOUR DAUGHTER AND THAT KID WITH THE GLASSES?
UM ...

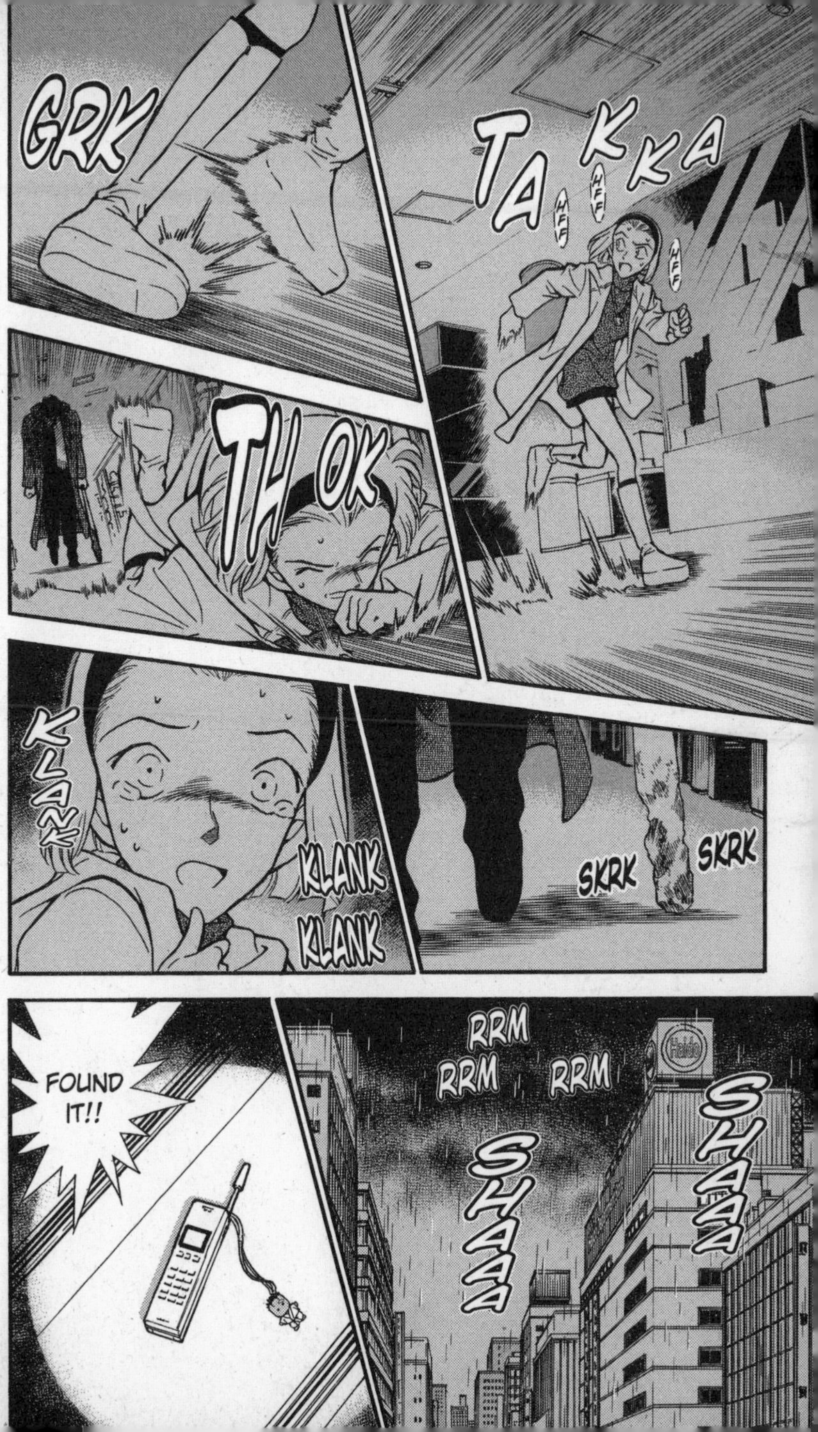
TA KKA
HFF
HFF
HFF
GRK
TH OK
SKRK
SKRK
KLANK KLANK
KLANK
KLANK
RRM
RRM
RRM
Haido
SHAAA
SHAAA
FOUND IT!!

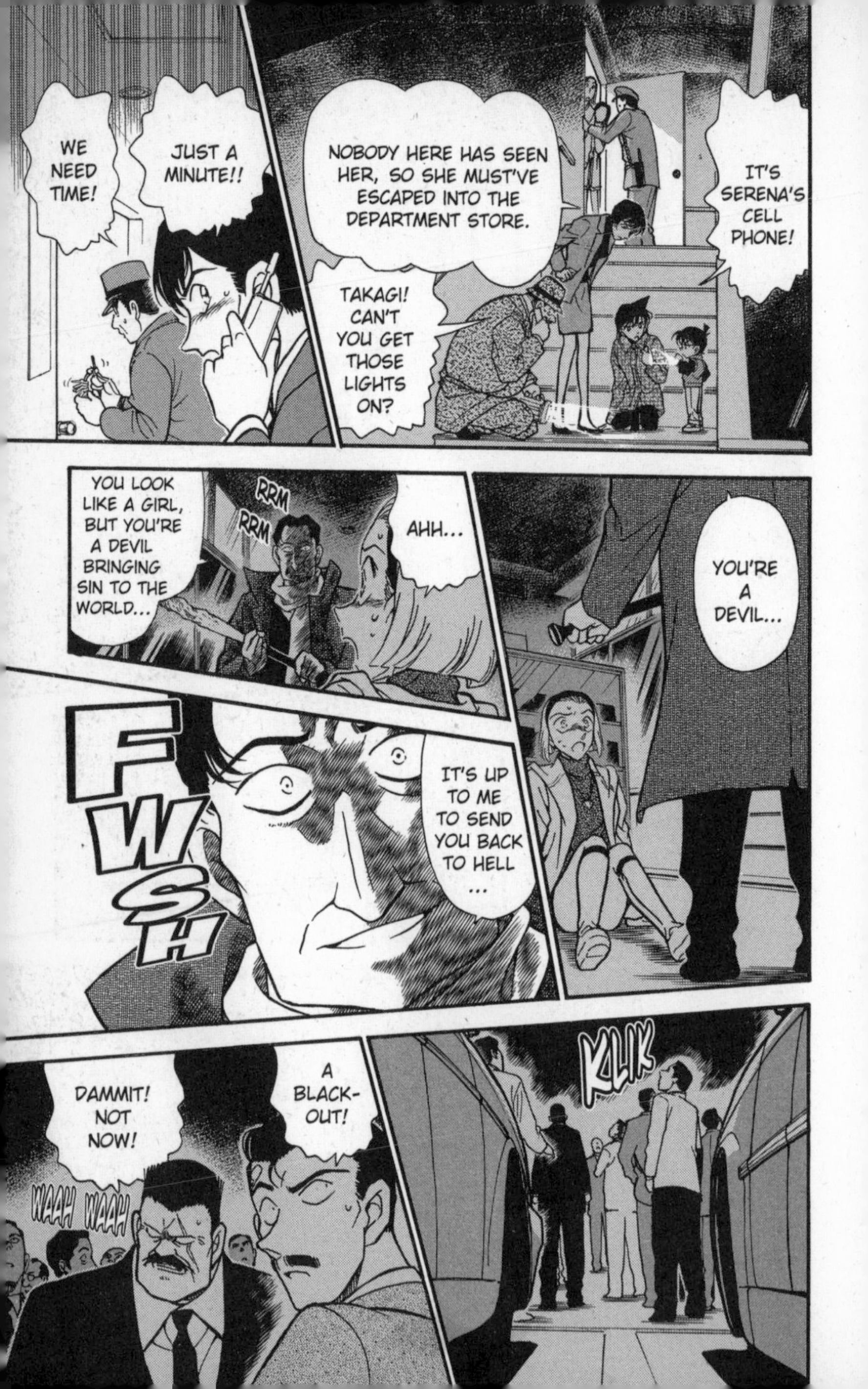
IT'S SERENA'S CELL PHONE!
NOBODY HERE HAS SEEN HER, SO SHE MUST'VE ESCAPED INTO THE DEPARTMENT STORE.
TAKAGI! CAN'T YOU GET THOSE LIGHTS ON?
JUST A MINUTE!!
WE NEED TIME!
YOU'RE A DEVIL...
AHH...
RRM RRM
YOU LOOK LIKE A GIRL, BUT YOU'RE A DEVIL BRINGING SIN TO THE WORLD...
IT'S UP TO ME TO SEND YOU BACK TO HELL...
FWSH
KLIK
A BLACK-OUT!
DAMMIT! NOT NOW!
WAAH WAAH

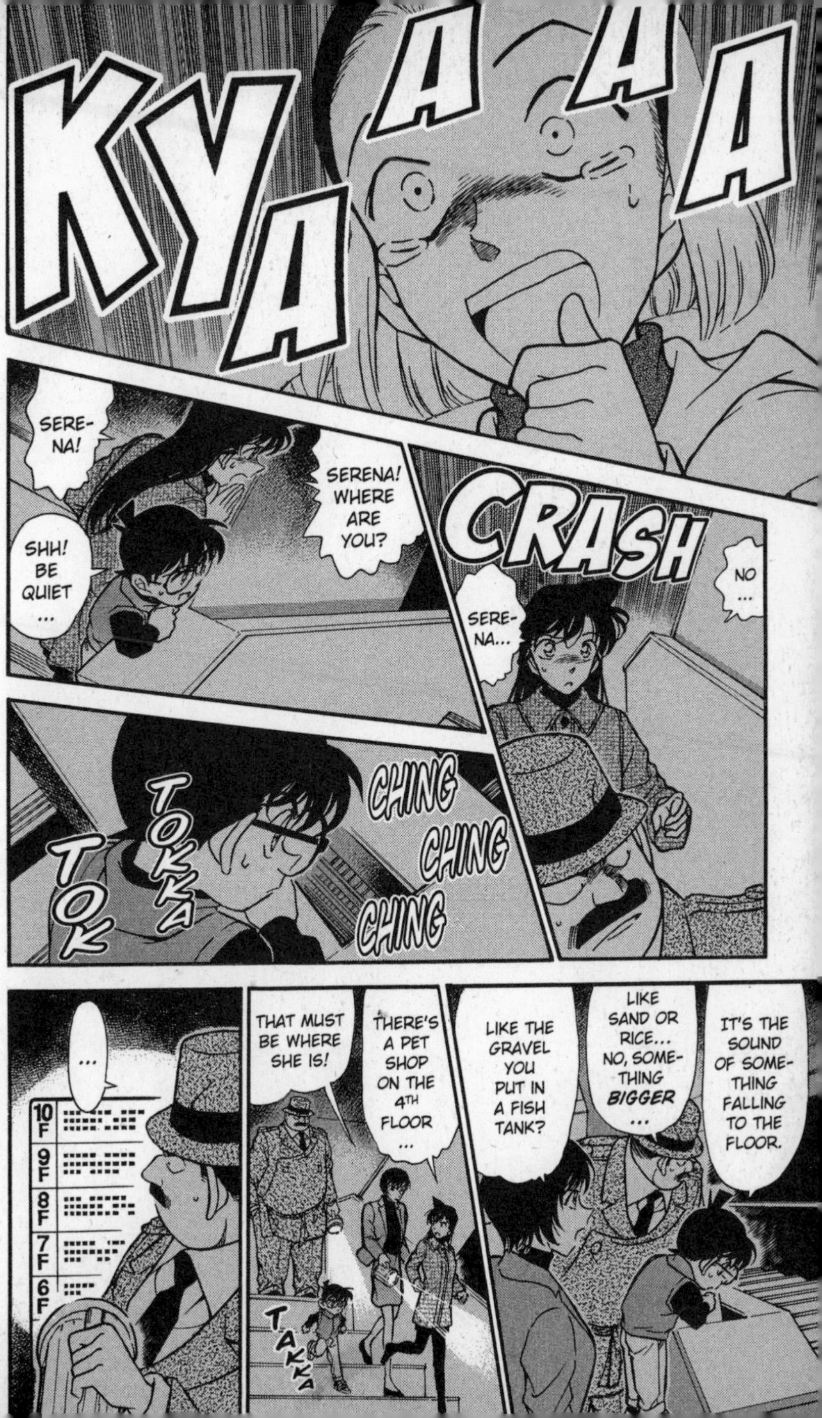
KYAAAAA
CRASH
NO...
SERE-NA...
SERE-NA!
SERENA! WHERE ARE YOU?
SHH! BE QUIET...
CHING CHING CHING
TOKKA TOK
IT'S THE SOUND OF SOME-THING FALLING TO THE FLOOR.
LIKE SAND OR RICE... NO, SOME-THING *BIGGER*...
LIKE THE GRAVEL YOU PUT IN A FISH TANK?
THERE'S A PET SHOP ON THE 4TH FLOOR...
THAT MUST BE WHERE SHE IS!
TAKKA
...
10F
9F
8F
7F
6F

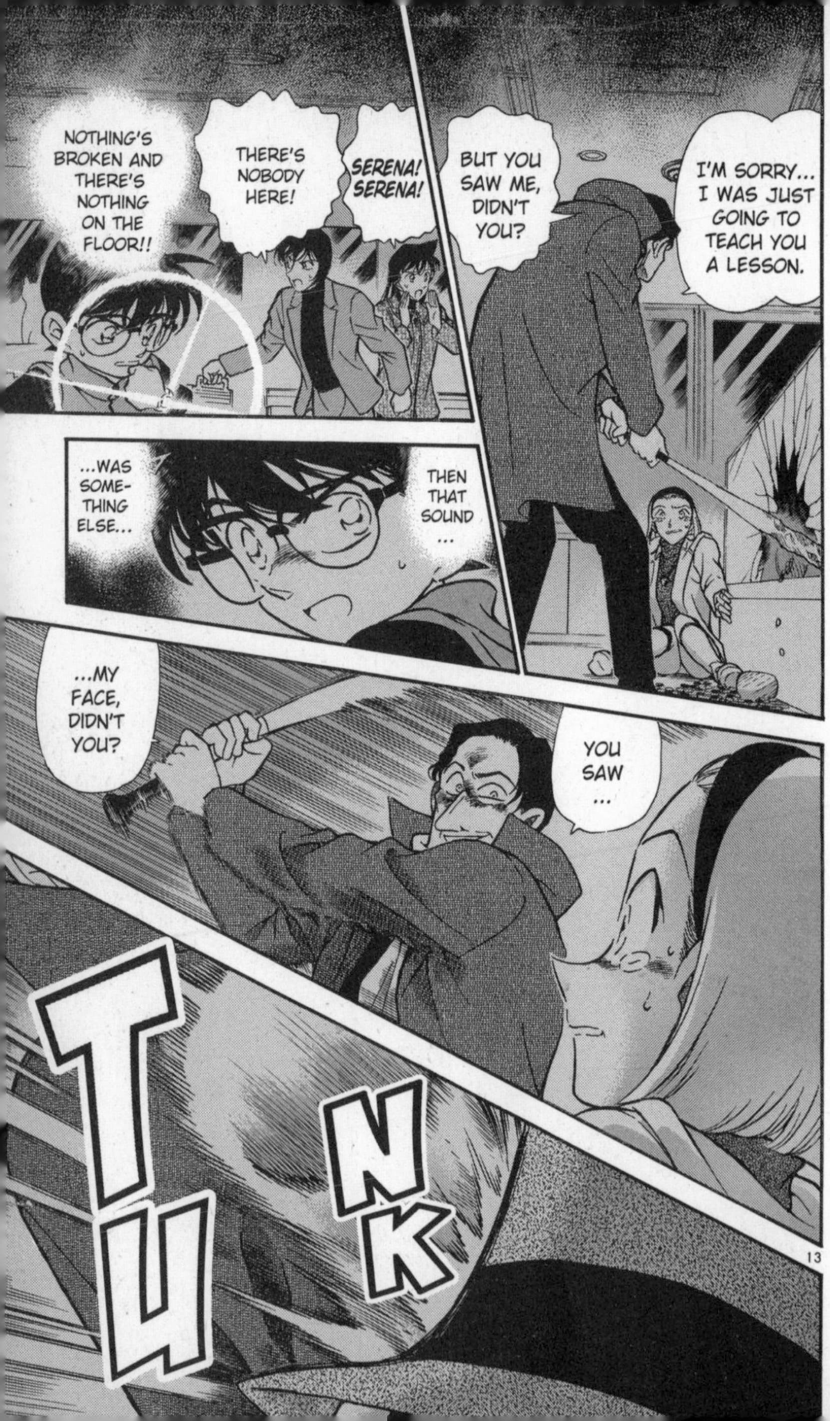
I'M SORRY... I WAS JUST GOING TO TEACH YOU A LESSON.
BUT YOU SAW ME, DIDN'T YOU?
SERENA! SERENA!
THERE'S NOBODY HERE!
NOTHING'S BROKEN AND THERE'S NOTHING ON THE FLOOR!!
THEN THAT SOUND ...
...WAS SOME-THING ELSE...
YOU SAW ...
...MY FACE, DIDN'T YOU?
THUNK

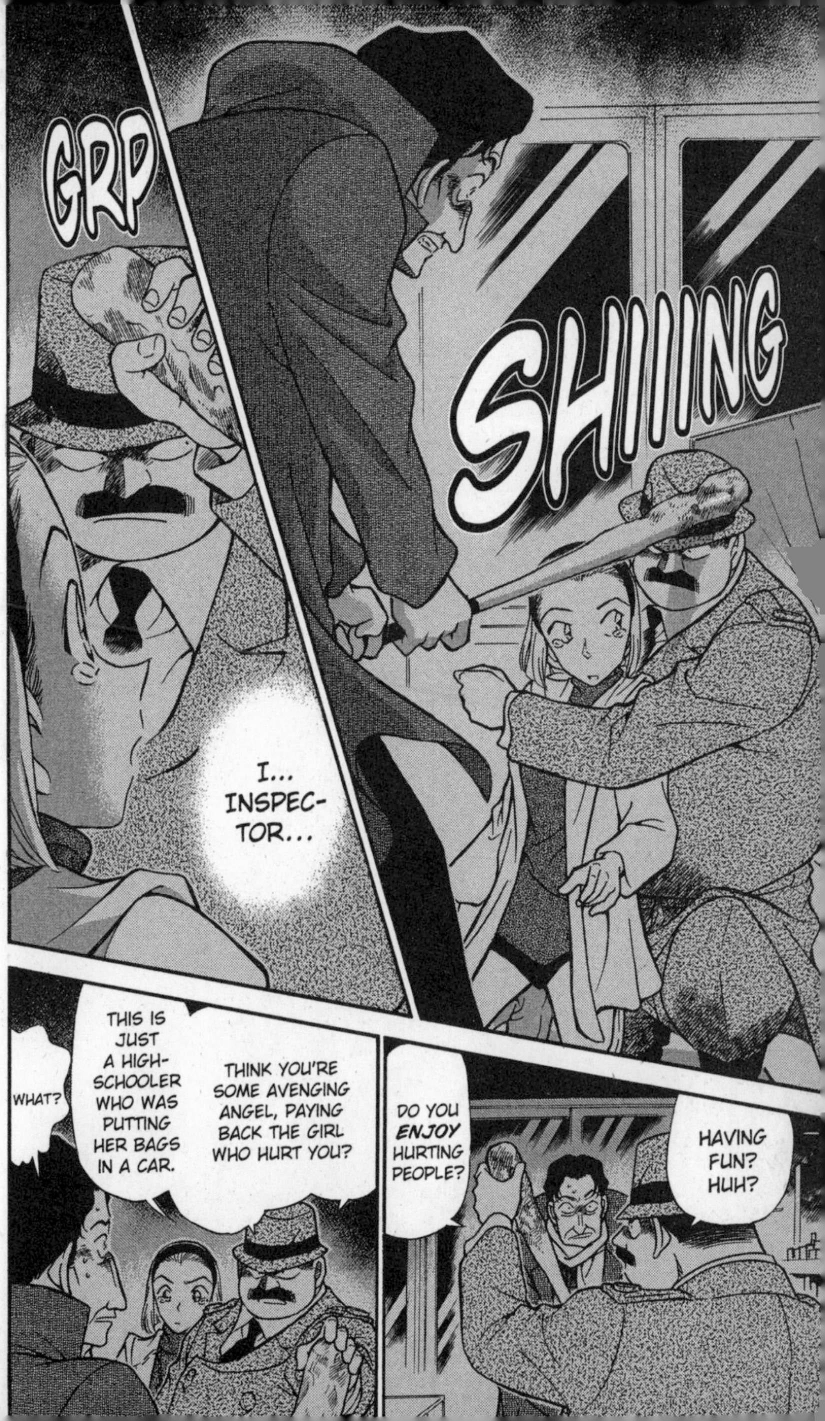

SHIIING
GRP
I... INSPECTOR...
HAVING FUN? HUH?
DO YOU *ENJOY* HURTING PEOPLE?
THINK YOU'RE SOME AVENGING ANGEL, PAYING BACK THE GIRL WHO HURT YOU?
THIS IS JUST A HIGH-SCHOOLER WHO WAS PUTTING HER BAGS IN A CAR.
WHAT?

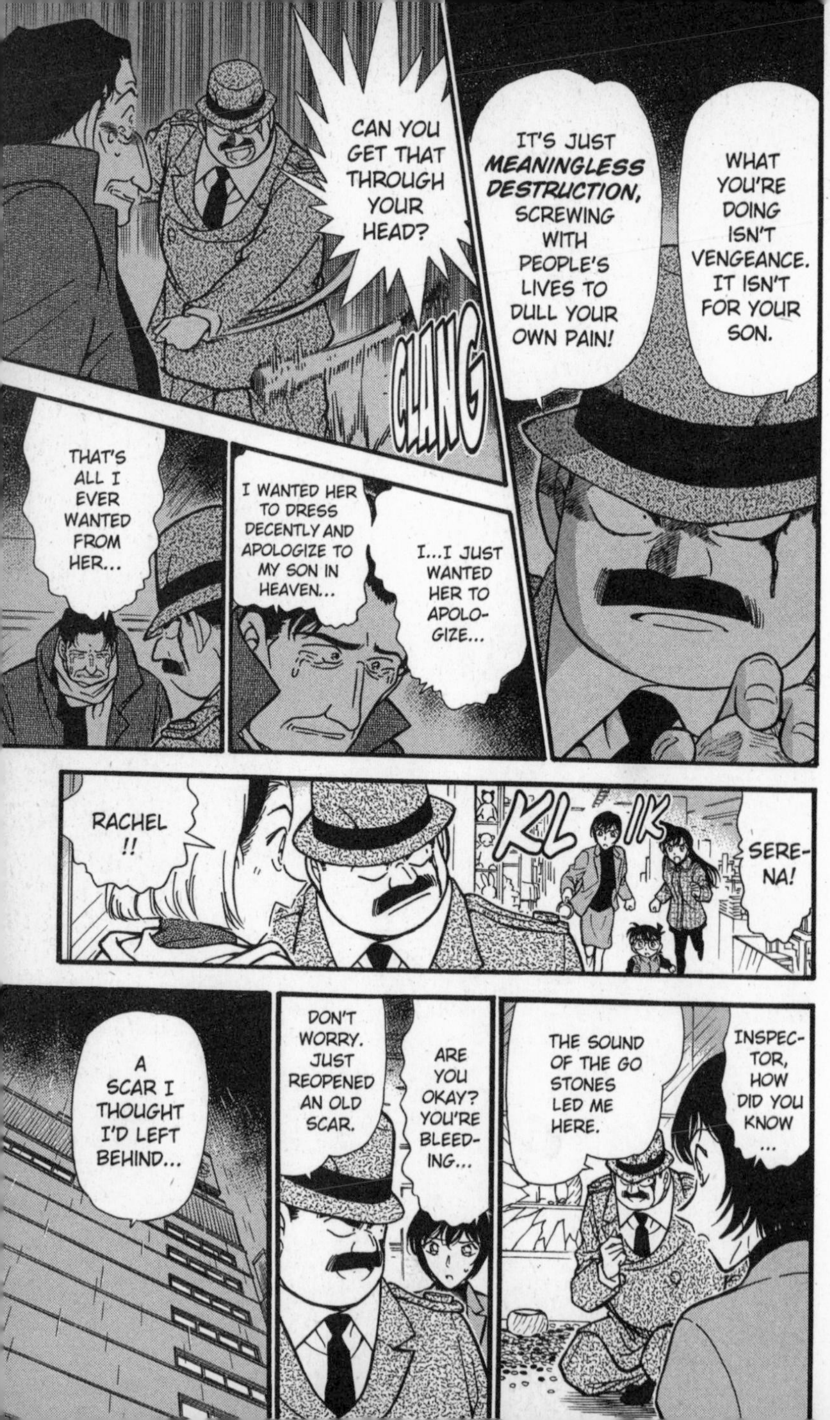
WHAT YOU'RE DOING ISN'T VENGEANCE. IT ISN'T FOR YOUR SON.
IT'S JUST **MEANINGLESS DESTRUCTION,** SCREWING WITH PEOPLE'S LIVES TO DULL YOUR OWN PAIN!
CAN YOU GET THAT THROUGH YOUR HEAD?
CLANG
I...I JUST WANTED HER TO APOLO-GIZE...
I WANTED HER TO DRESS DECENTLY AND APOLOGIZE TO MY SON IN HEAVEN...
THAT'S ALL I EVER WANTED FROM HER...
SERE-NA!
KL IK
RACHEL !!
INSPEC-TOR, HOW DID YOU KNOW ...
THE SOUND OF THE GO STONES LED ME HERE.
ARE YOU OKAY? YOU'RE BLEED-ING...
DON'T WORRY. JUST REOPENED AN OLD SCAR.
A SCAR I THOUGHT I'D LEFT BEHIND...

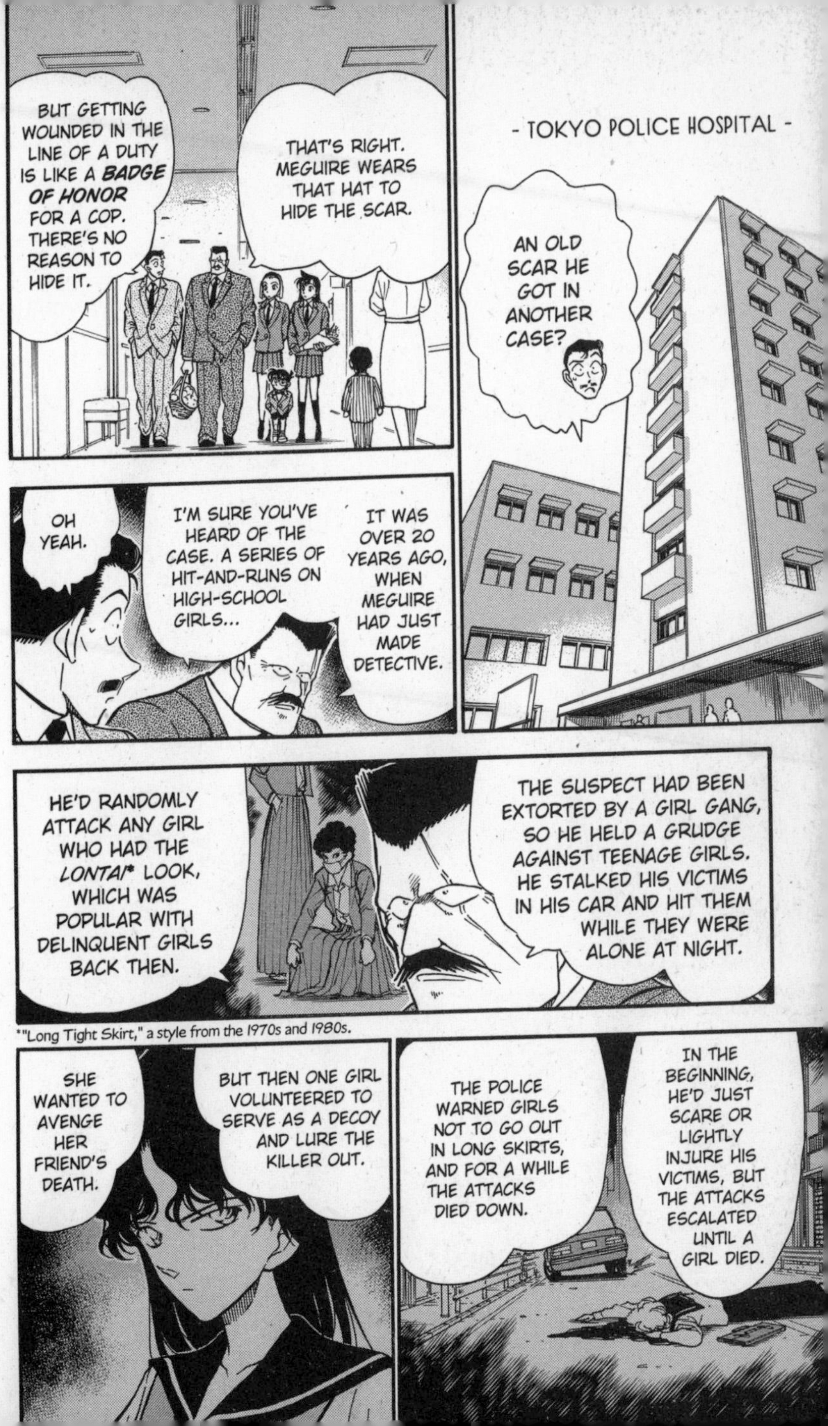
- TOKYO POLICE HOSPITAL -
AN OLD SCAR HE GOT IN ANOTHER CASE?
THAT'S RIGHT. MEGUIRE WEARS THAT HAT TO HIDE THE SCAR.
BUT GETTING WOUNDED IN THE LINE OF A DUTY IS LIKE A **BADGE OF HONOR** FOR A COP. THERE'S NO REASON TO HIDE IT.
IT WAS OVER 20 YEARS AGO, WHEN MEGUIRE HAD JUST MADE DETECTIVE.
I'M SURE YOU'VE HEARD OF THE CASE. A SERIES OF HIT-AND-RUNS ON HIGH-SCHOOL GIRLS...
OH YEAH.
THE SUSPECT HAD BEEN EXTORTED BY A GIRL GANG, SO HE HELD A GRUDGE AGAINST TEENAGE GIRLS. HE STALKED HIS VICTIMS IN HIS CAR AND HIT THEM WHILE THEY WERE ALONE AT NIGHT.
HE'D RANDOMLY ATTACK ANY GIRL WHO HAD THE *LONTAI** LOOK, WHICH WAS POPULAR WITH DELINQUENT GIRLS BACK THEN.
IN THE BEGINNING, HE'D JUST SCARE OR LIGHTLY INJURE HIS VICTIMS, BUT THE ATTACKS ESCALATED UNTIL A GIRL DIED.
THE POLICE WARNED GIRLS NOT TO GO OUT IN LONG SKIRTS, AND FOR A WHILE THE ATTACKS DIED DOWN.
BUT THEN ONE GIRL VOLUNTEERED TO SERVE AS A DECOY AND LURE THE KILLER OUT.
SHE WANTED TO AVENGE HER FRIEND'S DEATH.

*"Long Tight Skirt," a style from the 1970s and 1980s.

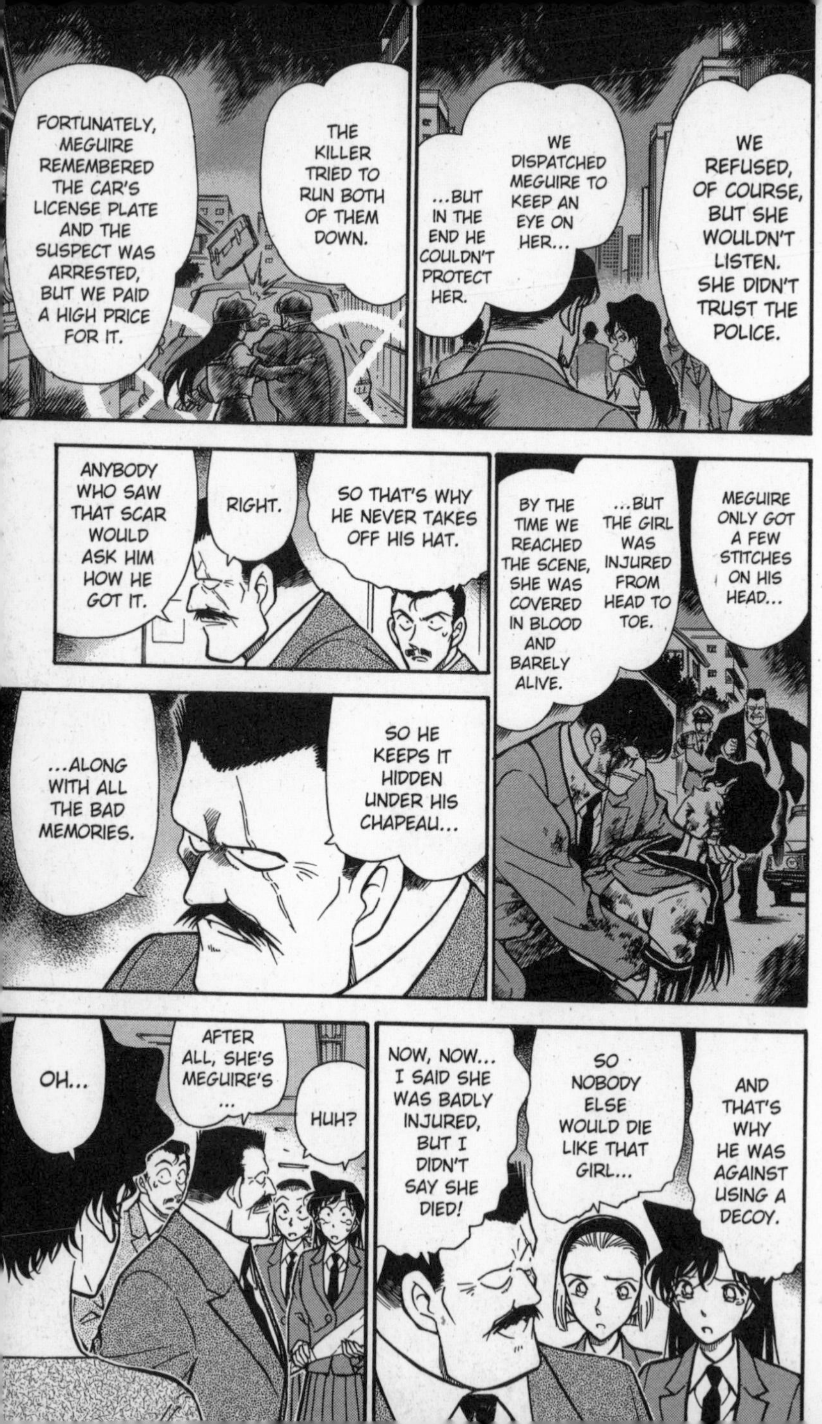
WE REFUSED, OF COURSE, BUT SHE WOULDN'T LISTEN. SHE DIDN'T TRUST THE POLICE.
WE DISPATCHED MEGUIRE TO KEEP AN EYE ON HER...
...BUT IN THE END HE COULDN'T PROTECT HER.
THE KILLER TRIED TO RUN BOTH OF THEM DOWN.
FORTUNATELY, MEGUIRE REMEMBERED THE CAR'S LICENSE PLATE AND THE SUSPECT WAS ARRESTED, BUT WE PAID A HIGH PRICE FOR IT.
MEGUIRE ONLY GOT A FEW STITCHES ON HIS HEAD...
...BUT THE GIRL WAS INJURED FROM HEAD TO TOE.
BY THE TIME WE REACHED THE SCENE, SHE WAS COVERED IN BLOOD AND BARELY ALIVE.
SO THAT'S WHY HE NEVER TAKES OFF HIS HAT.
RIGHT.
ANYBODY WHO SAW THAT SCAR WOULD ASK HIM HOW HE GOT IT.
SO HE KEEPS IT HIDDEN UNDER HIS CHAPEAU...
...ALONG WITH ALL THE BAD MEMORIES.
AND THAT'S WHY HE WAS AGAINST USING A DECOY.
SO NOBODY ELSE WOULD DIE LIKE THAT GIRL...
NOW, NOW... I SAID SHE WAS BADLY INJURED, BUT I DIDN'T SAY SHE DIED!
HUH?
AFTER ALL, SHE'S MEGUIRE'S ...
OH...

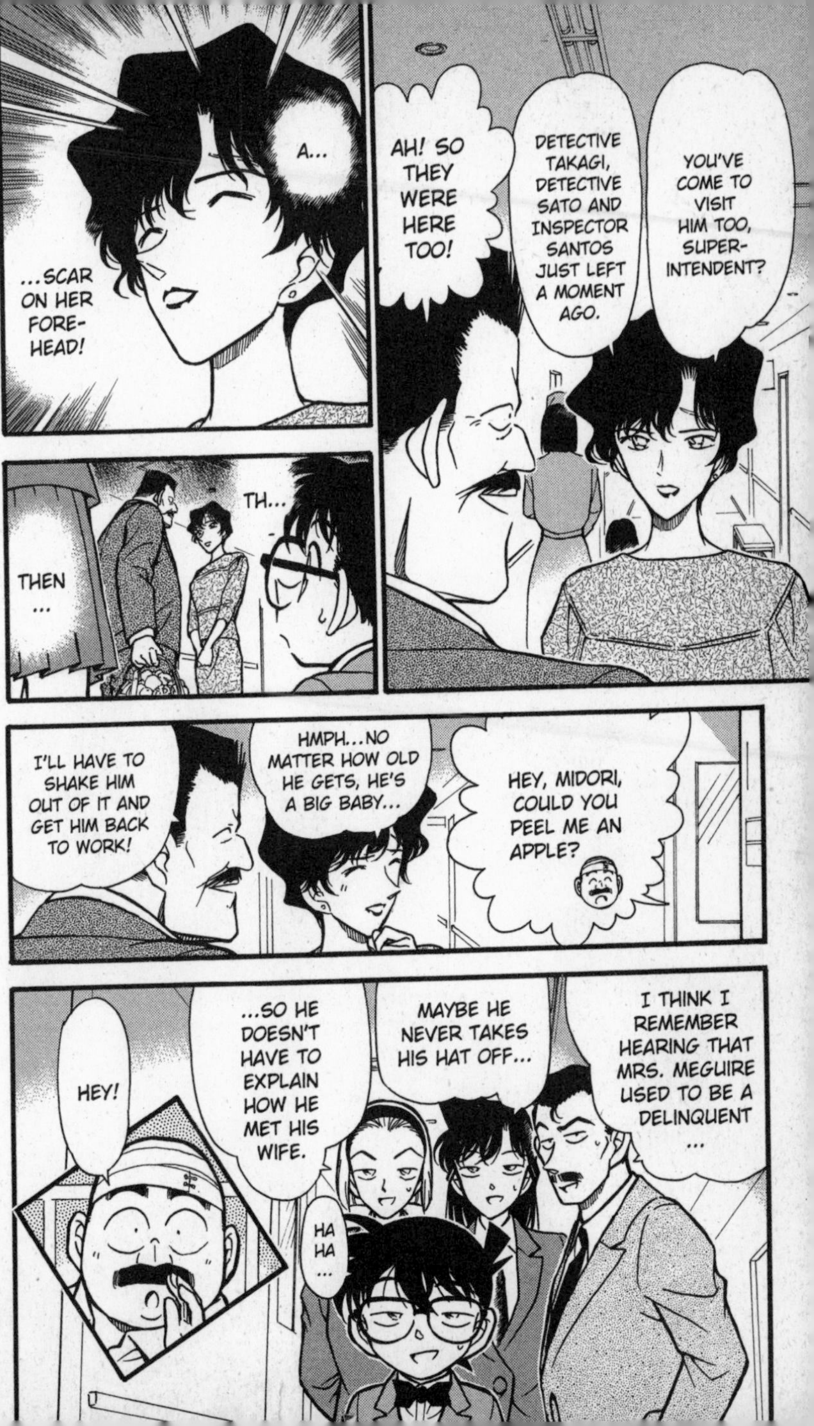
YOU'VE COME TO VISIT HIM TOO, SUPER-INTENDENT?
DETECTIVE TAKAGI, DETECTIVE SATO AND INSPECTOR SANTOS JUST LEFT A MOMENT AGO.
AH! SO THEY WERE HERE TOO!
A...
...SCAR ON HER FORE-HEAD!
TH...
THEN ...
HEY, MIDORI, COULD YOU PEEL ME AN APPLE?
HMPH...NO MATTER HOW OLD HE GETS, HE'S A BIG BABY...
I'LL HAVE TO SHAKE HIM OUT OF IT AND GET HIM BACK TO WORK!
I THINK I REMEMBER HEARING THAT MRS. MEGUIRE USED TO BE A DELINQUENT ...
MAYBE HE NEVER TAKES HIS HAT OFF...
...SO HE DOESN'T HAVE TO EXPLAIN HOW HE MET HIS WIFE.
HA HA ...
HEY!

FILE 3:
AN UNSEEN FEAR

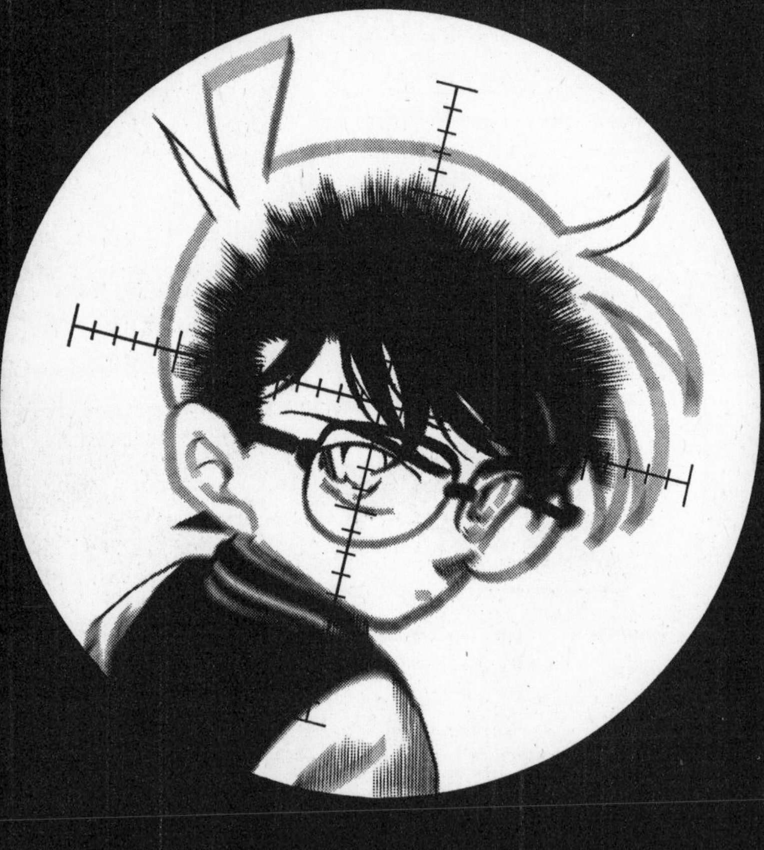

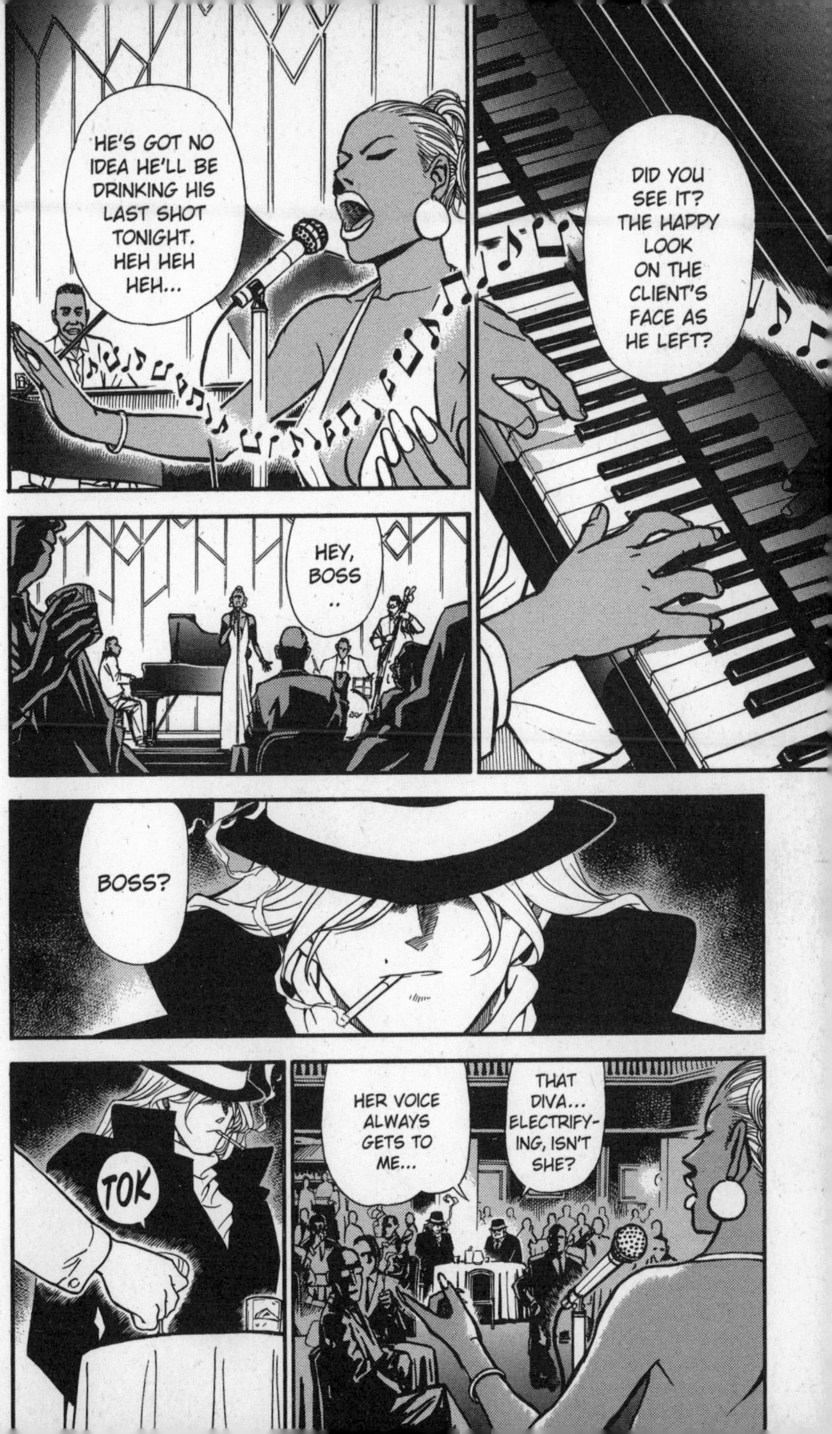
DID YOU SEE IT? THE HAPPY LOOK ON THE CLIENT'S FACE AS HE LEFT?
HE'S GOT NO IDEA HE'LL BE DRINKING HIS LAST SHOT TONIGHT. HEH HEH HEH...
HEY, BOSS ..
BOSS?
THAT DIVA... ELECTRIFY-ING, ISN'T SHE?
HER VOICE ALWAYS GETS TO ME...
TOK

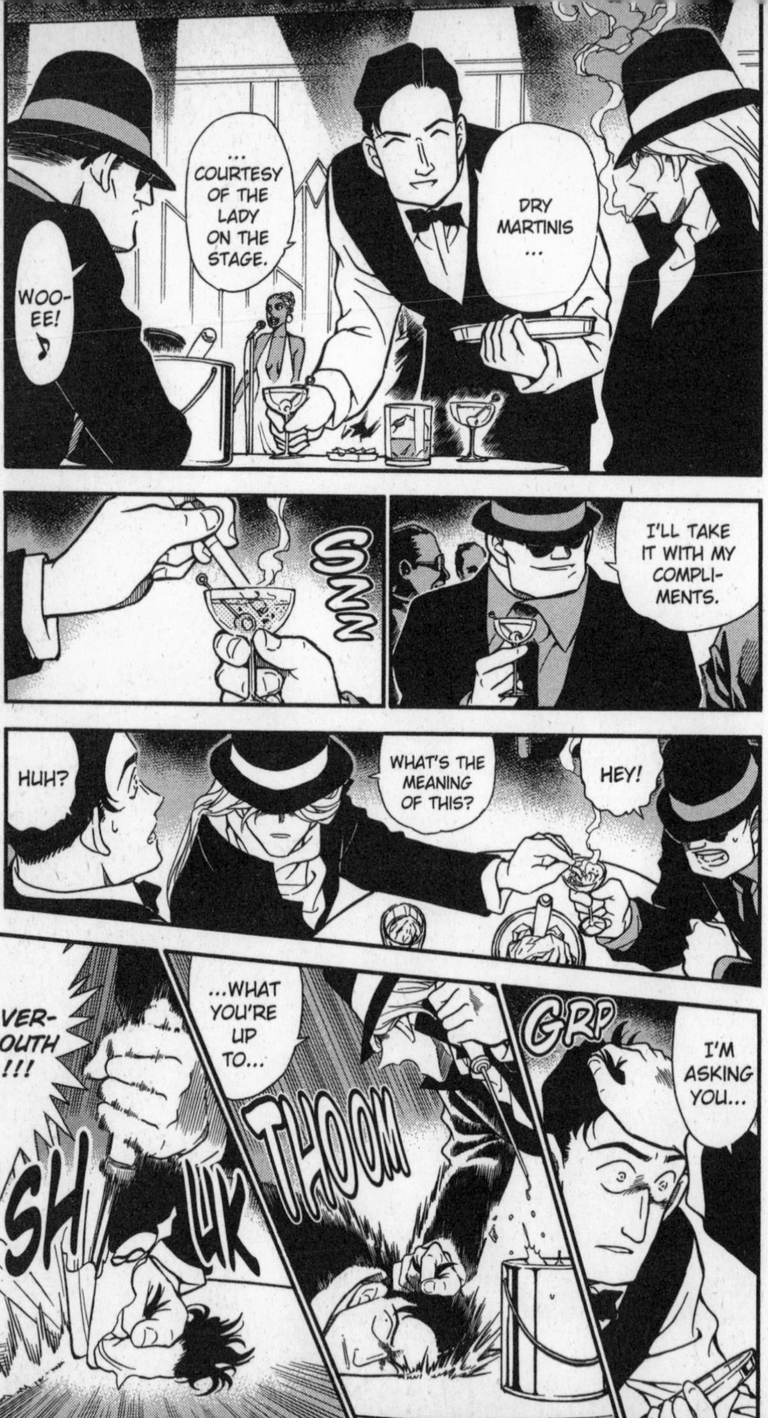
DRY MARTINIS ...
... COURTESY OF THE LADY ON THE STAGE.
WOO-EE! ♪
I'LL TAKE IT WITH MY COMPLIMENTS.
SZZ
HEY!
WHAT'S THE MEANING OF THIS?
HUH?
GRP
I'M ASKING YOU...
...WHAT YOU'RE UP TO...
THOOM
...VER-MOUTH!!!
SHLK

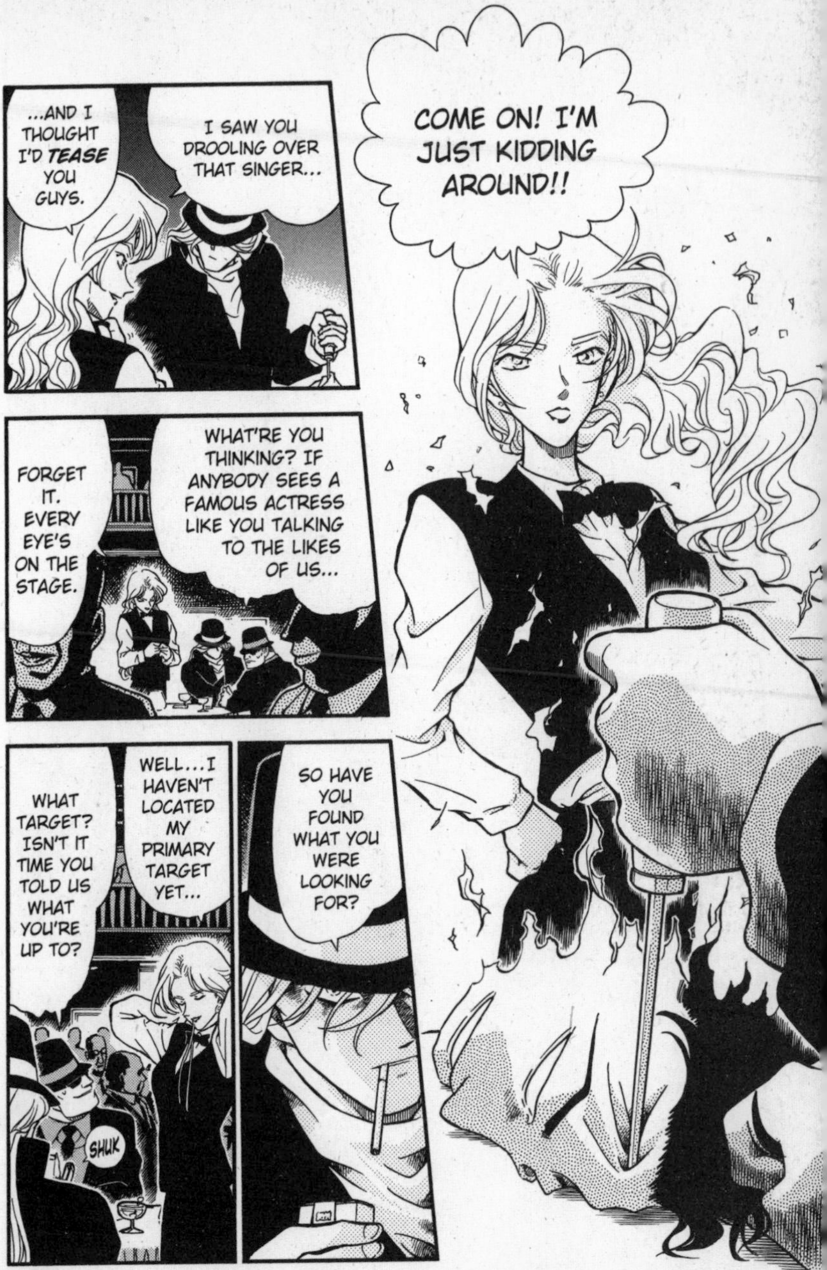
COME ON! I'M JUST KIDDING AROUND!!
I SAW YOU DROOLING OVER THAT SINGER...
...AND I THOUGHT I'D *TEASE* YOU GUYS.
WHAT'RE YOU THINKING? IF ANYBODY SEES A FAMOUS ACTRESS LIKE YOU TALKING TO THE LIKES OF US...
FORGET IT. EVERY EYE'S ON THE STAGE.
SO HAVE YOU FOUND WHAT YOU WERE LOOKING FOR?
WELL...I HAVEN'T LOCATED MY PRIMARY TARGET YET...
WHAT TARGET? ISN'T IT TIME YOU TOLD US WHAT YOU'RE UP TO?
SHUK

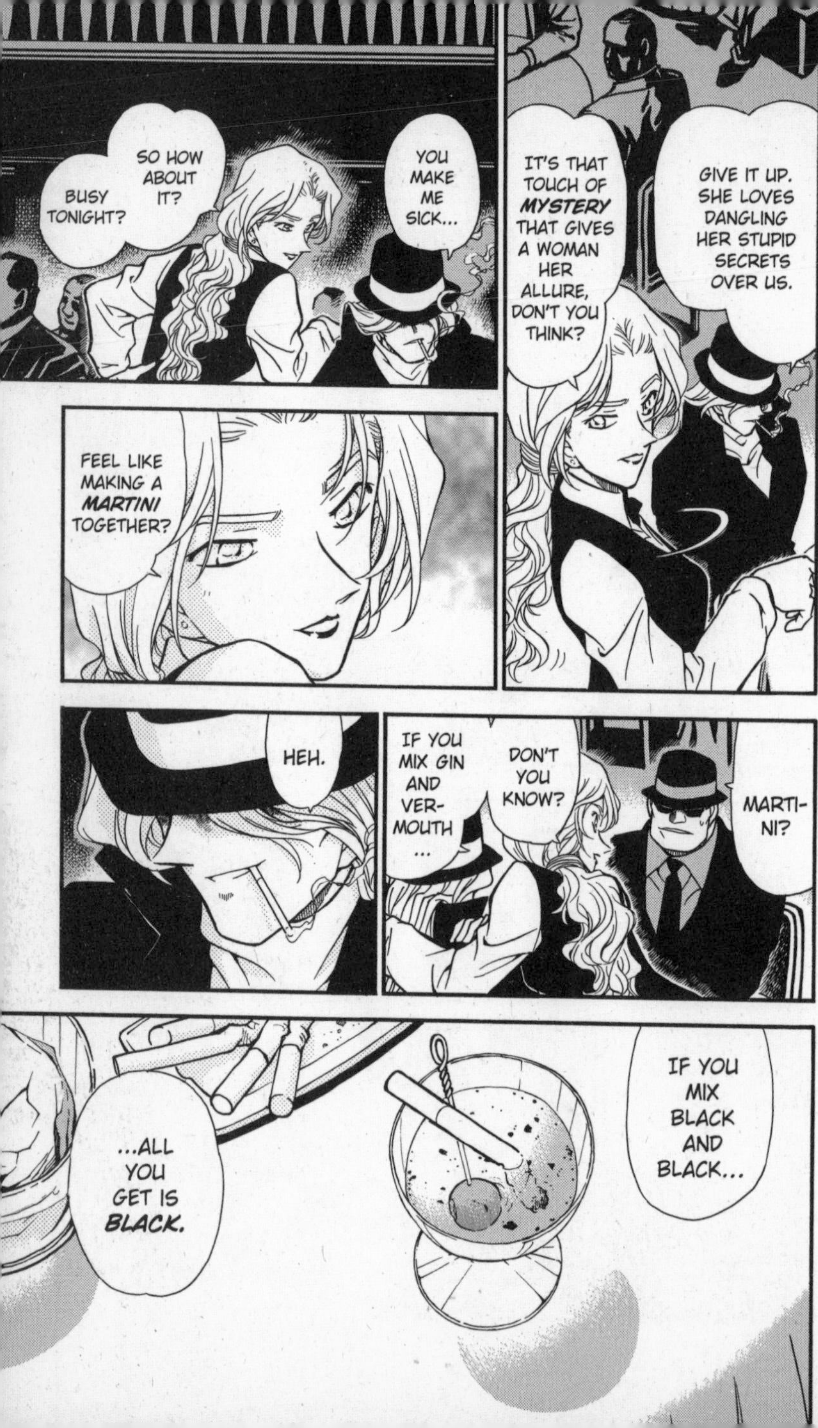
GIVE IT UP. SHE LOVES DANGLING HER STUPID SECRETS OVER US.
IT'S THAT TOUCH OF **MYSTERY** THAT GIVES A WOMAN HER ALLURE, DON'T YOU THINK?
YOU MAKE ME SICK...
SO HOW ABOUT IT?
BUSY TONIGHT?
FEEL LIKE MAKING A **MARTINI** TOGETHER?
MARTI-NI?
DON'T YOU KNOW?
IF YOU MIX GIN AND VER-MOUTH ...
HEH.
IF YOU MIX BLACK AND BLACK...
...ALL YOU GET IS **BLACK.**

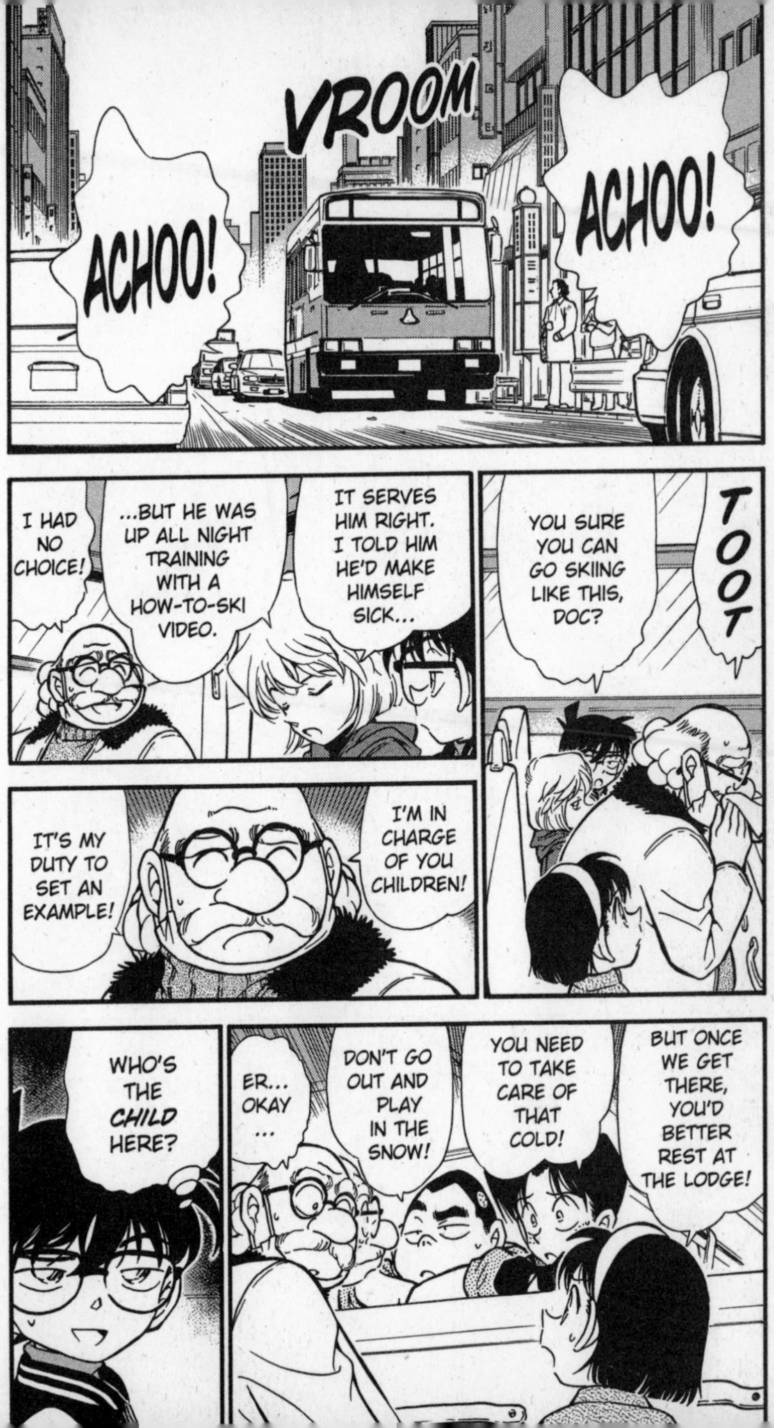
VROOM
ACHOO!
ACHOO!
TOOT
YOU SURE YOU CAN GO SKIING LIKE THIS, DOC?
IT SERVES HIM RIGHT. I TOLD HIM HE'D MAKE HIMSELF SICK...
...BUT HE WAS UP ALL NIGHT TRAINING WITH A HOW-TO-SKI VIDEO.
I HAD NO CHOICE!
I'M IN CHARGE OF YOU CHILDREN!
IT'S MY DUTY TO SET AN EXAMPLE!
BUT ONCE WE GET THERE, YOU'D BETTER REST AT THE LODGE!
YOU NEED TO TAKE CARE OF THAT COLD!
DON'T GO OUT AND PLAY IN THE SNOW!
ER... OKAY...
WHO'S THE *CHILD* HERE?

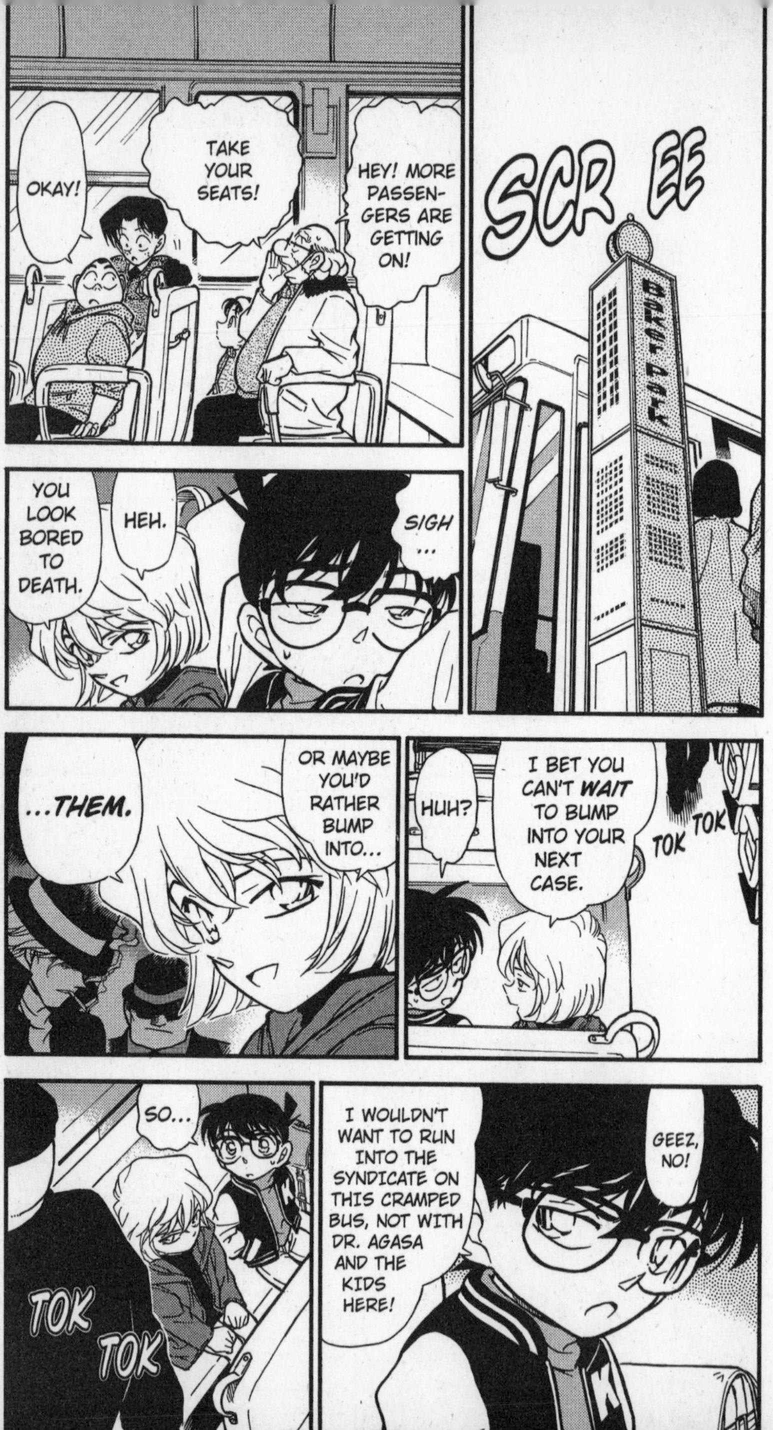
SCR EE
HEY! MORE PASSENGERS ARE GETTING ON!
TAKE YOUR SEATS!
OKAY!
SIGH ...
HEH.
YOU LOOK BORED TO DEATH.
TOK TOK
I BET YOU CAN'T *WAIT* TO BUMP INTO YOUR NEXT CASE.
HUH?
OR MAYBE YOU'D RATHER BUMP INTO...
...THEM.
GEEZ, NO!
I WOULDN'T WANT TO RUN INTO THE SYNDICATE ON THIS CRAMPED BUS, NOT WITH DR. AGASA AND THE KIDS HERE!
SO...
TOK TOK

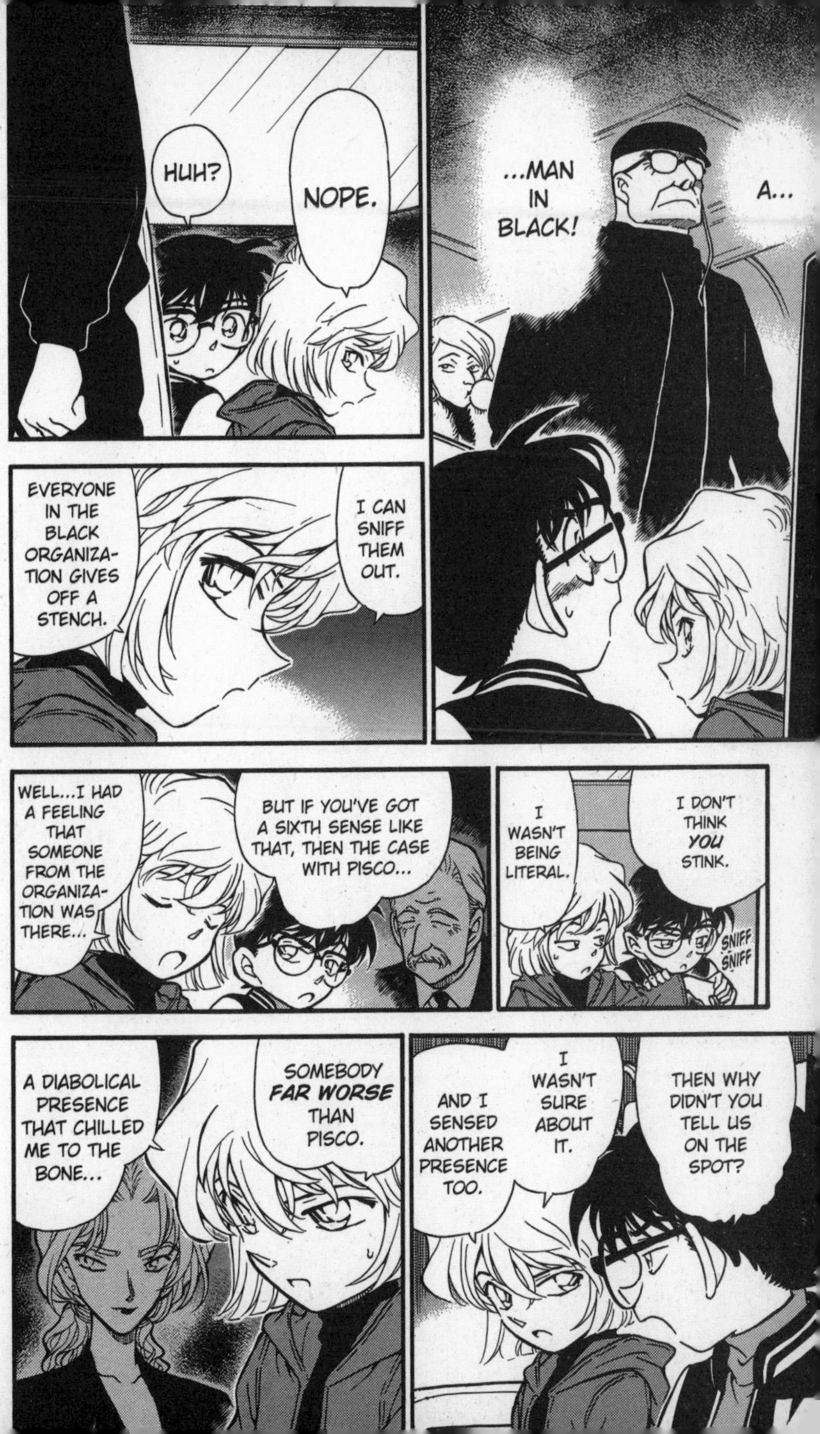

A...
...MAN IN BLACK!
NOPE.
HUH?
EVERYONE IN THE BLACK ORGANIZATION GIVES OFF A STENCH.
I CAN SNIFF THEM OUT.
I DON'T THINK *YOU* STINK.
SNIFF SNIFF
I WASN'T BEING LITERAL.
BUT IF YOU'VE GOT A SIXTH SENSE LIKE THAT, THEN THE CASE WITH PISCO...
WELL...I HAD A FEELING THAT SOMEONE FROM THE ORGANIZATION WAS THERE...
THEN WHY DIDN'T YOU TELL US ON THE SPOT?
I WASN'T SURE ABOUT IT.
AND I SENSED ANOTHER PRESENCE TOO.
SOMEBODY **FAR WORSE** THAN PISCO.
A DIABOLICAL PRESENCE THAT CHILLED ME TO THE BONE...

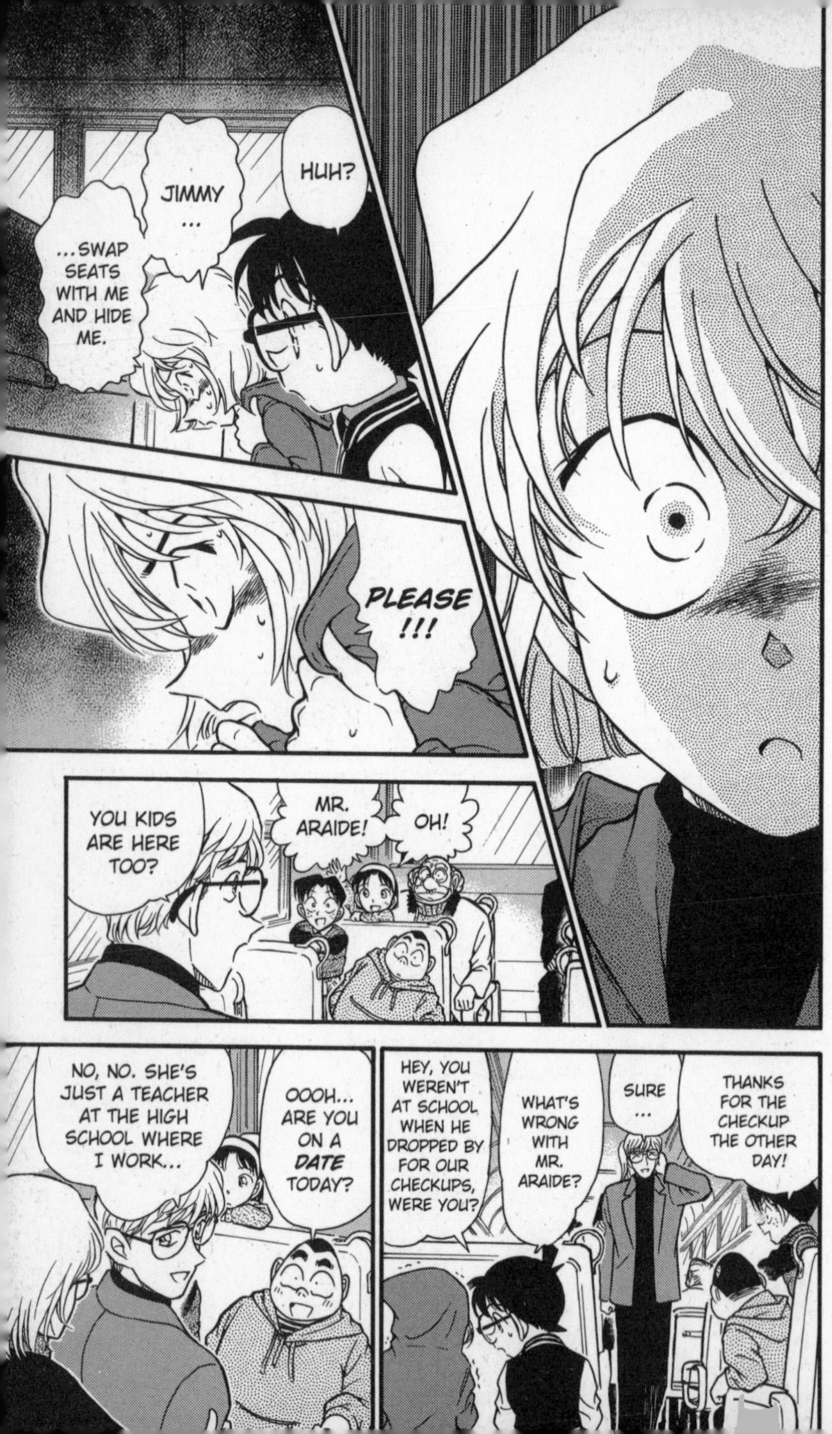
HUH?
JIMMY ...
...SWAP SEATS WITH ME AND HIDE ME.
PLEASE!!!
OH!
MR. ARAIDE!
YOU KIDS ARE HERE TOO?
THANKS FOR THE CHECKUP THE OTHER DAY!
SURE ...
WHAT'S WRONG WITH MR. ARAIDE?
HEY, YOU WEREN'T AT SCHOOL WHEN HE DROPPED BY FOR OUR CHECKUPS, WERE YOU?
OOOH... ARE YOU ON A *DATE* TODAY?
NO, NO. SHE'S JUST A TEACHER AT THE HIGH SCHOOL WHERE I WORK...

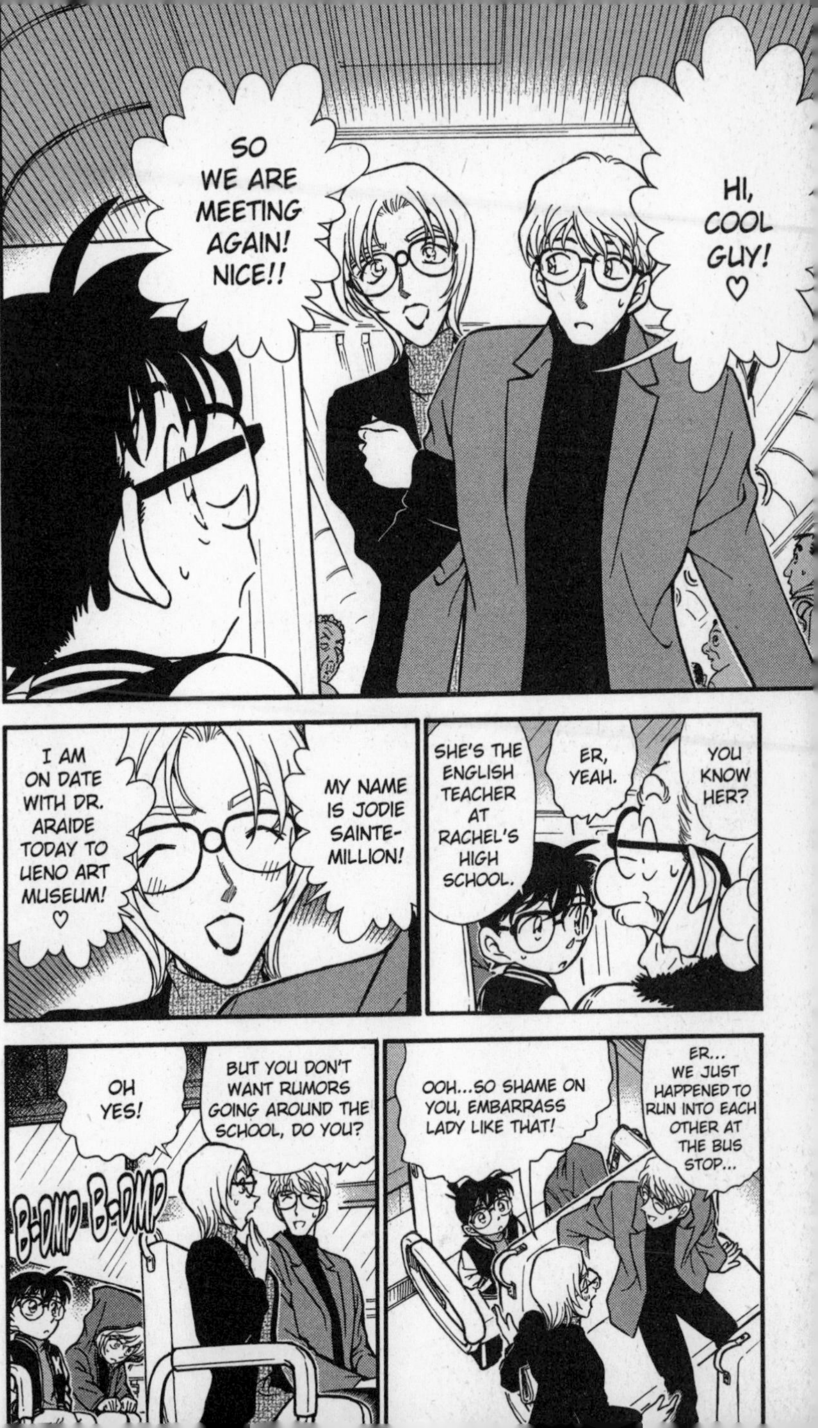
HI, COOL GUY! ♡
SO WE ARE MEETING AGAIN! NICE!!
YOU KNOW HER?
ER, YEAH.
SHE'S THE ENGLISH TEACHER AT RACHEL'S HIGH SCHOOL.
MY NAME IS JODIE SAINTE-MILLION!
I AM ON DATE WITH DR. ARAIDE TODAY TO UENO ART MUSEUM! ♡
ER... WE JUST HAPPENED TO RUN INTO EACH OTHER AT THE BUS STOP...
OOH...SO SHAME ON YOU, EMBARRASS LADY LIKE THAT!
BUT YOU DON'T WANT RUMORS GOING AROUND THE SCHOOL, DO YOU?
OH YES!
B-DMP B-DMP

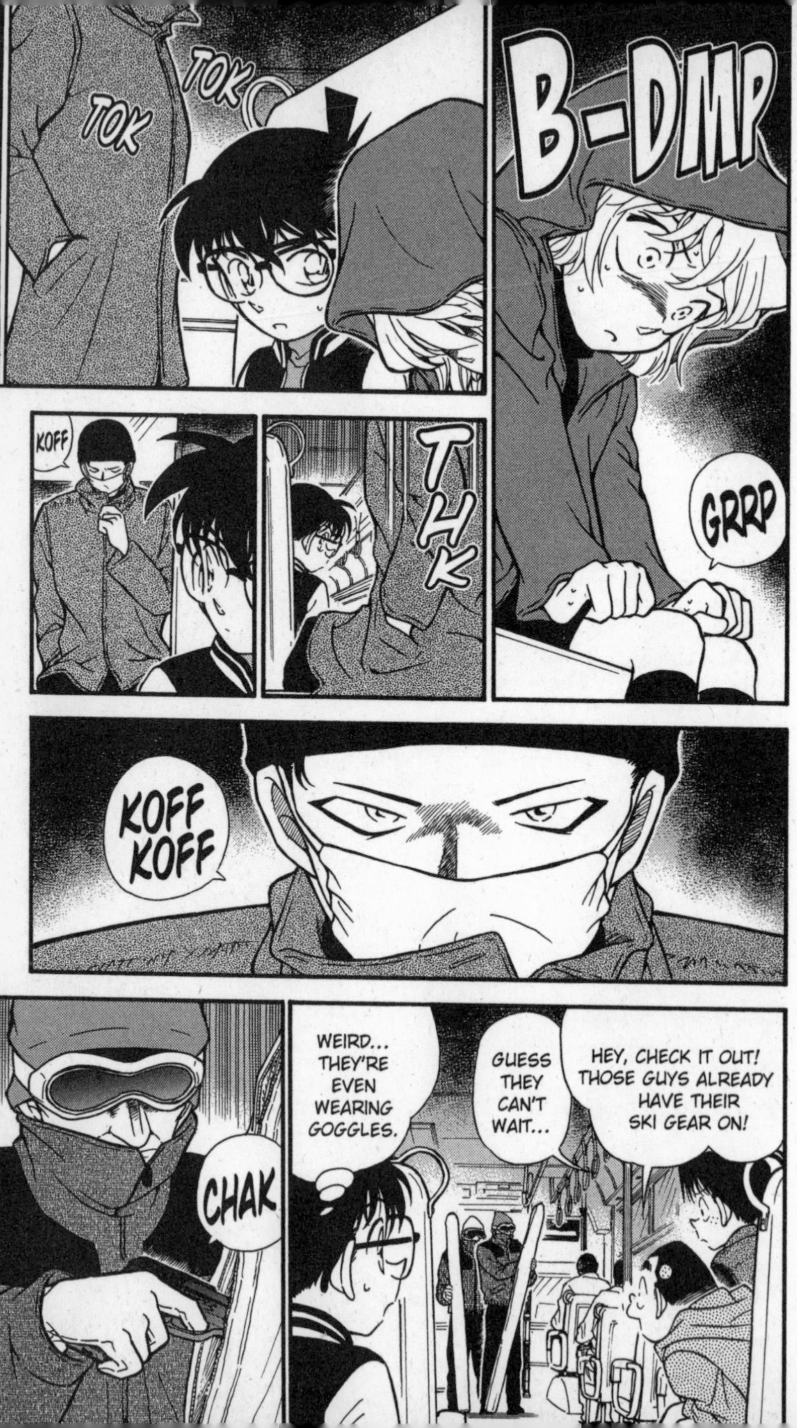
B-DMP
GRRP
TOK TOK
THK
KOFF
KOFF KOFF
HEY, CHECK IT OUT! THOSE GUYS ALREADY HAVE THEIR SKI GEAR ON!
GUESS THEY CAN'T WAIT...
WEIRD... THEY'RE EVEN WEARING GOGGLES.
CHAK

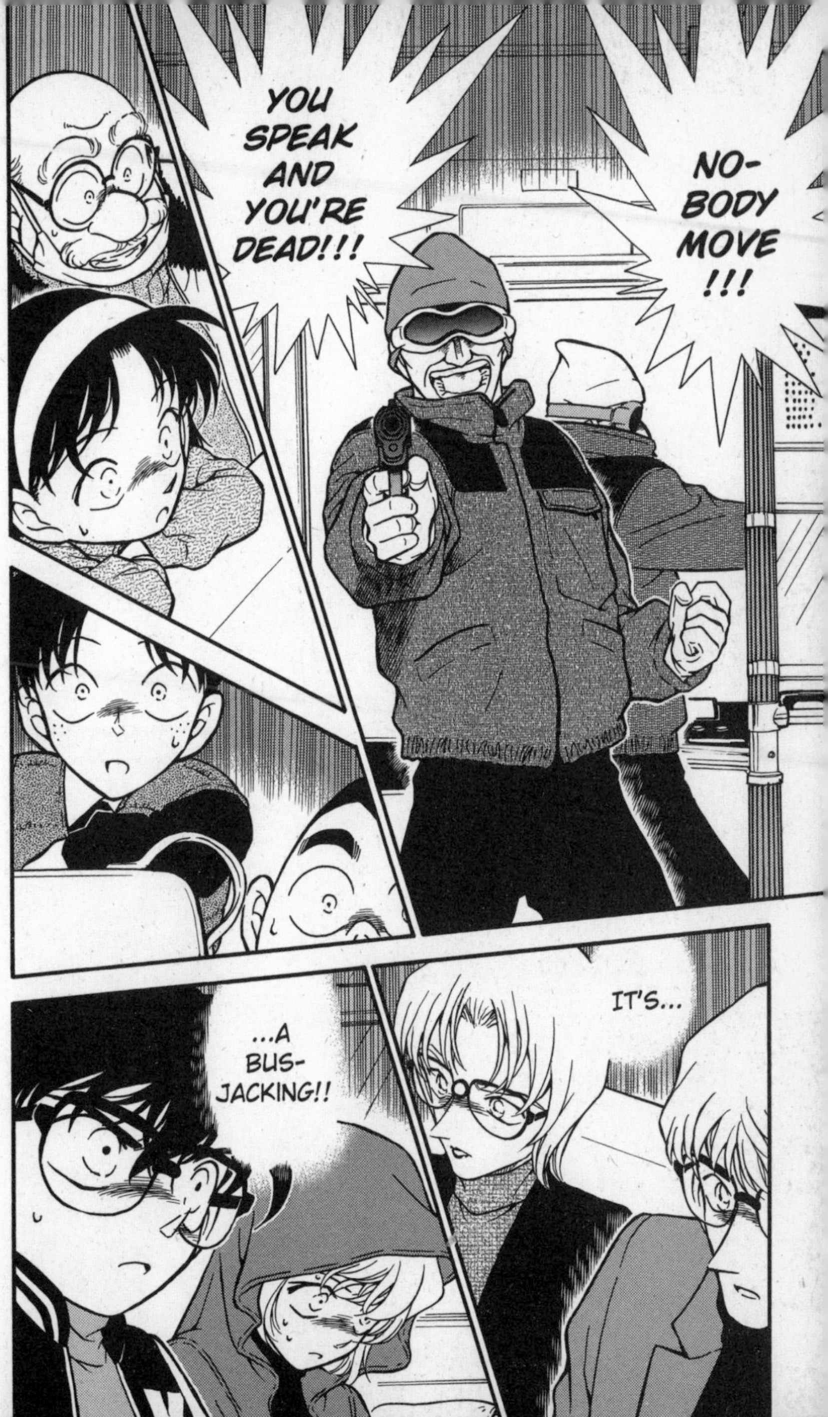
NO-BODY MOVE!!!
YOU SPEAK AND YOU'RE DEAD!!!
IT'S...
...A BUS-JACKING!!

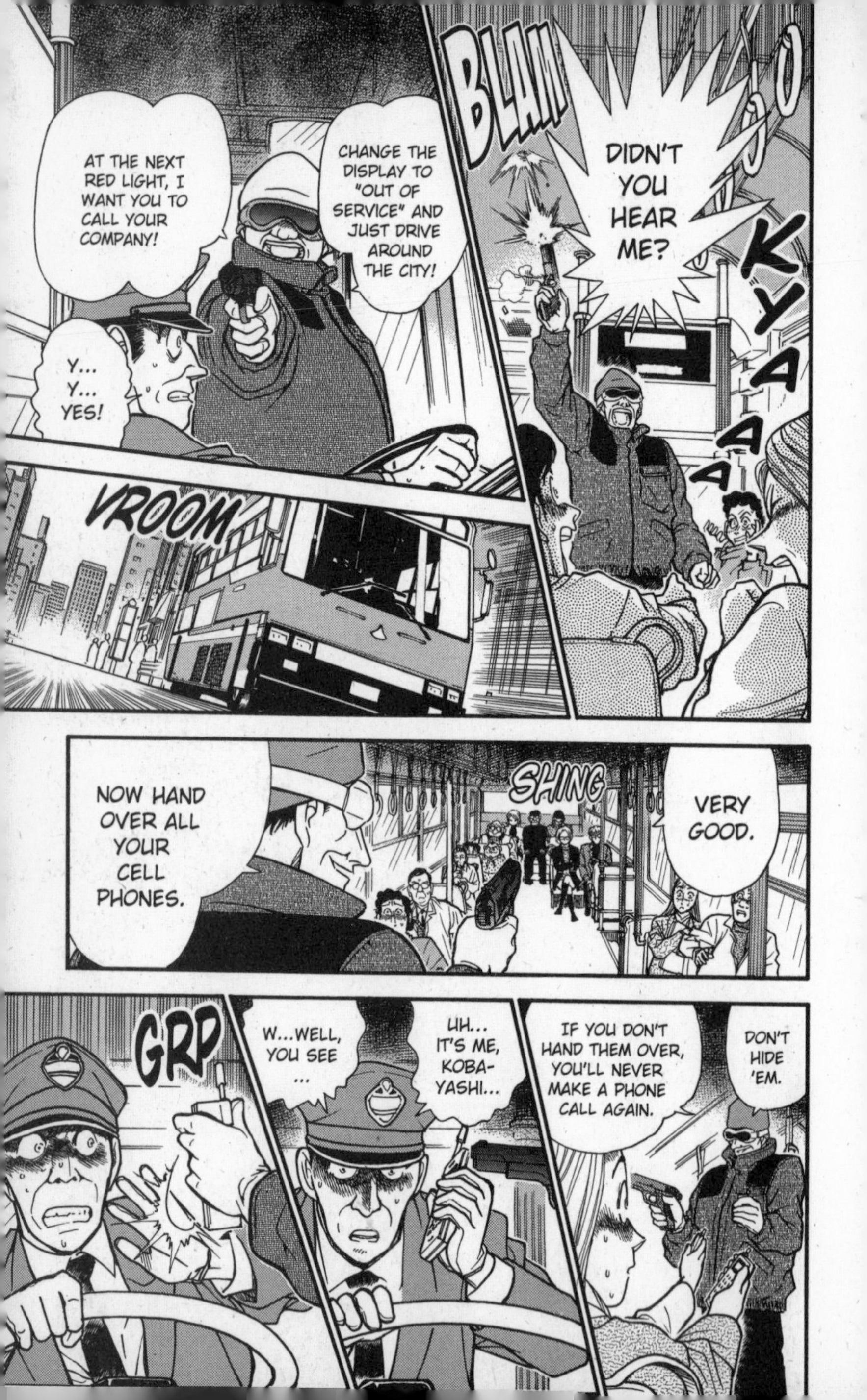
BLAM
DIDN'T YOU HEAR ME?
KYAAAA
CHANGE THE DISPLAY TO "OUT OF SERVICE" AND JUST DRIVE AROUND THE CITY!
AT THE NEXT RED LIGHT, I WANT YOU TO CALL YOUR COMPANY!
Y... Y... YES!
VROOM
VERY GOOD.
SHING
NOW HAND OVER ALL YOUR CELL PHONES.
DON'T HIDE 'EM.
IF YOU DON'T HAND THEM OVER, YOU'LL NEVER MAKE A PHONE CALL AGAIN.
UH... IT'S ME, KOBA-YASHI...
W...WELL, YOU SEE ...
GRP

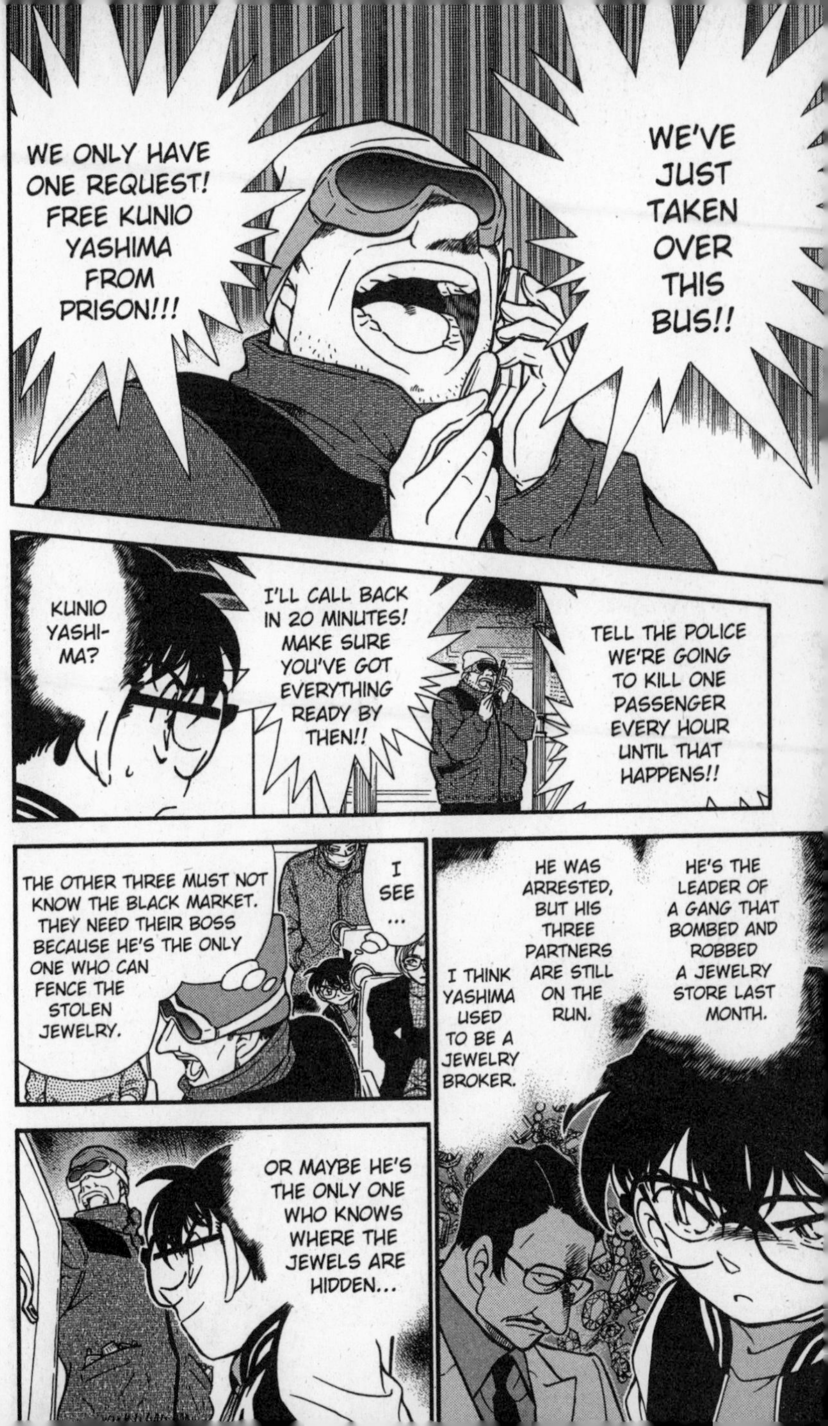
WE'VE JUST TAKEN OVER THIS BUS!!
WE ONLY HAVE ONE REQUEST! FREE KUNIO YASHIMA FROM PRISON!!!
TELL THE POLICE WE'RE GOING TO KILL ONE PASSENGER EVERY HOUR UNTIL THAT HAPPENS!!
I'LL CALL BACK IN 20 MINUTES! MAKE SURE YOU'VE GOT EVERYTHING READY BY THEN!!
KUNIO YASHI-MA?
HE'S THE LEADER OF A GANG THAT BOMBED AND ROBBED A JEWELRY STORE LAST MONTH.
HE WAS ARRESTED, BUT HIS THREE PARTNERS ARE STILL ON THE RUN.
I THINK YASHIMA USED TO BE A JEWELRY BROKER.
I SEE...
THE OTHER THREE MUST NOT KNOW THE BLACK MARKET. THEY NEED THEIR BOSS BECAUSE HE'S THE ONLY ONE WHO CAN FENCE THE STOLEN JEWELRY.
OR MAYBE HE'S THE ONLY ONE WHO KNOWS WHERE THE JEWELS ARE HIDDEN...

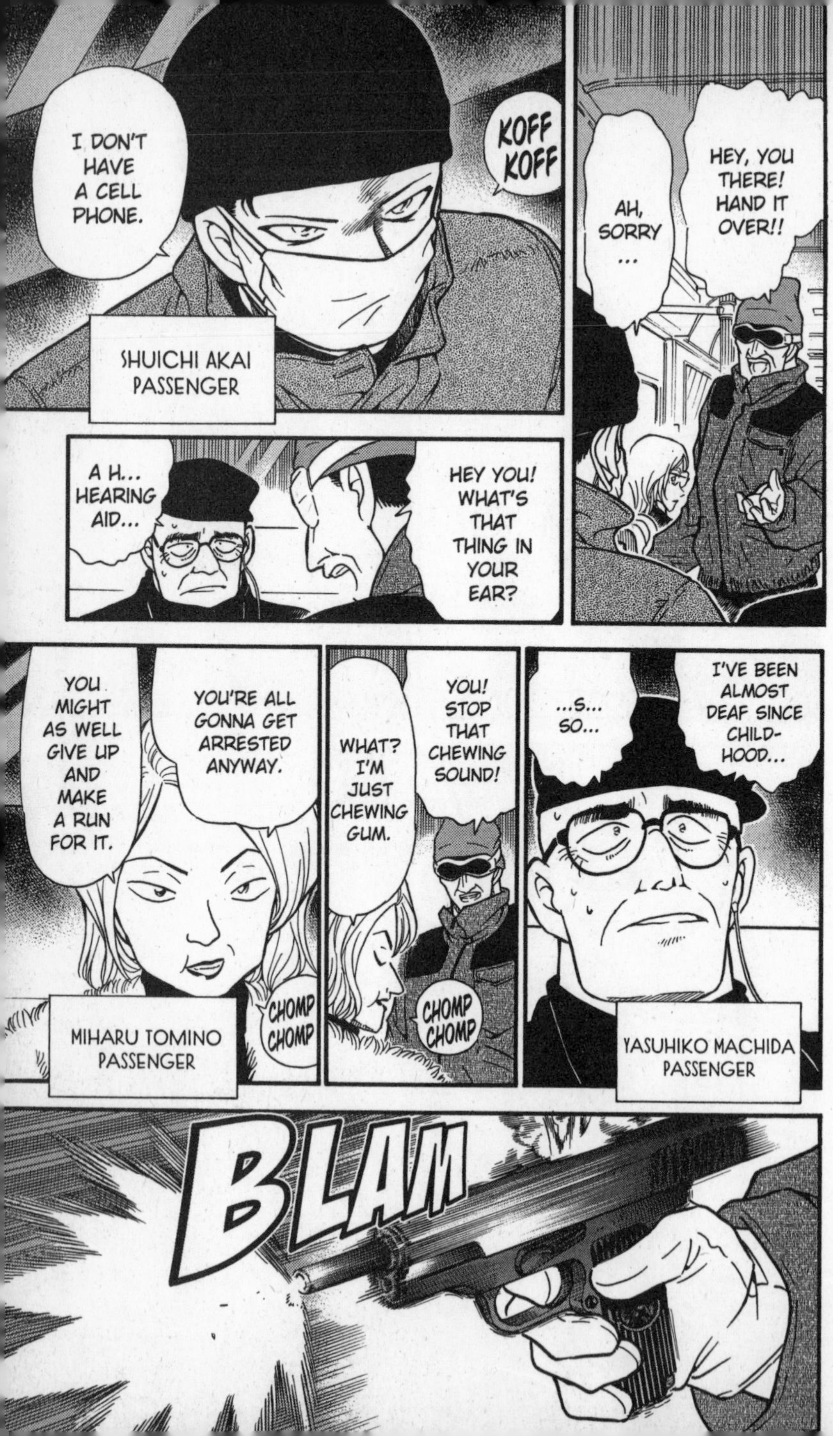
HEY, YOU THERE! HAND IT OVER!!
AH, SORRY ...
KOFF KOFF
I DON'T HAVE A CELL PHONE.
SHUICHI AKAI PASSENGER
HEY YOU! WHAT'S THAT THING IN YOUR EAR?
A H... HEARING AID...
I'VE BEEN ALMOST DEAF SINCE CHILD-HOOD...
...S... SO...
YASUHIKO MACHIDA PASSENGER
YOU! STOP THAT CHEWING SOUND!
WHAT? I'M JUST CHEWING GUM.
CHOMP CHOMP
CHOMP CHOMP
YOU'RE ALL GONNA GET ARRESTED ANYWAY.
YOU MIGHT AS WELL GIVE UP AND MAKE A RUN FOR IT.
MIHARU TOMINO PASSENGER
BLAM

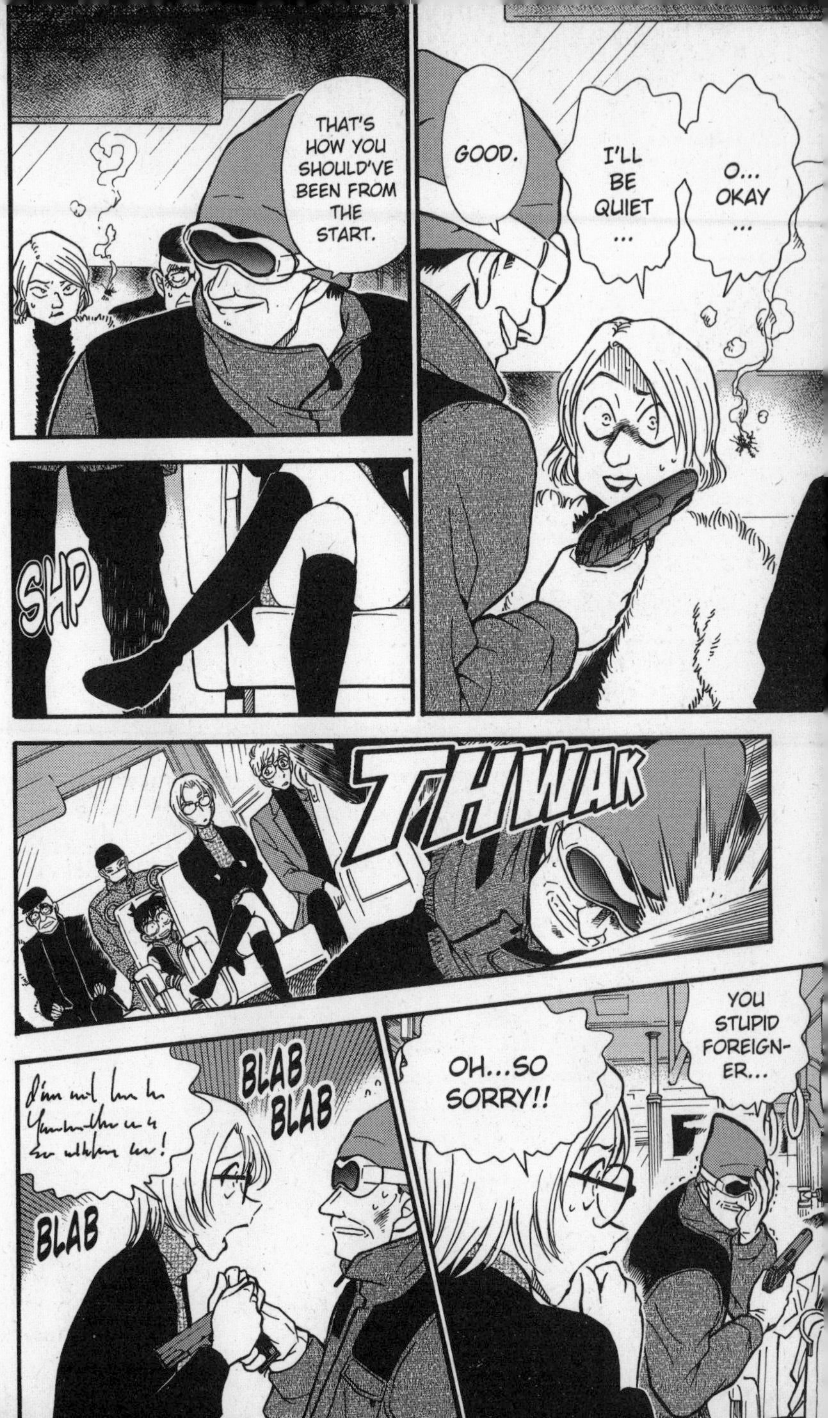
O... OKAY ...
I'LL BE QUIET ...
GOOD.
THAT'S HOW YOU SHOULD'VE BEEN FROM THE START.
SHP
THWAK
YOU STUPID FOREIGN-ER...
OH...SO SORRY!!
BLAB BLAB
BLAB

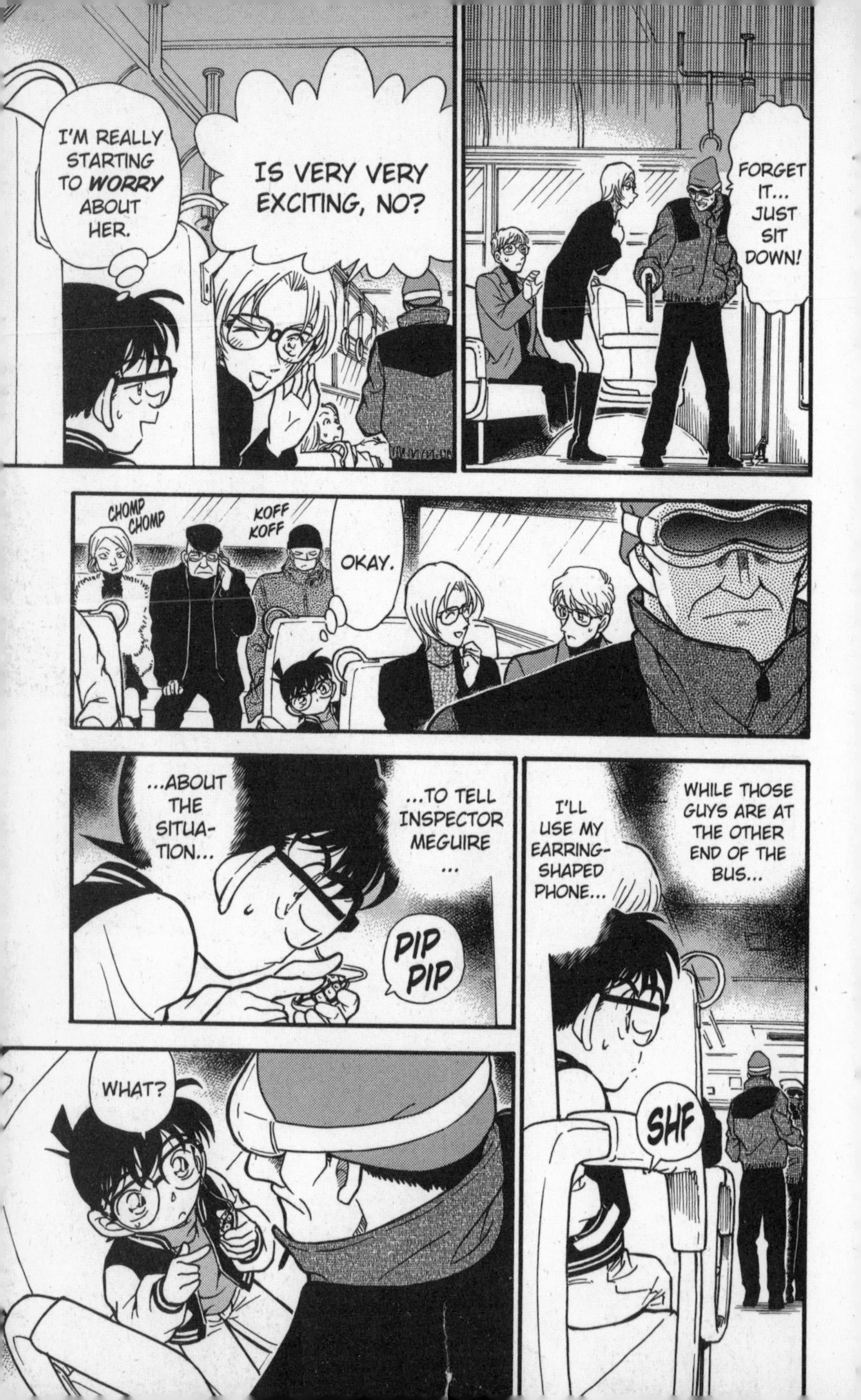
FORGET IT... JUST SIT DOWN!
IS VERY VERY EXCITING, NO?
I'M REALLY STARTING TO **WORRY** ABOUT HER.
OKAY.
KOFF KOFF
CHOMP CHOMP
WHILE THOSE GUYS ARE AT THE OTHER END OF THE BUS...
I'LL USE MY EARRING-SHAPED PHONE...
SHF
...TO TELL INSPECTOR MEGUIRE ...
...ABOUT THE SITUATION...
PIP PIP
WHAT?

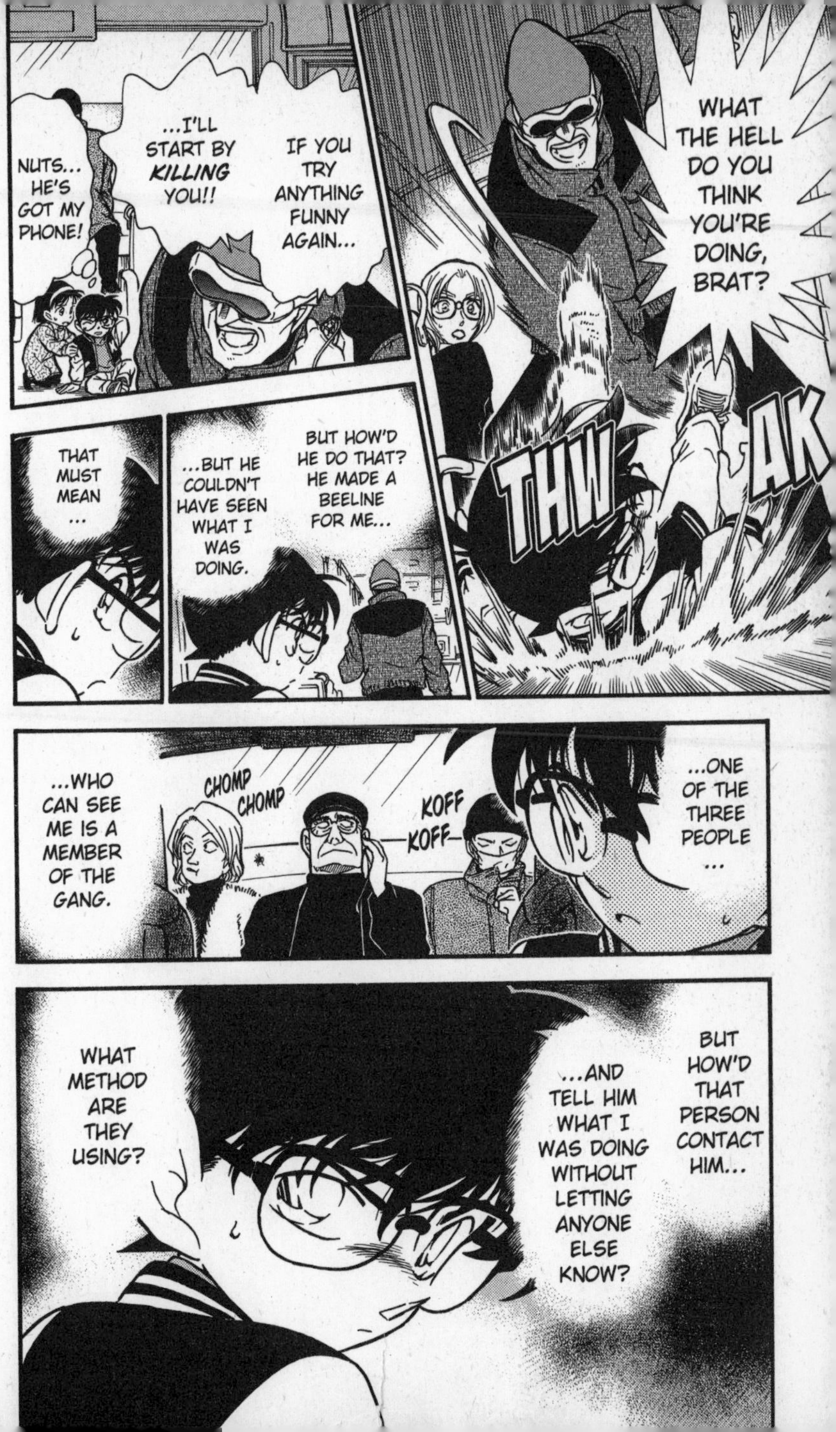
WHAT THE HELL DO YOU THINK YOU'RE DOING, BRAT?
THWAK
IF YOU TRY ANYTHING FUNNY AGAIN...
...I'LL START BY **KILLING** YOU!!
NUTS... HE'S GOT MY PHONE!
BUT HOW'D HE DO THAT? HE MADE A BEELINE FOR ME...
...BUT HE COULDN'T HAVE SEEN WHAT I WAS DOING.
THAT MUST MEAN ...
...ONE OF THE THREE PEOPLE ...
KOFF KOFF
CHOMP CHOMP
...WHO CAN SEE ME IS A MEMBER OF THE GANG.
BUT HOW'D THAT PERSON CONTACT HIM...
...AND TELL HIM WHAT I WAS DOING WITHOUT LETTING ANYONE ELSE KNOW?
WHAT METHOD ARE THEY USING?

FILE 4: RED ALERT

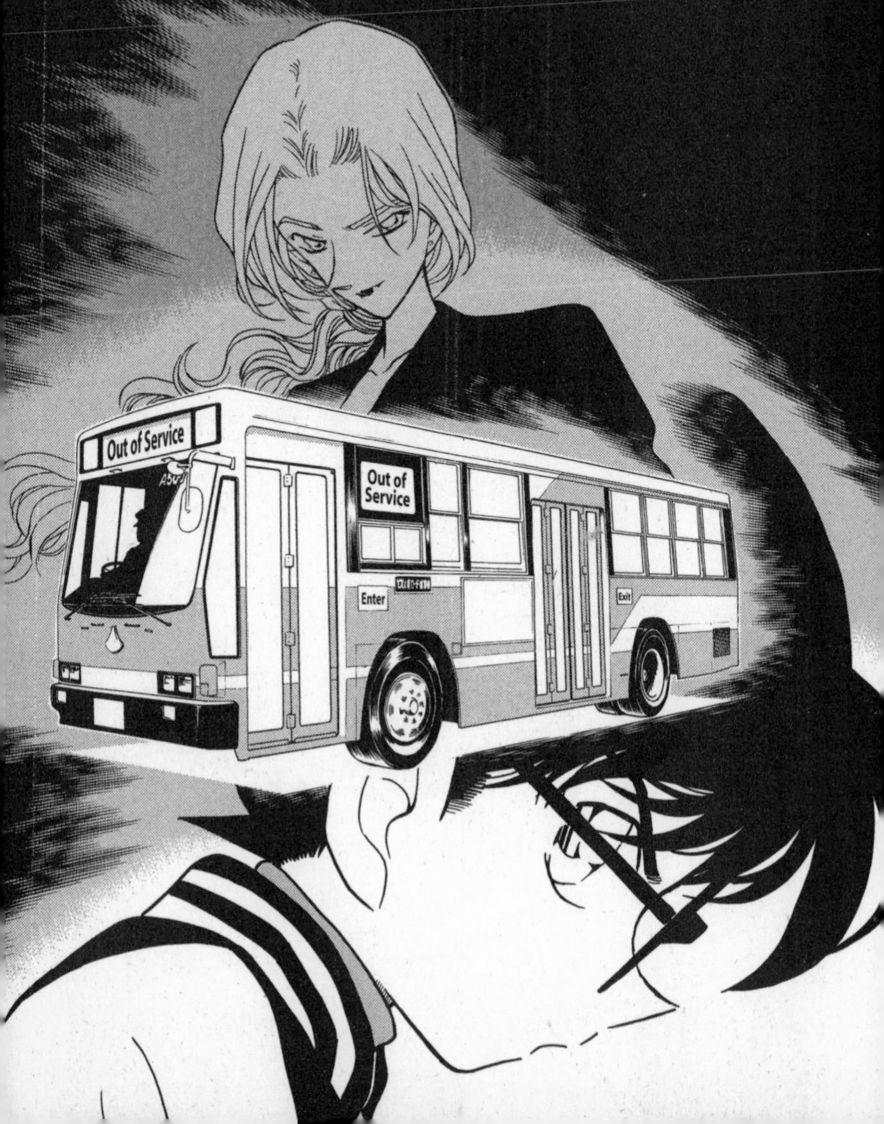
Out of Service
Out of Service
Enter
Exit

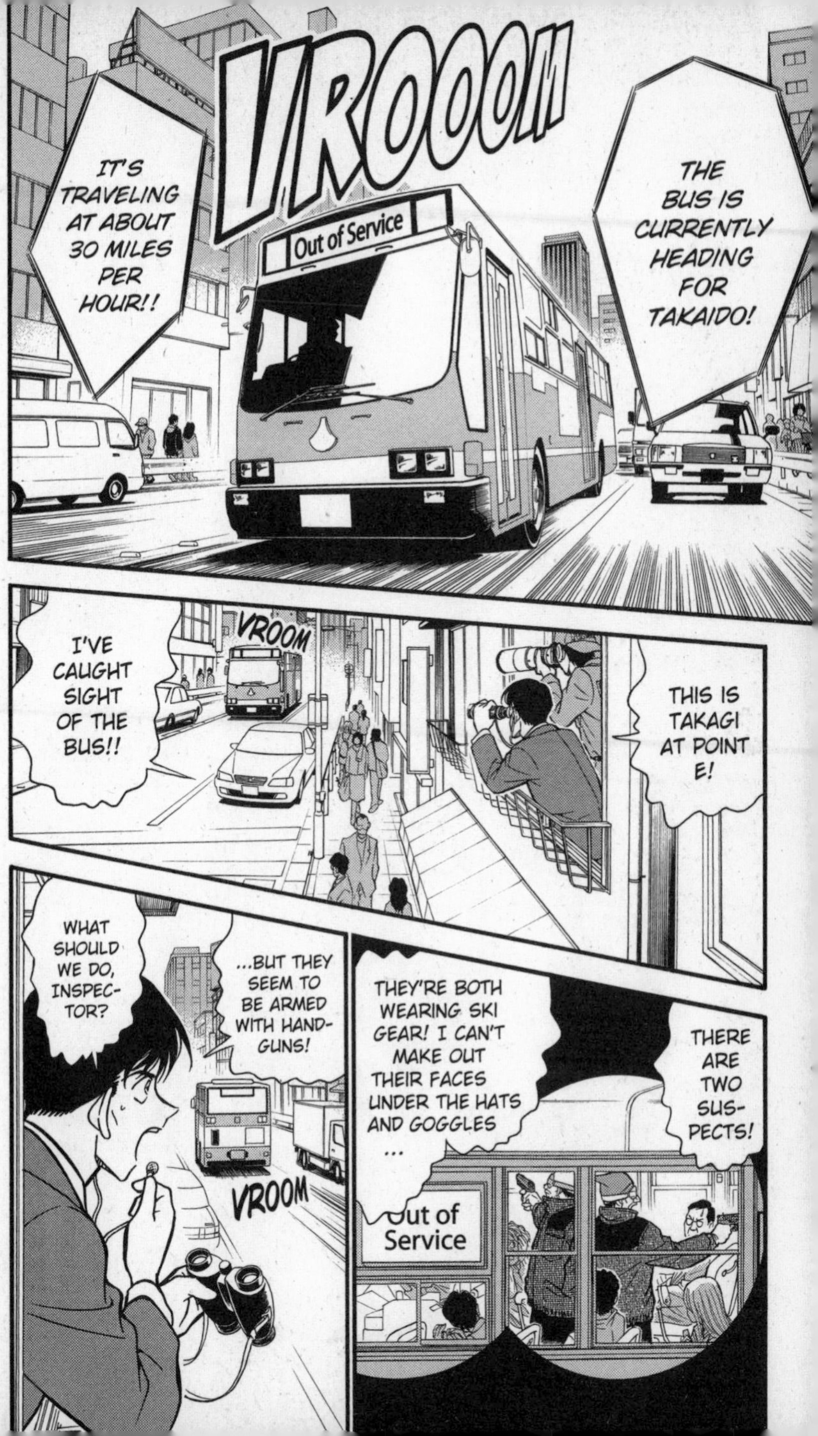
VROOOM
THE BUS IS CURRENTLY HEADING FOR TAKAIDO!
Out of Service
IT'S TRAVELING AT ABOUT 30 MILES PER HOUR!!
THIS IS TAKAGI AT POINT E!
VROOM
I'VE CAUGHT SIGHT OF THE BUS!!
THERE ARE TWO SUS-PECTS!
THEY'RE BOTH WEARING SKI GEAR! I CAN'T MAKE OUT THEIR FACES UNDER THE HATS AND GOGGLES ...
Out of Service
...BUT THEY SEEM TO BE ARMED WITH HAND-GUNS!
WHAT SHOULD WE DO, INSPEC-TOR?
VROOM

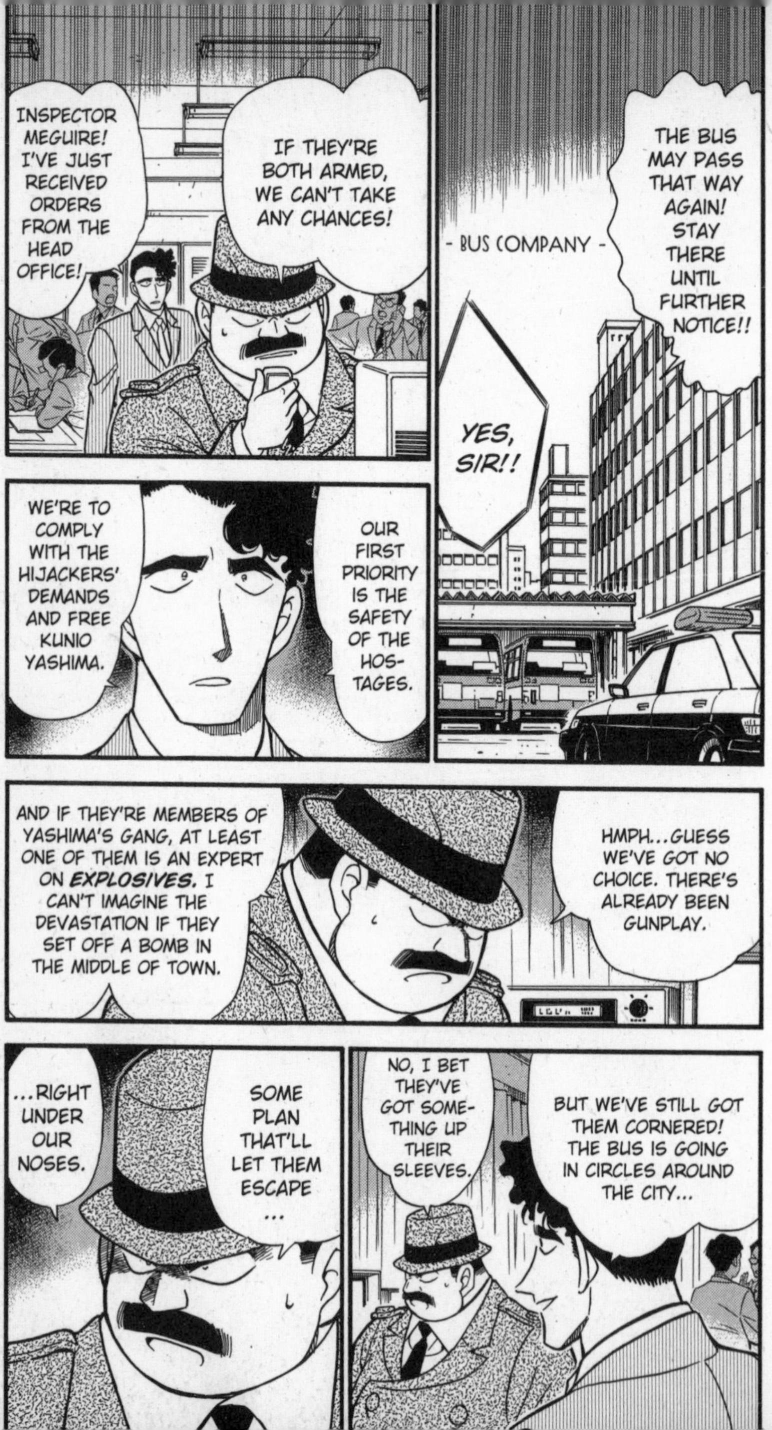
THE BUS MAY PASS THAT WAY AGAIN! STAY THERE UNTIL FURTHER NOTICE!!
- BUS COMPANY -
YES, SIR!!
IF THEY'RE BOTH ARMED, WE CAN'T TAKE ANY CHANCES!
INSPECTOR MEGUIRE! I'VE JUST RECEIVED ORDERS FROM THE HEAD OFFICE!
OUR FIRST PRIORITY IS THE SAFETY OF THE HOS-TAGES.
WE'RE TO COMPLY WITH THE HIJACKERS' DEMANDS AND FREE KUNIO YASHIMA.
HMPH...GUESS WE'VE GOT NO CHOICE. THERE'S ALREADY BEEN GUNPLAY.
AND IF THEY'RE MEMBERS OF YASHIMA'S GANG, AT LEAST ONE OF THEM IS AN EXPERT ON ***EXPLOSIVES.*** I CAN'T IMAGINE THE DEVASTATION IF THEY SET OFF A BOMB IN THE MIDDLE OF TOWN.
BUT WE'VE STILL GOT THEM CORNERED! THE BUS IS GOING IN CIRCLES AROUND THE CITY...
NO, I BET THEY'VE GOT SOME-THING UP THEIR SLEEVES.
SOME PLAN THAT'LL LET THEM ESCAPE...
...RIGHT UNDER OUR NOSES.

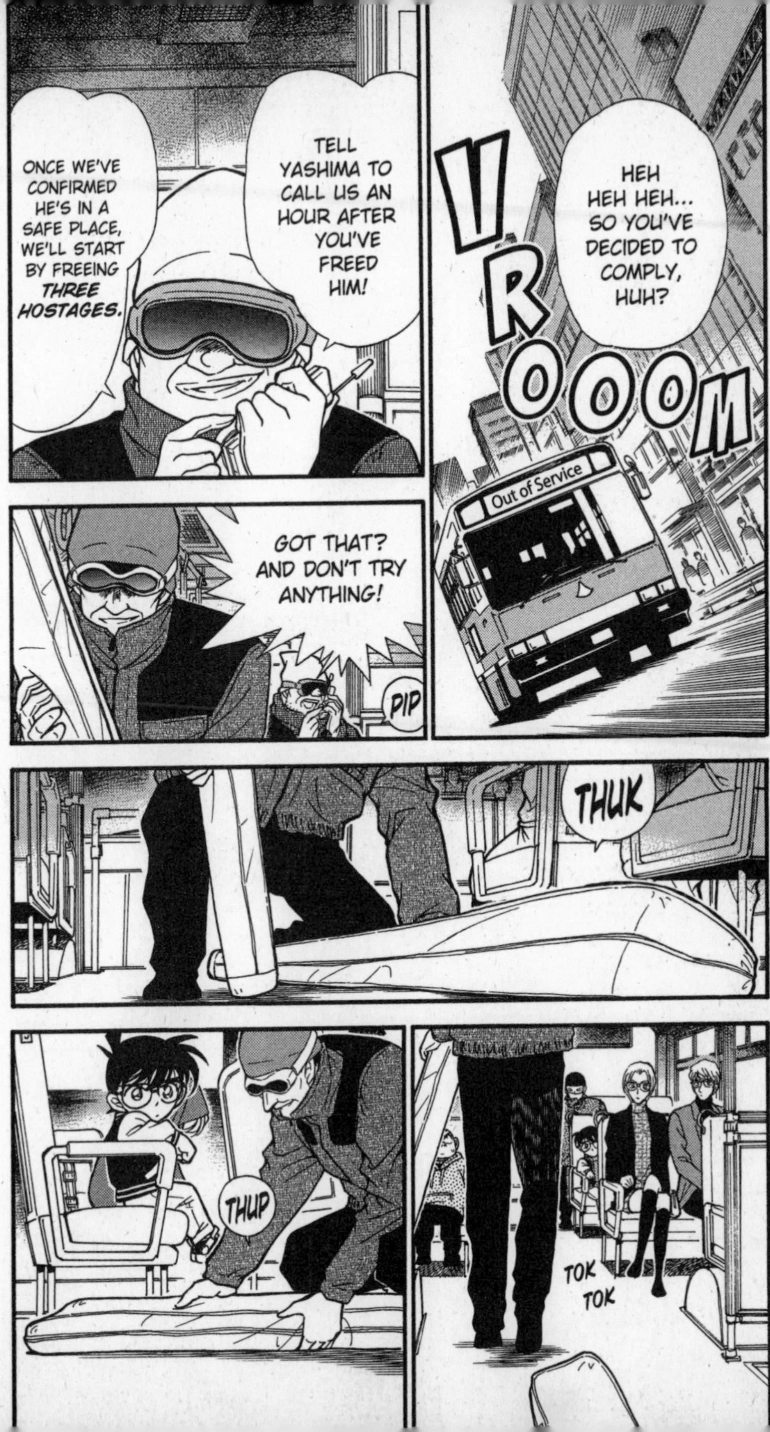
HEH HEH HEH... SO YOU'VE DECIDED TO COMPLY, HUH?
VROOOM
Out of Service
TELL YASHIMA TO CALL US AN HOUR AFTER YOU'VE FREED HIM!
ONCE WE'VE CONFIRMED HE'S IN A SAFE PLACE, WE'LL START BY FREEING *THREE HOSTAGES.*
GOT THAT? AND DON'T TRY ANYTHING!
PIP
THUK
TOK TOK
THUP

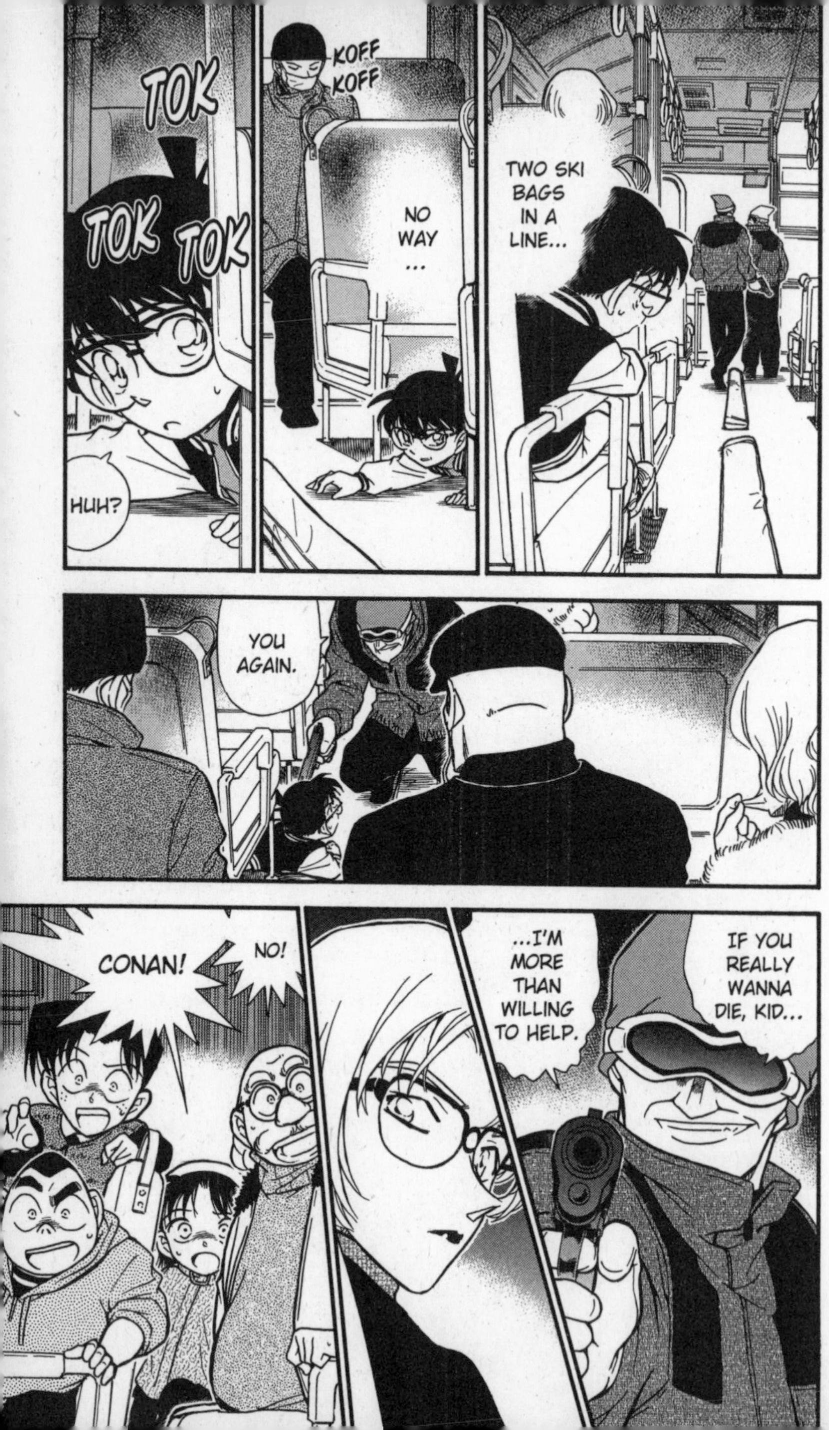
TWO SKI BAGS IN A LINE...
KOFF KOFF
NO WAY ...
TOK
TOK TOK
HUH?
YOU AGAIN.
IF YOU REALLY WANNA DIE, KID...
...I'M MORE THAN WILLING TO HELP.
NO!
CONAN!

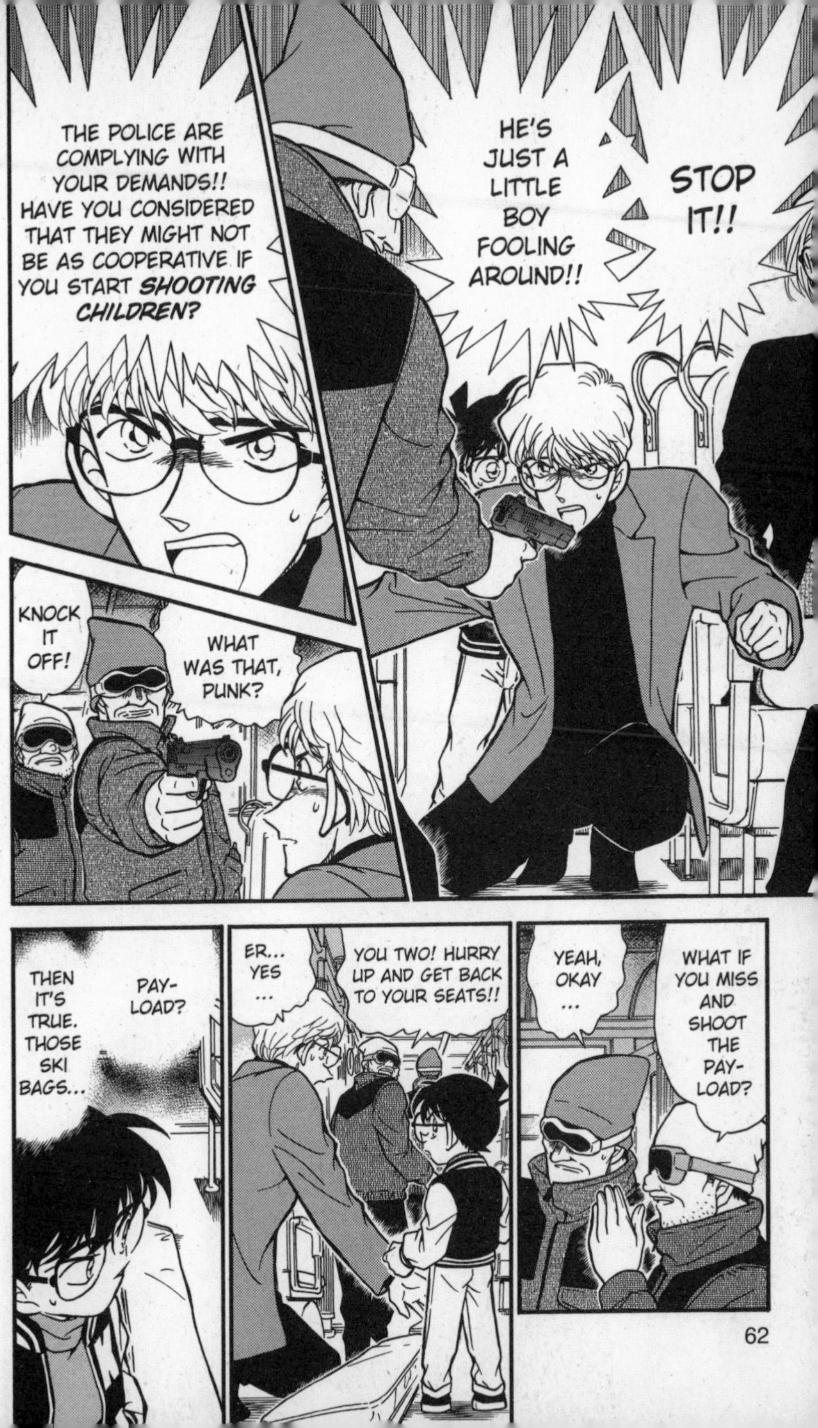
STOP IT!!
HE'S JUST A LITTLE BOY FOOLING AROUND!!
THE POLICE ARE COMPLYING WITH YOUR DEMANDS!! HAVE YOU CONSIDERED THAT THEY MIGHT NOT BE AS COOPERATIVE IF YOU START *SHOOTING CHILDREN?*
WHAT WAS THAT, PUNK?
KNOCK IT OFF!
WHAT IF YOU MISS AND SHOOT THE PAY-LOAD?
YEAH, OKAY ...
YOU TWO! HURRY UP AND GET BACK TO YOUR SEATS!!
ER... YES ...
PAY-LOAD?
THEN IT'S TRUE. THOSE SKI BAGS...

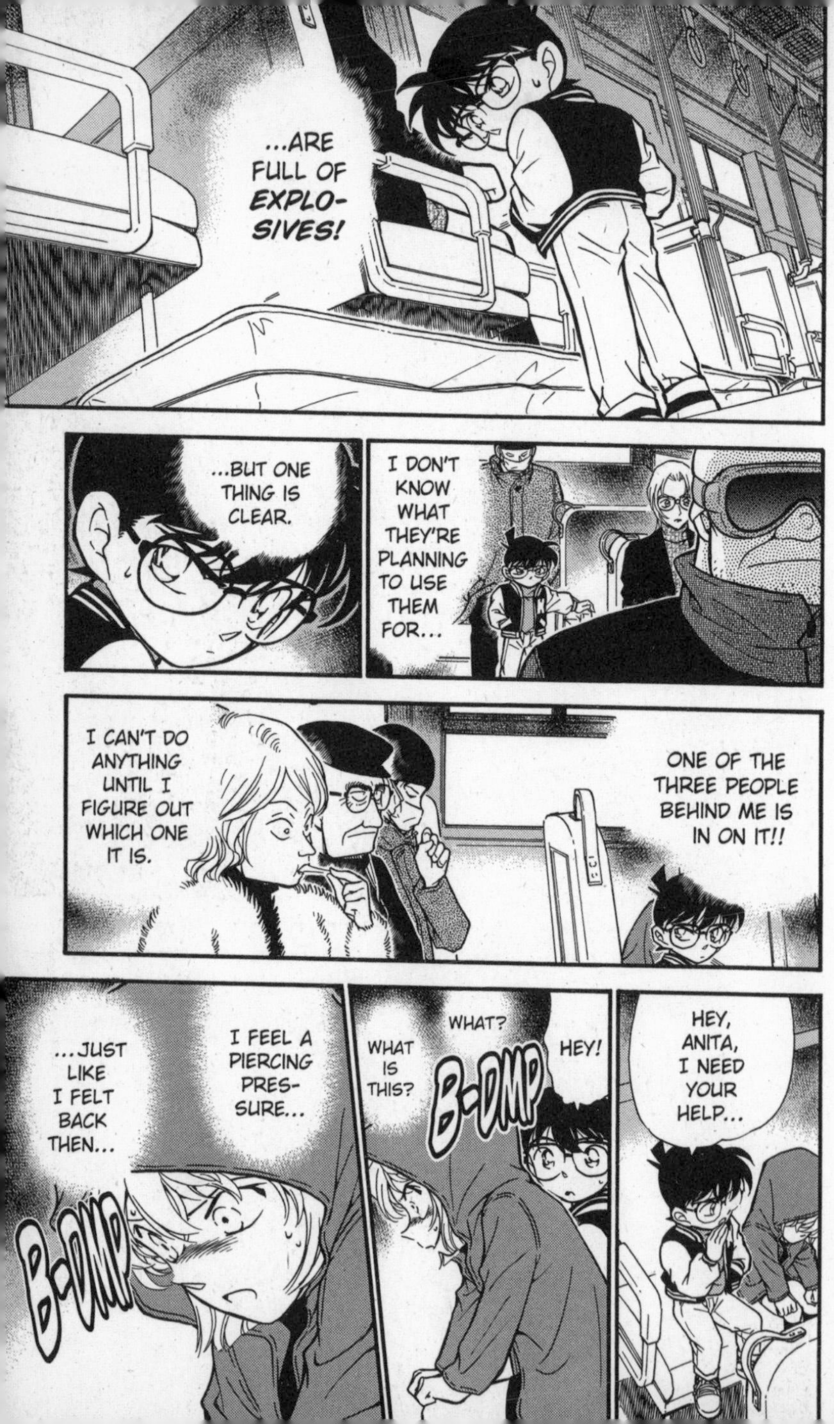
...ARE FULL OF EXPLOSIVES!
I DON'T KNOW WHAT THEY'RE PLANNING TO USE THEM FOR...
...BUT ONE THING IS CLEAR.
ONE OF THE THREE PEOPLE BEHIND ME IS IN ON IT!!
I CAN'T DO ANYTHING UNTIL I FIGURE OUT WHICH ONE IT IS.
HEY, ANITA, I NEED YOUR HELP...
HEY!
WHAT?
WHAT IS THIS?
B-DMP
I FEEL A PIERCING PRESSURE...
...JUST LIKE I FELT BACK THEN...
B-DMP

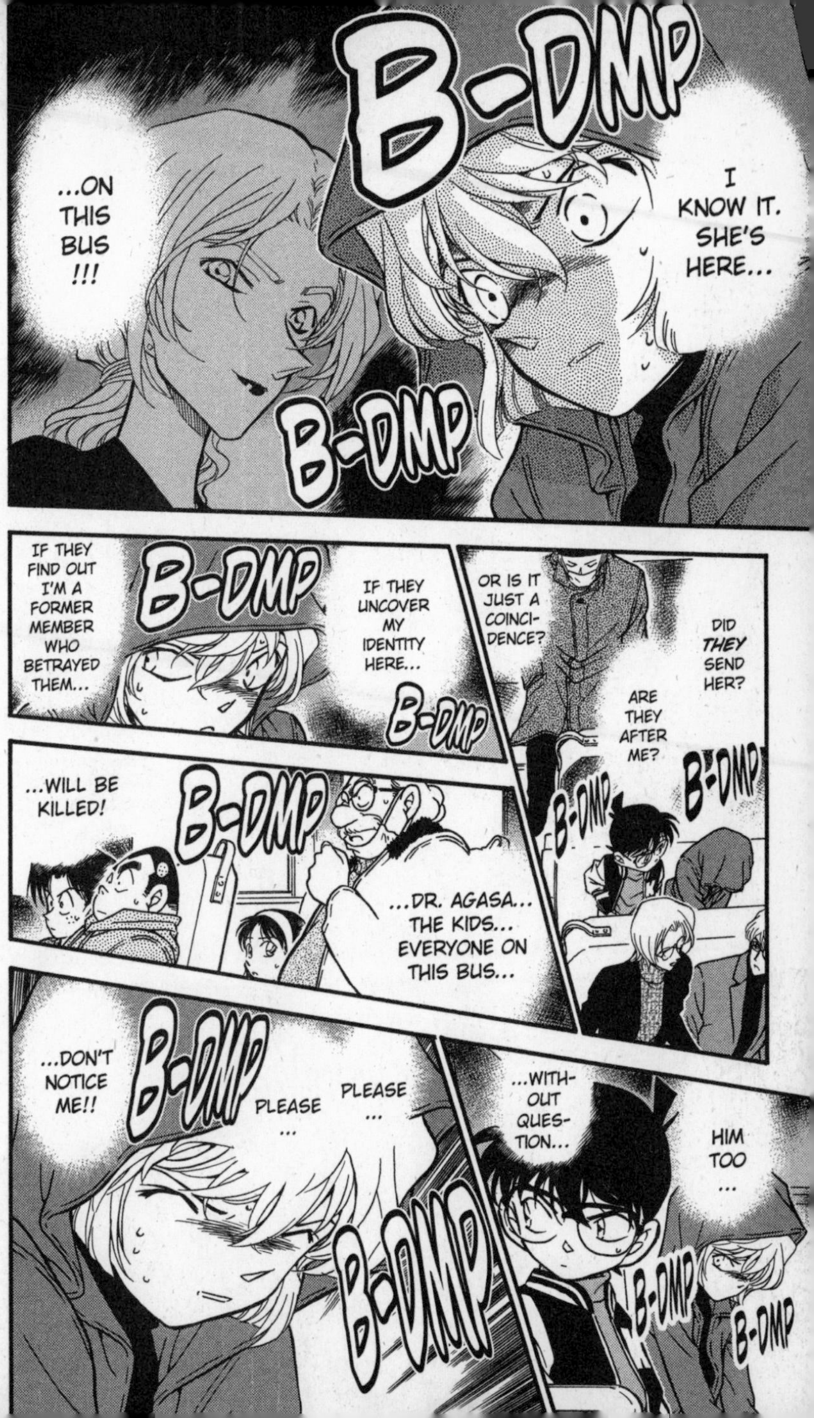
B-DMP
I KNOW IT. SHE'S HERE...
...ON THIS BUS!!!
B-DMP
DID *THEY* SEND HER?
OR IS IT JUST A COINCIDENCE?
ARE THEY AFTER ME?
B-DMP
B-DMP
IF THEY UNCOVER MY IDENTITY HERE...
B-DMP
IF THEY FIND OUT I'M A FORMER MEMBER WHO BETRAYED THEM...
B-DMP
...DR. AGASA... THE KIDS... EVERYONE ON THIS BUS...
B-DMP
...WILL BE KILLED!
HIM TOO...
B-DMP
B-DMP
...WITHOUT QUESTION...
B-DMP
PLEASE...
PLEASE...
B-DMP
...DON'T NOTICE ME!!

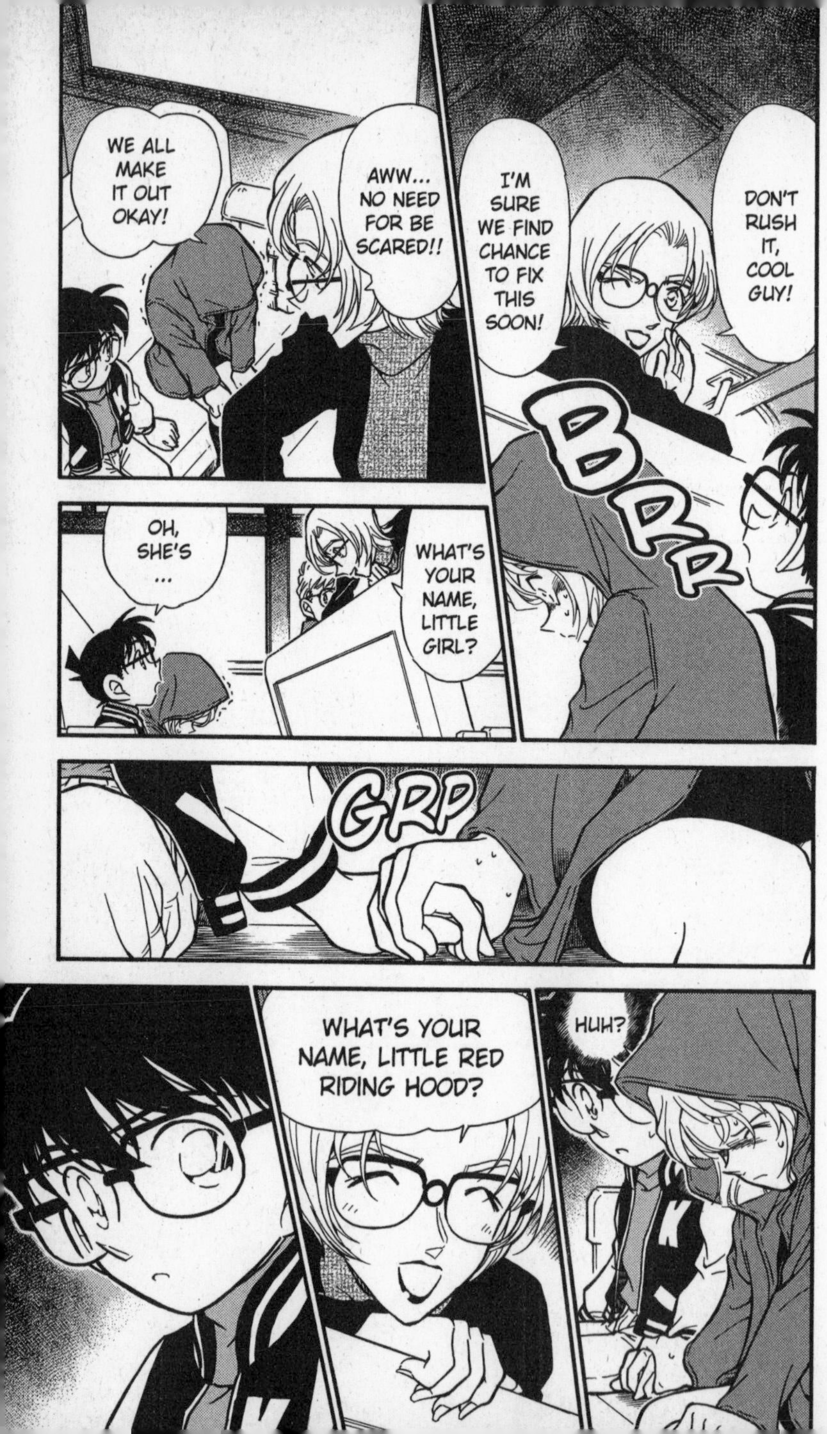
DON'T RUSH IT, COOL GUY!
I'M SURE WE FIND CHANCE TO FIX THIS SOON!
BRR
AWW... NO NEED FOR BE SCARED!!
WE ALL MAKE IT OUT OKAY!
WHAT'S YOUR NAME, LITTLE GIRL?
OH, SHE'S ...
GRP
HUH?
WHAT'S YOUR NAME, LITTLE RED RIDING HOOD?

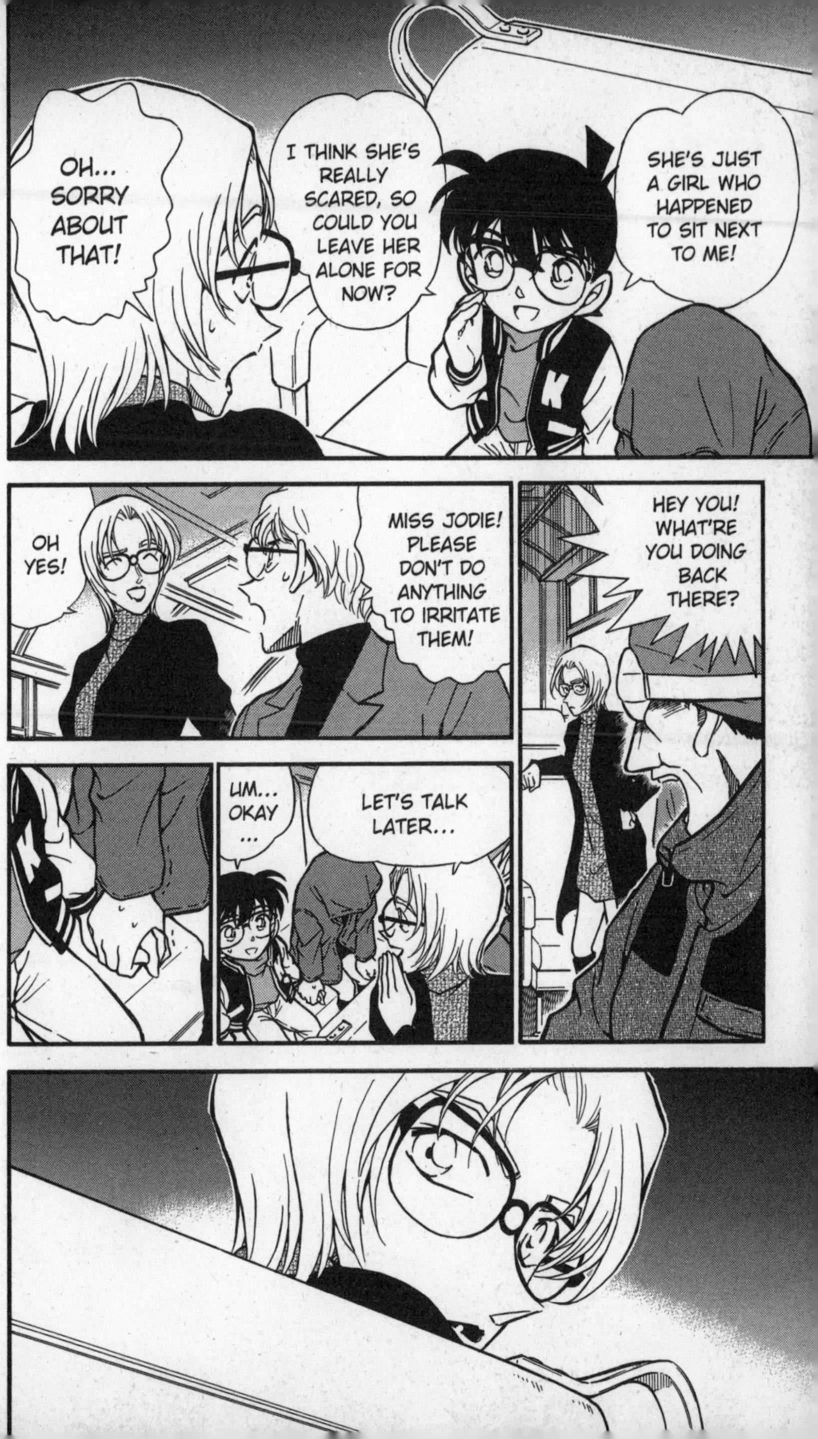
SHE'S JUST A GIRL WHO HAPPENED TO SIT NEXT TO ME!
I THINK SHE'S REALLY SCARED, SO COULD YOU LEAVE HER ALONE FOR NOW?
OH... SORRY ABOUT THAT!
HEY YOU! WHAT'RE YOU DOING BACK THERE?
MISS JODIE! PLEASE DON'T DO ANYTHING TO IRRITATE THEM!
OH YES!
LET'S TALK LATER...
UM... OKAY ...

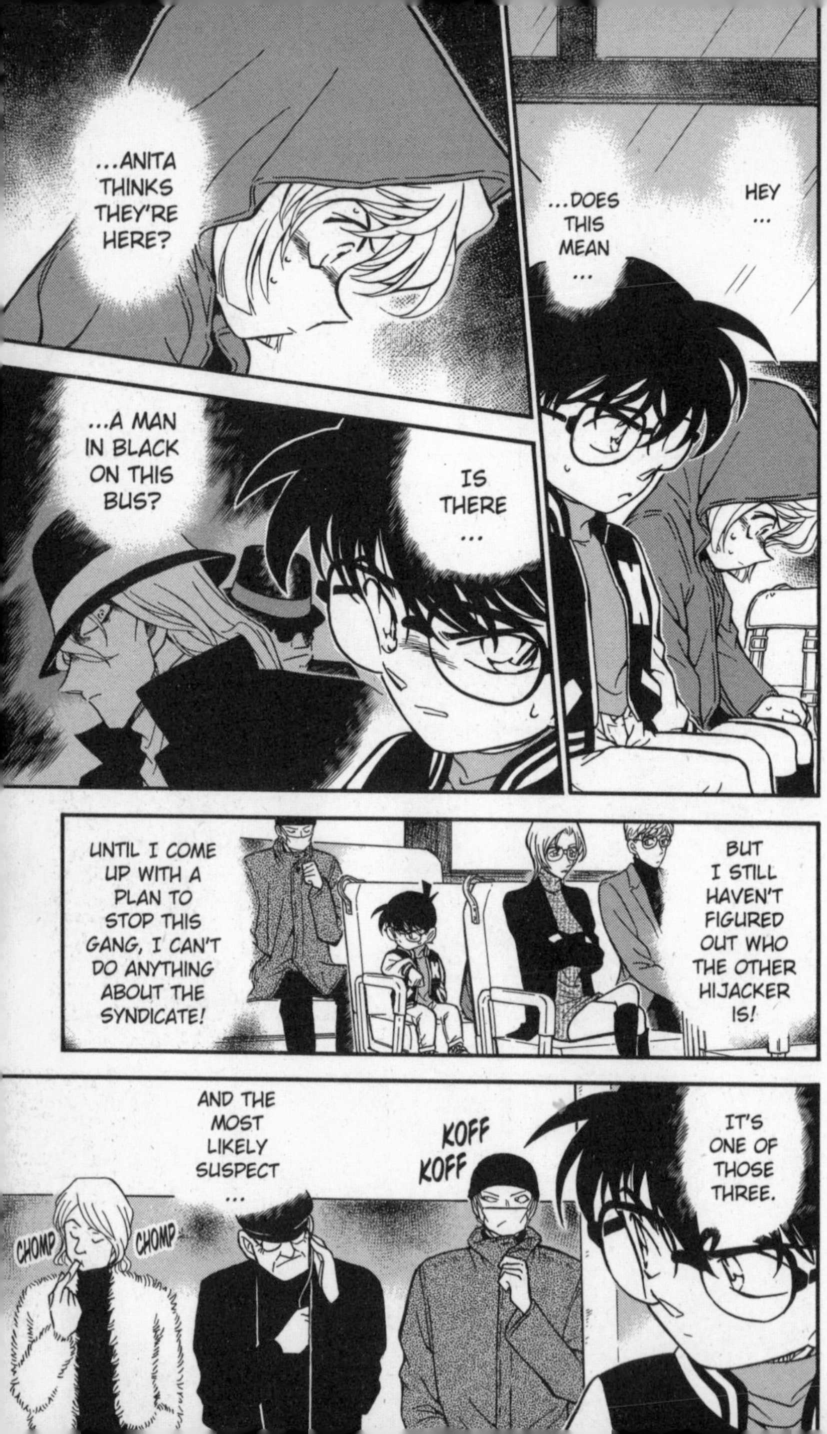
HEY ...
...DOES THIS MEAN ...
...ANITA THINKS THEY'RE HERE?
IS THERE ...
...A MAN IN BLACK ON THIS BUS?
BUT I STILL HAVEN'T FIGURED OUT WHO THE OTHER HIJACKER IS!
UNTIL I COME UP WITH A PLAN TO STOP THIS GANG, I CAN'T DO ANYTHING ABOUT THE SYNDICATE!
IT'S ONE OF THOSE THREE.
KOFF KOFF
AND THE MOST LIKELY SUSPECT ...
CHOMP
CHOMP

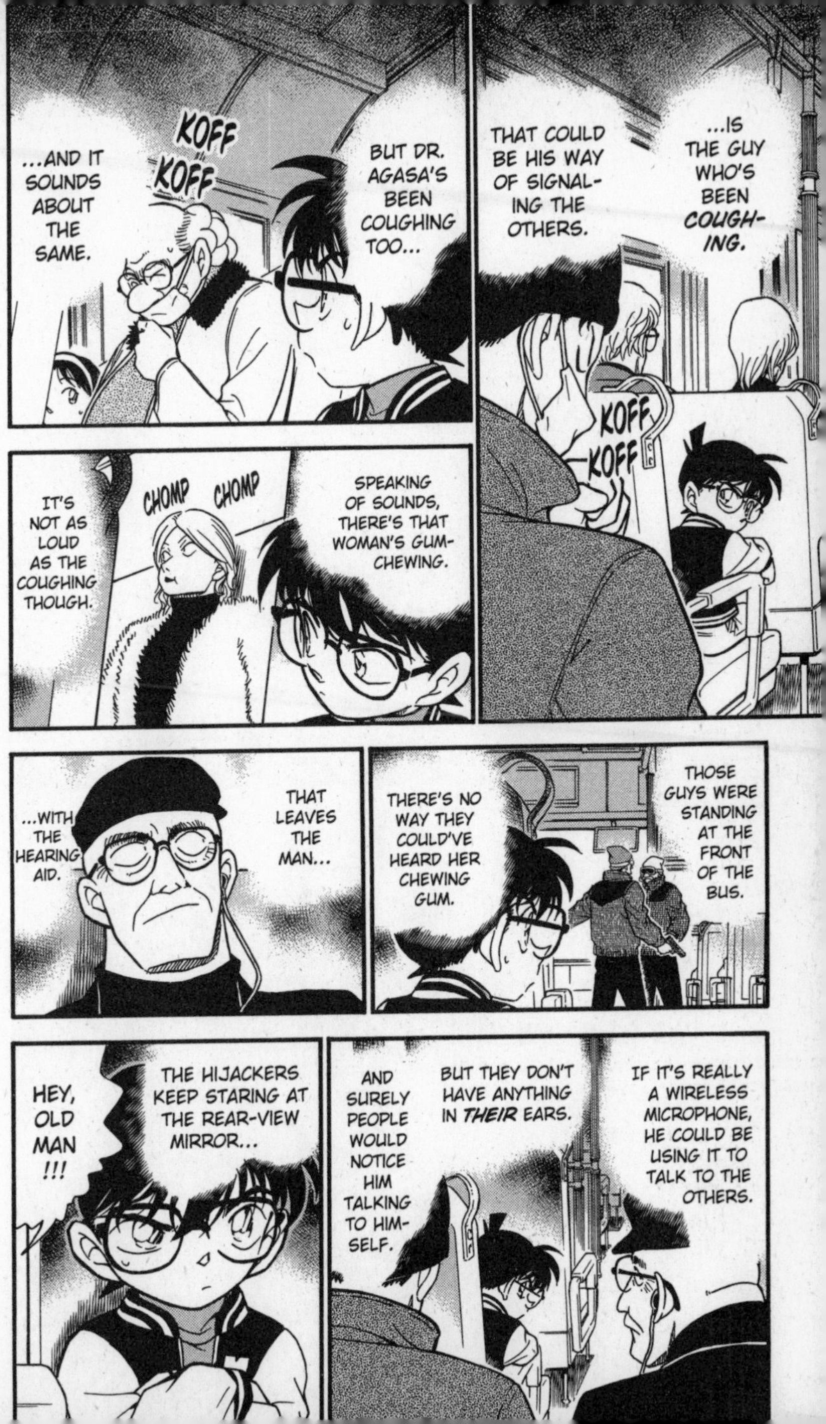
...IS THE GUY WHO'S BEEN *COUGHING.*
THAT COULD BE HIS WAY OF SIGNALING THE OTHERS.
KOFF KOFF
BUT DR. AGASA'S BEEN COUGHING TOO...
KOFF KOFF
...AND IT SOUNDS ABOUT THE SAME.
SPEAKING OF SOUNDS, THERE'S THAT WOMAN'S GUM-CHEWING.
CHOMP CHOMP
IT'S NOT AS LOUD AS THE COUGHING THOUGH.
THOSE GUYS WERE STANDING AT THE FRONT OF THE BUS.
THERE'S NO WAY THEY COULD'VE HEARD HER CHEWING GUM.
THAT LEAVES THE MAN...
...WITH THE HEARING AID.
IF IT'S REALLY A WIRELESS MICROPHONE, HE COULD BE USING IT TO TALK TO THE OTHERS.
BUT THEY DON'T HAVE ANYTHING IN *THEIR* EARS.
AND SURELY PEOPLE WOULD NOTICE HIM TALKING TO HIMSELF.
THE HIJACKERS KEEP STARING AT THE REAR-VIEW MIRROR...
HEY, OLD MAN!!!

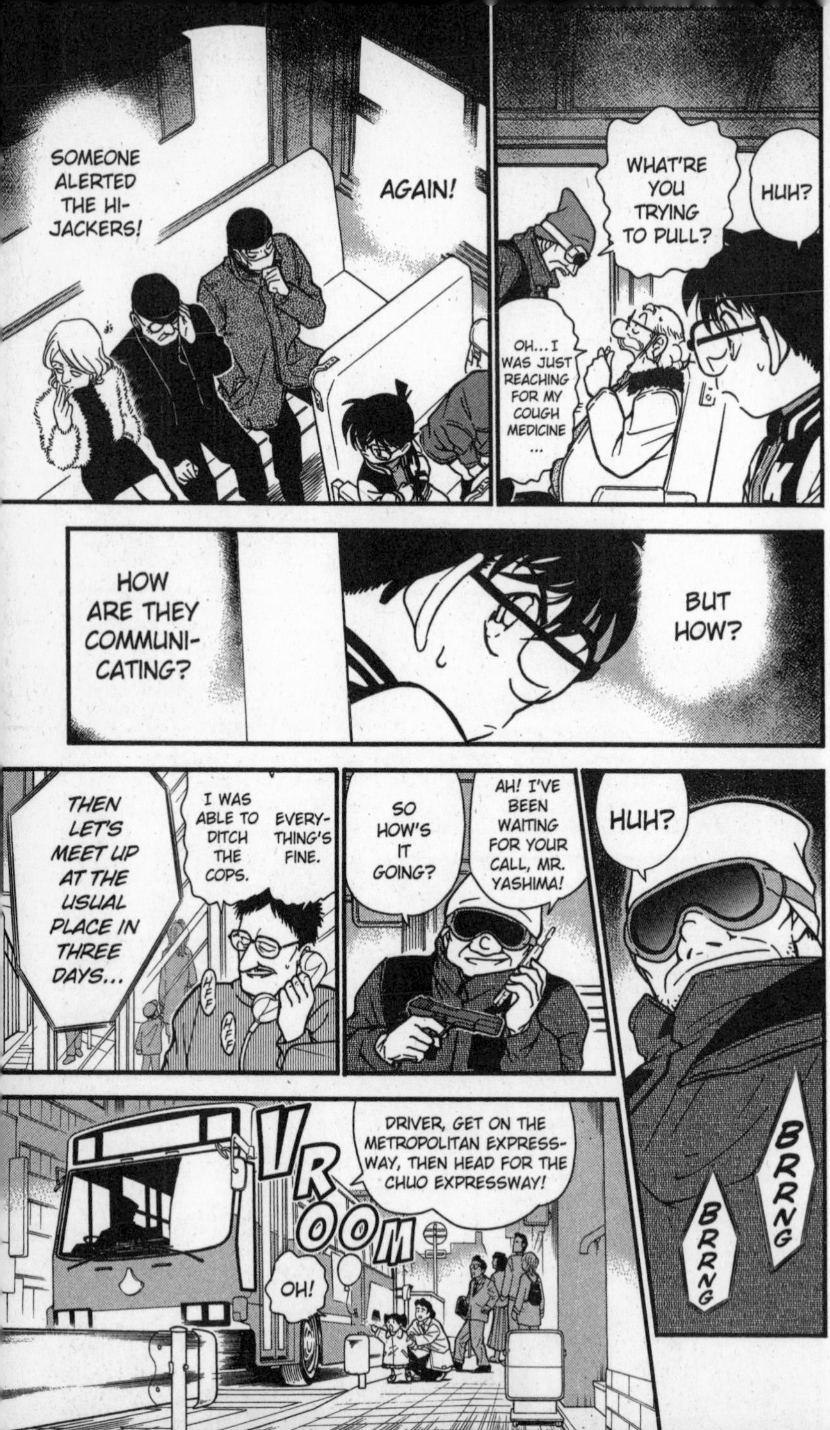
HUH?
WHAT'RE YOU TRYING TO PULL?
OH... I WAS JUST REACHING FOR MY COUGH MEDICINE ...
AGAIN!
SOMEONE ALERTED THE HI-JACKERS!
BUT HOW?
HOW ARE THEY COMMUNI-CATING?
HUH?
BRRNG
BRRNG
AH! I'VE BEEN WAITING FOR YOUR CALL, MR. YASHIMA!
SO HOW'S IT GOING?
EVERY-THING'S FINE.
I WAS ABLE TO DITCH THE COPS.
HFF
HFF
THEN LET'S MEET UP AT THE USUAL PLACE IN THREE DAYS...
DRIVER, GET ON THE METROPOLITAN EXPRESS-WAY, THEN HEAD FOR THE CHUO EXPRESSWAY!
VROOM
OH!

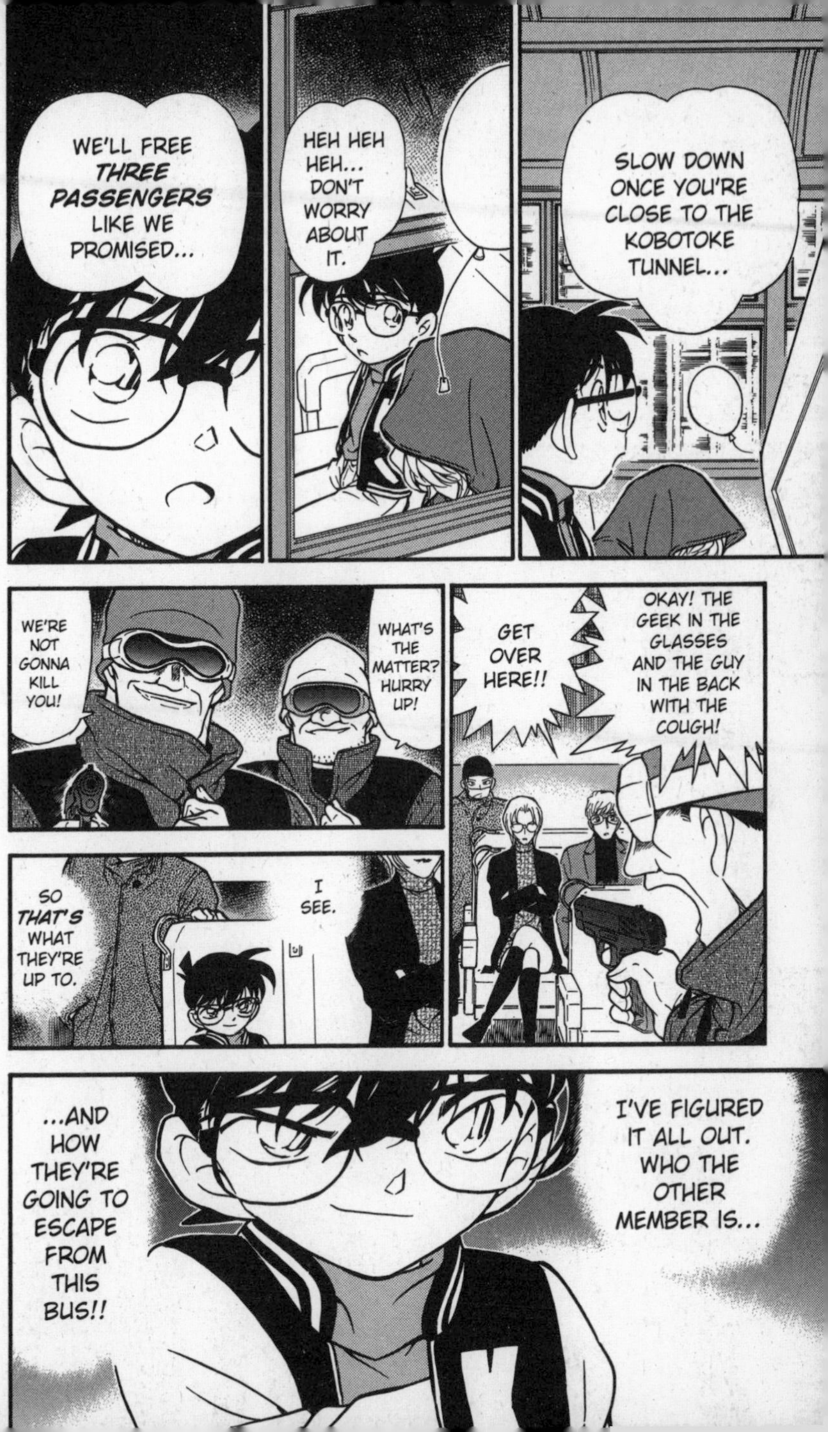
SLOW DOWN ONCE YOU'RE CLOSE TO THE KOBOTOKE TUNNEL...
HEH HEH HEH... DON'T WORRY ABOUT IT.
WE'LL FREE *THREE PASSENGERS* LIKE WE PROMISED...
OKAY! THE GEEK IN THE GLASSES AND THE GUY IN THE BACK WITH THE COUGH!
GET OVER HERE!!
WHAT'S THE MATTER? HURRY UP!
WE'RE NOT GONNA KILL YOU!
I SEE.
SO *THAT'S* WHAT THEY'RE UP TO.
I'VE FIGURED IT ALL OUT. WHO THE OTHER MEMBER IS...
...AND HOW THEY'RE GOING TO ESCAPE FROM THIS BUS!!

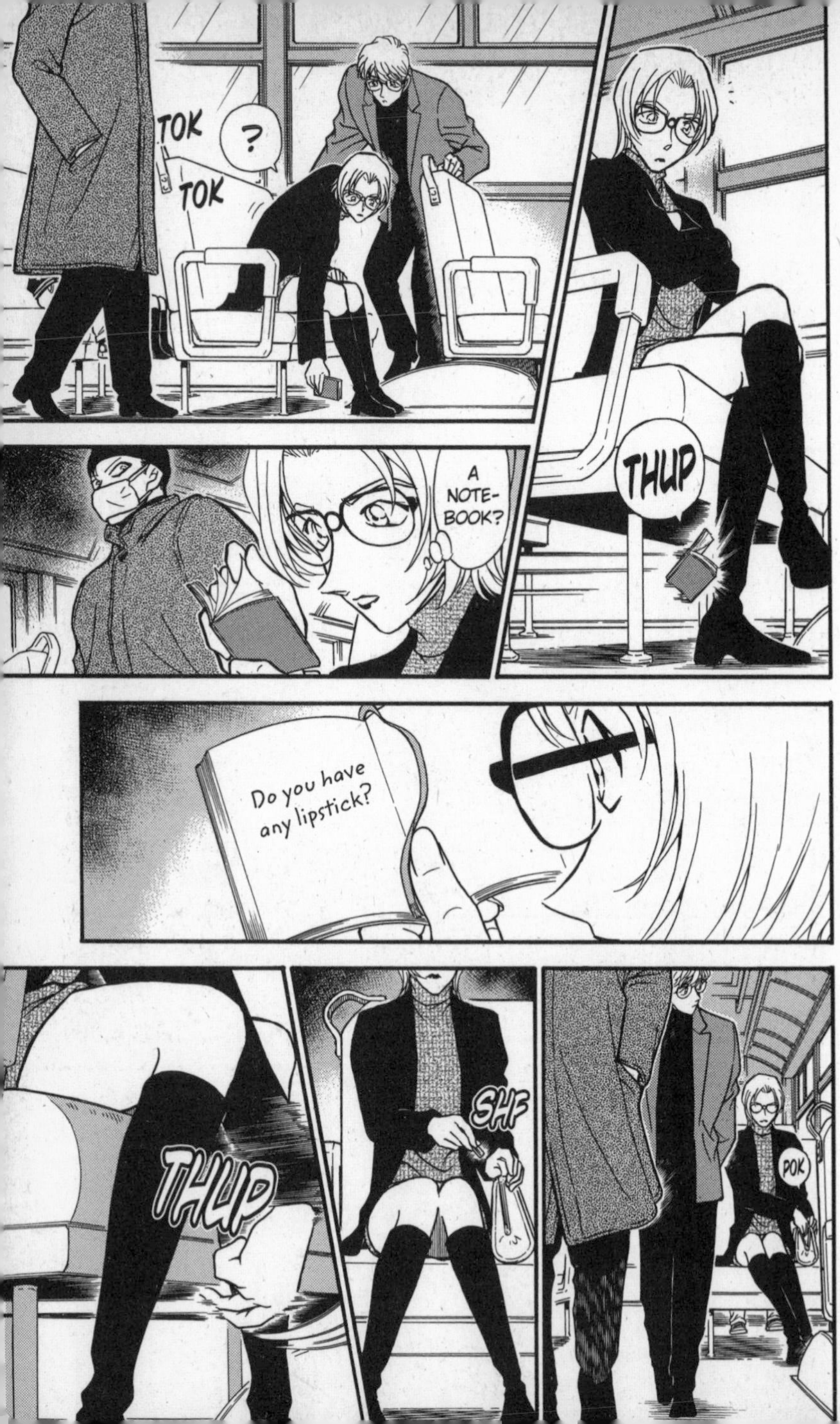
THUP
TOK
TOK
?
A NOTE-BOOK?
Do you have any lipstick?
POK
SHF
THUP

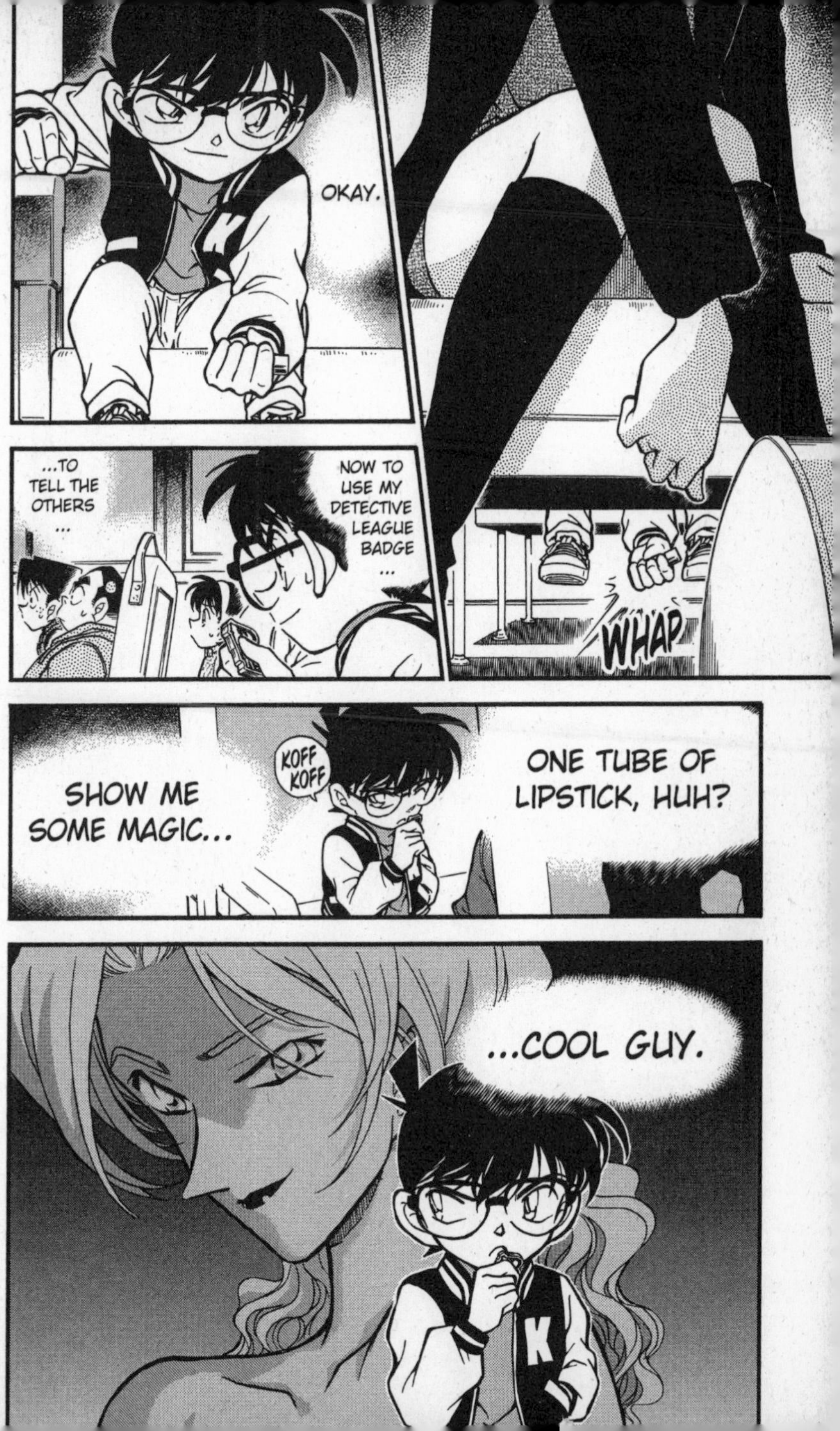
WHAP
OKAY.
NOW TO USE MY DETECTIVE LEAGUE BADGE ...
...TO TELL THE OTHERS ...
ONE TUBE OF LIPSTICK, HUH?
KOFF KOFF
SHOW ME SOME MAGIC...
...COOL GUY.

FILE 5:
IN PLAIN SIGHT

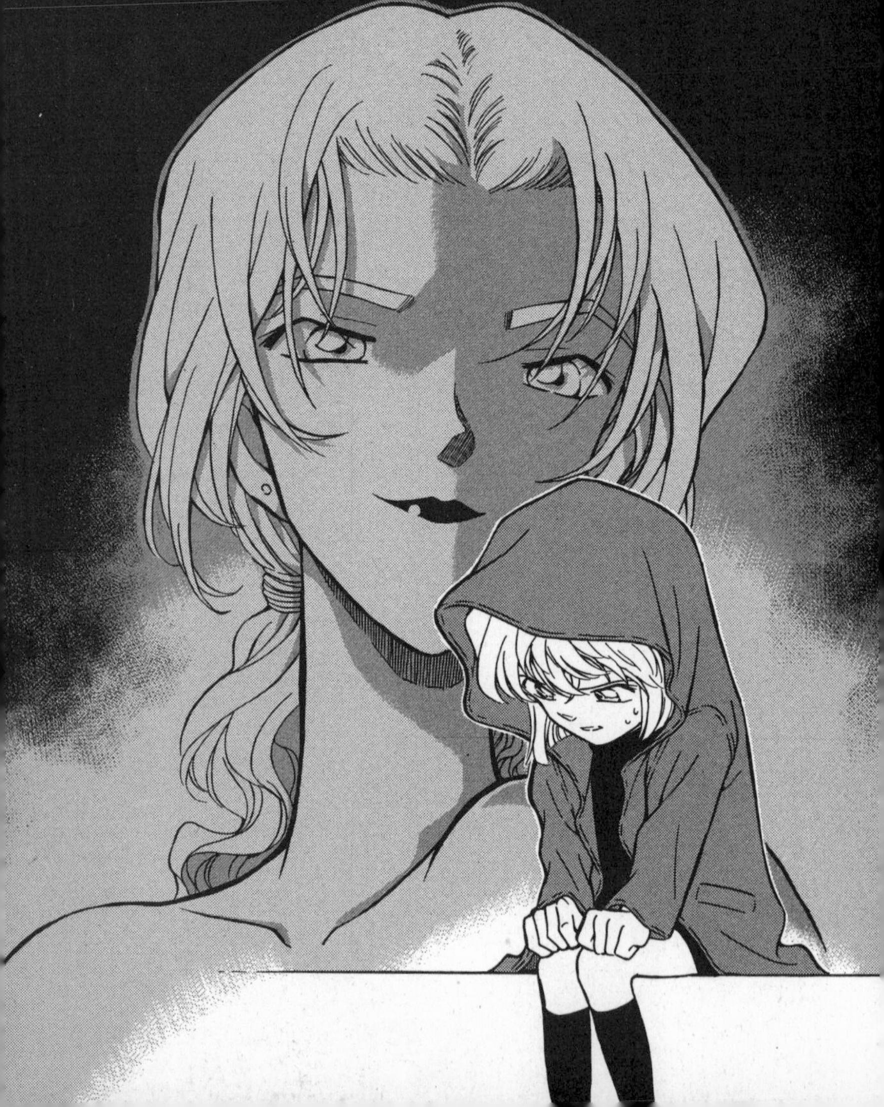

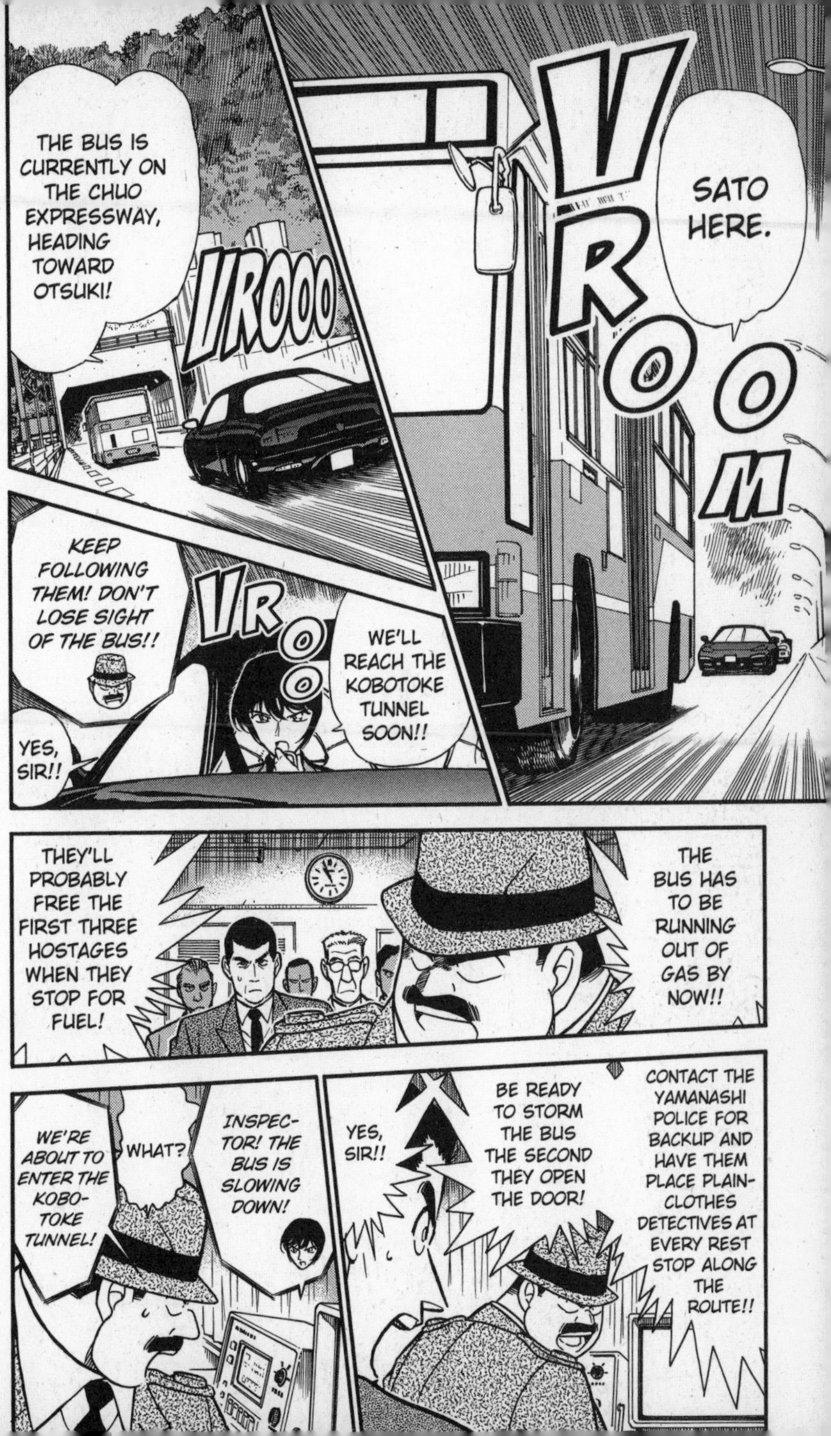
SATO HERE.
VROOOM
THE BUS IS CURRENTLY ON THE CHUO EXPRESSWAY, HEADING TOWARD OTSUKI!
VROOO
WE'LL REACH THE KOBOTOKE TUNNEL SOON!!
VROOO
KEEP FOLLOWING THEM! DON'T LOSE SIGHT OF THE BUS!!
YES, SIR!!
THE BUS HAS TO BE RUNNING OUT OF GAS BY NOW!!
THEY'LL PROBABLY FREE THE FIRST THREE HOSTAGES WHEN THEY STOP FOR FUEL!
CONTACT THE YAMANASHI POLICE FOR BACKUP AND HAVE THEM PLACE PLAIN-CLOTHES DETECTIVES AT EVERY REST STOP ALONG THE ROUTE!!
BE READY TO STORM THE BUS THE SECOND THEY OPEN THE DOOR!
YES, SIR!!
INSPECTOR! THE BUS IS SLOWING DOWN!
WHAT?
WE'RE ABOUT TO ENTER THE KOBO-TOKE TUNNEL!

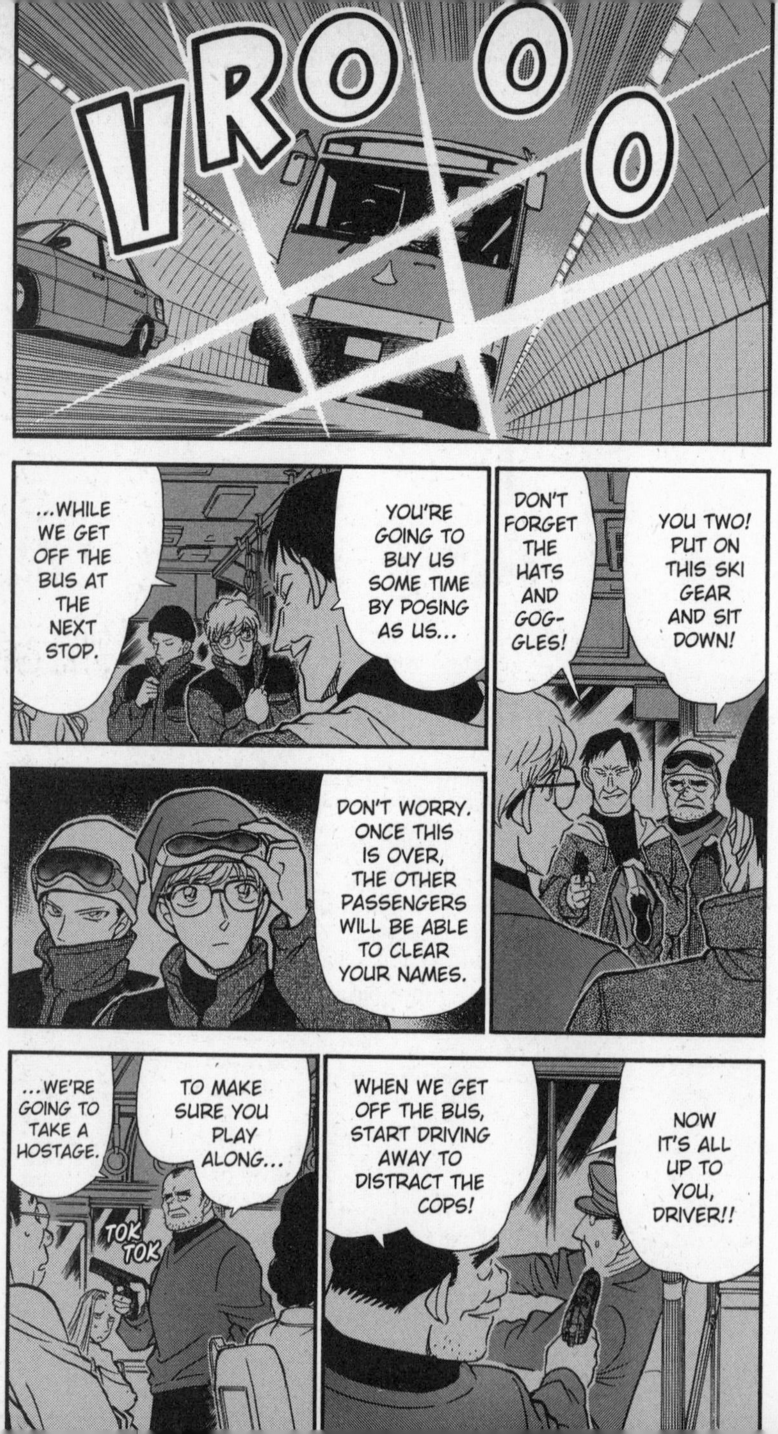
VROOO
YOU TWO! PUT ON THIS SKI GEAR AND SIT DOWN!
DON'T FORGET THE HATS AND GOG-GLES!
YOU'RE GOING TO BUY US SOME TIME BY POSING AS US...
...WHILE WE GET OFF THE BUS AT THE NEXT STOP.
DON'T WORRY. ONCE THIS IS OVER, THE OTHER PASSENGERS WILL BE ABLE TO CLEAR YOUR NAMES.
NOW IT'S ALL UP TO YOU, DRIVER!!
WHEN WE GET OFF THE BUS, START DRIVING AWAY TO DISTRACT THE COPS!
TO MAKE SURE YOU PLAY ALONG...
...WE'RE GOING TO TAKE A HOSTAGE.
TOK TOK

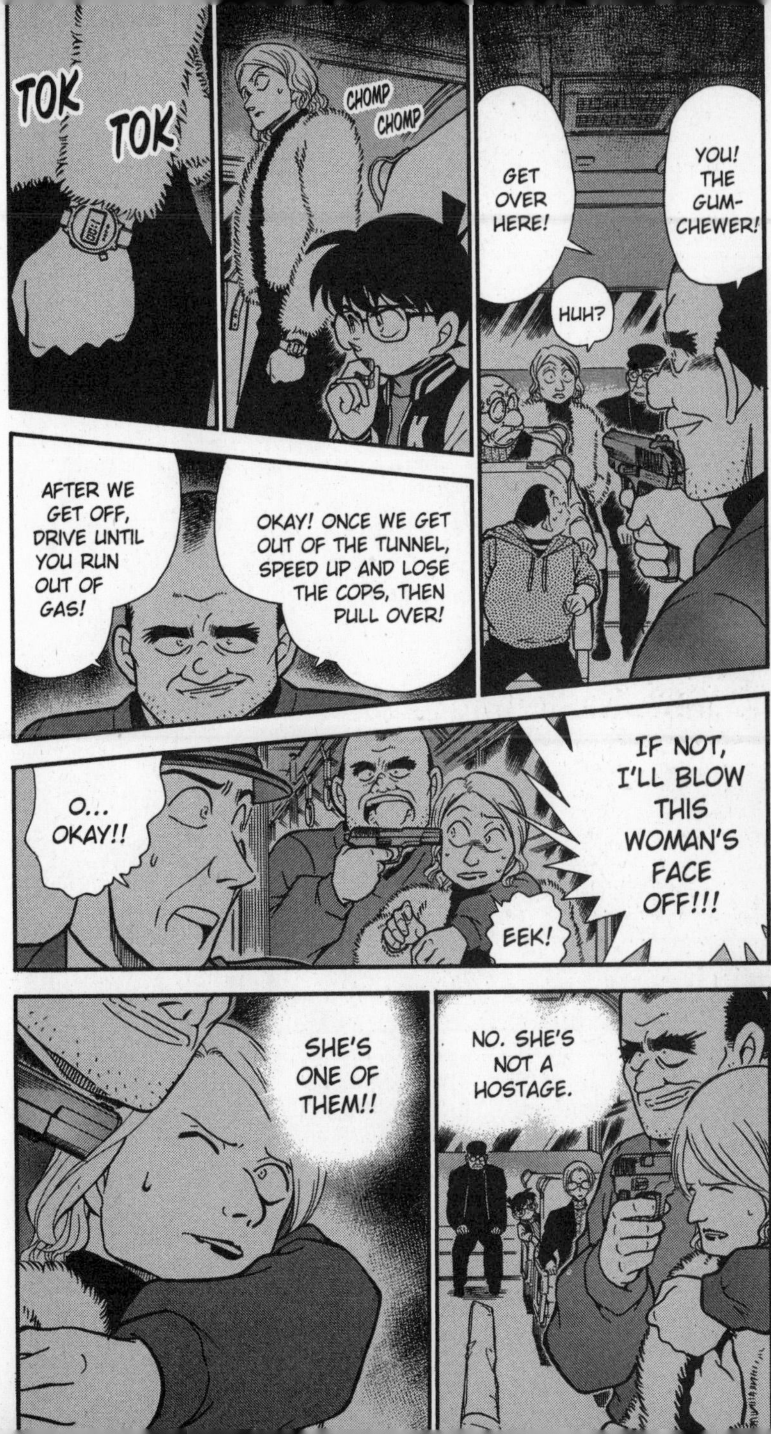
YOU! THE GUM-CHEWER!
GET OVER HERE!
HUH?
CHOMP
CHOMP
TOK
TOK
OKAY! ONCE WE GET OUT OF THE TUNNEL, SPEED UP AND LOSE THE COPS, THEN PULL OVER!
AFTER WE GET OFF, DRIVE UNTIL YOU RUN OUT OF GAS!
IF NOT, I'LL BLOW THIS WOMAN'S FACE OFF!!!
EEK!
O... OKAY!!
NO. SHE'S NOT A HOSTAGE.
SHE'S ONE OF THEM!!

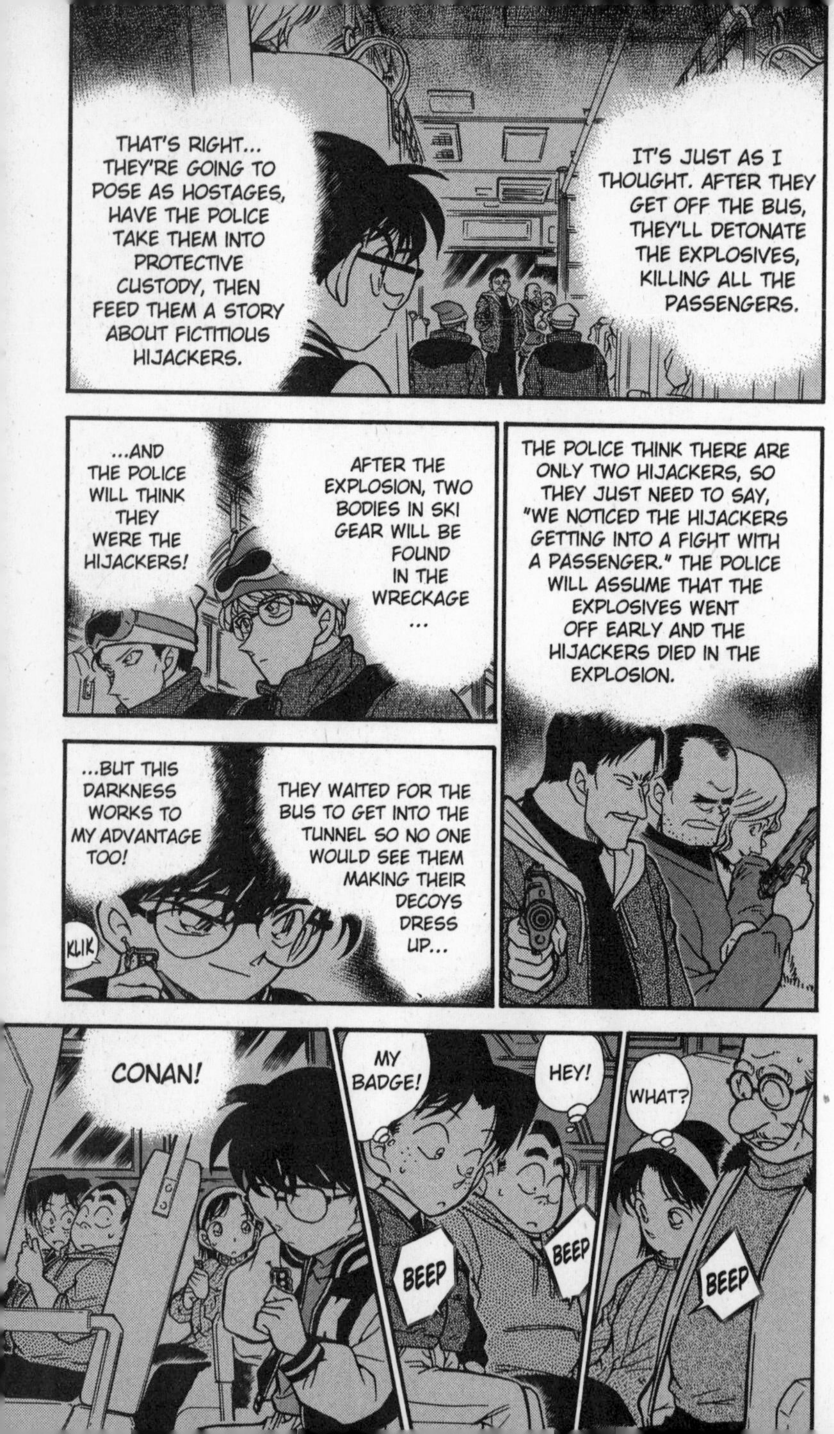

IT'S JUST AS I THOUGHT. AFTER THEY GET OFF THE BUS, THEY'LL DETONATE THE EXPLOSIVES, KILLING ALL THE PASSENGERS.
THAT'S RIGHT... THEY'RE GOING TO POSE AS HOSTAGES, HAVE THE POLICE TAKE THEM INTO PROTECTIVE CUSTODY, THEN FEED THEM A STORY ABOUT FICTITIOUS HIJACKERS.
THE POLICE THINK THERE ARE ONLY TWO HIJACKERS, SO THEY JUST NEED TO SAY, "WE NOTICED THE HIJACKERS GETTING INTO A FIGHT WITH A PASSENGER." THE POLICE WILL ASSUME THAT THE EXPLOSIVES WENT OFF EARLY AND THE HIJACKERS DIED IN THE EXPLOSION.
AFTER THE EXPLOSION, TWO BODIES IN SKI GEAR WILL BE FOUND IN THE WRECKAGE...
...AND THE POLICE WILL THINK THEY WERE THE HIJACKERS!
THEY WAITED FOR THE BUS TO GET INTO THE TUNNEL SO NO ONE WOULD SEE THEM MAKING THEIR DECOYS DRESS UP...
...BUT THIS DARKNESS WORKS TO MY ADVANTAGE TOO!
KLIK
WHAT?
BEEP
HEY!
BEEP
MY BADGE!
BEEP
CONAN!

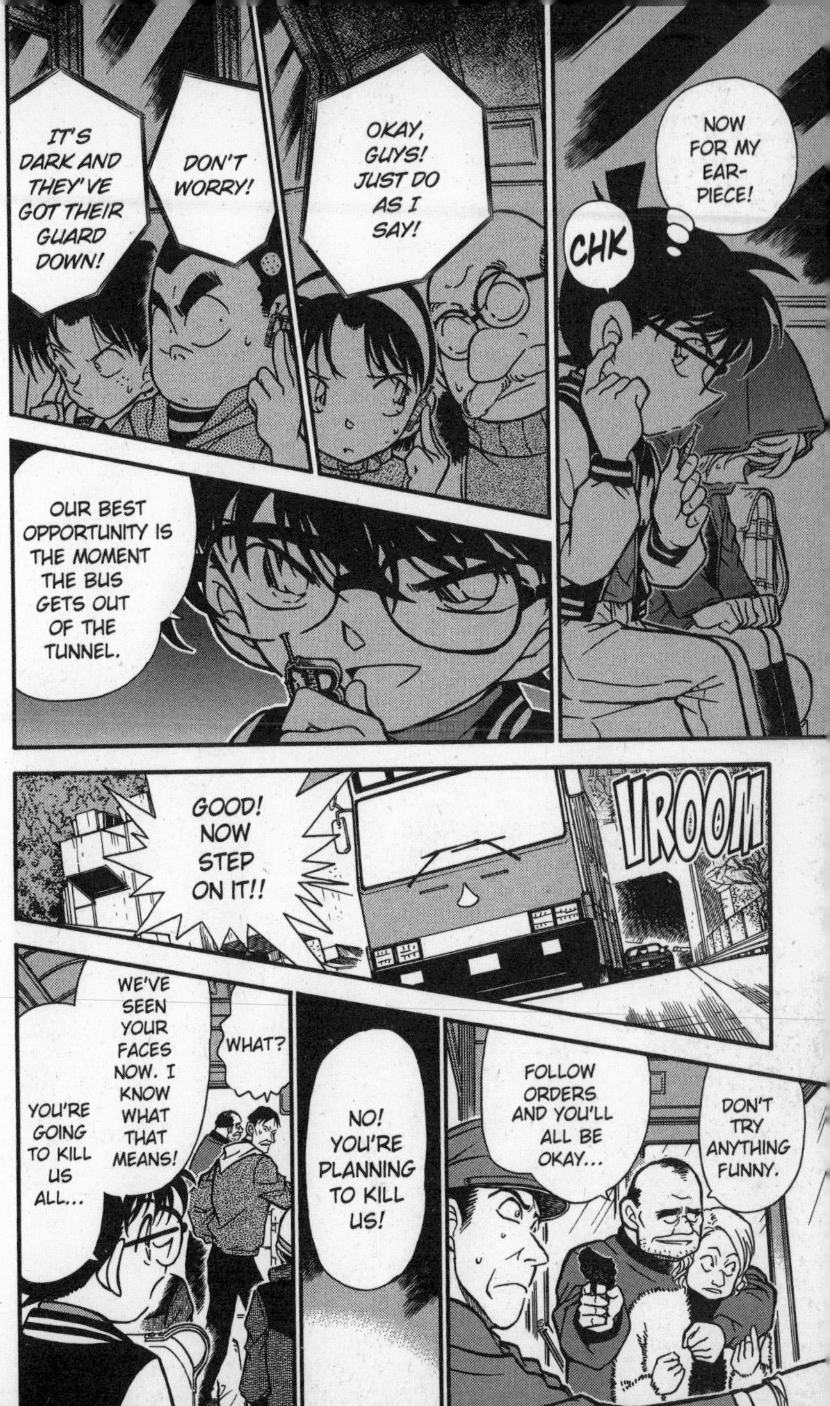
NOW FOR MY EAR-PIECE!
CHK
OKAY, GUYS! JUST DO AS I SAY!
DON'T WORRY!
IT'S DARK AND THEY'VE GOT THEIR GUARD DOWN!
OUR BEST OPPORTUNITY IS THE MOMENT THE BUS GETS OUT OF THE TUNNEL.
VROOM
GOOD! NOW STEP ON IT!!
DON'T TRY ANYTHING FUNNY.
FOLLOW ORDERS AND YOU'LL ALL BE OKAY...
NO! YOU'RE PLANNING TO KILL US!
WHAT?
WE'VE SEEN YOUR FACES NOW. I KNOW WHAT THAT MEANS!
YOU'RE GOING TO KILL US ALL...

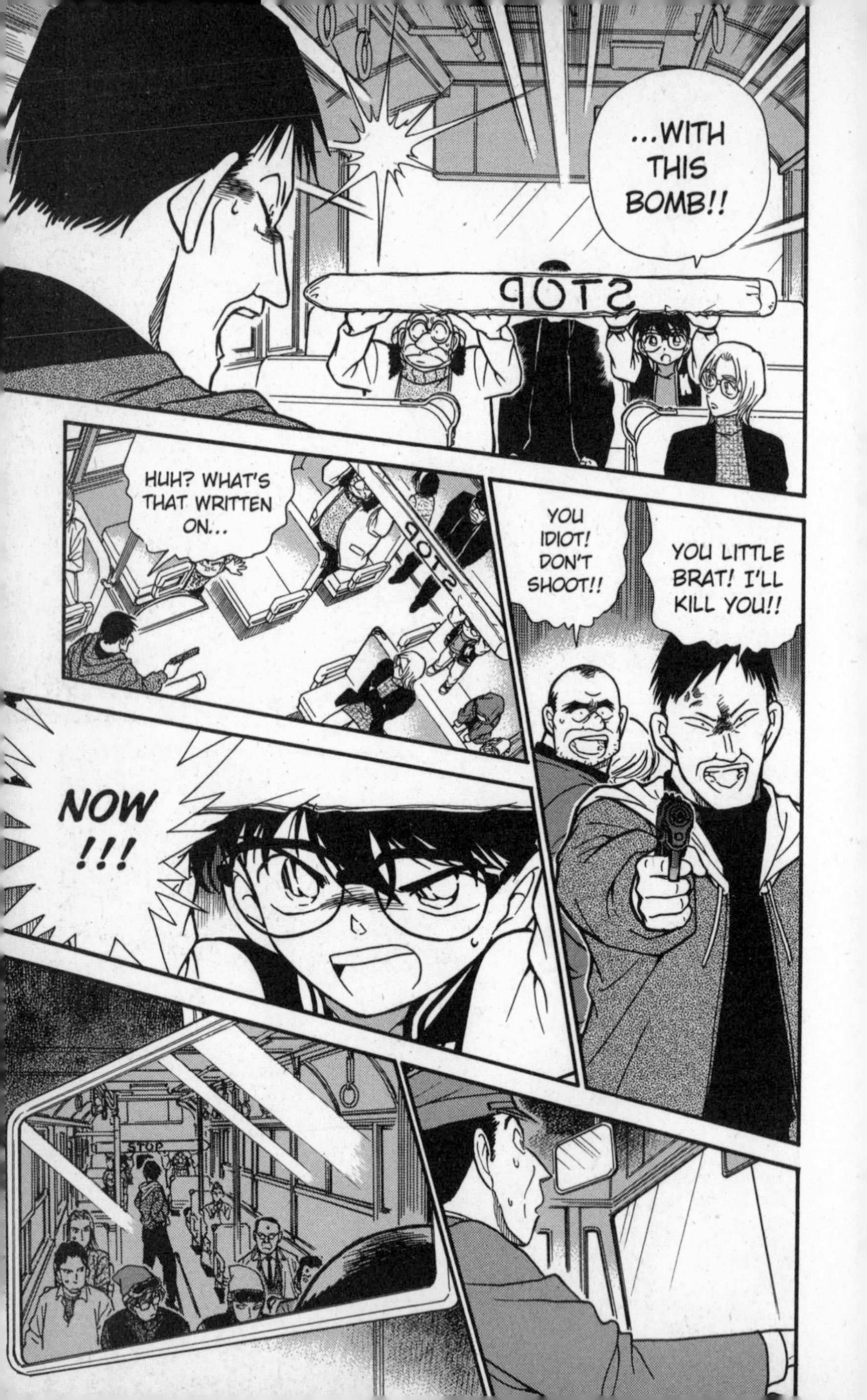
...WITH THIS BOMB!!
YOU LITTLE BRAT! I'LL KILL YOU!!
YOU IDIOT! DON'T SHOOT!!
HUH? WHAT'S THAT WRITTEN ON...
STOP
NOW !!!
STOP

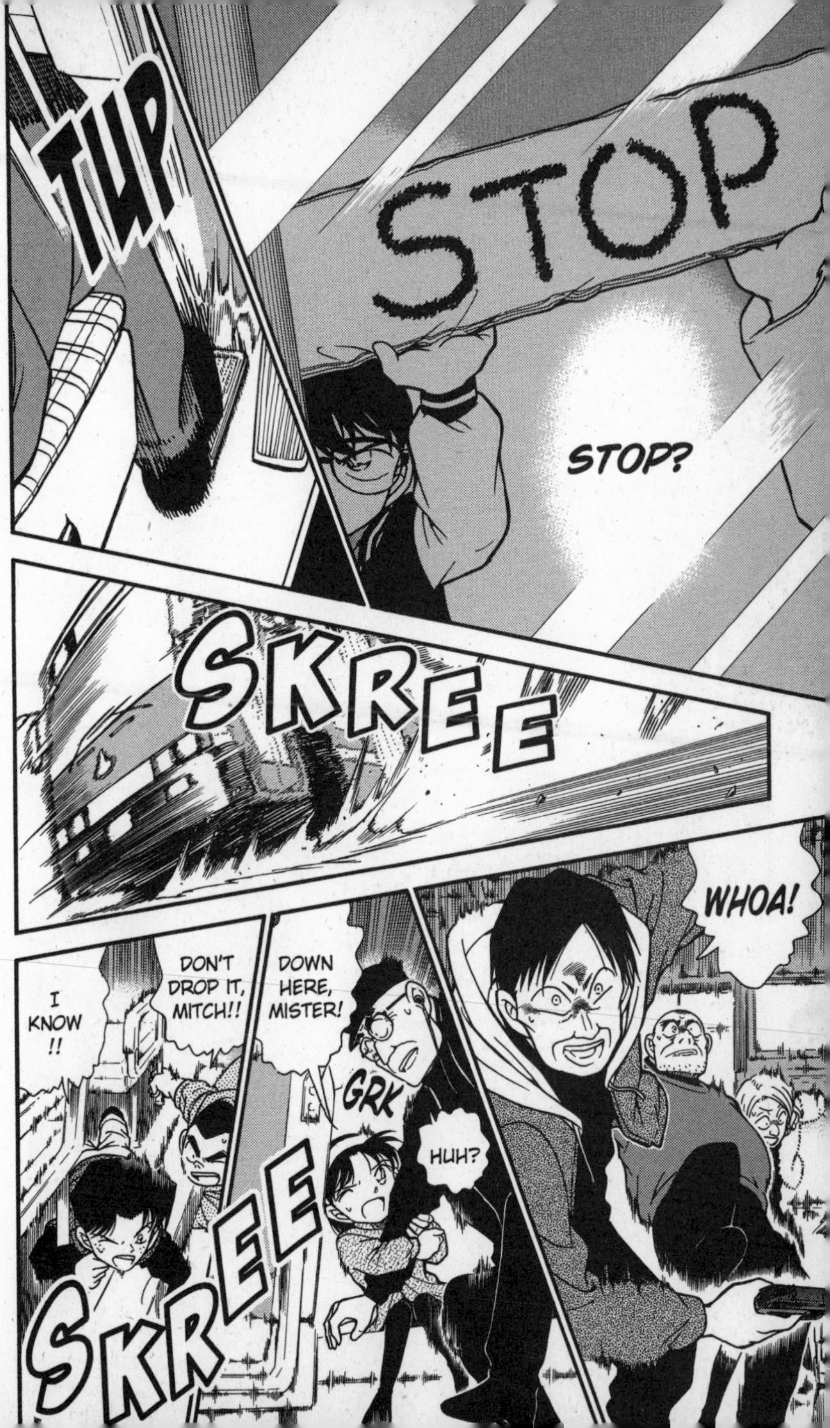
STOP
STOP?
TMP
SKREE
WHOA!
DOWN HERE, MISTER!
GRK
HUH?
DON'T DROP IT, MITCH!!
I KNOW!!
SKREE

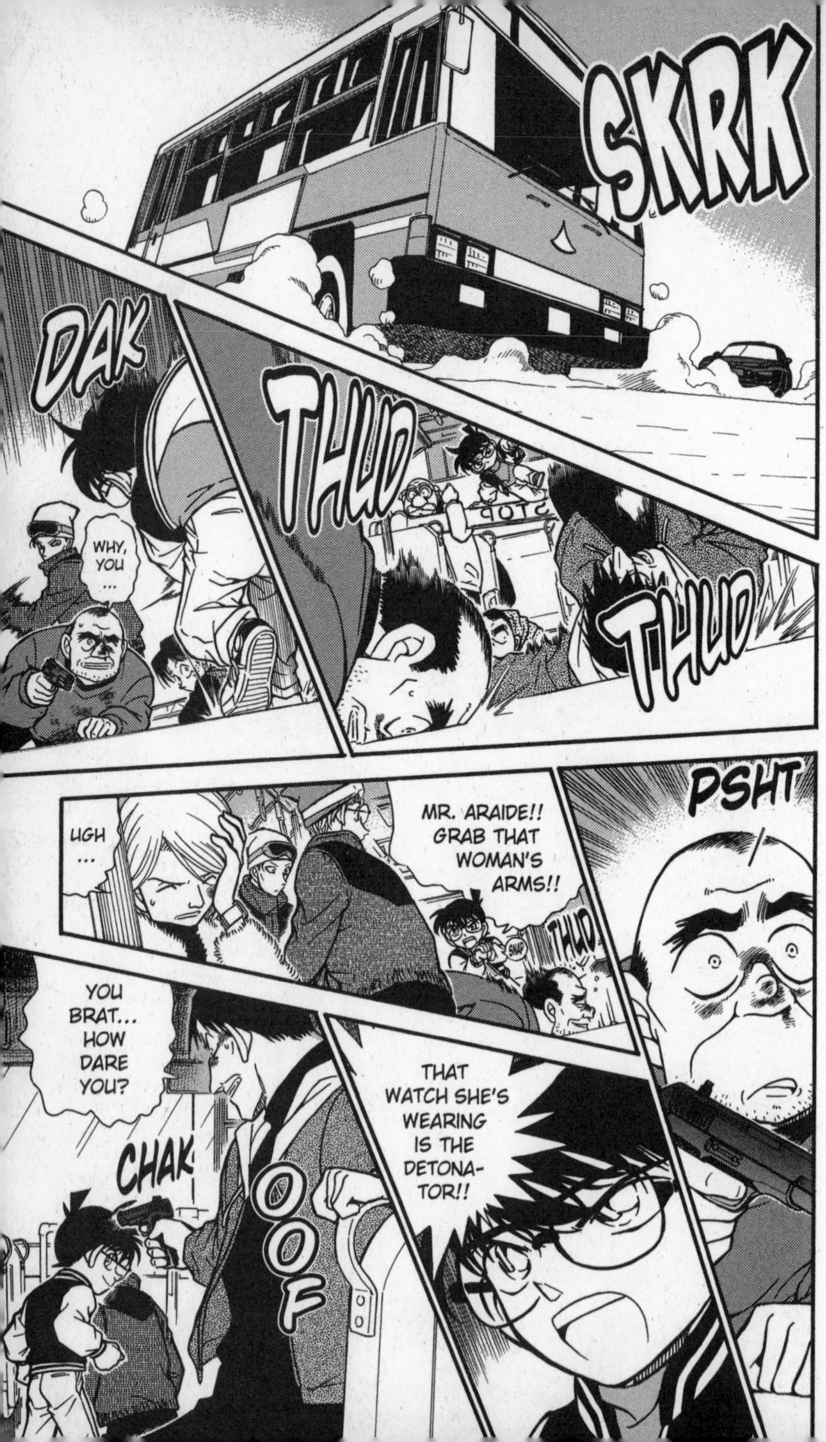
SKRK
THUD
THUD
DAK
WHY, YOU ...
PSHT
MR. ARAIDE!! GRAB THAT WOMAN'S ARMS!!
THUD
SNAP
UGH ...
THAT WATCH SHE'S WEARING IS THE DETONA-TOR!!
OOF
YOU BRAT... HOW DARE YOU?
CHAK

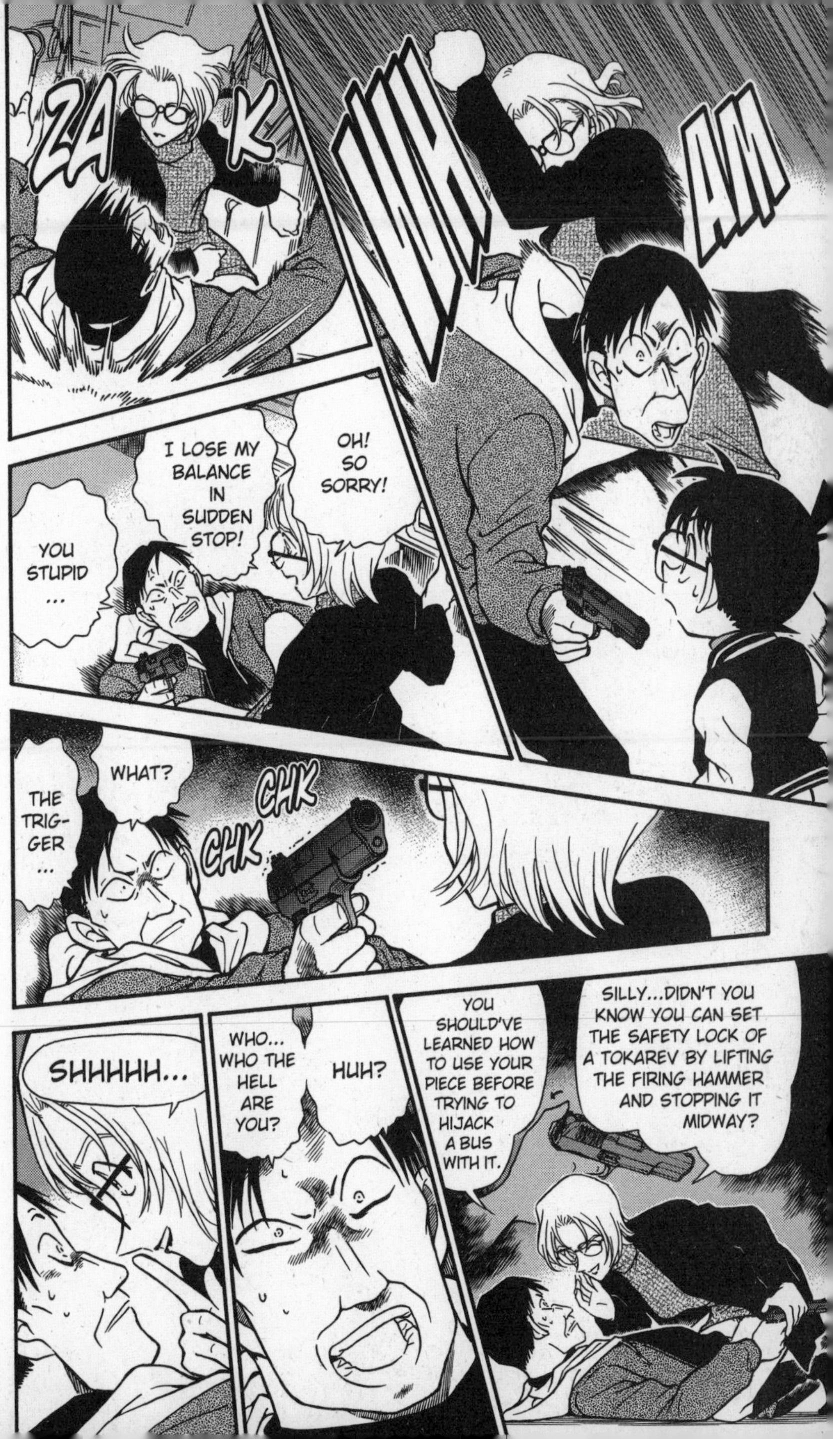
WHA
AM
ZA K
OH! SO SORRY!
I LOSE MY BALANCE IN SUDDEN STOP!
YOU STUPID ...
CHK
CHK
WHAT?
THE TRIG-GER ...
SILLY...DIDN'T YOU KNOW YOU CAN SET THE SAFETY LOCK OF A TOKAREV BY LIFTING THE FIRING HAMMER AND STOPPING IT MIDWAY?
YOU SHOULD'VE LEARNED HOW TO USE YOUR PIECE BEFORE TRYING TO HIJACK A BUS WITH IT.
HUH?
WHO... WHO THE HELL ARE YOU?
SHHHHH...

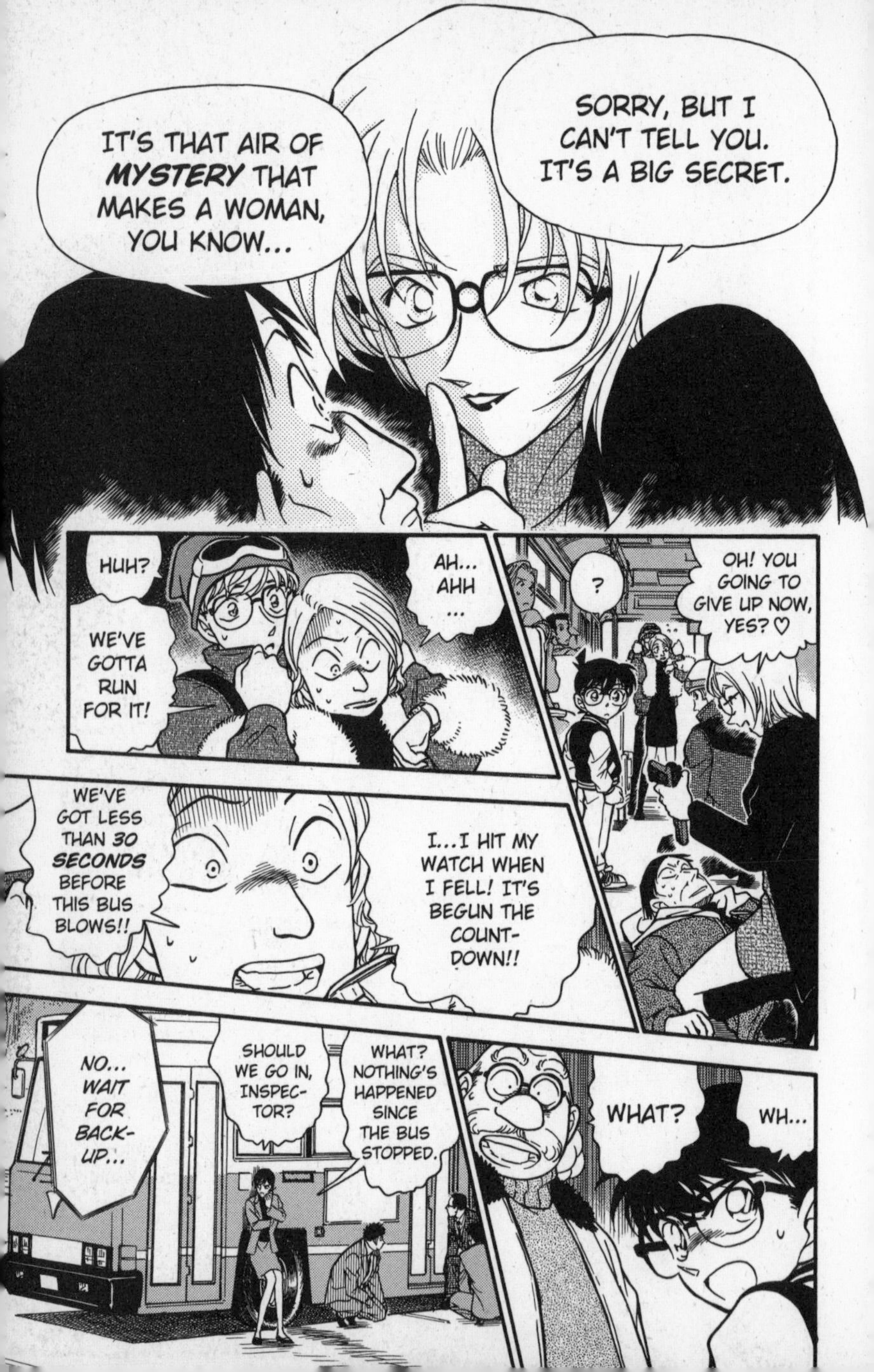
SORRY, BUT I CAN'T TELL YOU. IT'S A BIG SECRET.
IT'S THAT AIR OF *MYSTERY* THAT MAKES A WOMAN, YOU KNOW...
OH! YOU GOING TO GIVE UP NOW, YES? ♡
?
AH... AHH ...
HUH?
WE'VE GOTTA RUN FOR IT!
I...I HIT MY WATCH WHEN I FELL! IT'S BEGUN THE COUNT-DOWN!!
WE'VE GOT LESS THAN 30 SECONDS BEFORE THIS BUS BLOWS!!
WH...
WHAT?
WHAT? NOTHING'S HAPPENED SINCE THE BUS STOPPED.
SHOULD WE GO IN, INSPEC-TOR?
NO... WAIT FOR BACK-UP...

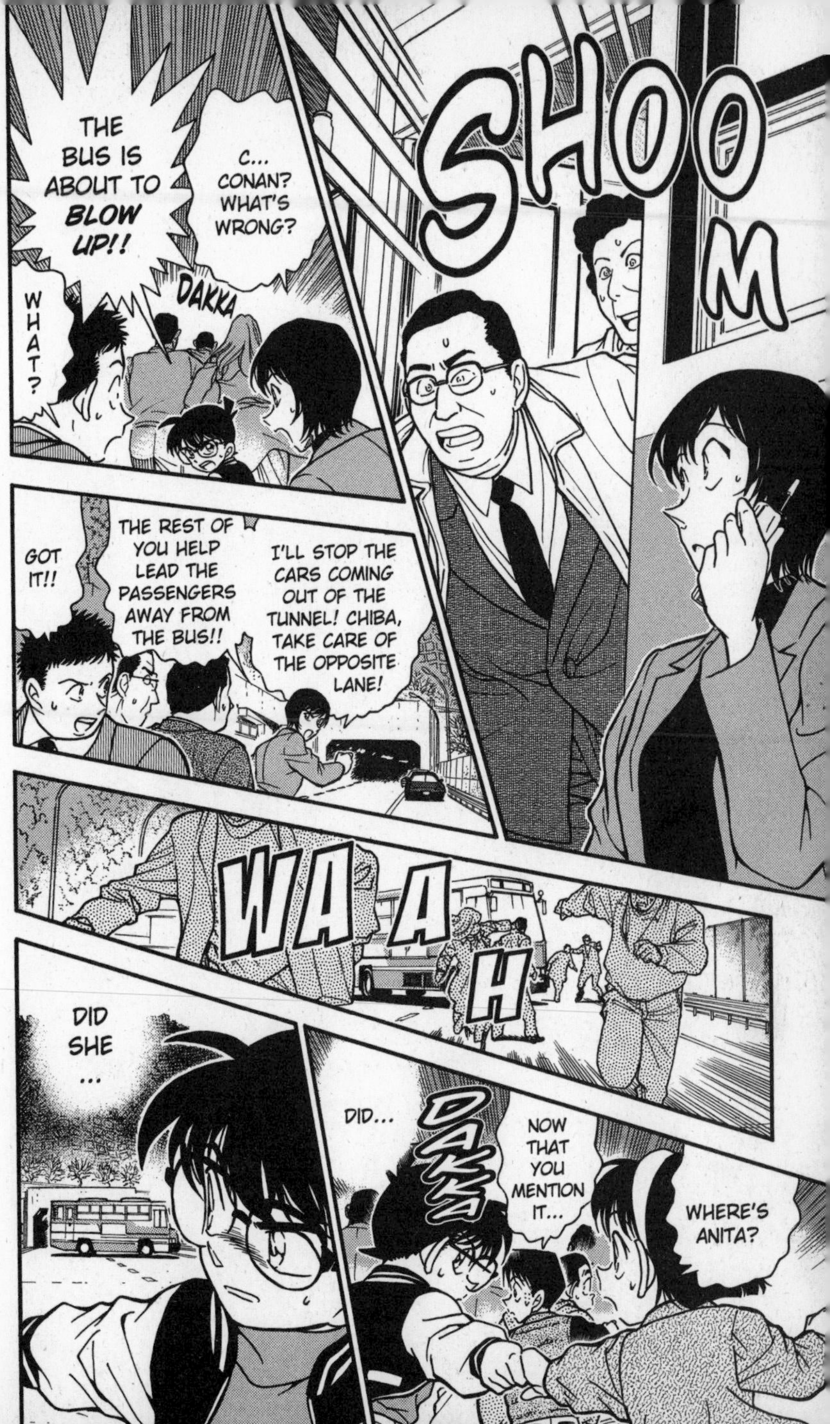
SHOOOM
C... CONAN? WHAT'S WRONG?
THE BUS IS ABOUT TO *BLOW UP!!*
DAKKA
WHAT?
I'LL STOP THE CARS COMING OUT OF THE TUNNEL! CHIBA, TAKE CARE OF THE OPPOSITE LANE!
THE REST OF YOU HELP LEAD THE PASSENGERS AWAY FROM THE BUS!!
GOT IT!!
WAAAH
WHERE'S ANITA?
NOW THAT YOU MENTION IT...
DAKKA
DID...
DID SHE ...

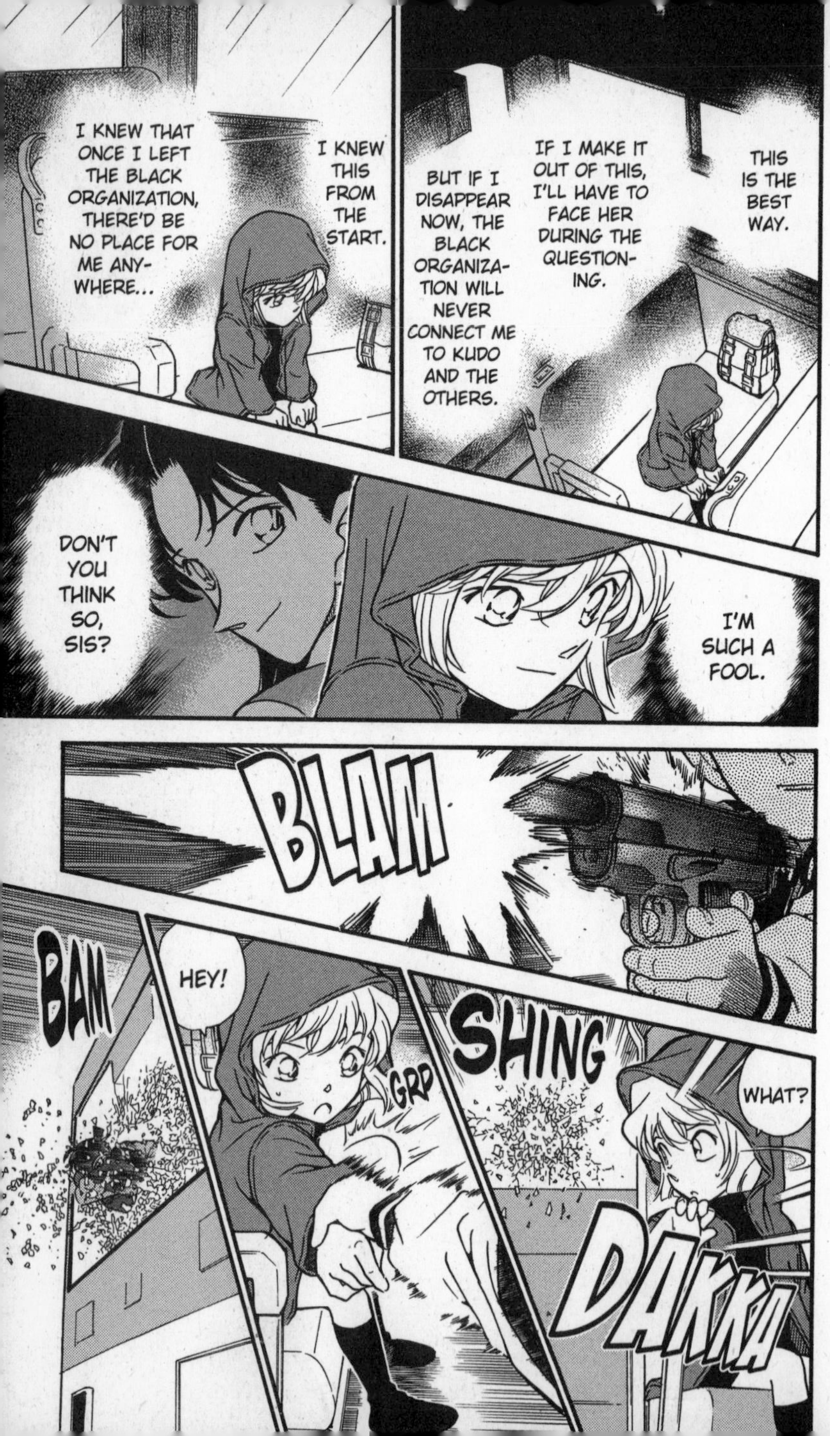
THIS IS THE BEST WAY.
IF I MAKE IT OUT OF THIS, I'LL HAVE TO FACE HER DURING THE QUESTIONING.
BUT IF I DISAPPEAR NOW, THE BLACK ORGANIZATION WILL NEVER CONNECT ME TO KUDO AND THE OTHERS.
I KNEW THIS FROM THE START.
I KNEW THAT ONCE I LEFT THE BLACK ORGANIZATION, THERE'D BE NO PLACE FOR ME ANYWHERE...
I'M SUCH A FOOL.
DON'T YOU THINK SO, SIS?
BLAM
SHING
WHAT?
DAKKA
HEY!
GRP
BAM

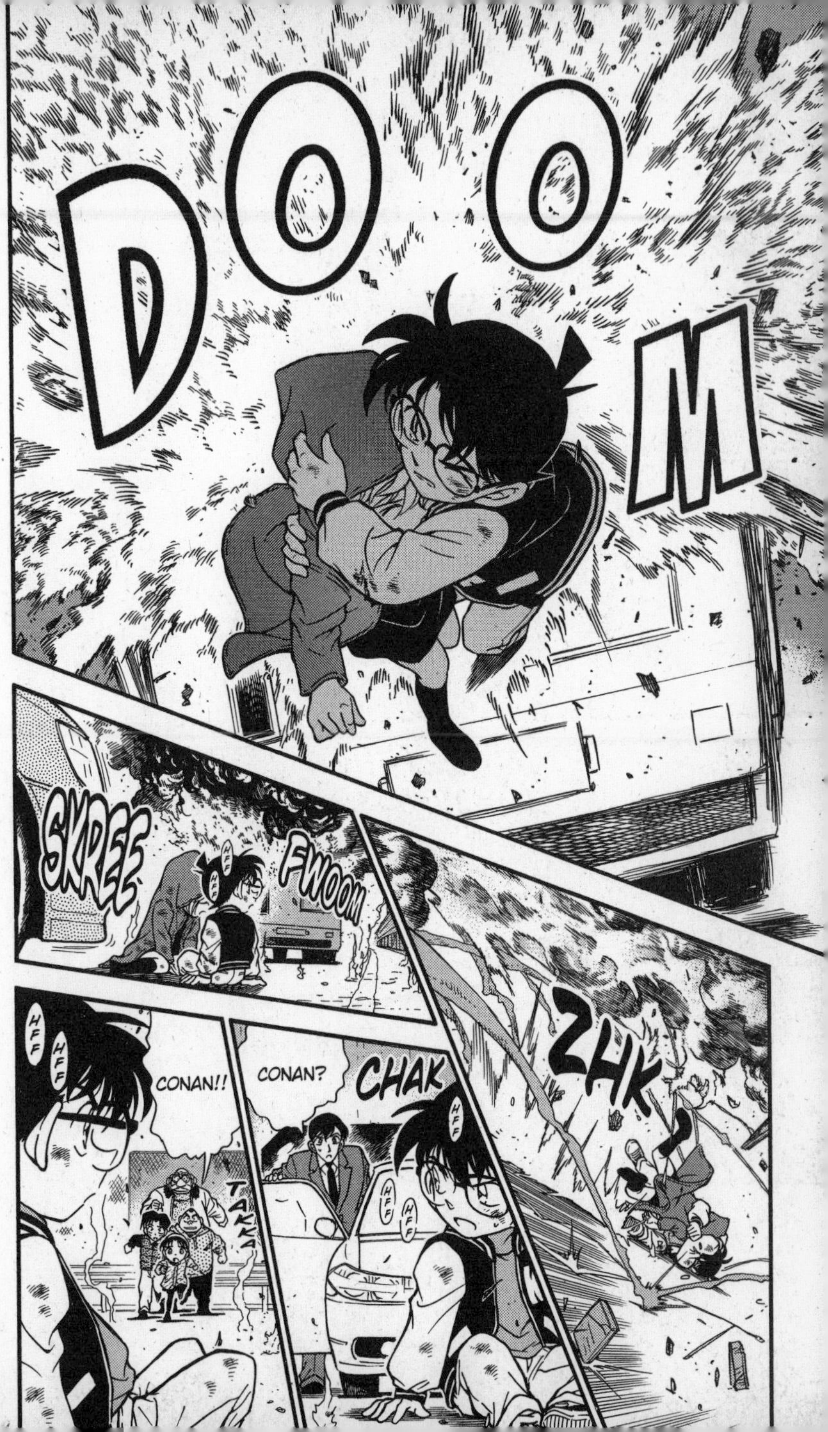
DOOOM
ZHK
FWOOM
HFF HFF
SKREE
HFF
CHAK
CONAN?
HFF HFF
CONAN!!
HFF HFF
TAKKA

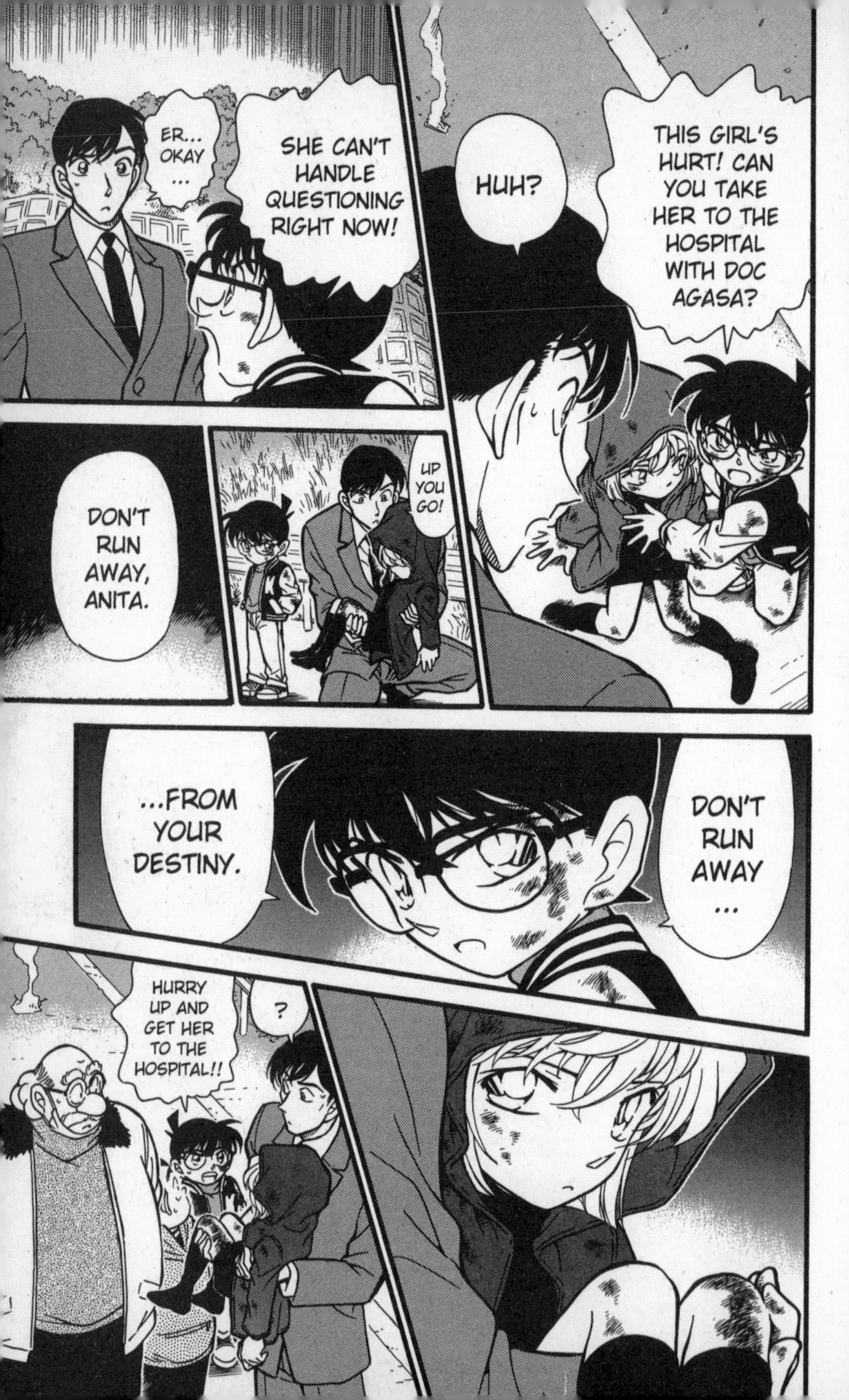
THIS GIRL'S HURT! CAN YOU TAKE HER TO THE HOSPITAL WITH DOC AGASA?
HUH?
SHE CAN'T HANDLE QUESTIONING RIGHT NOW!
ER... OKAY ...
UP YOU GO!
DON'T RUN AWAY, ANITA.
DON'T RUN AWAY ...
...FROM YOUR DESTINY.
?
HURRY UP AND GET HER TO THE HOSPITAL!!

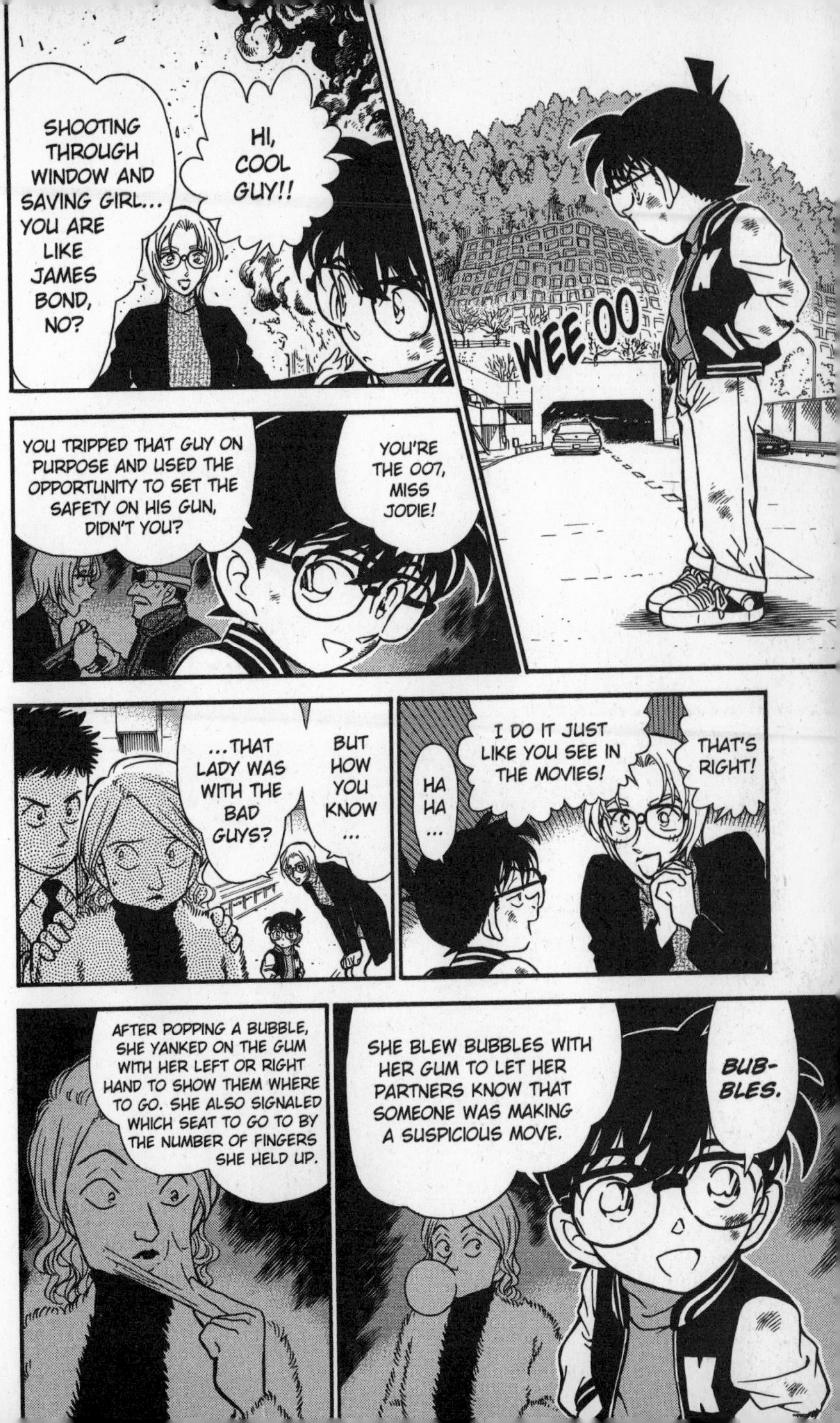
WEE OO
HI, COOL GUY!!
SHOOTING THROUGH WINDOW AND SAVING GIRL... YOU ARE LIKE JAMES BOND, NO?
YOU'RE THE 007, MISS JODIE!
YOU TRIPPED THAT GUY ON PURPOSE AND USED THE OPPORTUNITY TO SET THE SAFETY ON HIS GUN, DIDN'T YOU?
THAT'S RIGHT!
I DO IT JUST LIKE YOU SEE IN THE MOVIES!
HA HA ...
BUT HOW YOU KNOW ...
...THAT LADY WAS WITH THE BAD GUYS?
BUB-BLES.
SHE BLEW BUBBLES WITH HER GUM TO LET HER PARTNERS KNOW THAT SOMEONE WAS MAKING A SUSPICIOUS MOVE.
AFTER POPPING A BUBBLE, SHE YANKED ON THE GUM WITH HER LEFT OR RIGHT HAND TO SHOW THEM WHERE TO GO. SHE ALSO SIGNALED WHICH SEAT TO GO TO BY THE NUMBER OF FINGERS SHE HELD UP.

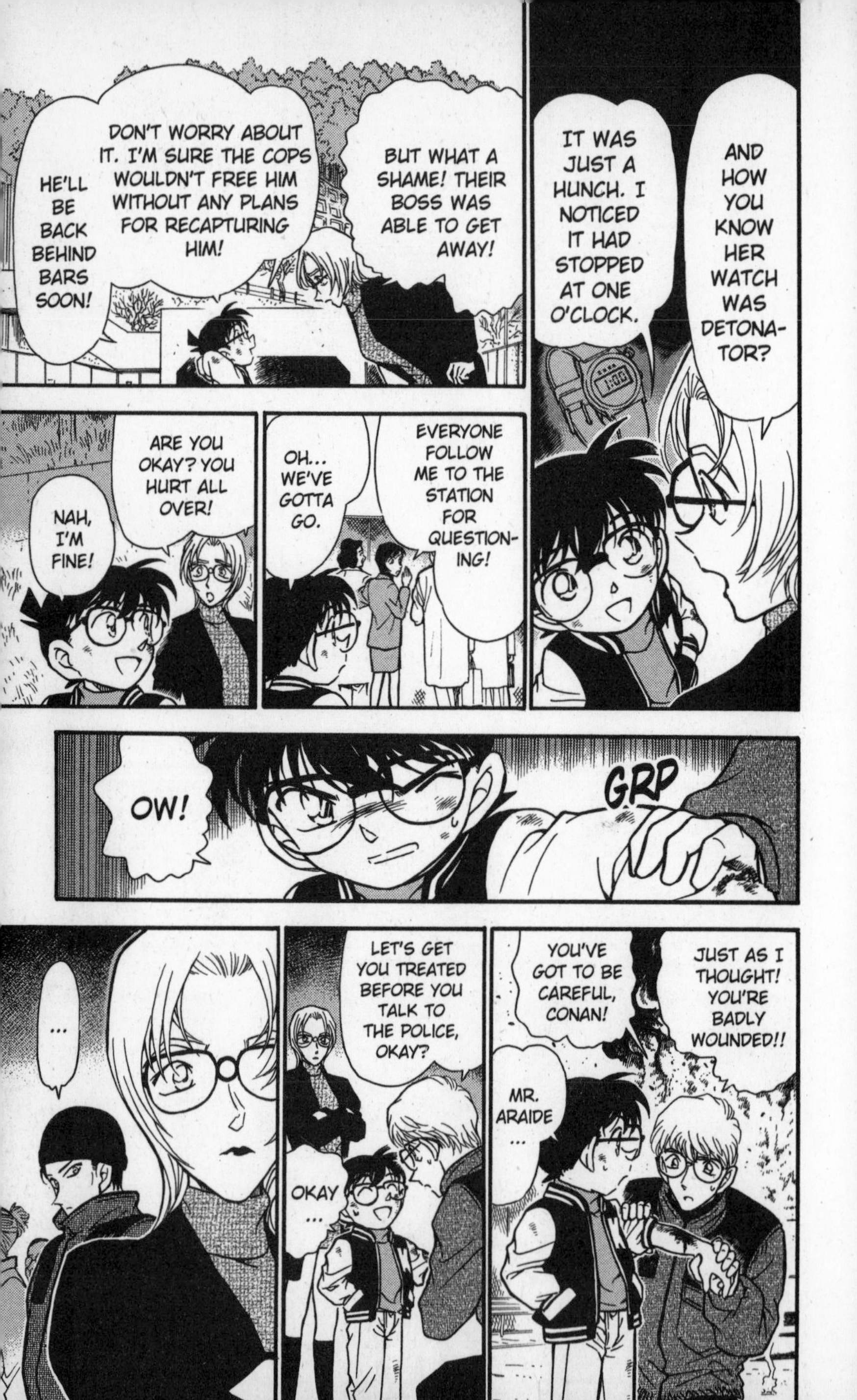
AND HOW YOU KNOW HER WATCH WAS DETONATOR?
IT WAS JUST A HUNCH. I NOTICED IT HAD STOPPED AT ONE O'CLOCK.
BUT WHAT A SHAME! THEIR BOSS WAS ABLE TO GET AWAY!
DON'T WORRY ABOUT IT. I'M SURE THE COPS WOULDN'T FREE HIM WITHOUT ANY PLANS FOR RECAPTURING HIM!
HE'LL BE BACK BEHIND BARS SOON!
EVERYONE FOLLOW ME TO THE STATION FOR QUESTIONING!
OH... WE'VE GOTTA GO.
ARE YOU OKAY? YOU HURT ALL OVER!
NAH, I'M FINE!
GRP
OW!
JUST AS I THOUGHT! YOU'RE BADLY WOUNDED!!
YOU'VE GOT TO BE CAREFUL, CONAN!
MR. ARAIDE ...
LET'S GET YOU TREATED BEFORE YOU TALK TO THE POLICE, OKAY?
OKAY ...
...

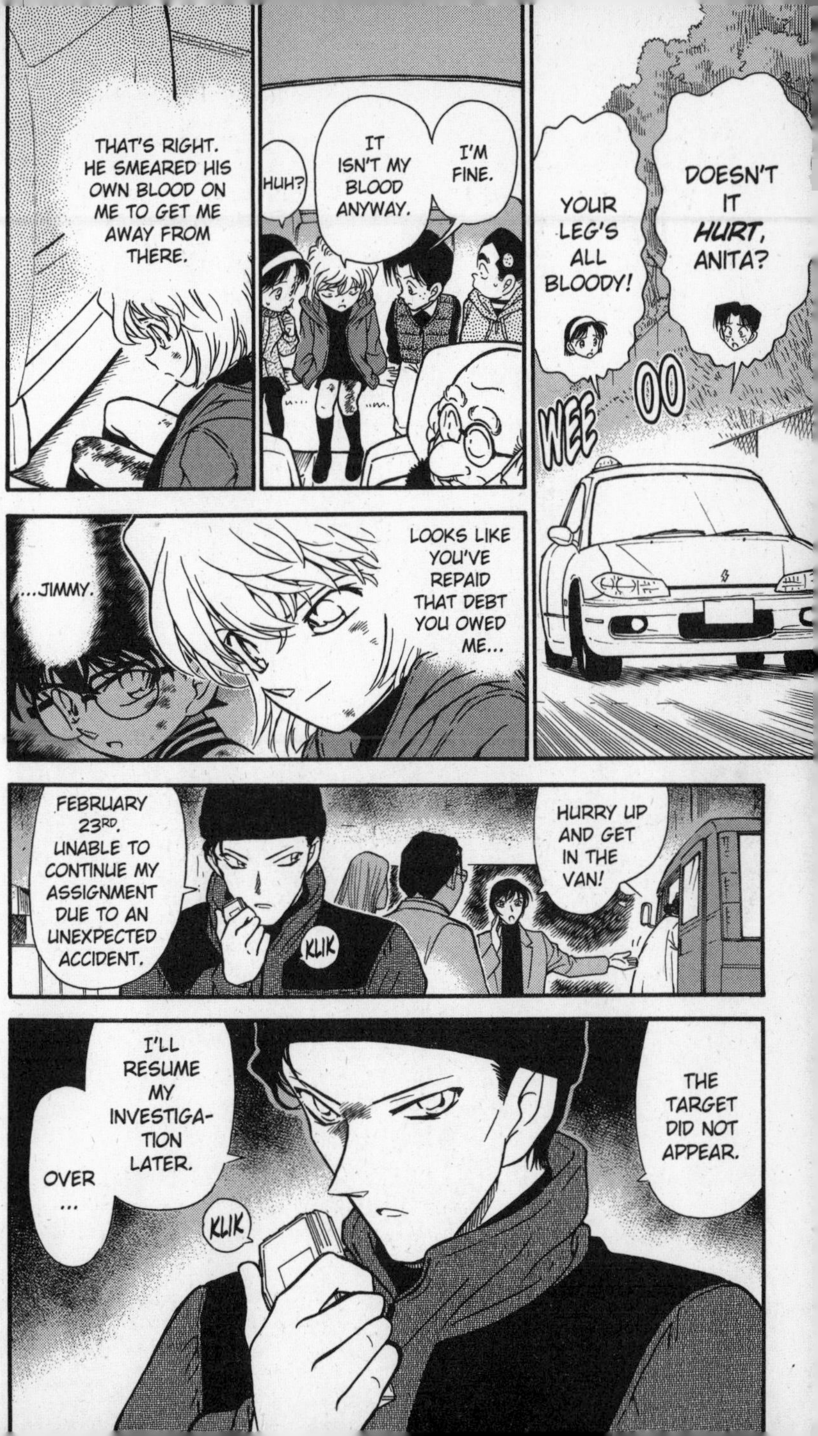
DOESN'T IT HURT, ANITA?
YOUR LEG'S ALL BLOODY!
WEE OO
I'M FINE.
IT ISN'T MY BLOOD ANYWAY.
HUH?
THAT'S RIGHT. HE SMEARED HIS OWN BLOOD ON ME TO GET ME AWAY FROM THERE.
LOOKS LIKE YOU'VE REPAID THAT DEBT YOU OWED ME...
...JIMMY.
HURRY UP AND GET IN THE VAN!
FEBRUARY 23RD. UNABLE TO CONTINUE MY ASSIGNMENT DUE TO AN UNEXPECTED ACCIDENT.
KLIK
THE TARGET DID NOT APPEAR.
I'LL RESUME MY INVESTIGATION LATER.
OVER...
KLIK

FILE 6: DOG LOVERS

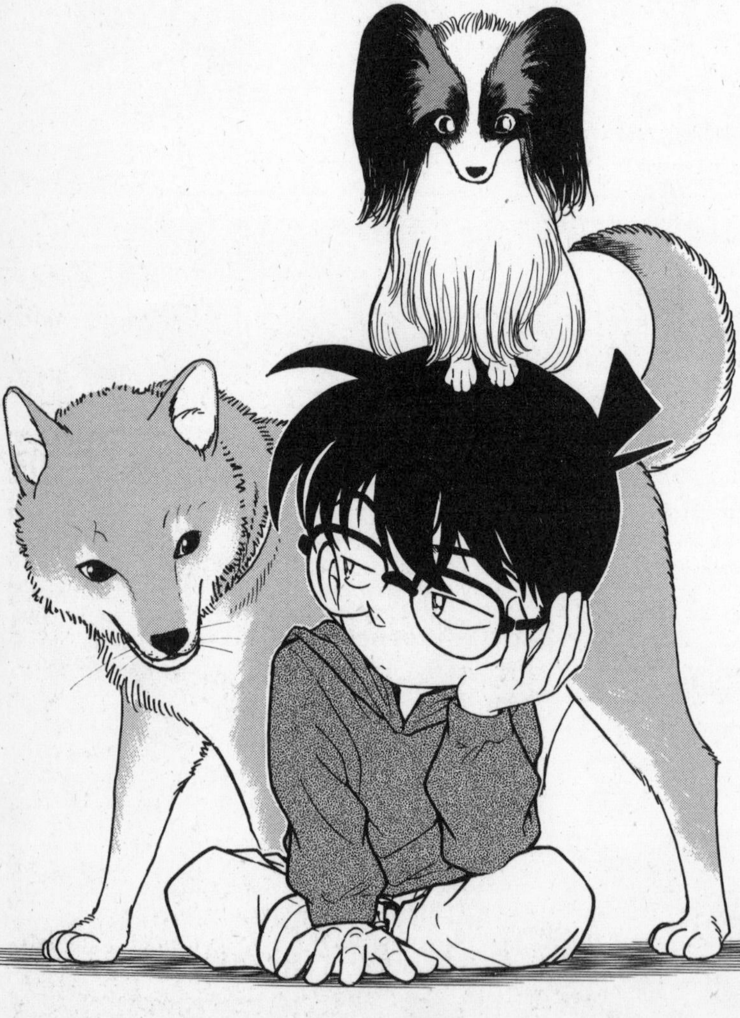

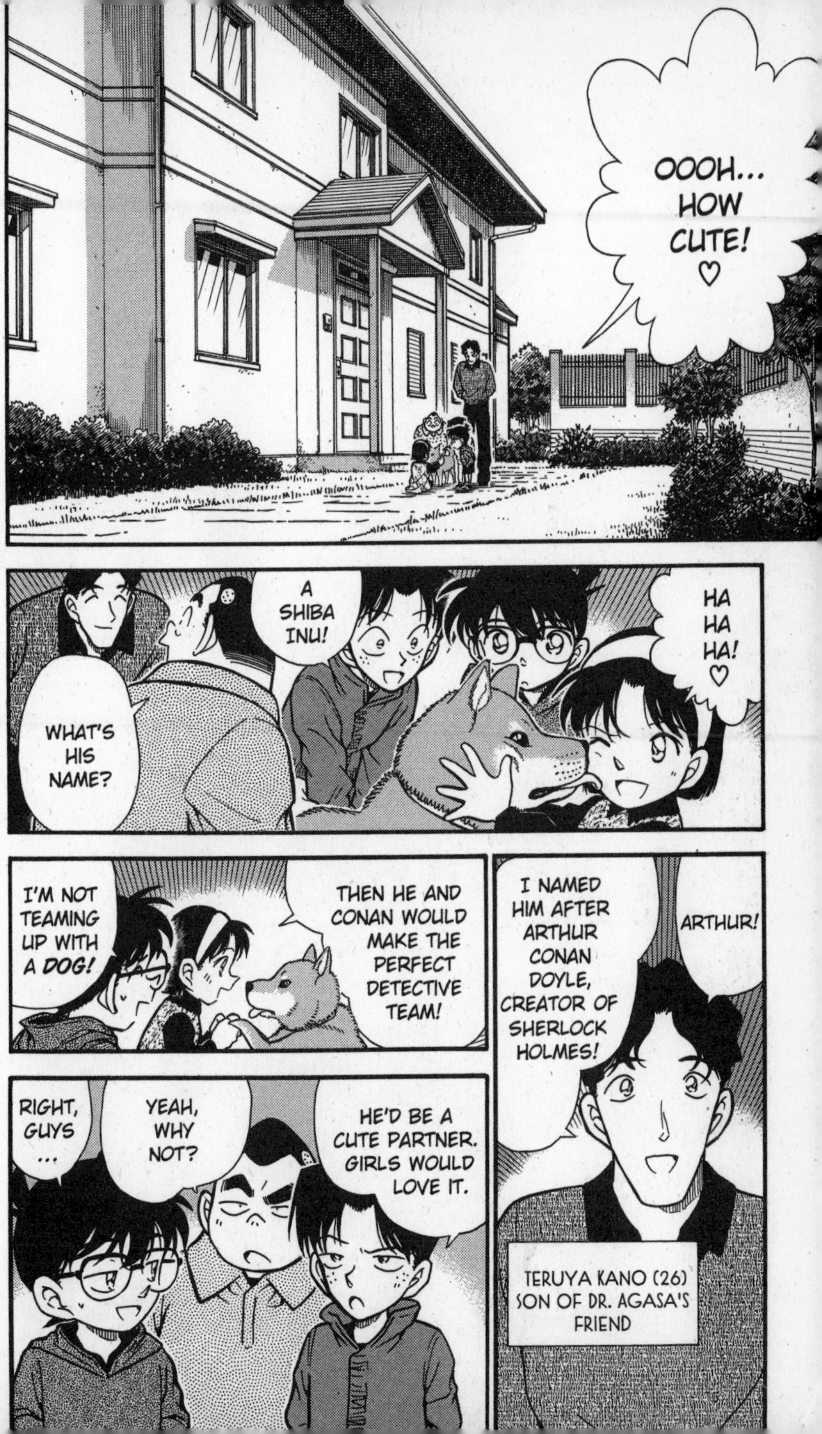
OOOH... HOW CUTE! ♡
HA HA HA! ♡
A SHIBA INU!
WHAT'S HIS NAME?
ARTHUR!
I NAMED HIM AFTER ARTHUR CONAN DOYLE, CREATOR OF SHERLOCK HOLMES!
TERUYA KANO (26) SON OF DR. AGASA'S FRIEND
THEN HE AND CONAN WOULD MAKE THE PERFECT DETECTIVE TEAM!
I'M NOT TEAMING UP WITH A *DOG!*
HE'D BE A CUTE PARTNER. GIRLS WOULD LOVE IT.
YEAH, WHY NOT?
RIGHT, GUYS ...

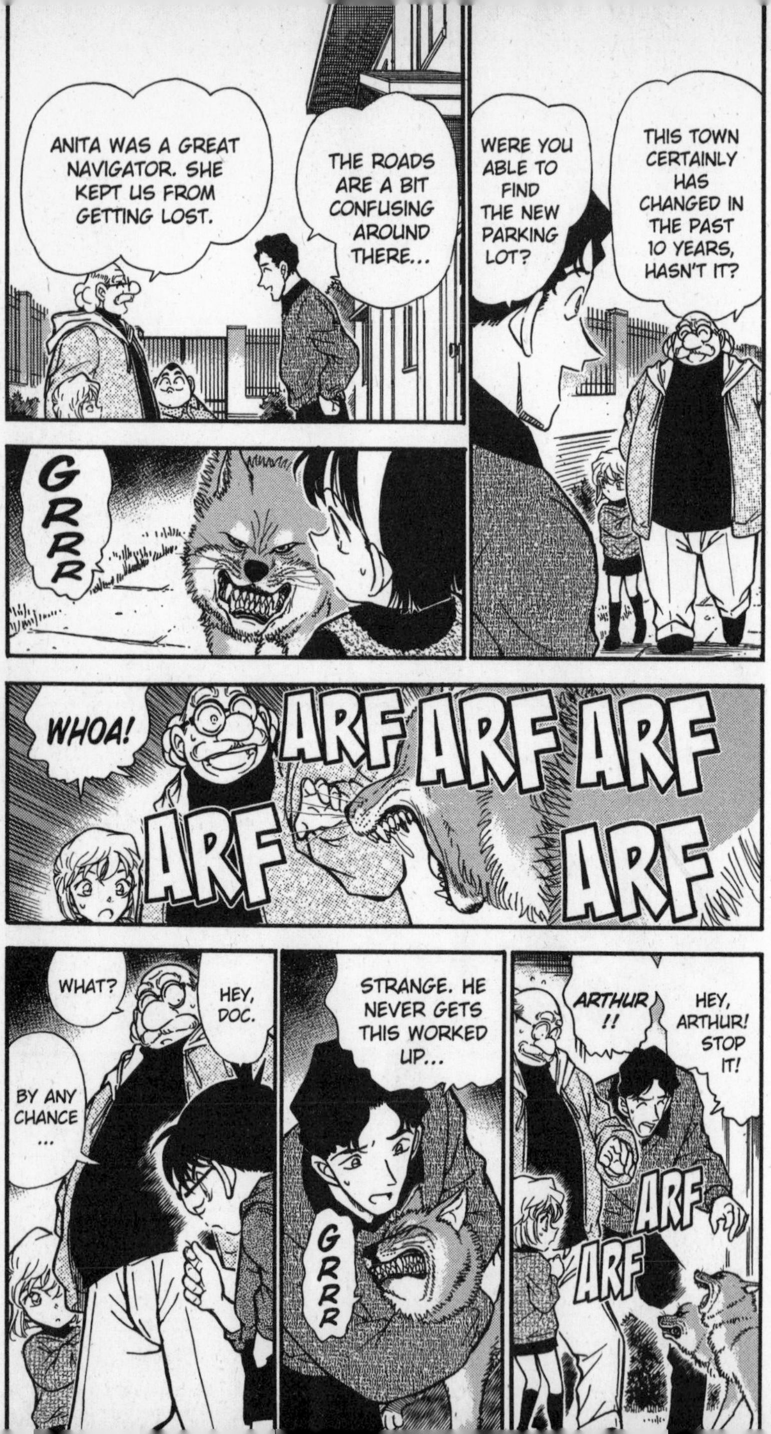
THIS TOWN CERTAINLY HAS CHANGED IN THE PAST 10 YEARS, HASN'T IT?
WERE YOU ABLE TO FIND THE NEW PARKING LOT?
THE ROADS ARE A BIT CONFUSING AROUND THERE...
ANITA WAS A GREAT NAVIGATOR. SHE KEPT US FROM GETTING LOST.
GRRR
ARF ARF ARF
ARF
ARF
WHOA!
HEY, ARTHUR! STOP IT!
ARTHUR!!
ARF
ARF
STRANGE. HE NEVER GETS THIS WORKED UP...
GRRR
HEY, DOC.
WHAT?
BY ANY CHANCE...

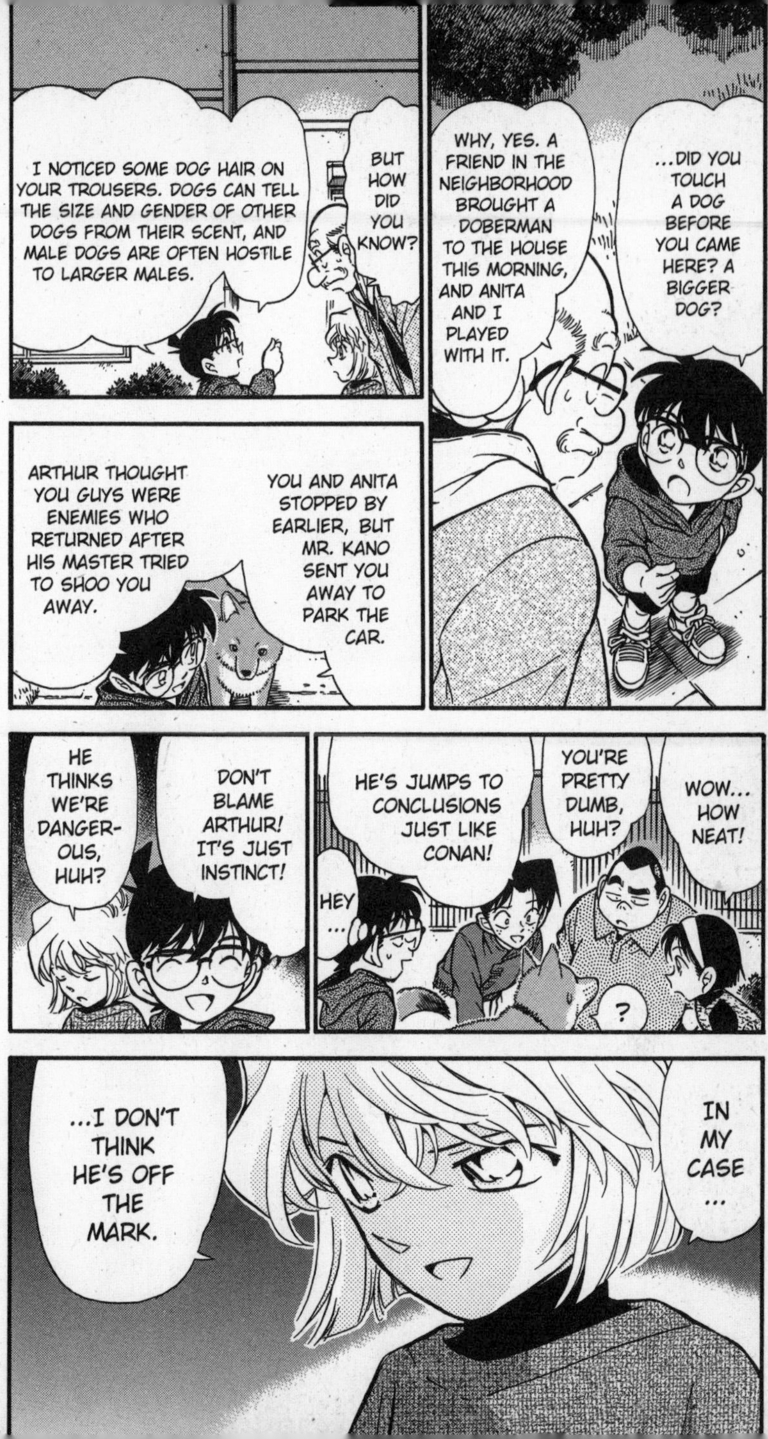
...DID YOU TOUCH A DOG BEFORE YOU CAME HERE? A BIGGER DOG?
WHY, YES. A FRIEND IN THE NEIGHBORHOOD BROUGHT A DOBERMAN TO THE HOUSE THIS MORNING, AND ANITA AND I PLAYED WITH IT.
BUT HOW DID YOU KNOW?
I NOTICED SOME DOG HAIR ON YOUR TROUSERS. DOGS CAN TELL THE SIZE AND GENDER OF OTHER DOGS FROM THEIR SCENT, AND MALE DOGS ARE OFTEN HOSTILE TO LARGER MALES.
YOU AND ANITA STOPPED BY EARLIER, BUT MR. KANO SENT YOU AWAY TO PARK THE CAR.
ARTHUR THOUGHT YOU GUYS WERE ENEMIES WHO RETURNED AFTER HIS MASTER TRIED TO SHOO YOU AWAY.
WOW... HOW NEAT!
YOU'RE PRETTY DUMB, HUH?
HE'S JUMPS TO CONCLUSIONS JUST LIKE CONAN!
?
HEY ...
DON'T BLAME ARTHUR! IT'S JUST INSTINCT!
HE THINKS WE'RE DANGER-OUS, HUH?
IN MY CASE ...
...I DON'T THINK HE'S OFF THE MARK.

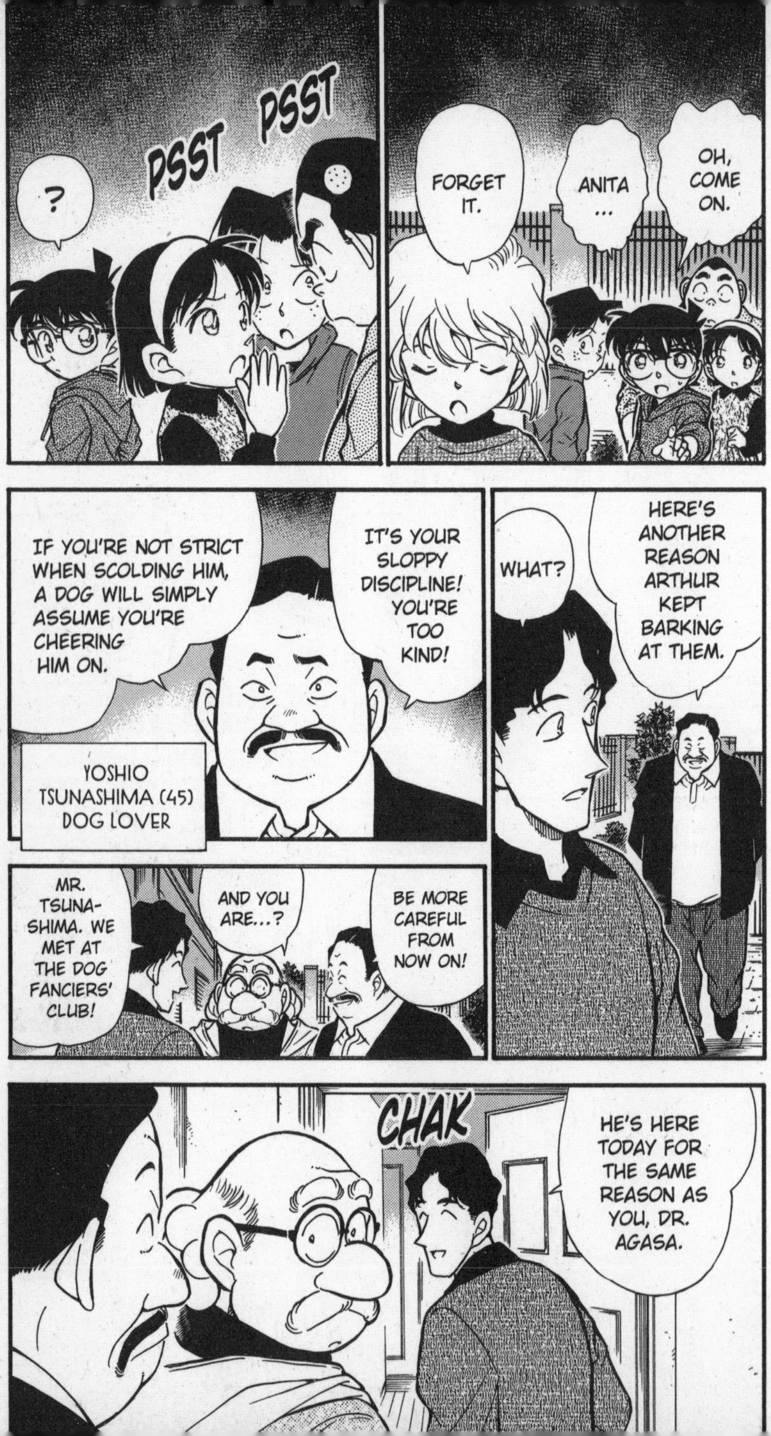
OH, COME ON.
ANITA...
FORGET IT.
PSST
PSST
?
HERE'S ANOTHER REASON ARTHUR KEPT BARKING AT THEM.
WHAT?
IT'S YOUR SLOPPY DISCIPLINE! YOU'RE TOO KIND!
IF YOU'RE NOT STRICT WHEN SCOLDING HIM, A DOG WILL SIMPLY ASSUME YOU'RE CHEERING HIM ON.
YOSHIO TSUNASHIMA (45) DOG LOVER
BE MORE CAREFUL FROM NOW ON!
AND YOU ARE...?
MR. TSUNA-SHIMA. WE MET AT THE DOG FANCIERS' CLUB!
HE'S HERE TODAY FOR THE SAME REASON AS YOU, DR. AGASA.
CHAK

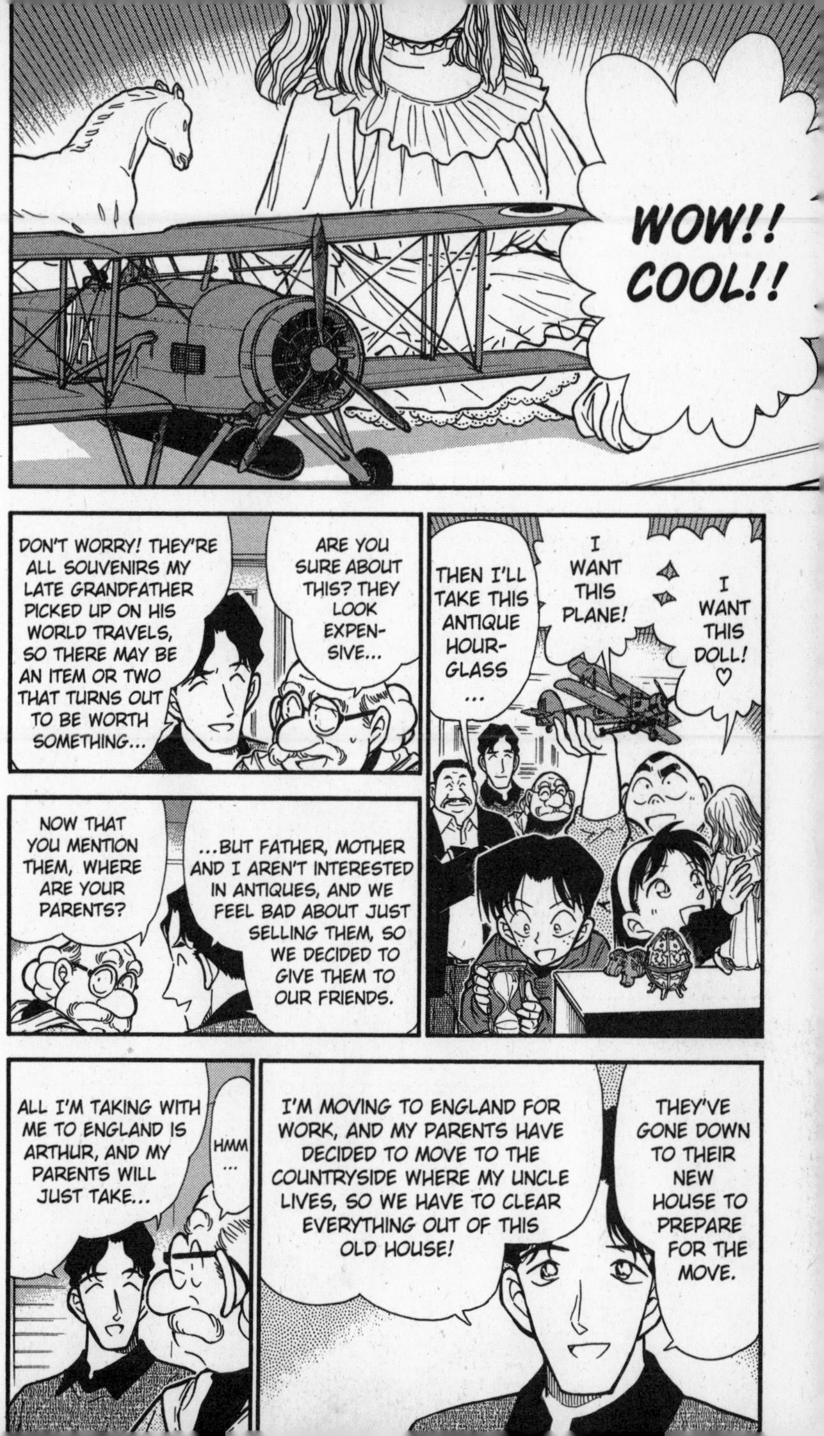
WOW!! COOL!!
I WANT THIS DOLL! ♡
I WANT THIS PLANE!
THEN I'LL TAKE THIS ANTIQUE HOUR-GLASS...
ARE YOU SURE ABOUT THIS? THEY LOOK EXPEN-SIVE...
DON'T WORRY! THEY'RE ALL SOUVENIRS MY LATE GRANDFATHER PICKED UP ON HIS WORLD TRAVELS, SO THERE MAY BE AN ITEM OR TWO THAT TURNS OUT TO BE WORTH SOMETHING...
...BUT FATHER, MOTHER AND I AREN'T INTERESTED IN ANTIQUES, AND WE FEEL BAD ABOUT JUST SELLING THEM, SO WE DECIDED TO GIVE THEM TO OUR FRIENDS.
NOW THAT YOU MENTION THEM, WHERE ARE YOUR PARENTS?
THEY'VE GONE DOWN TO THEIR NEW HOUSE TO PREPARE FOR THE MOVE.
I'M MOVING TO ENGLAND FOR WORK, AND MY PARENTS HAVE DECIDED TO MOVE TO THE COUNTRYSIDE WHERE MY UNCLE LIVES, SO WE HAVE TO CLEAR EVERYTHING OUT OF THIS OLD HOUSE!
HMM...
ALL I'M TAKING WITH ME TO ENGLAND IS ARTHUR, AND MY PARENTS WILL JUST TAKE...

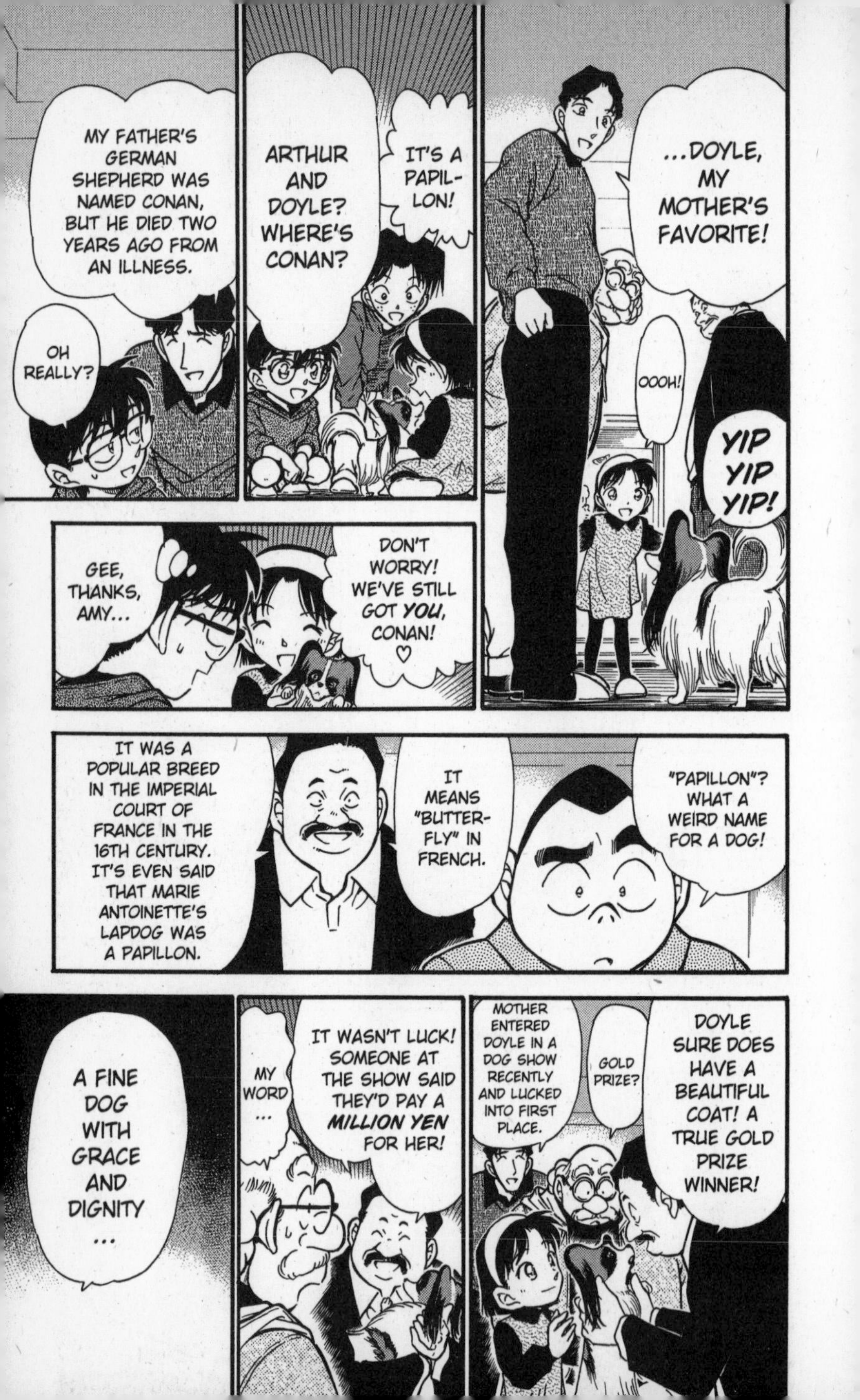
...DOYLE, MY MOTHER'S FAVORITE!
OOOH!
YIP YIP YIP!
IT'S A PAPILLON!
ARTHUR AND DOYLE? WHERE'S CONAN?
MY FATHER'S GERMAN SHEPHERD WAS NAMED CONAN, BUT HE DIED TWO YEARS AGO FROM AN ILLNESS.
OH REALLY?
DON'T WORRY! WE'VE STILL GOT *YOU*, CONAN! ♡
GEE, THANKS, AMY...
"PAPILLON"? WHAT A WEIRD NAME FOR A DOG!
IT MEANS "BUTTERFLY" IN FRENCH.
IT WAS A POPULAR BREED IN THE IMPERIAL COURT OF FRANCE IN THE 16TH CENTURY. IT'S EVEN SAID THAT MARIE ANTOINETTE'S LAPDOG WAS A PAPILLON.
DOYLE SURE DOES HAVE A BEAUTIFUL COAT! A TRUE GOLD PRIZE WINNER!
GOLD PRIZE?
MOTHER ENTERED DOYLE IN A DOG SHOW RECENTLY AND LUCKED INTO FIRST PLACE.
IT WASN'T LUCK! SOMEONE AT THE SHOW SAID THEY'D PAY A *MILLION YEN* FOR HER!
MY WORD...
A FINE DOG WITH GRACE AND DIGNITY...

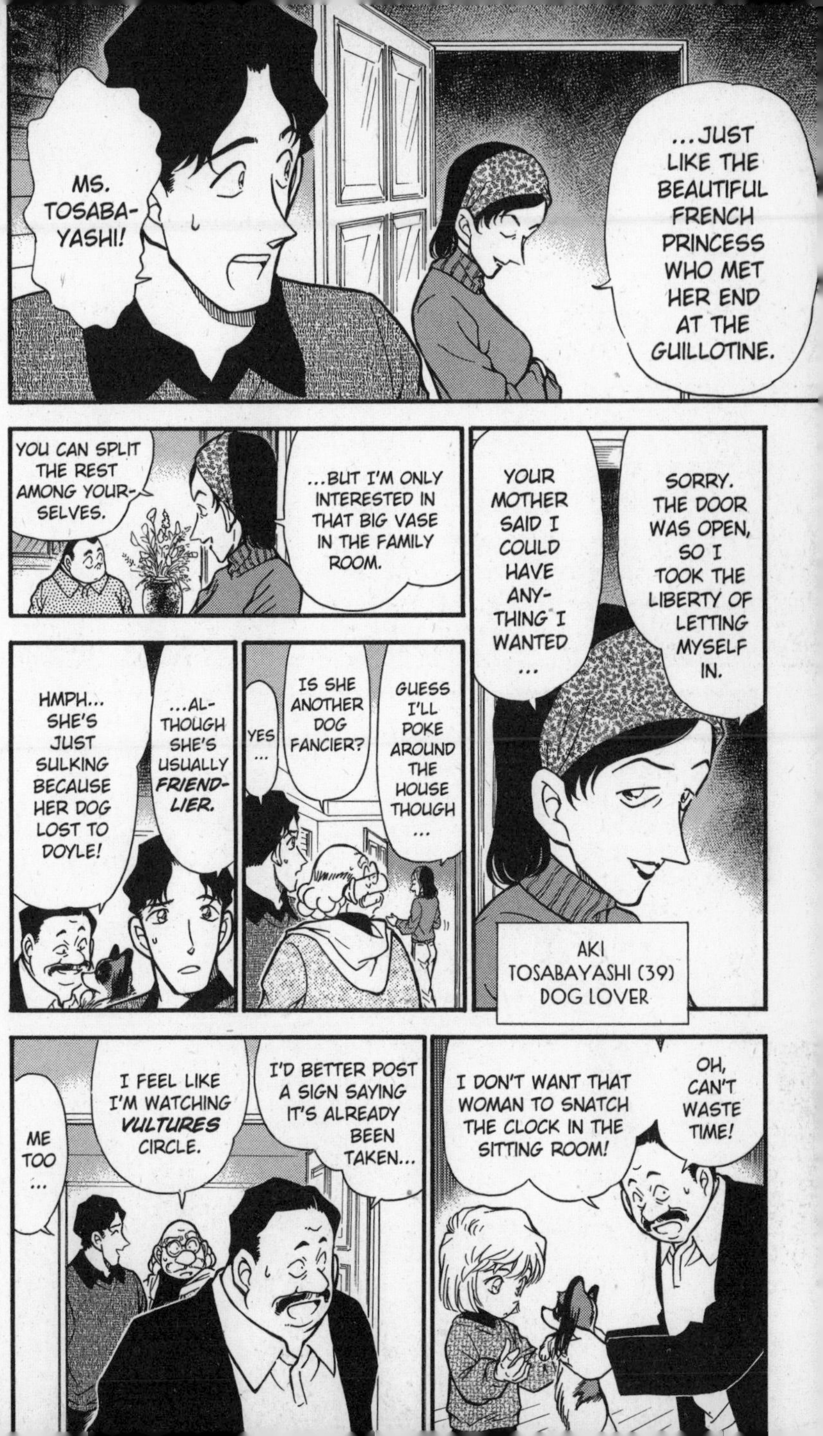
...JUST LIKE THE BEAUTIFUL FRENCH PRINCESS WHO MET HER END AT THE GUILLOTINE.
MS. TOSABA-YASHI!
SORRY. THE DOOR WAS OPEN, SO I TOOK THE LIBERTY OF LETTING MYSELF IN.
YOUR MOTHER SAID I COULD HAVE ANY-THING I WANTED...
AKI TOSABAYASHI (39) DOG LOVER
...BUT I'M ONLY INTERESTED IN THAT BIG VASE IN THE FAMILY ROOM.
YOU CAN SPLIT THE REST AMONG YOUR-SELVES.
GUESS I'LL POKE AROUND THE HOUSE THOUGH...
IS SHE ANOTHER DOG FANCIER?
YES...
...AL-THOUGH SHE'S USUALLY *FRIEND-LIER.*
HMPH... SHE'S JUST SULKING BECAUSE HER DOG LOST TO DOYLE!
OH, CAN'T WASTE TIME!
I DON'T WANT THAT WOMAN TO SNATCH THE CLOCK IN THE SITTING ROOM!
I'D BETTER POST A SIGN SAYING IT'S ALREADY BEEN TAKEN...
I FEEL LIKE I'M WATCHING *VULTURES* CIRCLE.
ME TOO...

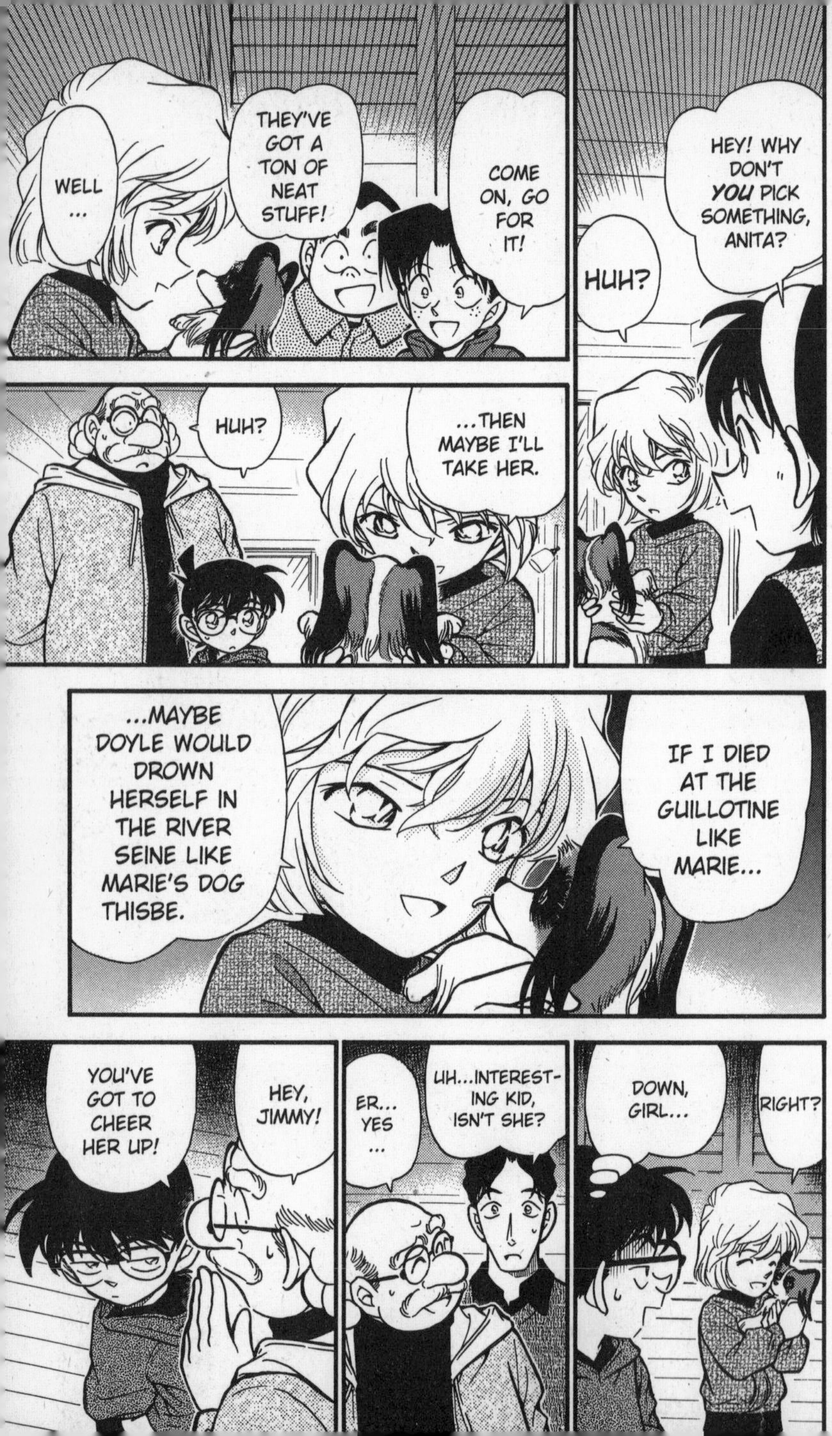
HEY! WHY DON'T *YOU* PICK SOMETHING, ANITA?
HUH?
COME ON, GO FOR IT!
THEY'VE GOT A TON OF NEAT STUFF!
WELL ...
...THEN MAYBE I'LL TAKE HER.
HUH?
IF I DIED AT THE GUILLOTINE LIKE MARIE...
...MAYBE DOYLE WOULD DROWN HERSELF IN THE RIVER SEINE LIKE MARIE'S DOG THISBE.
RIGHT?
DOWN, GIRL...
UH...INTERESTING KID, ISN'T SHE?
ER... YES ...
HEY, JIMMY!
YOU'VE GOT TO CHEER HER UP!

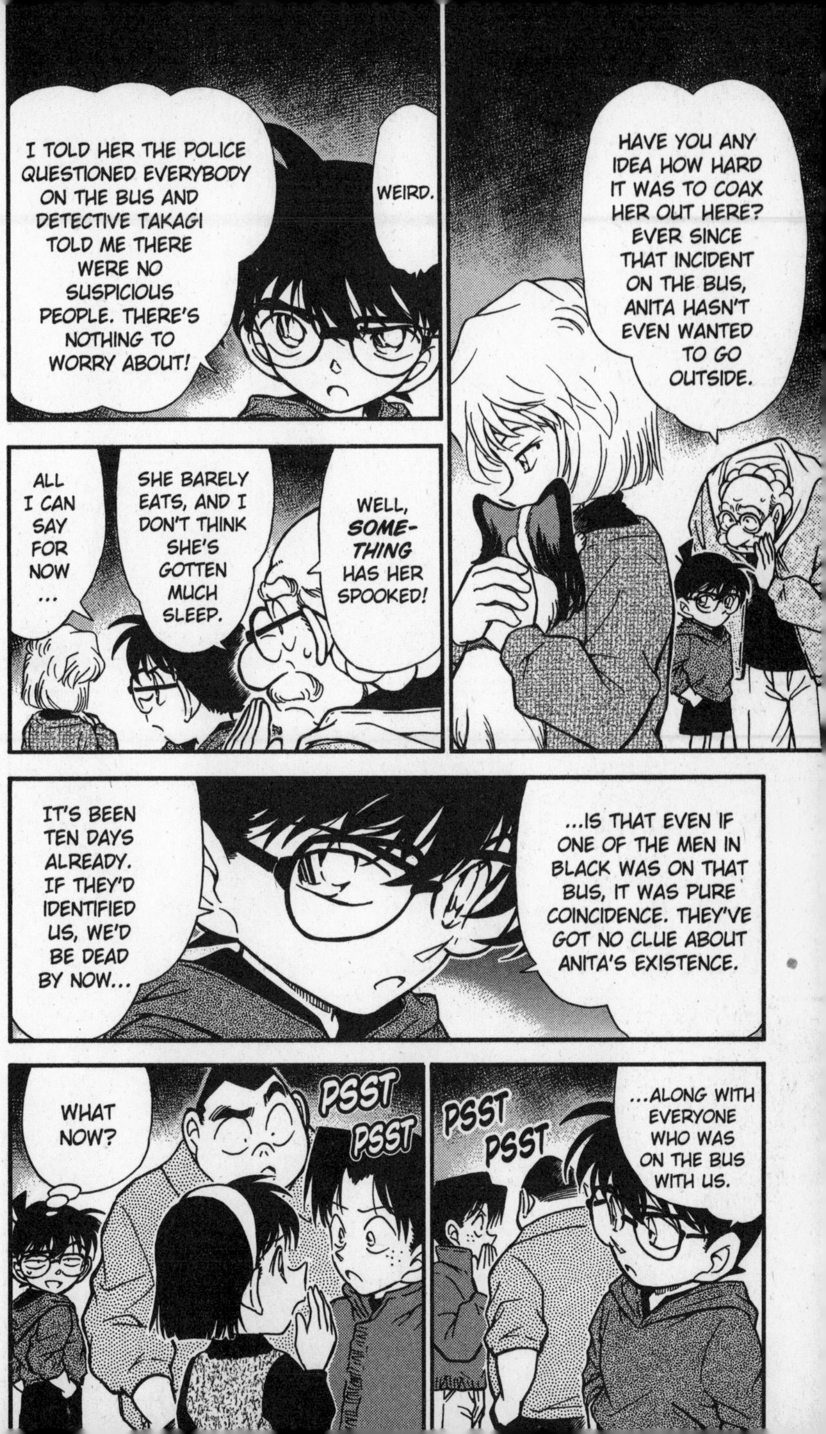
HAVE YOU ANY IDEA HOW HARD IT WAS TO COAX HER OUT HERE? EVER SINCE THAT INCIDENT ON THE BUS, ANITA HASN'T EVEN WANTED TO GO OUTSIDE.
WEIRD.
I TOLD HER THE POLICE QUESTIONED EVERYBODY ON THE BUS AND DETECTIVE TAKAGI TOLD ME THERE WERE NO SUSPICIOUS PEOPLE. THERE'S NOTHING TO WORRY ABOUT!
WELL, *SOMETHING* HAS HER SPOOKED!
SHE BARELY EATS, AND I DON'T THINK SHE'S GOTTEN MUCH SLEEP.
ALL I CAN SAY FOR NOW ...
...IS THAT EVEN IF ONE OF THE MEN IN BLACK WAS ON THAT BUS, IT WAS PURE COINCIDENCE. THEY'VE GOT NO CLUE ABOUT ANITA'S EXISTENCE.
IT'S BEEN TEN DAYS ALREADY. IF THEY'D IDENTIFIED US, WE'D BE DEAD BY NOW...
...ALONG WITH EVERYONE WHO WAS ON THE BUS WITH US.
PSST PSST
PSST PSST
WHAT NOW?

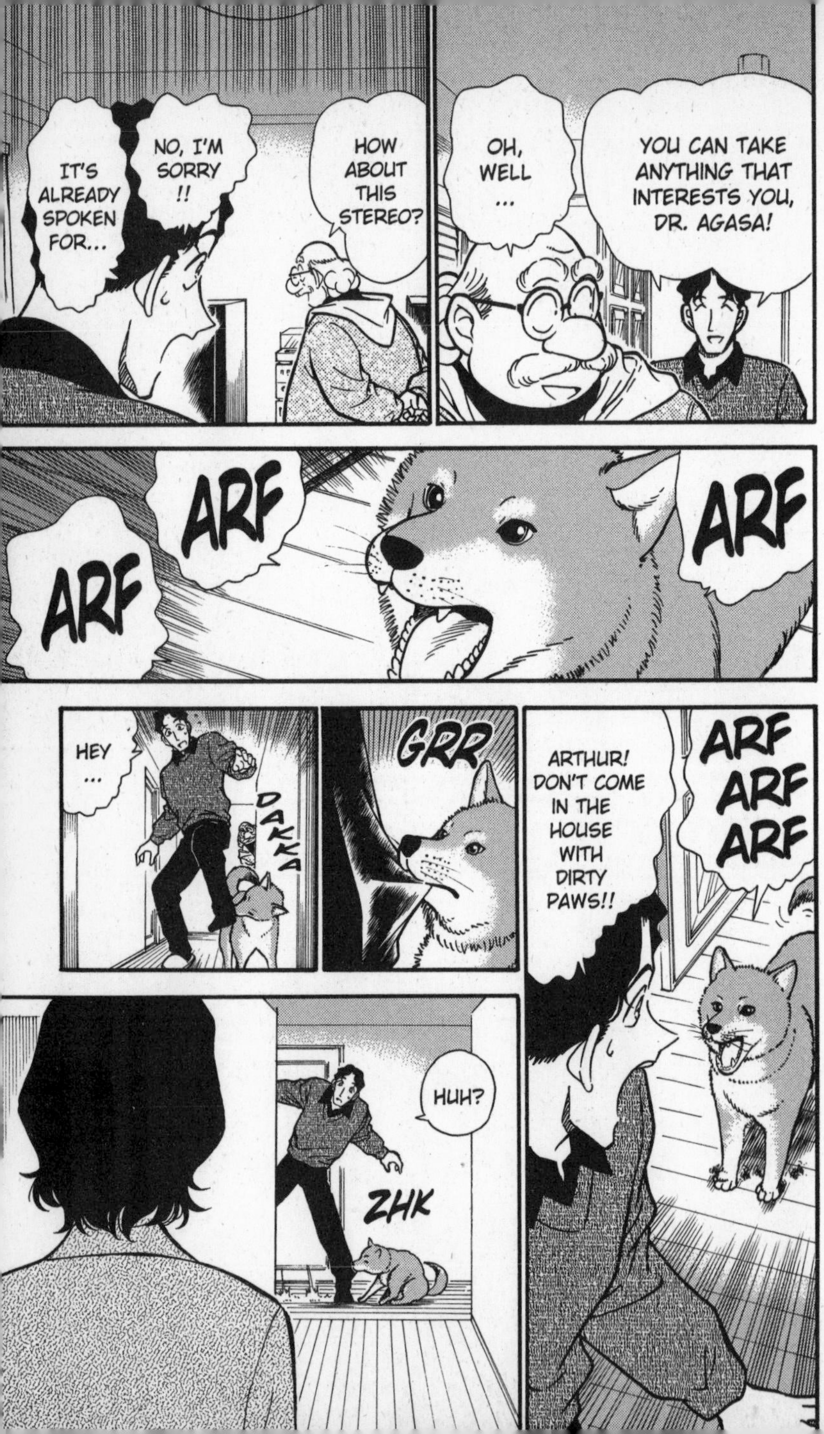
YOU CAN TAKE ANYTHING THAT INTERESTS YOU, DR. AGASA!
OH, WELL ...
HOW ABOUT THIS STEREO?
NO, I'M SORRY !!
IT'S ALREADY SPOKEN FOR...
ARF
ARF
ARF
ARF ARF ARF
ARTHUR! DON'T COME IN THE HOUSE WITH DIRTY PAWS!!
GRR
HEY ...
DAKKA
HUH?
ZHK

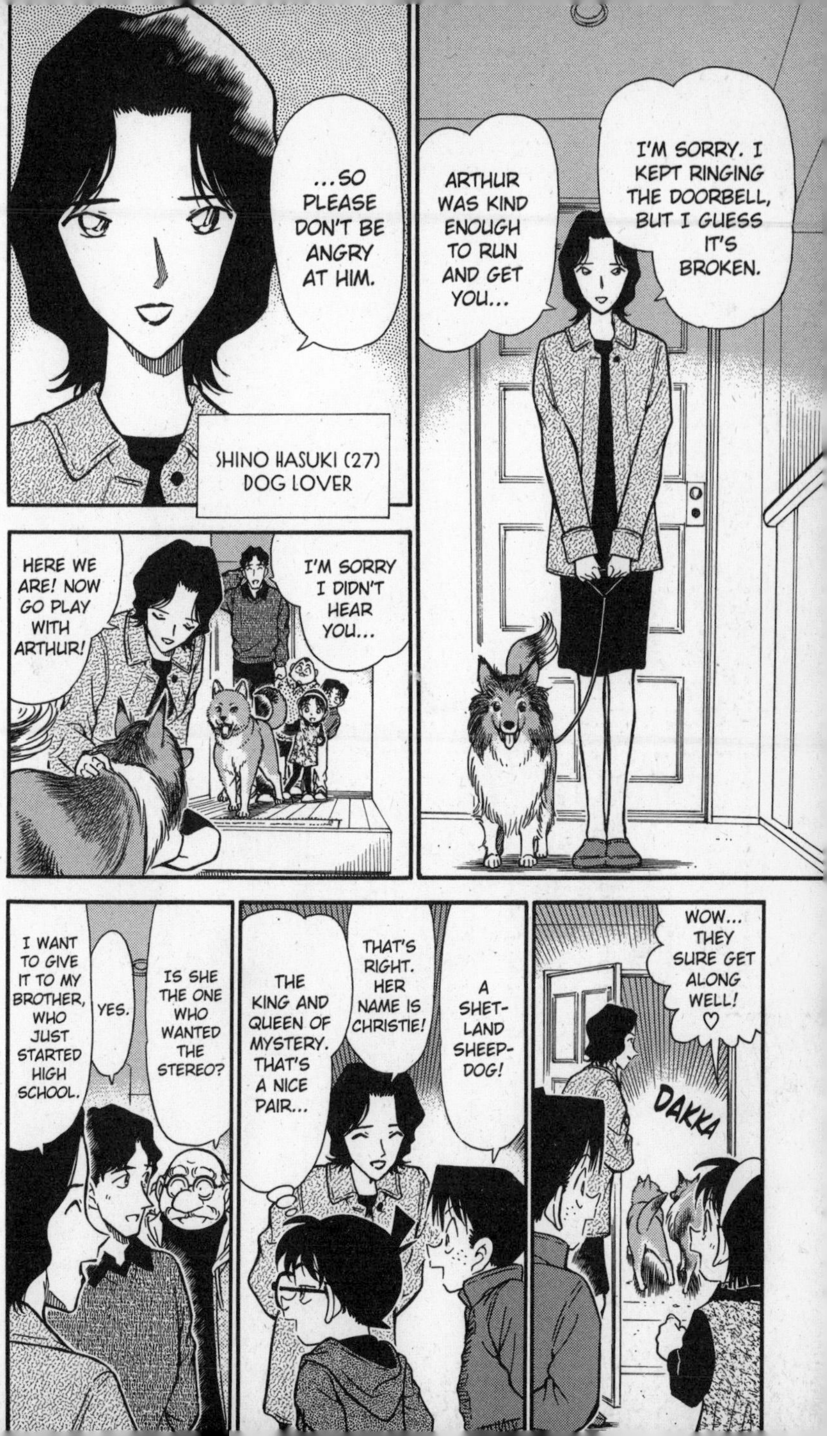
I'M SORRY. I KEPT RINGING THE DOORBELL, BUT I GUESS IT'S BROKEN.
ARTHUR WAS KIND ENOUGH TO RUN AND GET YOU...
...SO PLEASE DON'T BE ANGRY AT HIM.
SHINO HASUKI (27) DOG LOVER
I'M SORRY I DIDN'T HEAR YOU...
HERE WE ARE! NOW GO PLAY WITH ARTHUR!
WOW... THEY SURE GET ALONG WELL! ♡
DAKKA
A SHET-LAND SHEEP-DOG!
THAT'S RIGHT. HER NAME IS CHRISTIE!
THE KING AND QUEEN OF MYSTERY. THAT'S A NICE PAIR...
IS SHE THE ONE WHO WANTED THE STEREO?
YES.
I WANT TO GIVE IT TO MY BROTHER, WHO JUST STARTED HIGH SCHOOL.

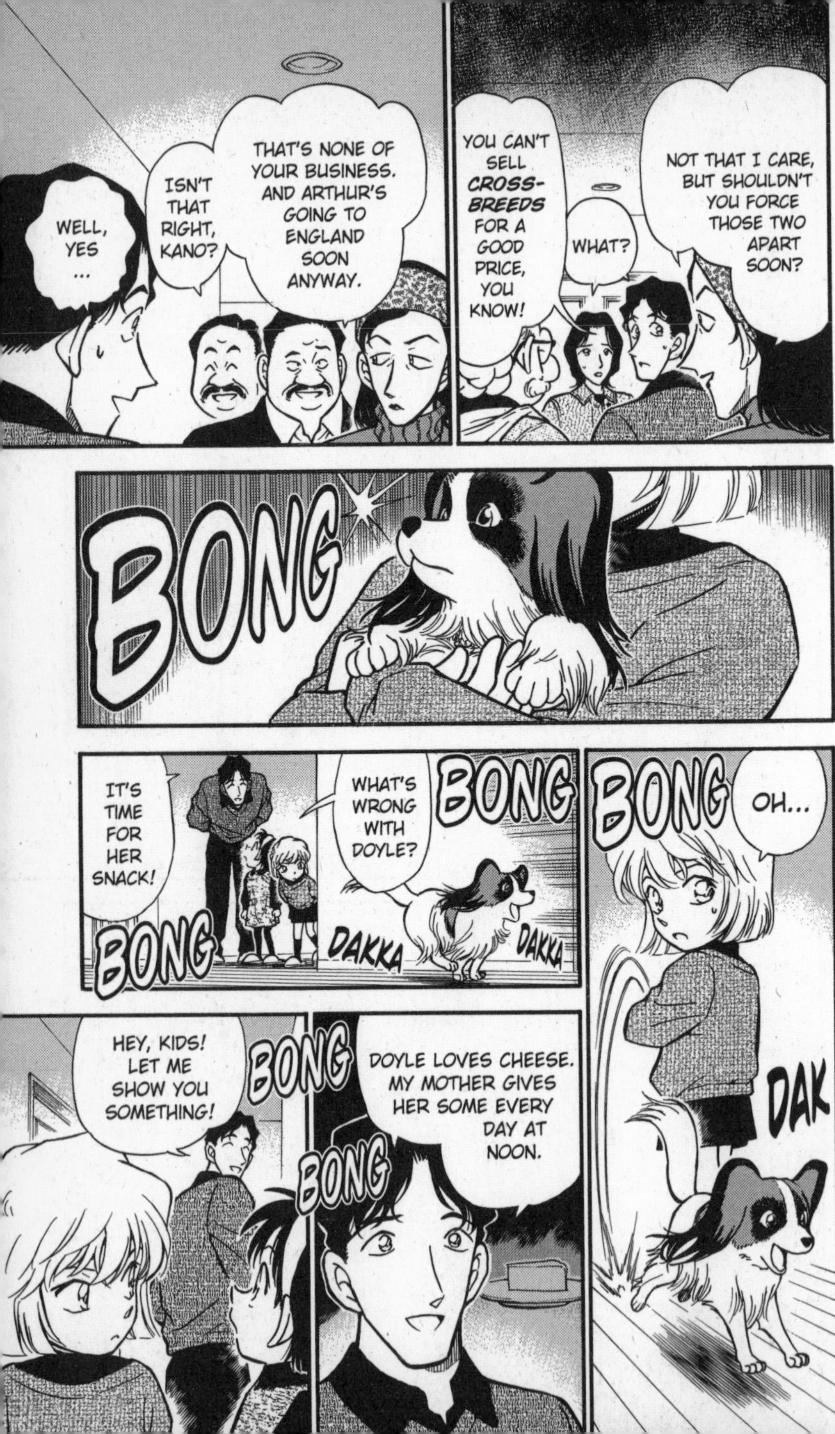
NOT THAT I CARE, BUT SHOULDN'T YOU FORCE THOSE TWO APART SOON?
WHAT?
YOU CAN'T SELL CROSS-BREEDS FOR A GOOD PRICE, YOU KNOW!
THAT'S NONE OF YOUR BUSINESS. AND ARTHUR'S GOING TO ENGLAND SOON ANYWAY.
ISN'T THAT RIGHT, KANO?
WELL, YES ...
BONG
BONG
OH...
DAK
BONG
WHAT'S WRONG WITH DOYLE?
DAKKA
DAKKA
IT'S TIME FOR HER SNACK!
BONG
DOYLE LOVES CHEESE. MY MOTHER GIVES HER SOME EVERY DAY AT NOON.
BONG
BONG
HEY, KIDS! LET ME SHOW YOU SOMETHING!

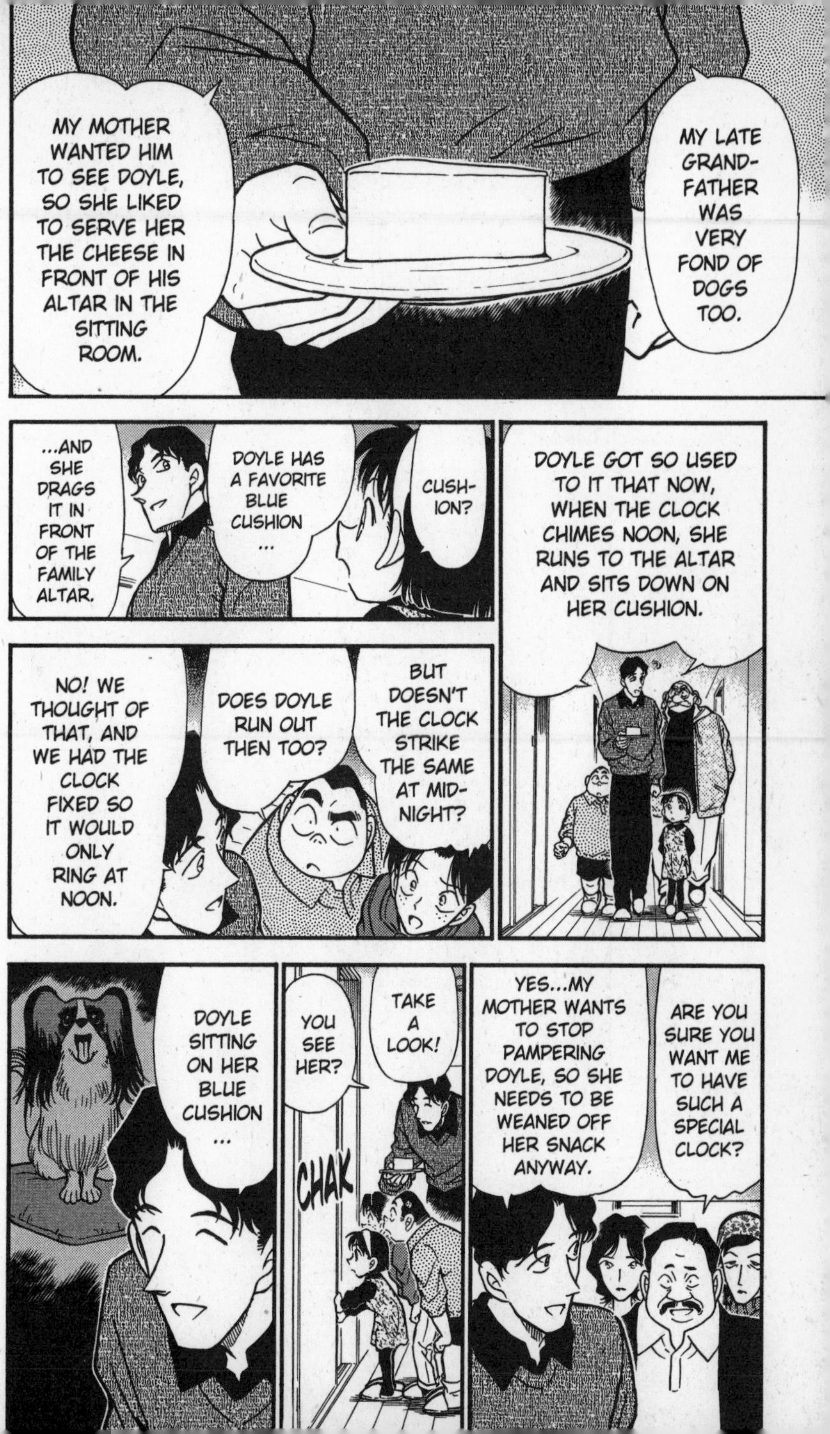
MY LATE GRAND-FATHER WAS VERY FOND OF DOGS TOO.
MY MOTHER WANTED HIM TO SEE DOYLE, SO SHE LIKED TO SERVE HER THE CHEESE IN FRONT OF HIS ALTAR IN THE SITTING ROOM.
DOYLE GOT SO USED TO IT THAT NOW, WHEN THE CLOCK CHIMES NOON, SHE RUNS TO THE ALTAR AND SITS DOWN ON HER CUSHION.
CUSH-ION?
DOYLE HAS A FAVORITE BLUE CUSHION ...
...AND SHE DRAGS IT IN FRONT OF THE FAMILY ALTAR.
BUT DOESN'T THE CLOCK STRIKE THE SAME AT MID-NIGHT?
DOES DOYLE RUN OUT THEN TOO?
NO! WE THOUGHT OF THAT, AND WE HAD THE CLOCK FIXED SO IT WOULD ONLY RING AT NOON.
ARE YOU SURE YOU WANT ME TO HAVE SUCH A SPECIAL CLOCK?
YES...MY MOTHER WANTS TO STOP PAMPERING DOYLE, SO SHE NEEDS TO BE WEANED OFF HER SNACK ANYWAY.
TAKE A LOOK!
YOU SEE HER?
CHAK
DOYLE SITTING ON HER BLUE CUSHION ...

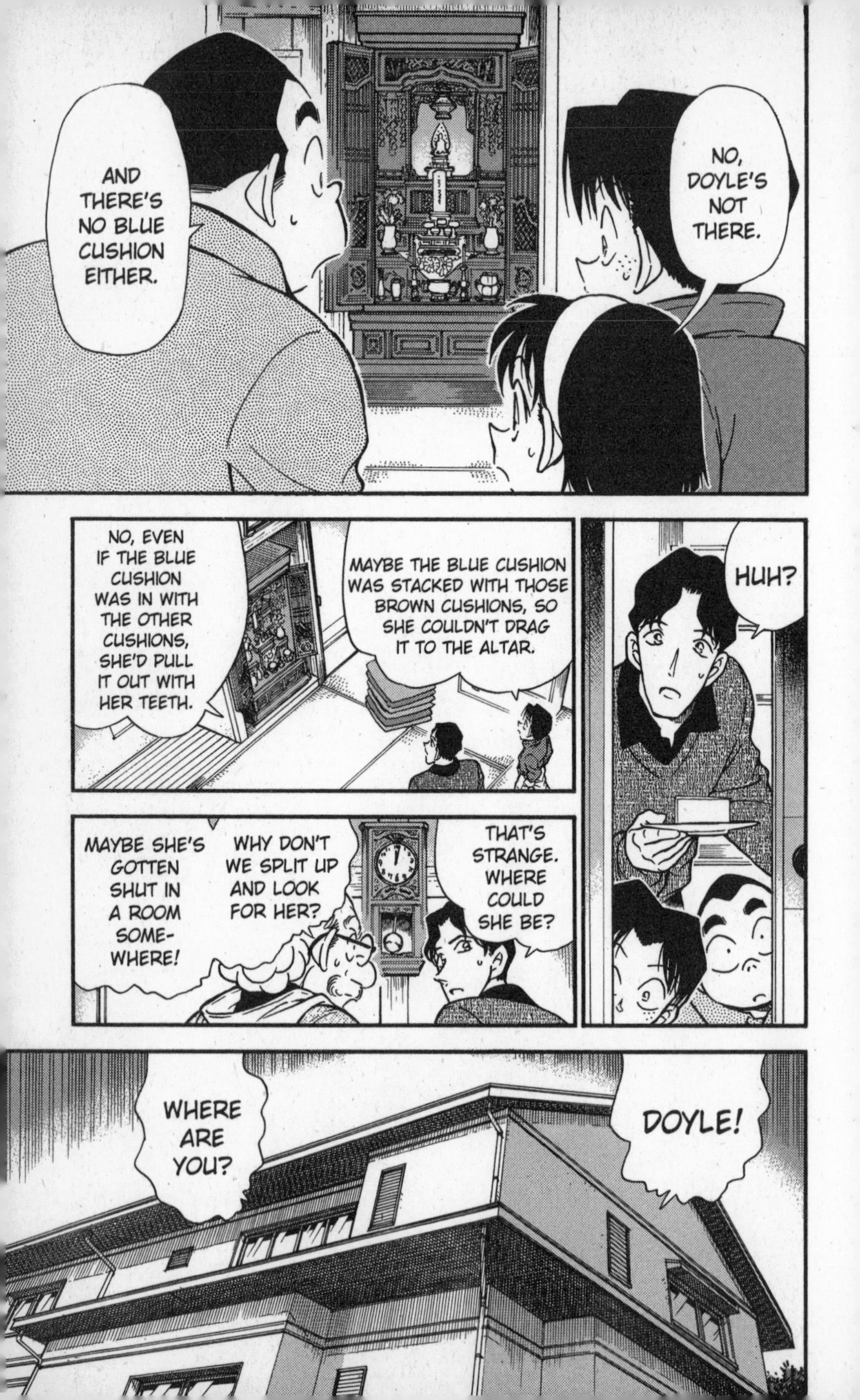
NO, DOYLE'S NOT THERE.
AND THERE'S NO BLUE CUSHION EITHER.
HUH?
MAYBE THE BLUE CUSHION WAS STACKED WITH THOSE BROWN CUSHIONS, SO SHE COULDN'T DRAG IT TO THE ALTAR.
NO, EVEN IF THE BLUE CUSHION WAS IN WITH THE OTHER CUSHIONS, SHE'D PULL IT OUT WITH HER TEETH.
THAT'S STRANGE. WHERE COULD SHE BE?
WHY DON'T WE SPLIT UP AND LOOK FOR HER?
MAYBE SHE'S GOTTEN SHUT IN A ROOM SOME-WHERE!
DOYLE!
WHERE ARE YOU?

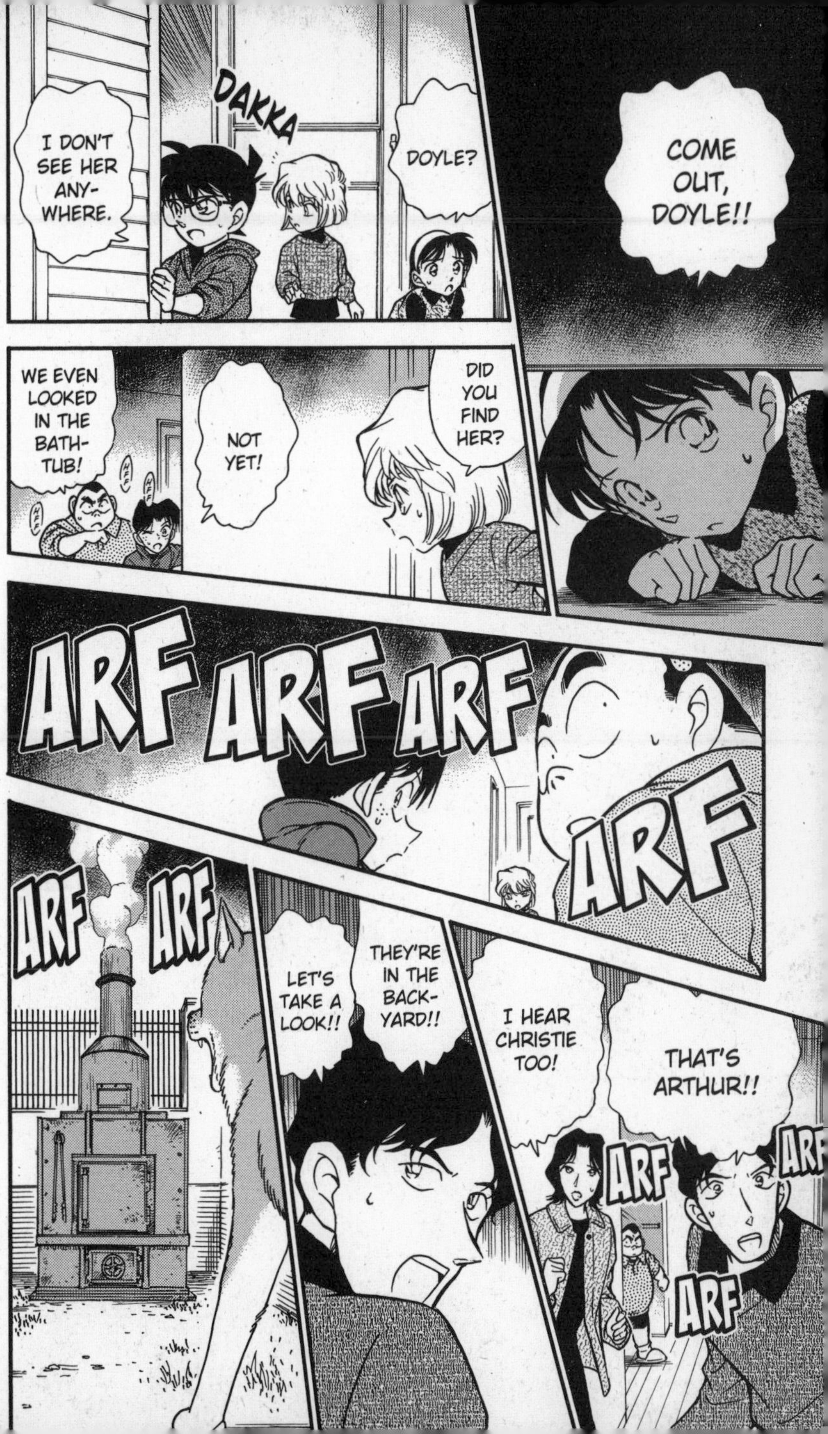
COME OUT, DOYLE!!
DOYLE?
DAKKA
I DON'T SEE HER ANY-WHERE.
DID YOU FIND HER?
NOT YET!
WE EVEN LOOKED IN THE BATH-TUB!
ARF ARF ARF
ARF
THAT'S ARTHUR!!
ARF
ARF
ARF
I HEAR CHRISTIE TOO!
THEY'RE IN THE BACK-YARD!!
LET'S TAKE A LOOK!!
ARF
ARF

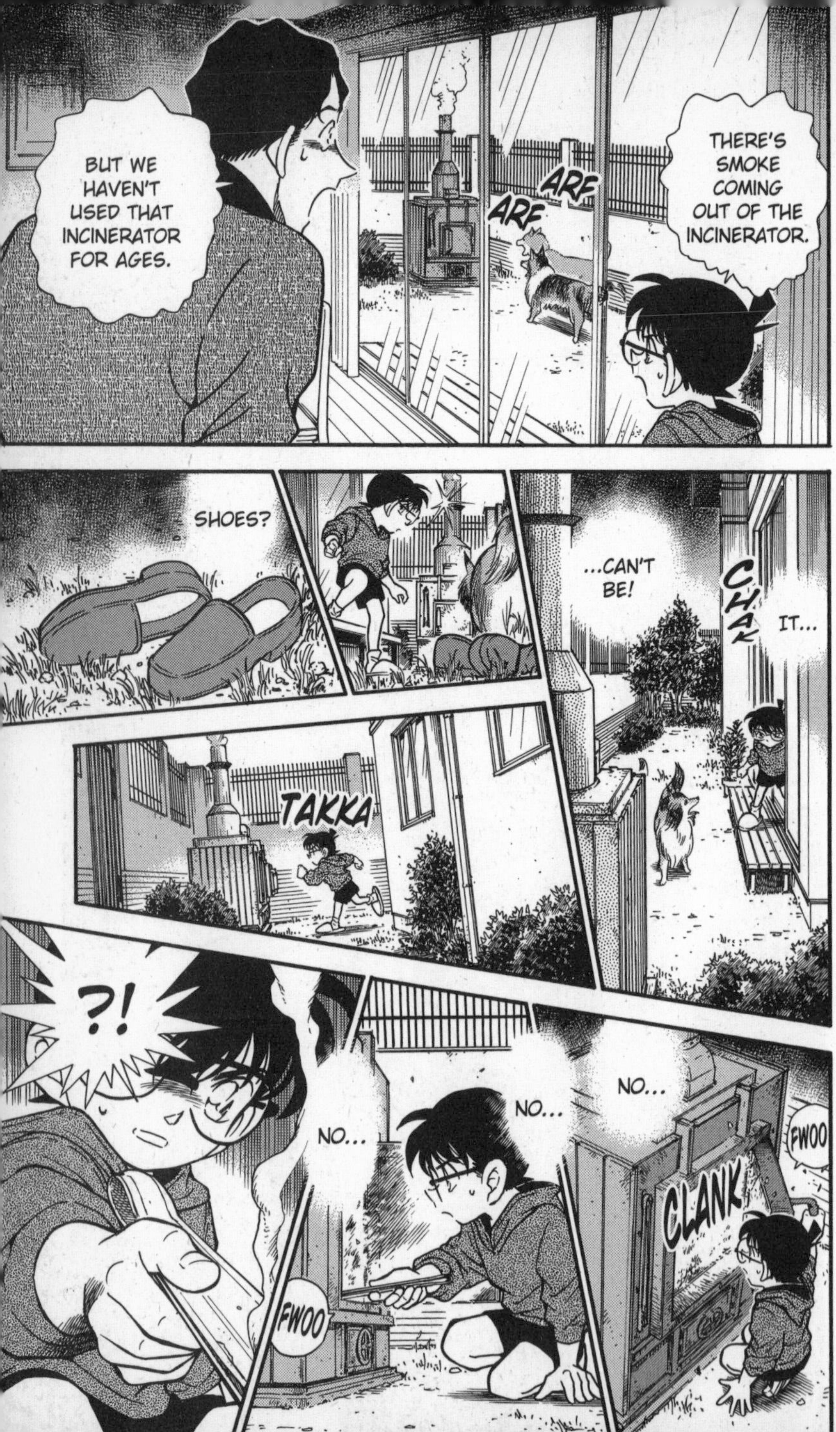

THERE'S SMOKE COMING OUT OF THE INCINERATOR.
ARF
ARF
BUT WE HAVEN'T USED THAT INCINERATOR FOR AGES.
IT...
CHAK
...CAN'T BE!
SHOES?
TAKKA
FWOO
CLANK
NO...
NO...
NO...
FWOO
?!

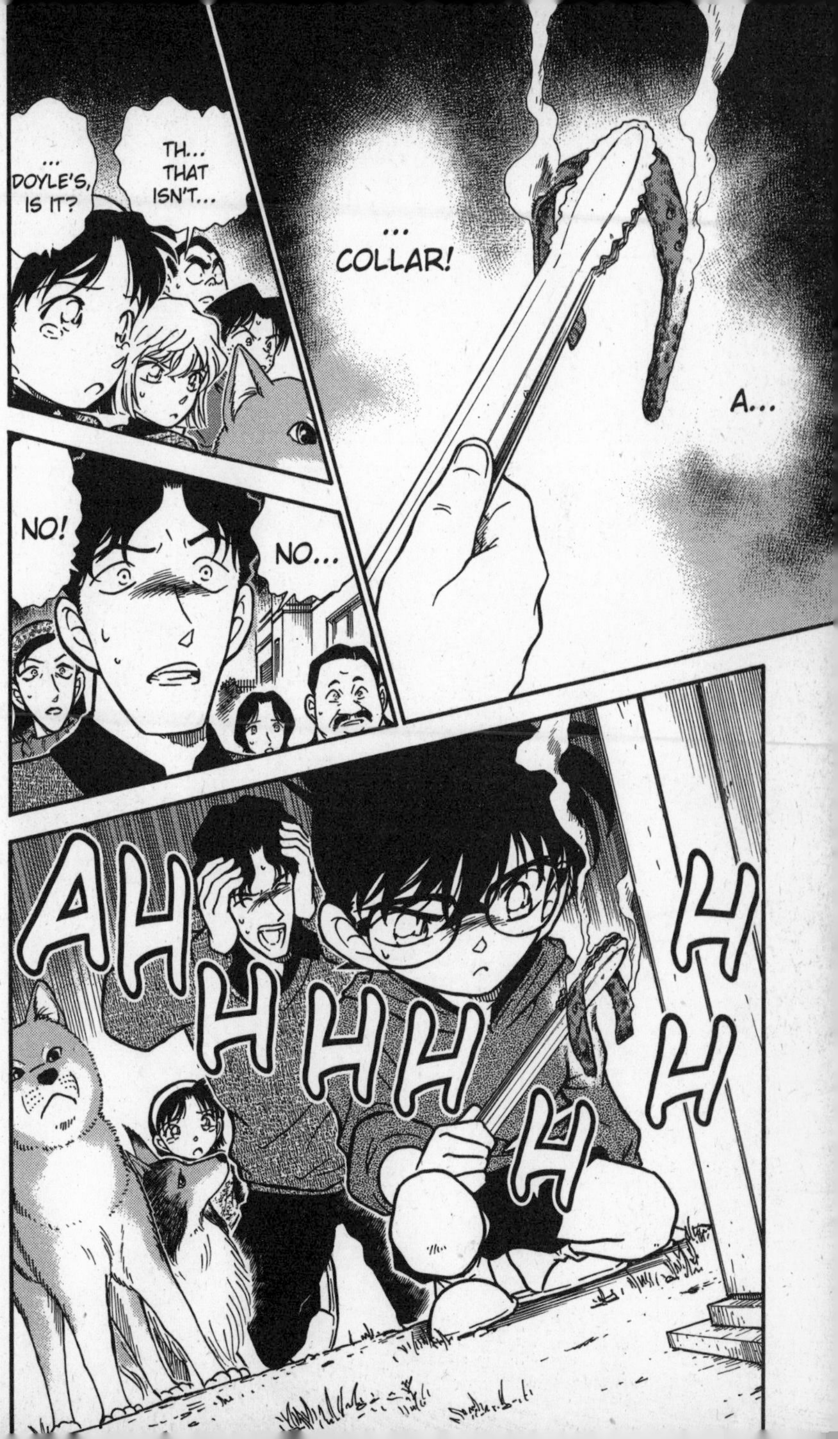
A...
... COLLAR!
TH... THAT ISN'T...
... DOYLE'S, IS IT?
NO...
NO!
AHHHHHHHHHH

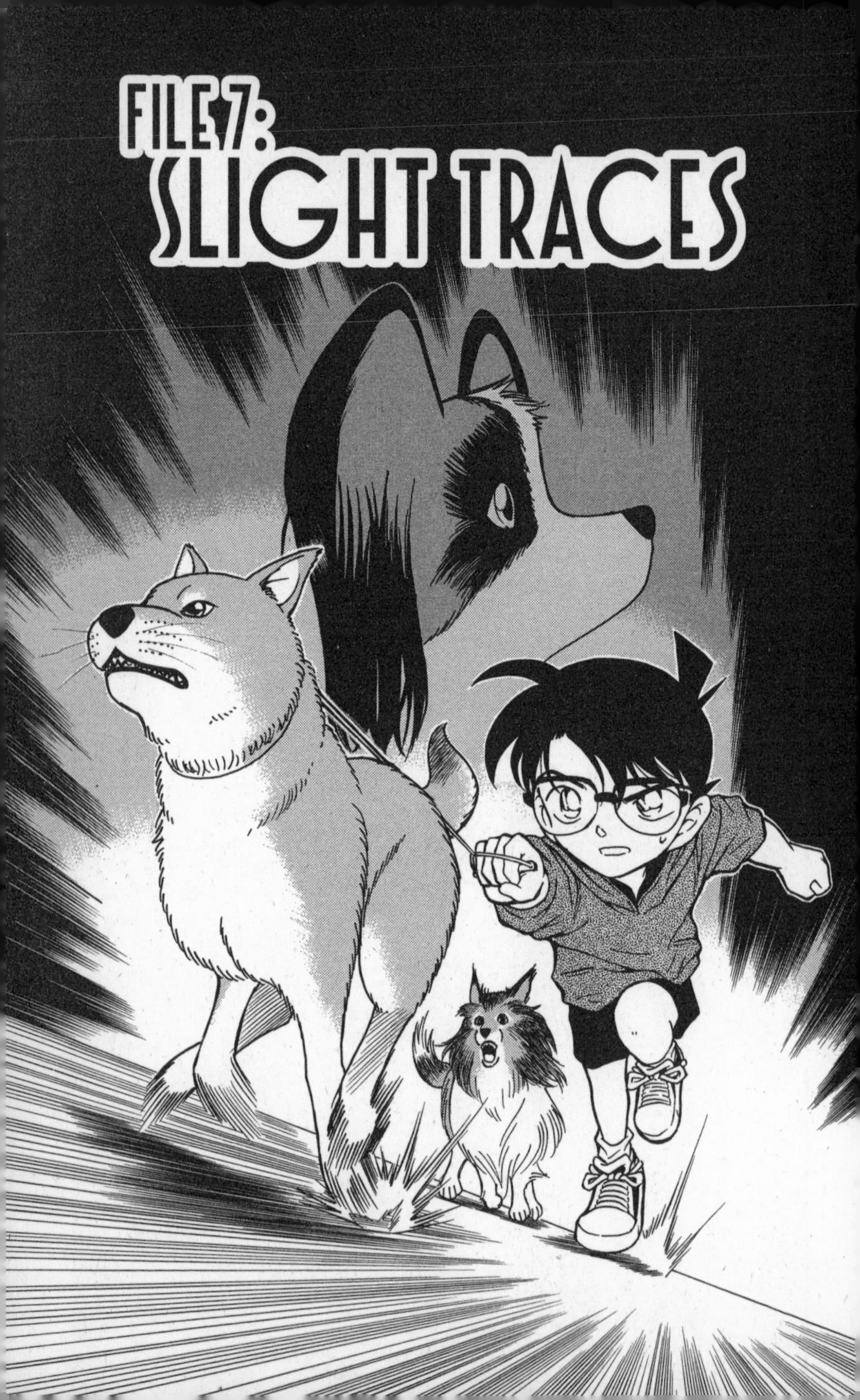
FILE 7:
SLIGHT TRACES

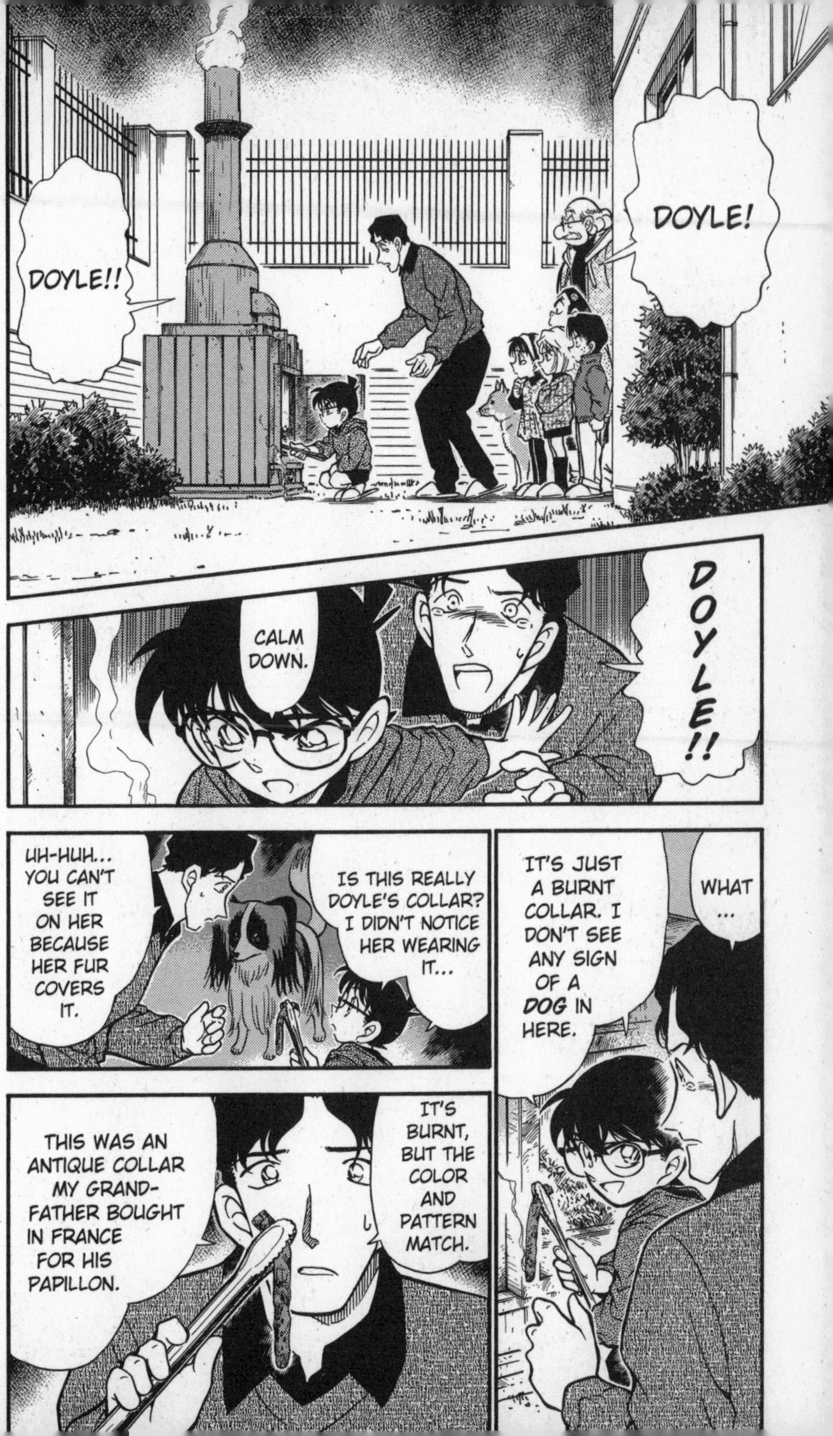
DOYLE!
DOYLE!!
DOYLE!!
CALM DOWN.
WHAT ...
IT'S JUST A BURNT COLLAR. I DON'T SEE ANY SIGN OF A **DOG** IN HERE.
IS THIS REALLY DOYLE'S COLLAR? I DIDN'T NOTICE HER WEARING IT...
UH-HUH... YOU CAN'T SEE IT ON HER BECAUSE HER FUR COVERS IT.
IT'S BURNT, BUT THE COLOR AND PATTERN MATCH.
THIS WAS AN ANTIQUE COLLAR MY GRAND-FATHER BOUGHT IN FRANCE FOR HIS PAPILLON.

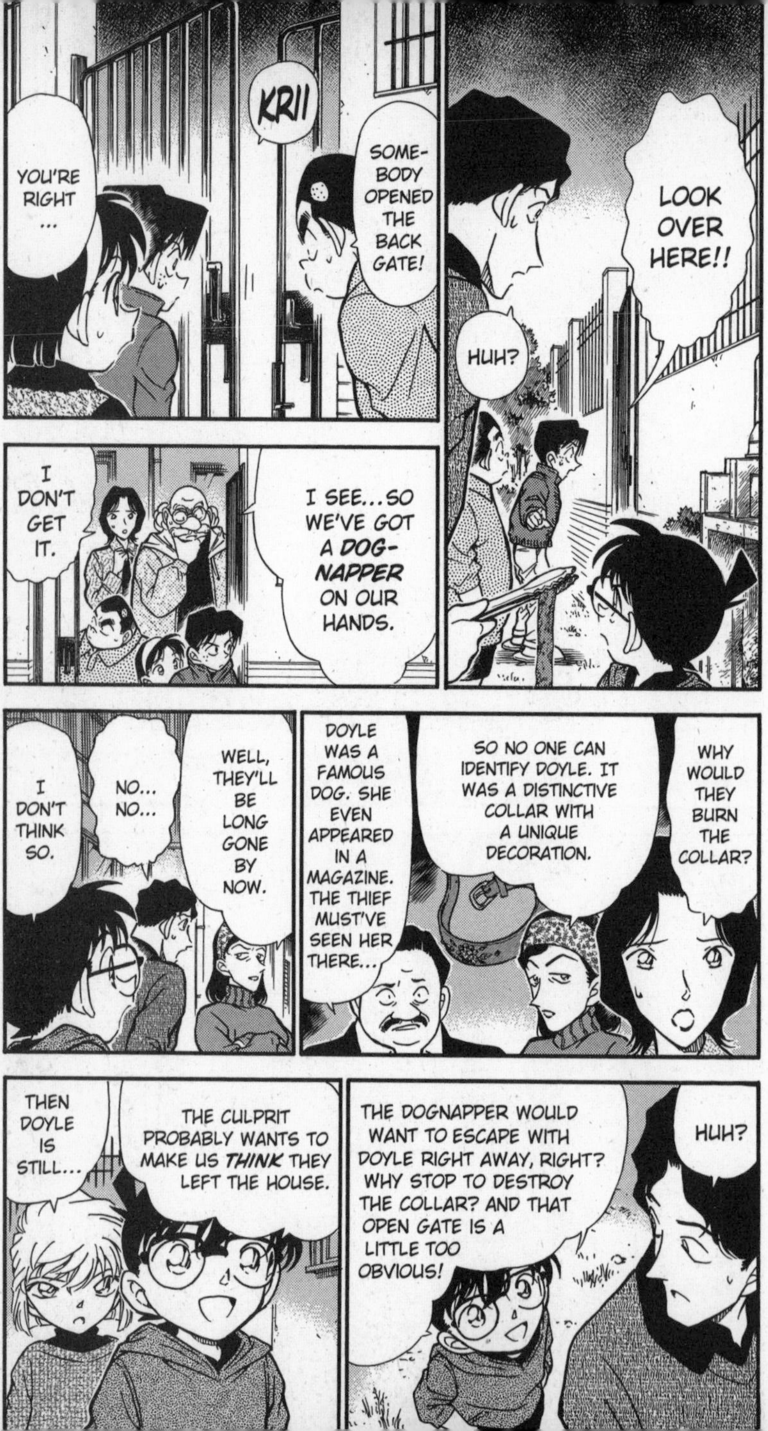

LOOK OVER HERE!!
HUH?
KRII
SOME-BODY OPENED THE BACK GATE!
YOU'RE RIGHT ...
I SEE...SO WE'VE GOT A ***DOG-NAPPER*** ON OUR HANDS.
I DON'T GET IT.
WHY WOULD THEY BURN THE COLLAR?
SO NO ONE CAN IDENTIFY DOYLE. IT WAS A DISTINCTIVE COLLAR WITH A UNIQUE DECORATION.
DOYLE WAS A FAMOUS DOG. SHE EVEN APPEARED IN A MAGAZINE. THE THIEF MUST'VE SEEN HER THERE...
WELL, THEY'LL BE LONG GONE BY NOW.
NO... NO...
I DON'T THINK SO.
HUH?
THE DOGNAPPER WOULD WANT TO ESCAPE WITH DOYLE RIGHT AWAY, RIGHT? WHY STOP TO DESTROY THE COLLAR? AND THAT OPEN GATE IS A LITTLE TOO OBVIOUS!
THE CULPRIT PROBABLY WANTS TO MAKE US ***THINK*** THEY LEFT THE HOUSE.
THEN DOYLE IS STILL...

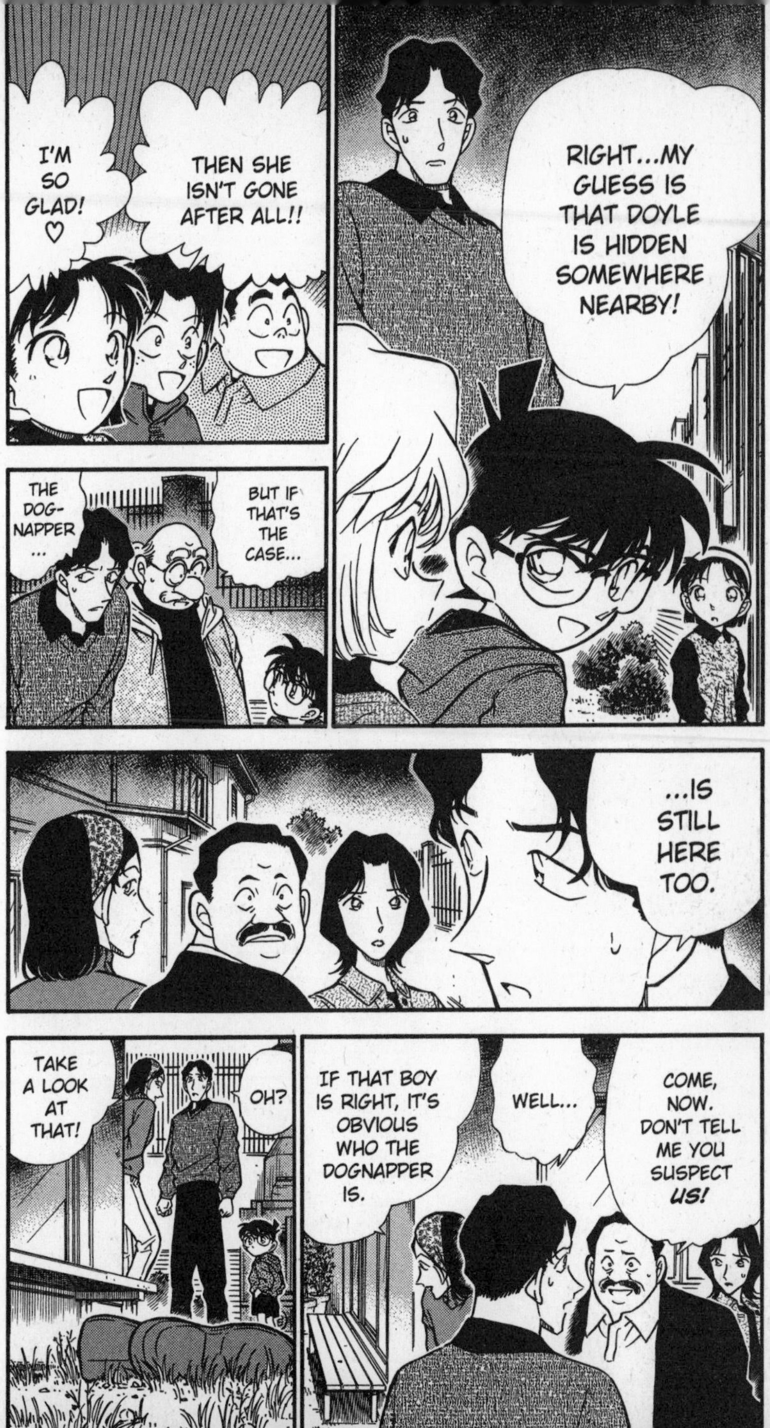

RIGHT...MY GUESS IS THAT DOYLE IS HIDDEN SOMEWHERE NEARBY!
THEN SHE ISN'T GONE AFTER ALL!!
I'M SO GLAD! ♡
BUT IF THAT'S THE CASE...
THE DOG-NAPPER ...
...IS STILL HERE TOO.
COME, NOW. DON'T TELL ME YOU SUSPECT *US!*
WELL...
IF THAT BOY IS RIGHT, IT'S OBVIOUS WHO THE DOGNAPPER IS.
OH?
TAKE A LOOK AT THAT!

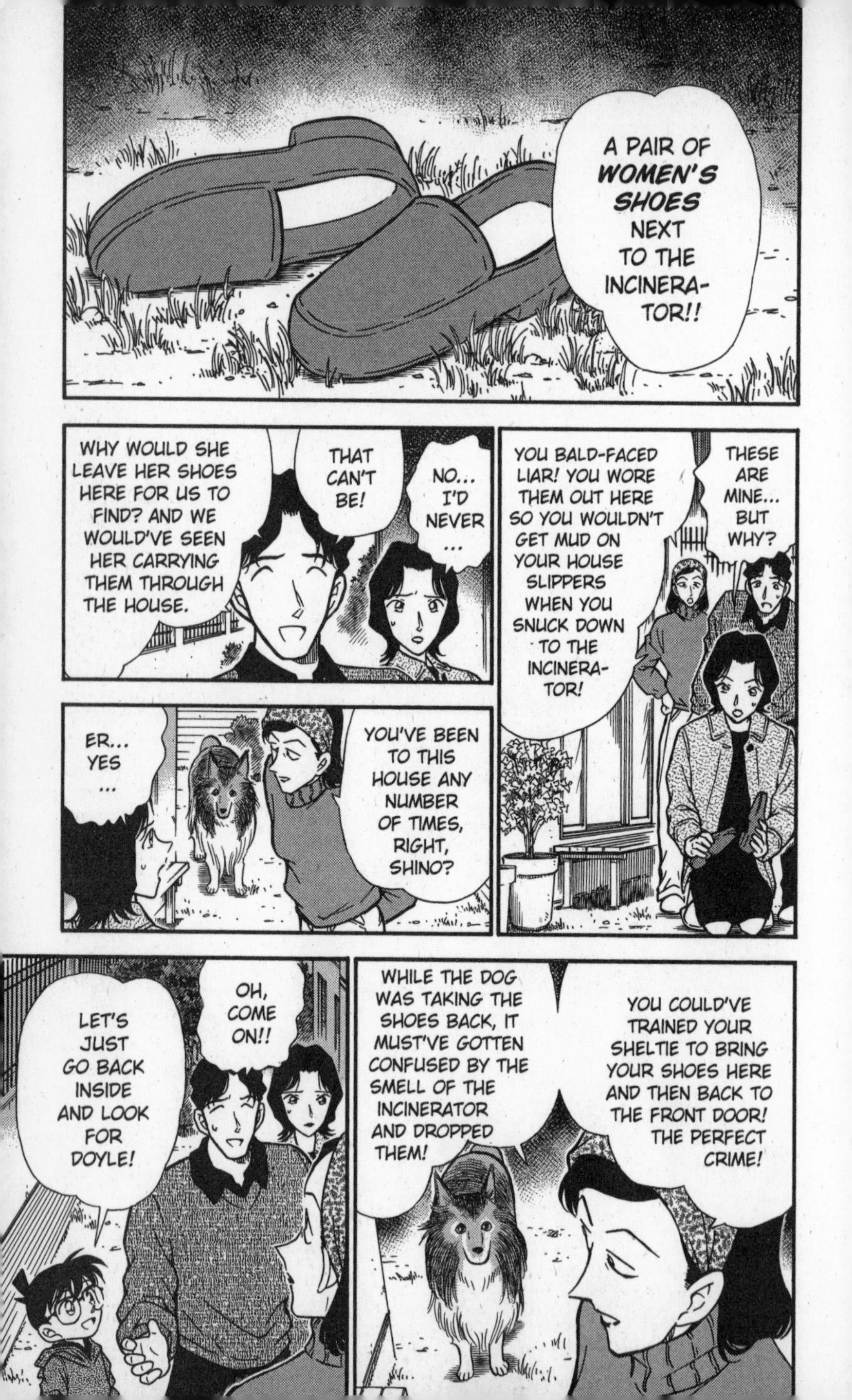
A PAIR OF ***WOMEN'S SHOES*** NEXT TO THE INCINERATOR!!
THESE ARE MINE... BUT WHY?
YOU BALD-FACED LIAR! YOU WORE THEM OUT HERE SO YOU WOULDN'T GET MUD ON YOUR HOUSE SLIPPERS WHEN YOU SNUCK DOWN TO THE INCINERATOR!
NO... I'D NEVER...
THAT CAN'T BE!
WHY WOULD SHE LEAVE HER SHOES HERE FOR US TO FIND? AND WE WOULD'VE SEEN HER CARRYING THEM THROUGH THE HOUSE.
YOU'VE BEEN TO THIS HOUSE ANY NUMBER OF TIMES, RIGHT, SHINO?
ER... YES...
YOU COULD'VE TRAINED YOUR SHELTIE TO BRING YOUR SHOES HERE AND THEN BACK TO THE FRONT DOOR! THE PERFECT CRIME!
WHILE THE DOG WAS TAKING THE SHOES BACK, IT MUST'VE GOTTEN CONFUSED BY THE SMELL OF THE INCINERATOR AND DROPPED THEM!
OH, COME ON!!
LET'S JUST GO BACK INSIDE AND LOOK FOR DOYLE!

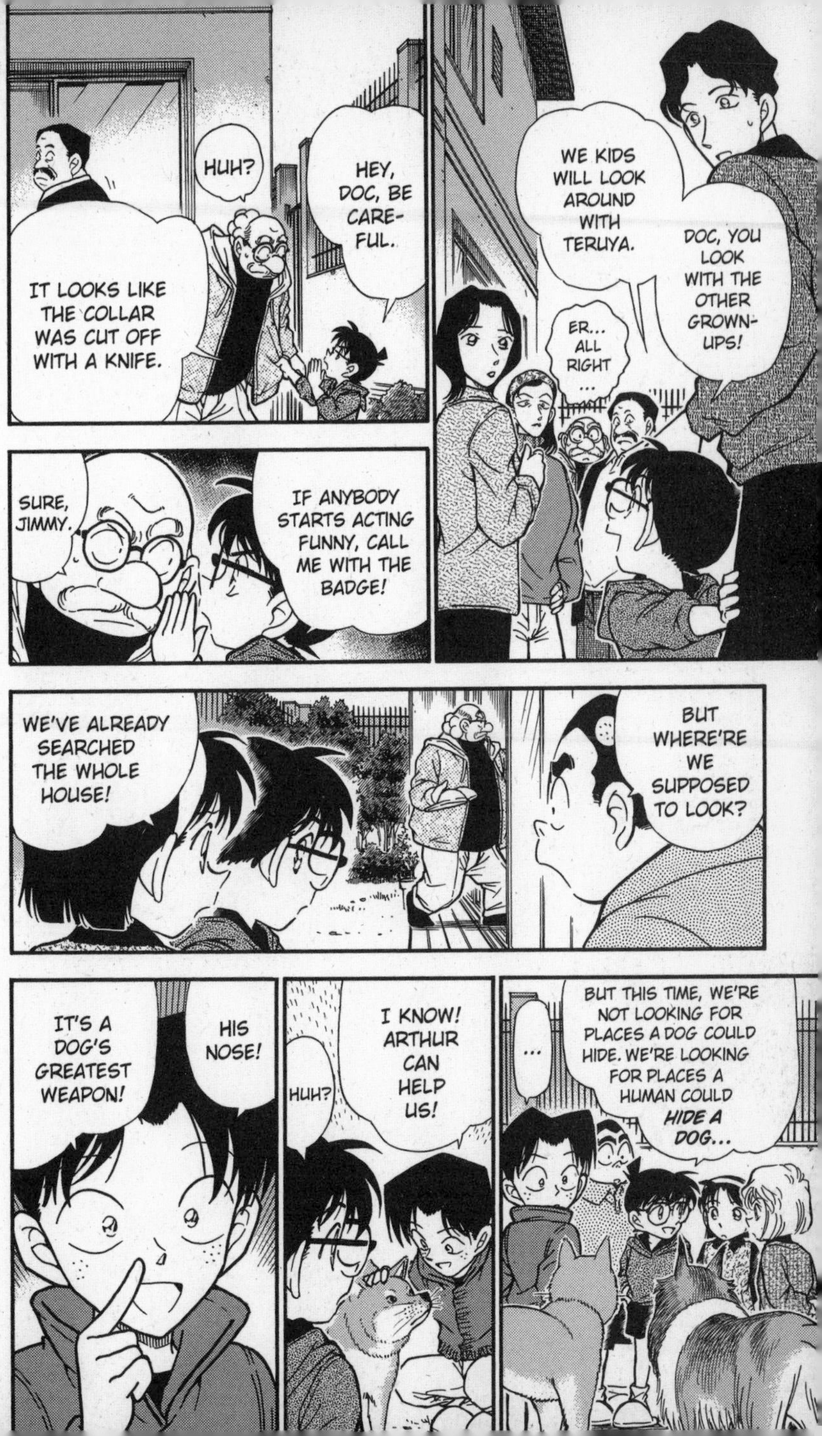
WE KIDS WILL LOOK AROUND WITH TERUYA.
DOC, YOU LOOK WITH THE OTHER GROWN-UPS!
ER... ALL RIGHT...
HEY, DOC, BE CAREFUL.
HUH?
IT LOOKS LIKE THE COLLAR WAS CUT OFF WITH A KNIFE.
IF ANYBODY STARTS ACTING FUNNY, CALL ME WITH THE BADGE!
SURE, JIMMY.
BUT WHERE'RE WE SUPPOSED TO LOOK?
WE'VE ALREADY SEARCHED THE WHOLE HOUSE!
BUT THIS TIME, WE'RE NOT LOOKING FOR PLACES A DOG COULD HIDE. WE'RE LOOKING FOR PLACES A HUMAN COULD *HIDE A DOG...*
...
I KNOW! ARTHUR CAN HELP US!
HUH?
HIS NOSE!
IT'S A DOG'S GREATEST WEAPON!

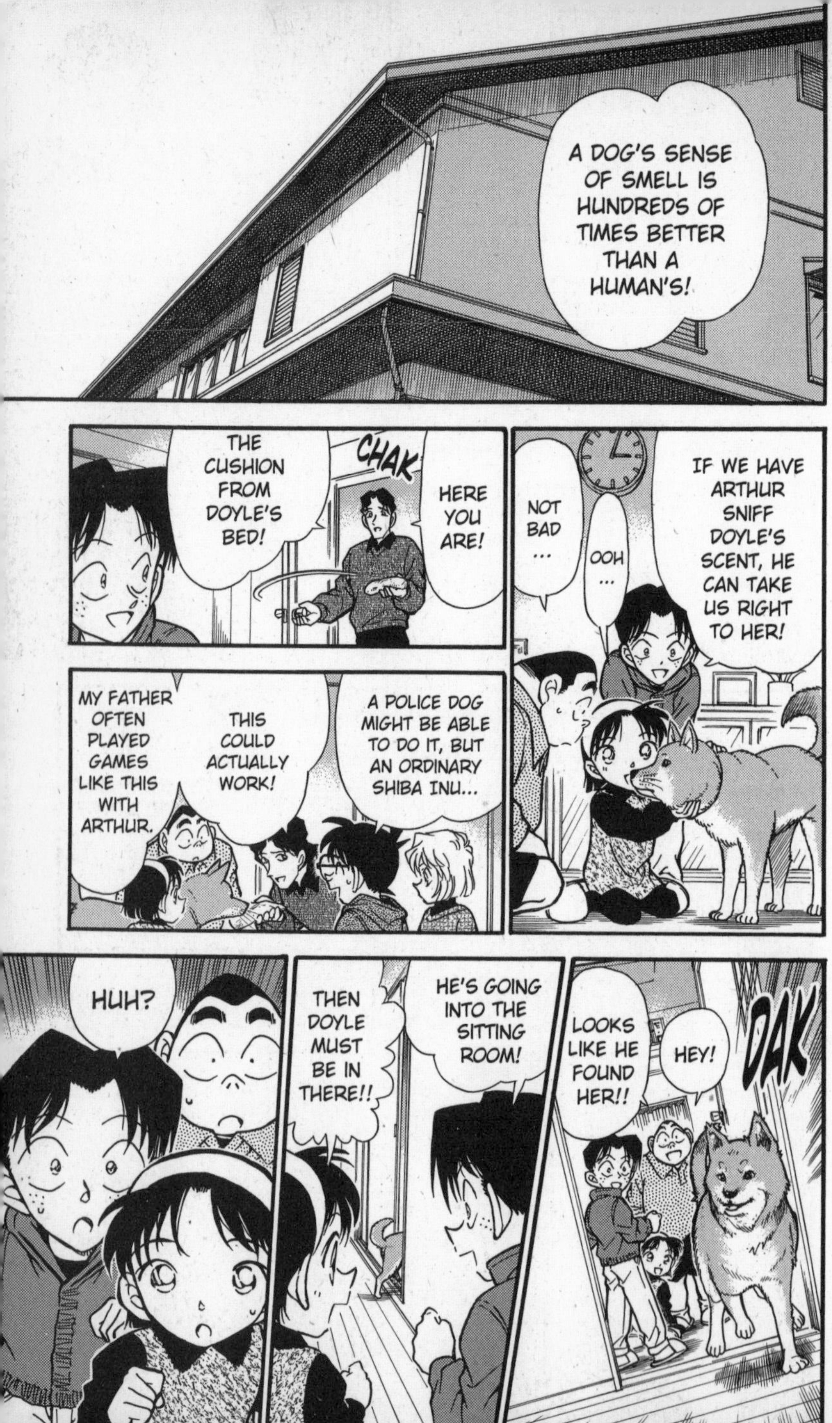
A DOG'S SENSE OF SMELL IS HUNDREDS OF TIMES BETTER THAN A HUMAN'S!
IF WE HAVE ARTHUR SNIFF DOYLE'S SCENT, HE CAN TAKE US RIGHT TO HER!
OOH ...
NOT BAD ...
HERE YOU ARE!
CHAK
THE CUSHION FROM DOYLE'S BED!
A POLICE DOG MIGHT BE ABLE TO DO IT, BUT AN ORDINARY SHIBA INU...
THIS COULD ACTUALLY WORK!
MY FATHER OFTEN PLAYED GAMES LIKE THIS WITH ARTHUR.
DAK
HEY!
LOOKS LIKE HE FOUND HER!!
HE'S GOING INTO THE SITTING ROOM!
THEN DOYLE MUST BE IN THERE!!
HUH?

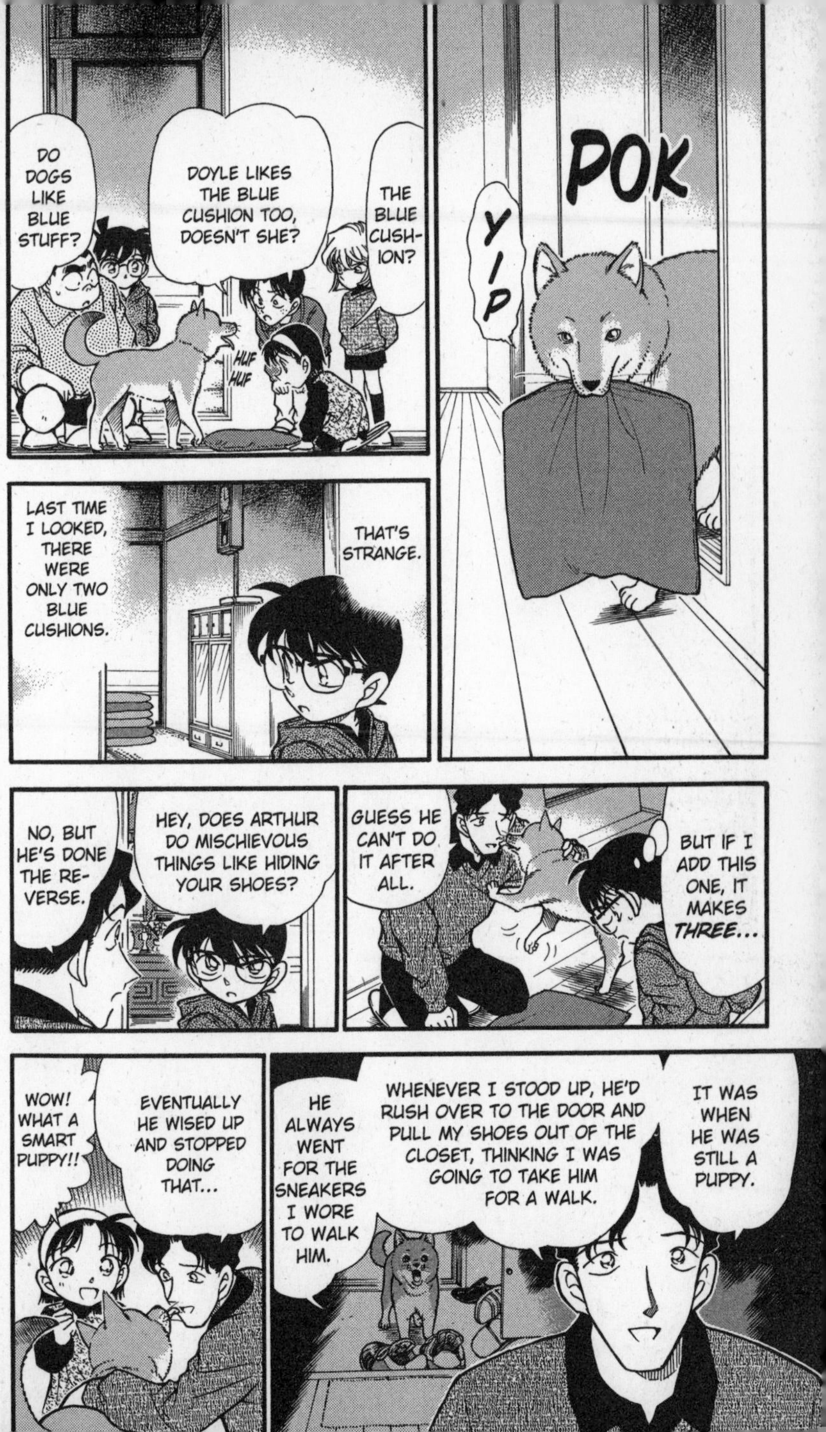
POK
YIP
THE BLUE CUSHION?
DOYLE LIKES THE BLUE CUSHION TOO, DOESN'T SHE?
DO DOGS LIKE BLUE STUFF?
HUF HUF
THAT'S STRANGE.
LAST TIME I LOOKED, THERE WERE ONLY TWO BLUE CUSHIONS.
BUT IF I ADD THIS ONE, IT MAKES *THREE*...
GUESS HE CAN'T DO IT AFTER ALL.
HEY, DOES ARTHUR DO MISCHIEVOUS THINGS LIKE HIDING YOUR SHOES?
NO, BUT HE'S DONE THE REVERSE.
IT WAS WHEN HE WAS STILL A PUPPY.
WHENEVER I STOOD UP, HE'D RUSH OVER TO THE DOOR AND PULL MY SHOES OUT OF THE CLOSET, THINKING I WAS GOING TO TAKE HIM FOR A WALK.
HE ALWAYS WENT FOR THE SNEAKERS I WORE TO WALK HIM.
EVENTUALLY HE WISED UP AND STOPPED DOING THAT...
WOW! WHAT A SMART PUPPY!!

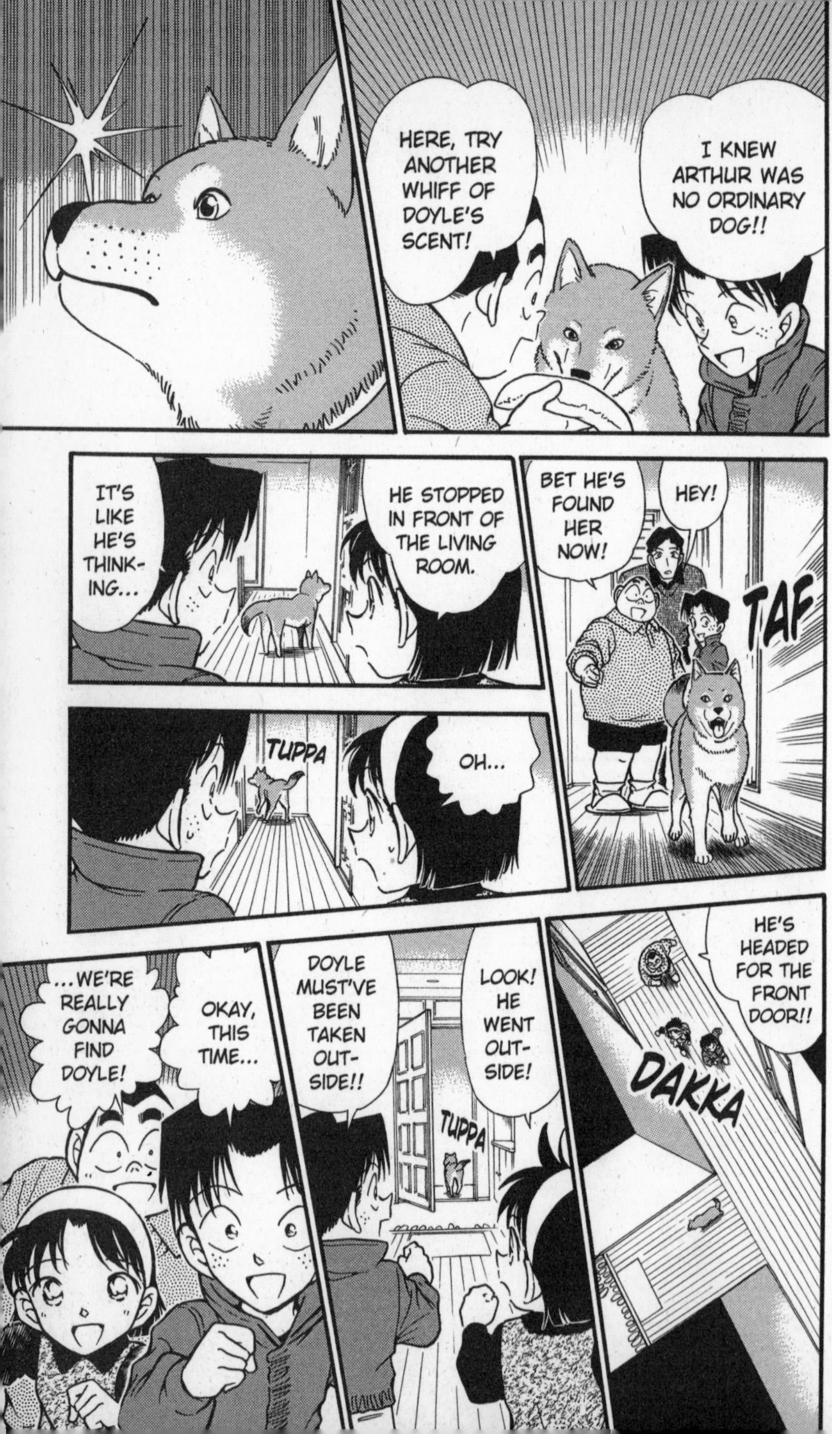
I KNEW ARTHUR WAS NO ORDINARY DOG!!
HERE, TRY ANOTHER WHIFF OF DOYLE'S SCENT!
HEY!
BET HE'S FOUND HER NOW!
TAF
HE STOPPED IN FRONT OF THE LIVING ROOM.
IT'S LIKE HE'S THINKING...
OH...
TUPPA
HE'S HEADED FOR THE FRONT DOOR!!
DAKKA
LOOK! HE WENT OUTSIDE!
DOYLE MUST'VE BEEN TAKEN OUTSIDE!!
TUPPA
OKAY, THIS TIME...
...WE'RE REALLY GONNA FIND DOYLE!

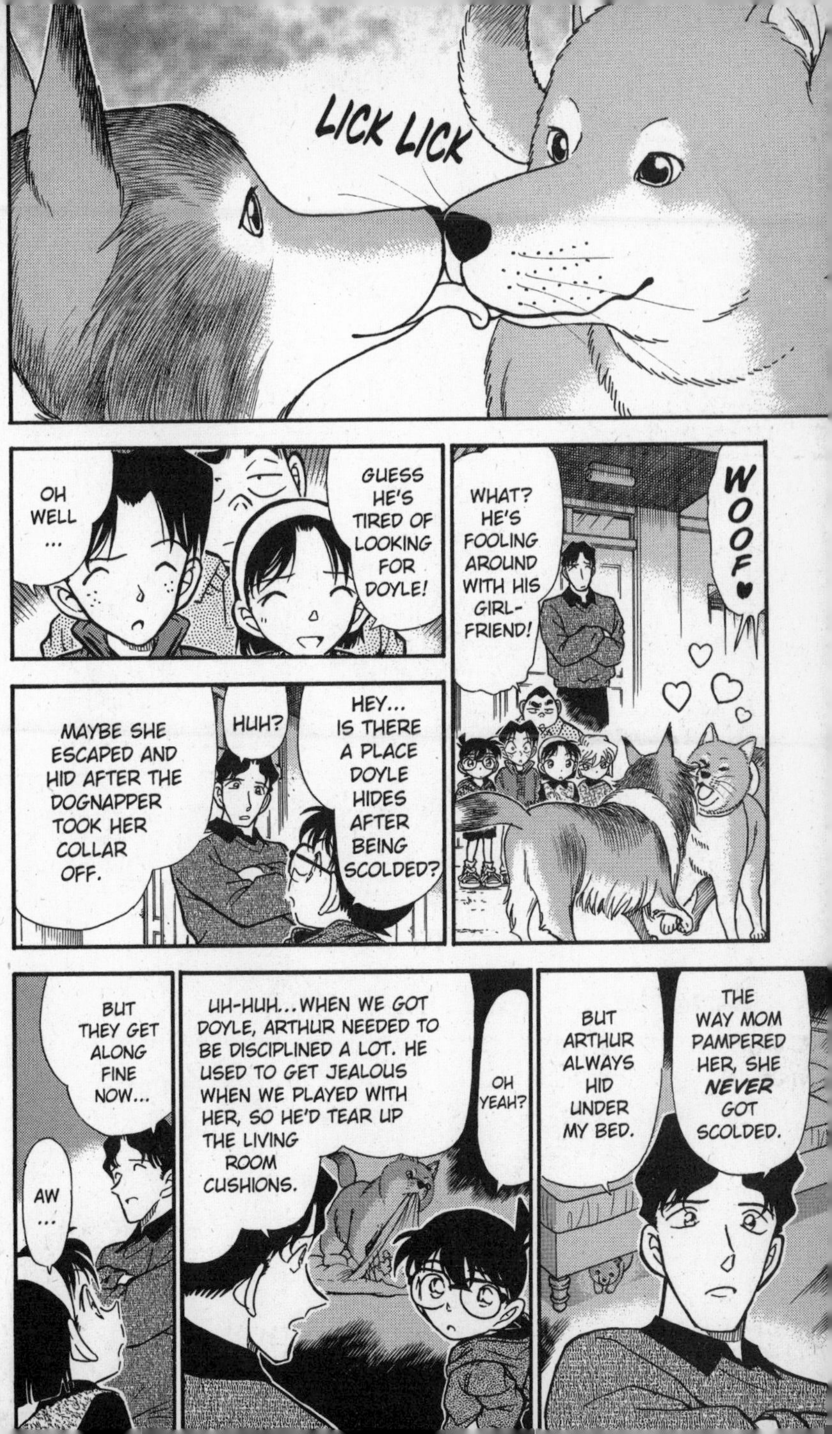
LICK LICK
WOOF♥
WHAT? HE'S FOOLING AROUND WITH HIS GIRL-FRIEND!
GUESS HE'S TIRED OF LOOKING FOR DOYLE!
OH WELL...
HEY... IS THERE A PLACE DOYLE HIDES AFTER BEING SCOLDED?
HUH?
MAYBE SHE ESCAPED AND HID AFTER THE DOGNAPPER TOOK HER COLLAR OFF.
THE WAY MOM PAMPERED HER, SHE NEVER GOT SCOLDED.
BUT ARTHUR ALWAYS HID UNDER MY BED.
OH YEAH?
UH-HUH...WHEN WE GOT DOYLE, ARTHUR NEEDED TO BE DISCIPLINED A LOT. HE USED TO GET JEALOUS WHEN WE PLAYED WITH HER, SO HE'D TEAR UP THE LIVING ROOM CUSHIONS.
BUT THEY GET ALONG FINE NOW...
AW...

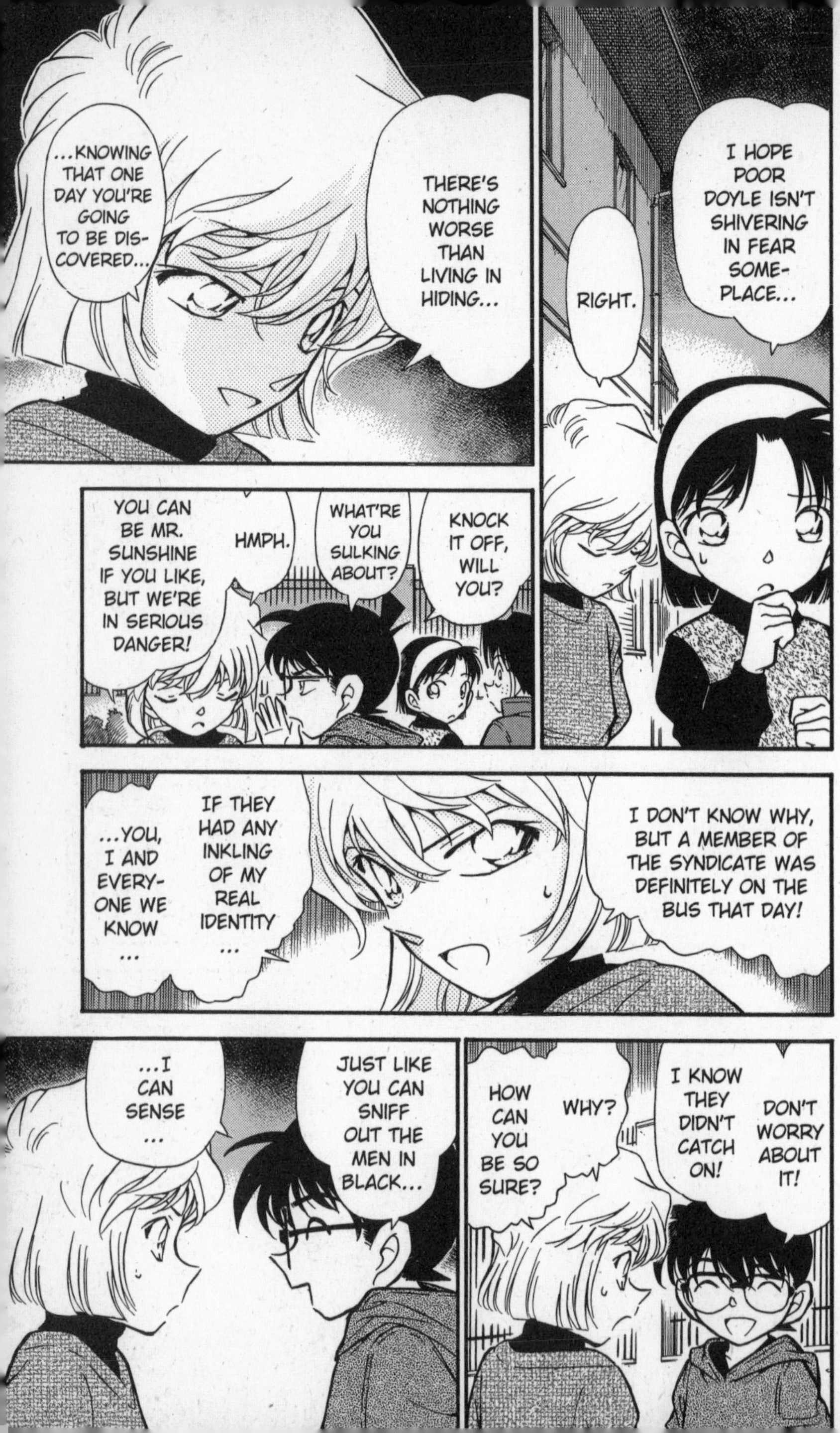
I HOPE POOR DOYLE ISN'T SHIVERING IN FEAR SOMEPLACE...
RIGHT.
THERE'S NOTHING WORSE THAN LIVING IN HIDING...
...KNOWING THAT ONE DAY YOU'RE GOING TO BE DISCOVERED...
KNOCK IT OFF, WILL YOU?
WHAT'RE YOU SULKING ABOUT?
HMPH.
YOU CAN BE MR. SUNSHINE IF YOU LIKE, BUT WE'RE IN SERIOUS DANGER!
I DON'T KNOW WHY, BUT A MEMBER OF THE SYNDICATE WAS DEFINITELY ON THE BUS THAT DAY!
IF THEY HAD ANY INKLING OF MY REAL IDENTITY...
...YOU, I AND EVERYONE WE KNOW...
DON'T WORRY ABOUT IT!
I KNOW THEY DIDN'T CATCH ON!
WHY?
HOW CAN YOU BE SO SURE?
JUST LIKE YOU CAN SNIFF OUT THE MEN IN BLACK...
...I CAN SENSE...

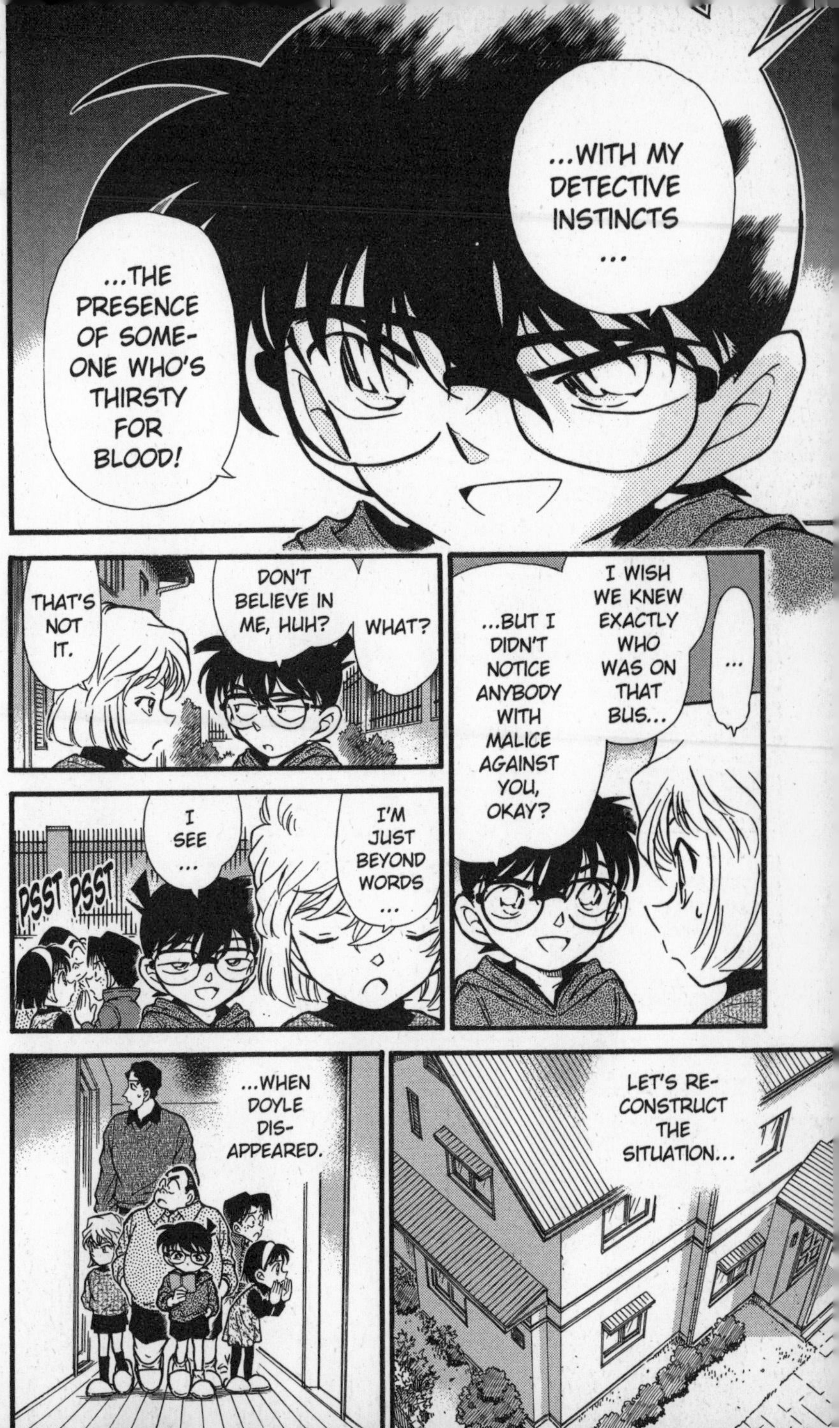
...WITH MY DETECTIVE INSTINCTS ...
...THE PRESENCE OF SOME-ONE WHO'S THIRSTY FOR BLOOD!
...
I WISH WE KNEW EXACTLY WHO WAS ON THAT BUS...
...BUT I DIDN'T NOTICE ANYBODY WITH MALICE AGAINST YOU, OKAY?
WHAT?
DON'T BELIEVE IN ME, HUH?
THAT'S NOT IT.
I'M JUST BEYOND WORDS ...
I SEE ...
PSST PSST
LET'S RE-CONSTRUCT THE SITUATION...
...WHEN DOYLE DIS-APPEARED.

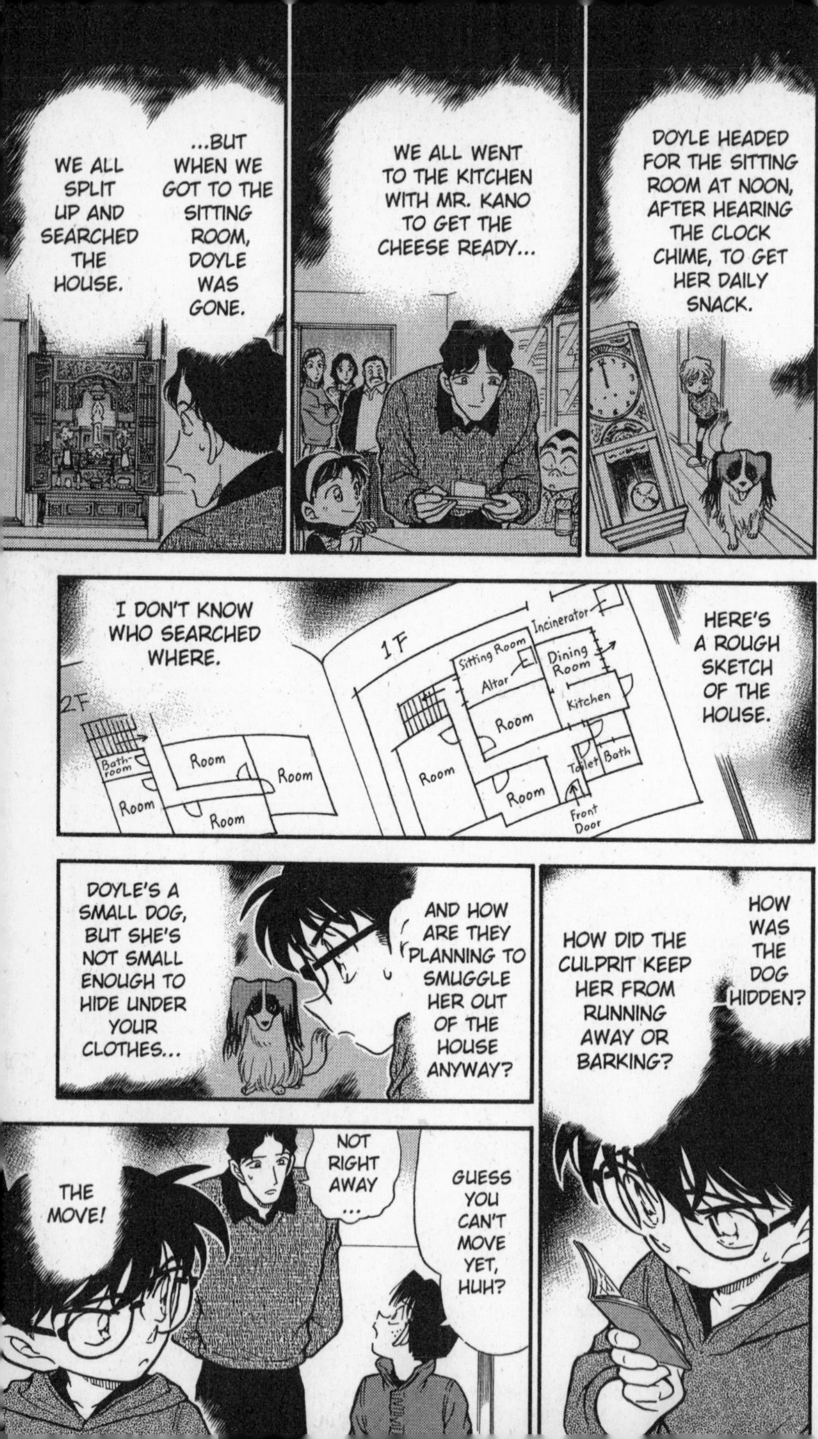
DOYLE HEADED FOR THE SITTING ROOM AT NOON, AFTER HEARING THE CLOCK CHIME, TO GET HER DAILY SNACK.
WE ALL WENT TO THE KITCHEN WITH MR. KANO TO GET THE CHEESE READY...
...BUT WHEN WE GOT TO THE SITTING ROOM, DOYLE WAS GONE.
WE ALL SPLIT UP AND SEARCHED THE HOUSE.
HERE'S A ROUGH SKETCH OF THE HOUSE.
I DON'T KNOW WHO SEARCHED WHERE.
1F
Incinerator
Sitting Room
Altar
Dining Room
Kitchen
Room
Room
Room
Toilet
Bath
Front Door
2F
Bathroom
Room
Room
Room
Room
HOW WAS THE DOG HIDDEN?
HOW DID THE CULPRIT KEEP HER FROM RUNNING AWAY OR BARKING?
DOYLE'S A SMALL DOG, BUT SHE'S NOT SMALL ENOUGH TO HIDE UNDER YOUR CLOTHES...
AND HOW ARE THEY PLANNING TO SMUGGLE HER OUT OF THE HOUSE ANYWAY?
GUESS YOU CAN'T MOVE YET, HUH?
NOT RIGHT AWAY ...
THE MOVE!

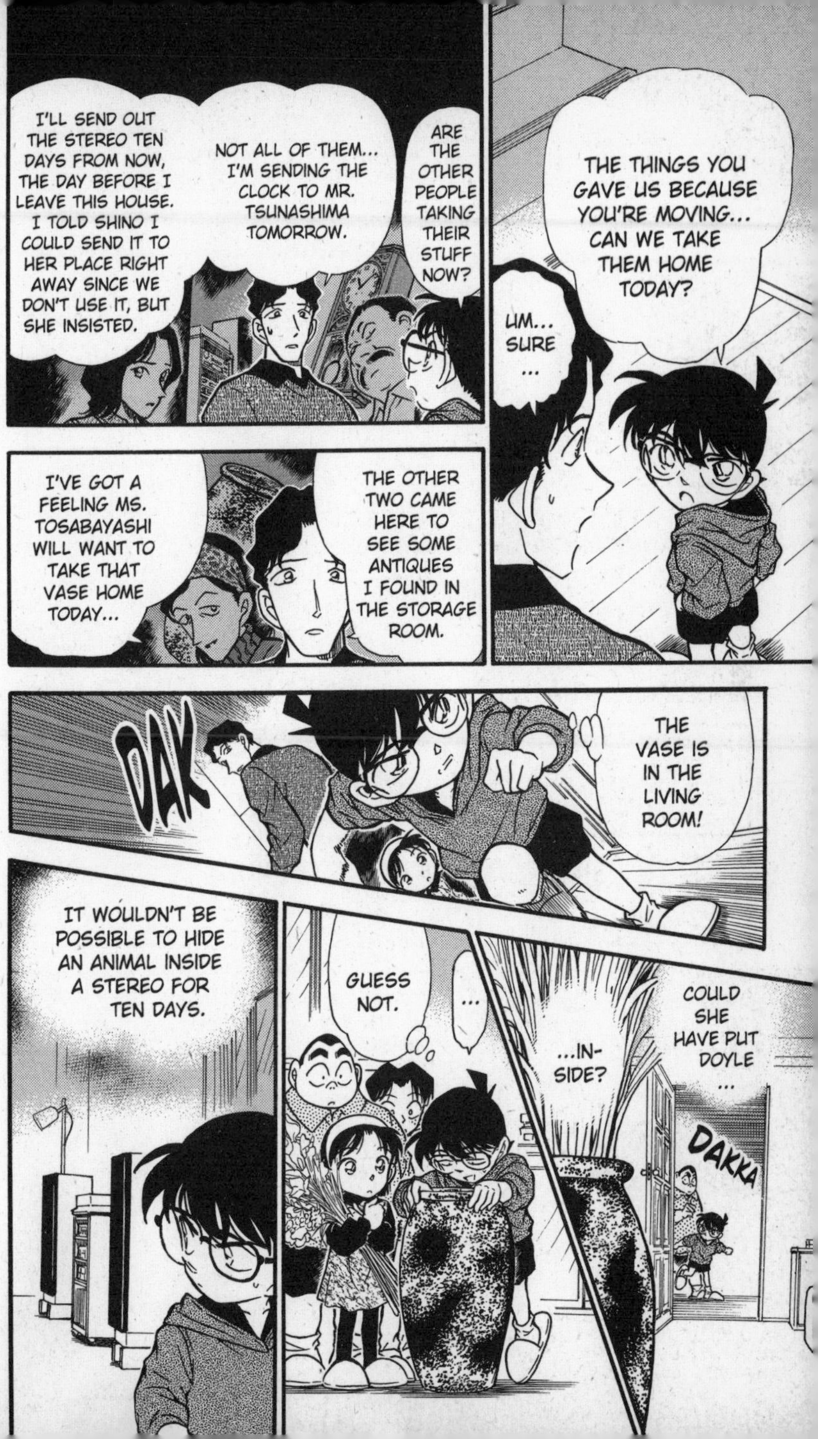
THE THINGS YOU GAVE US BECAUSE YOU'RE MOVING... CAN WE TAKE THEM HOME TODAY?
UM... SURE ...
ARE THE OTHER PEOPLE TAKING THEIR STUFF NOW?
NOT ALL OF THEM... I'M SENDING THE CLOCK TO MR. TSUNASHIMA TOMORROW.
I'LL SEND OUT THE STEREO TEN DAYS FROM NOW, THE DAY BEFORE I LEAVE THIS HOUSE. I TOLD SHINO I COULD SEND IT TO HER PLACE RIGHT AWAY SINCE WE DON'T USE IT, BUT SHE INSISTED.
THE OTHER TWO CAME HERE TO SEE SOME ANTIQUES I FOUND IN THE STORAGE ROOM.
I'VE GOT A FEELING MS. TOSABAYASHI WILL WANT TO TAKE THAT VASE HOME TODAY...
THE VASE IS IN THE LIVING ROOM!
DAK
COULD SHE HAVE PUT DOYLE ...
...IN-SIDE?
DAKKA
...
GUESS NOT.
IT WOULDN'T BE POSSIBLE TO HIDE AN ANIMAL INSIDE A STEREO FOR TEN DAYS.

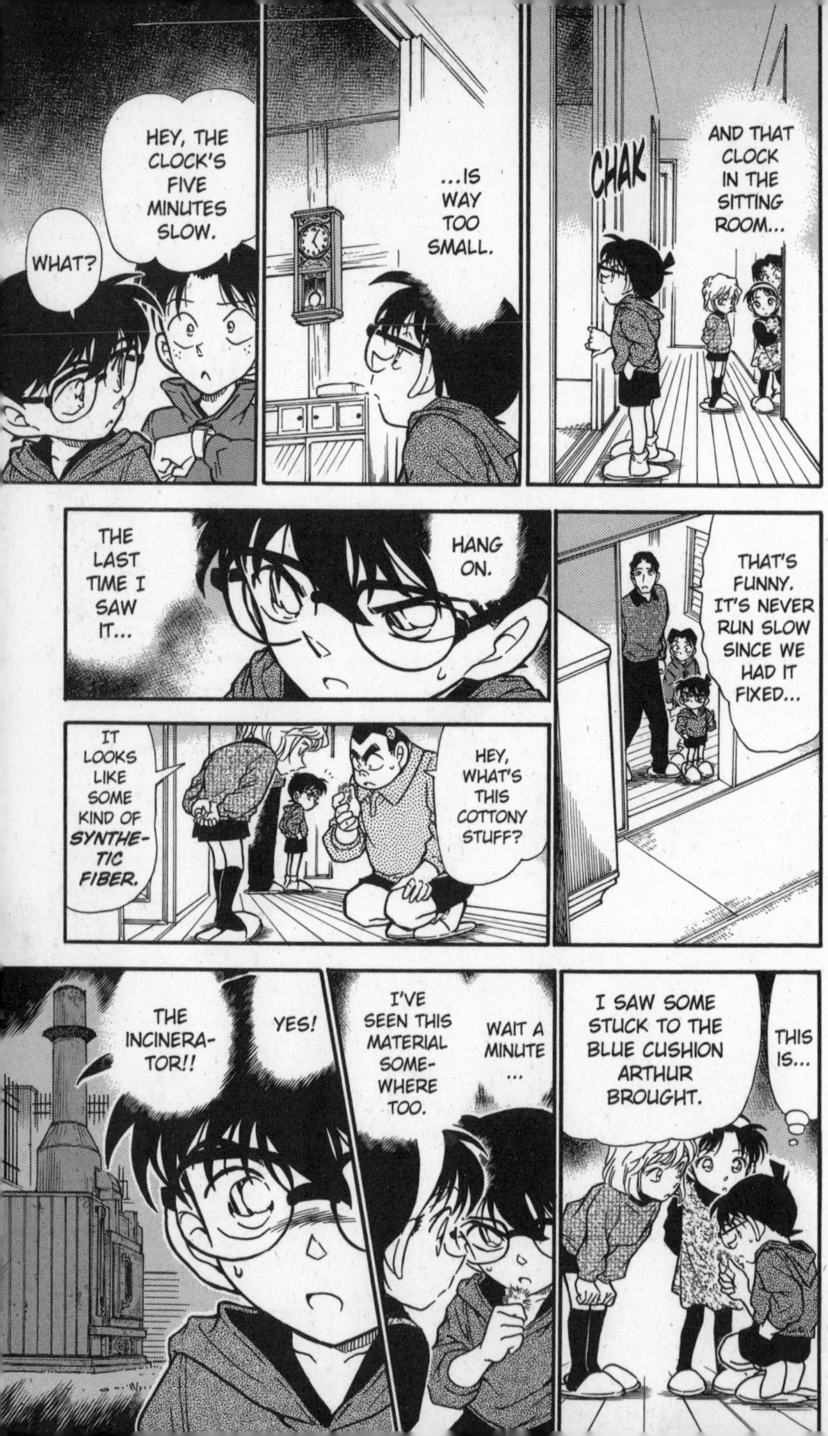

AND THAT CLOCK IN THE SITTING ROOM...
CHAK
...IS WAY TOO SMALL.
HEY, THE CLOCK'S FIVE MINUTES SLOW.
WHAT?
THAT'S FUNNY. IT'S NEVER RUN SLOW SINCE WE HAD IT FIXED...
HANG ON.
THE LAST TIME I SAW IT...
HEY, WHAT'S THIS COTTONY STUFF?
IT LOOKS LIKE SOME KIND OF *SYNTHETIC FIBER.*
THIS IS...
I SAW SOME STUCK TO THE BLUE CUSHION ARTHUR BROUGHT.
WAIT A MINUTE...
I'VE SEEN THIS MATERIAL SOMEWHERE TOO.
YES!
THE INCINERATOR!!

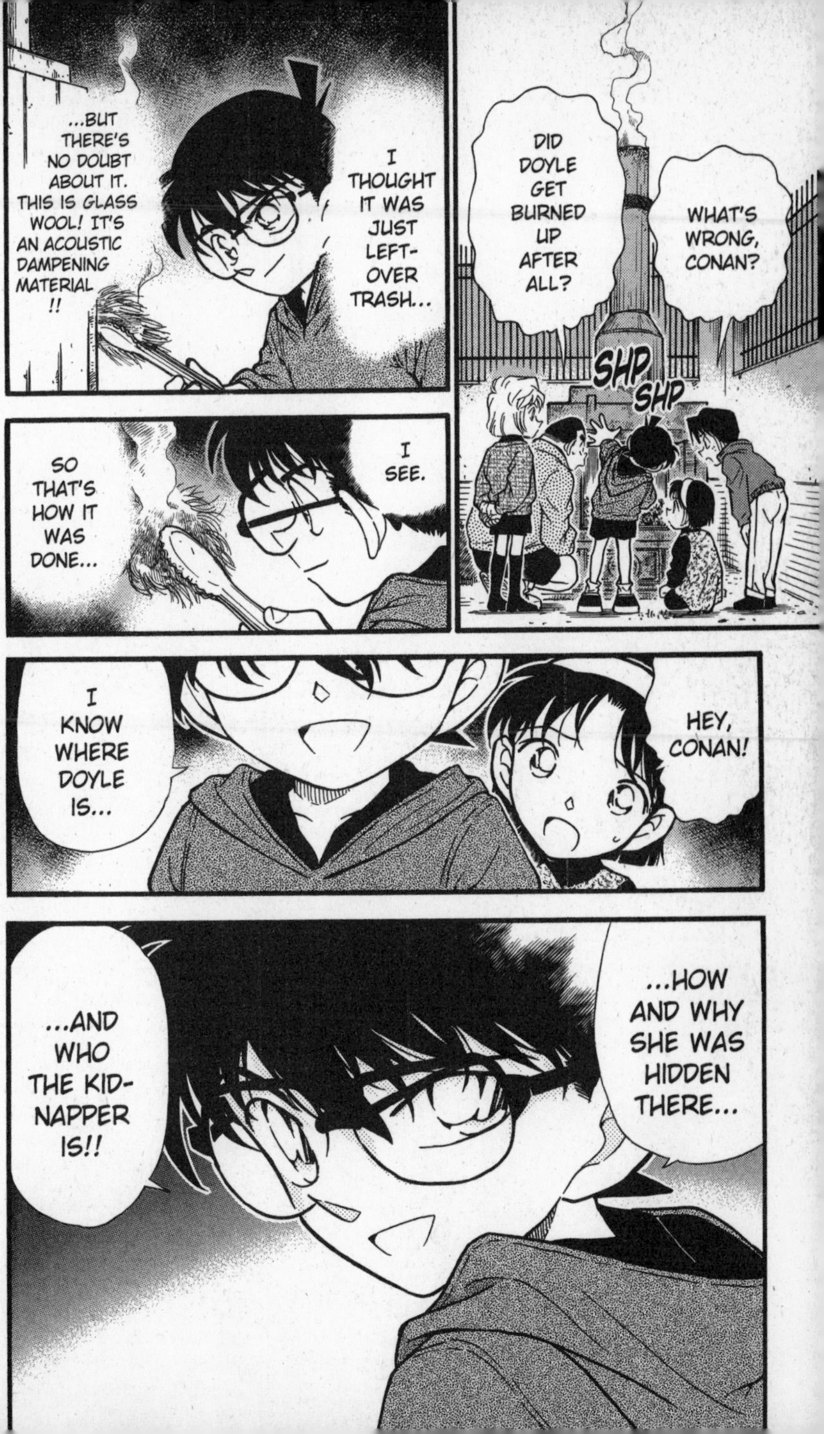
WHAT'S WRONG, CONAN?
DID DOYLE GET BURNED UP AFTER ALL?
SHP SHP
I THOUGHT IT WAS JUST LEFT-OVER TRASH...
...BUT THERE'S NO DOUBT ABOUT IT. THIS IS GLASS WOOL! IT'S AN ACOUSTIC DAMPENING MATERIAL !!
I SEE.
SO THAT'S HOW IT WAS DONE...
HEY, CONAN!
I KNOW WHERE DOYLE IS...
...HOW AND WHY SHE WAS HIDDEN THERE...
...AND WHO THE KID-NAPPER IS!!

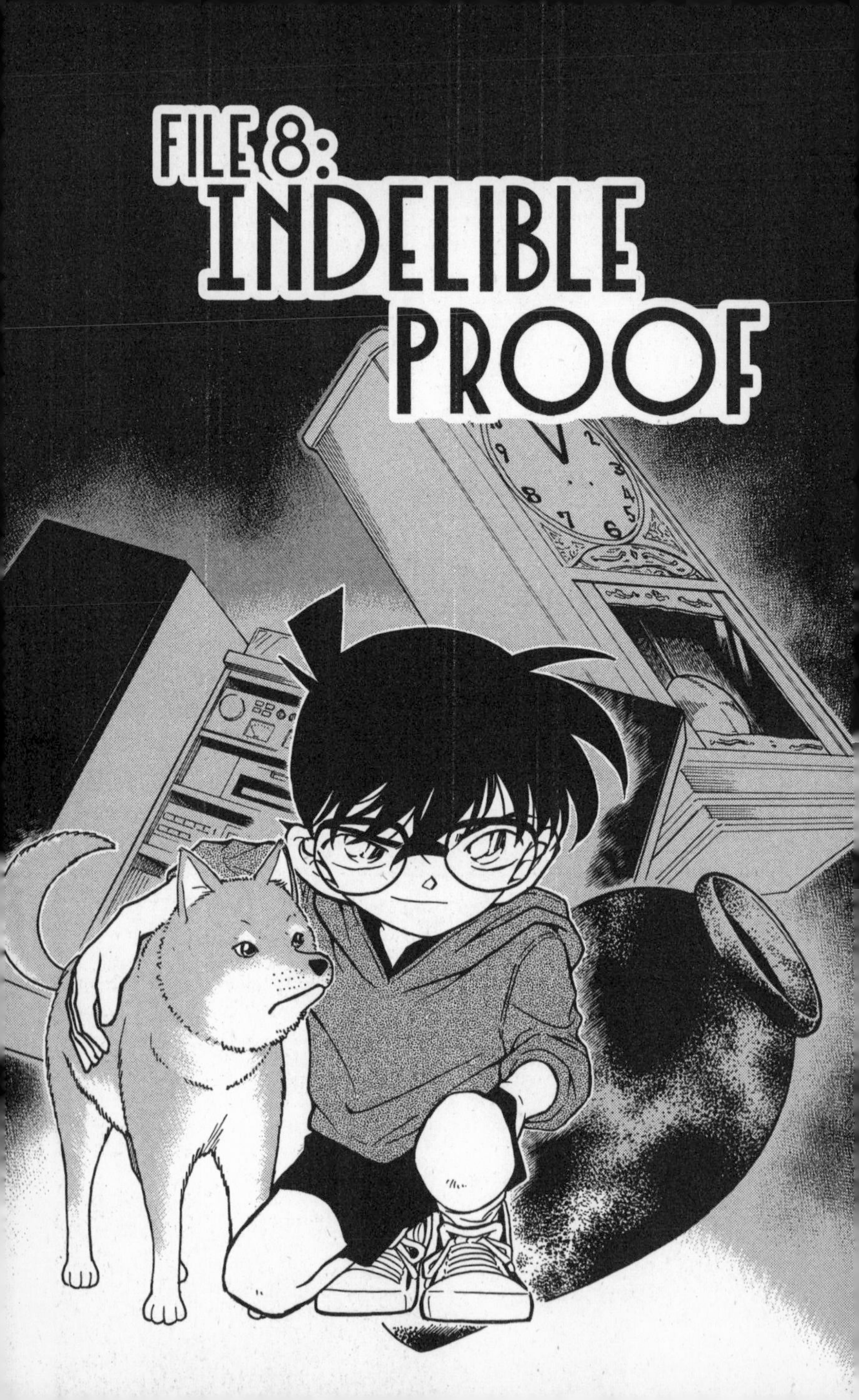
FILE 8:
INDELIBLE PROOF

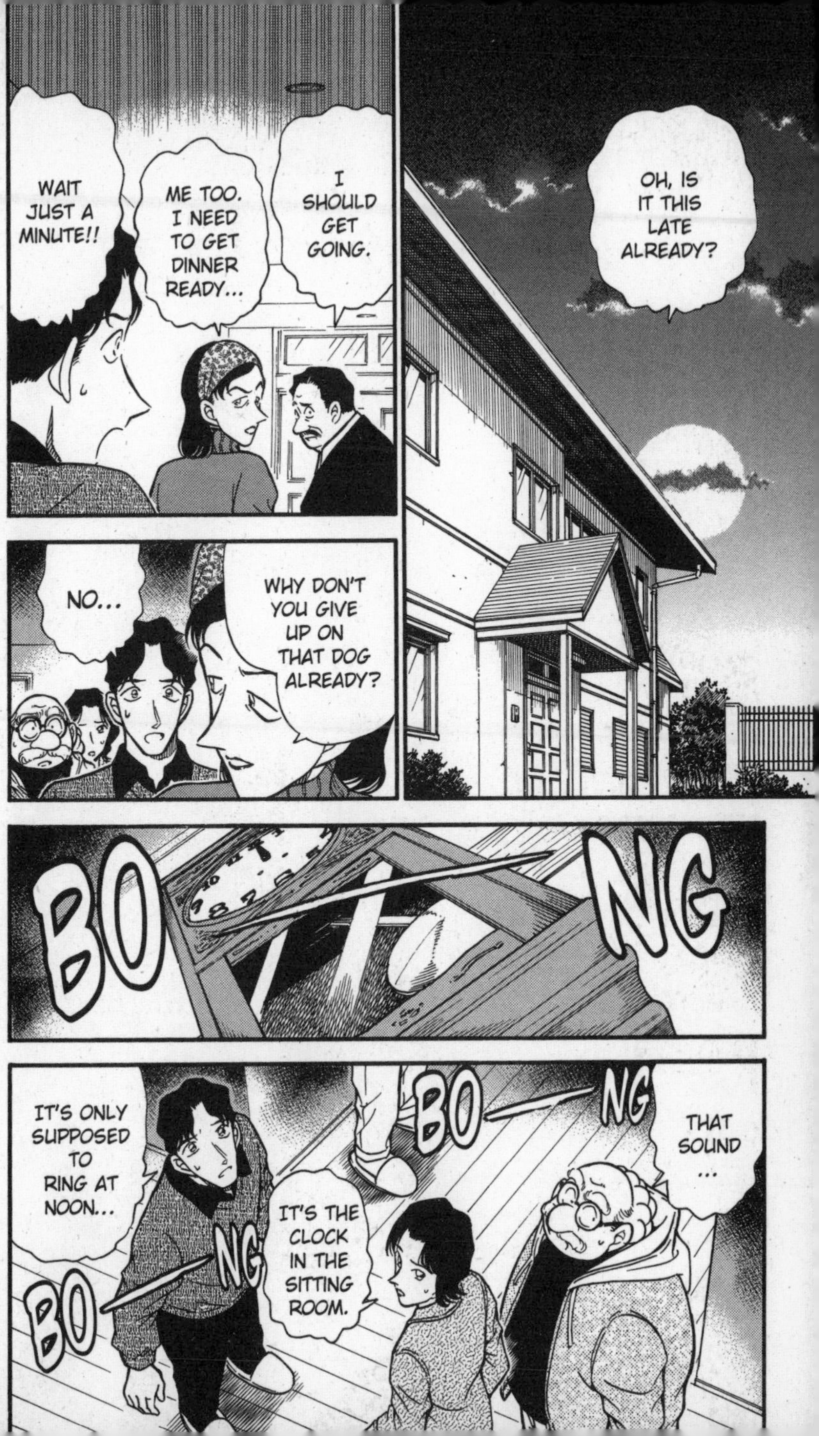
OH, IS IT THIS LATE ALREADY?
I SHOULD GET GOING.
ME TOO. I NEED TO GET DINNER READY...
WAIT JUST A MINUTE!!
WHY DON'T YOU GIVE UP ON THAT DOG ALREADY?
NO...
BONG
THAT SOUND...
BONG
IT'S THE CLOCK IN THE SITTING ROOM.
IT'S ONLY SUPPOSED TO RING AT NOON...
BONG

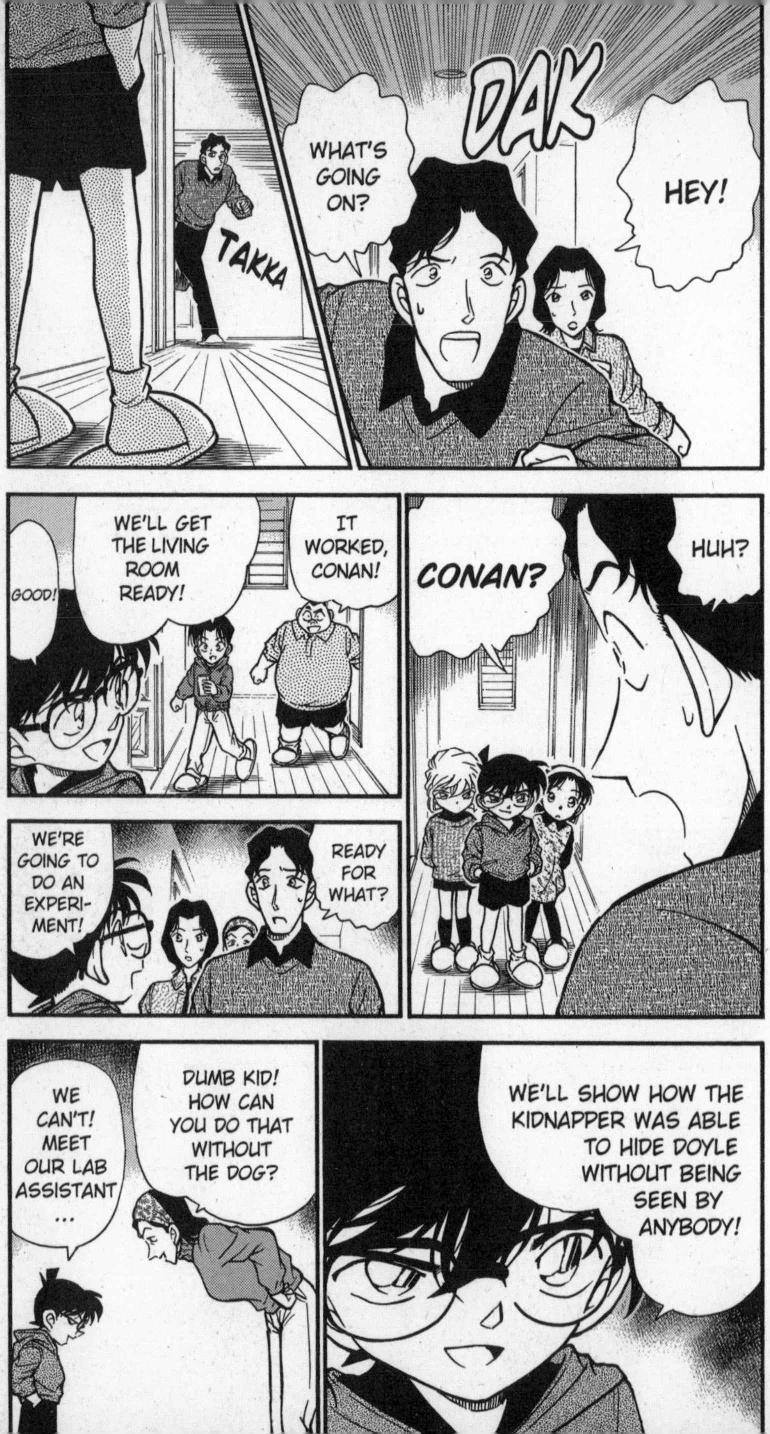
DAK
HEY!
WHAT'S GOING ON?
TAKKA
HUH?
CONAN?
IT WORKED, CONAN!
WE'LL GET THE LIVING ROOM READY!
GOOD!
READY FOR WHAT?
WE'RE GOING TO DO AN EXPERI-MENT!
WE'LL SHOW HOW THE KIDNAPPER WAS ABLE TO HIDE DOYLE WITHOUT BEING SEEN BY ANYBODY!
DUMB KID! HOW CAN YOU DO THAT WITHOUT THE DOG?
WE CAN'T! MEET OUR LAB ASSISTANT ...

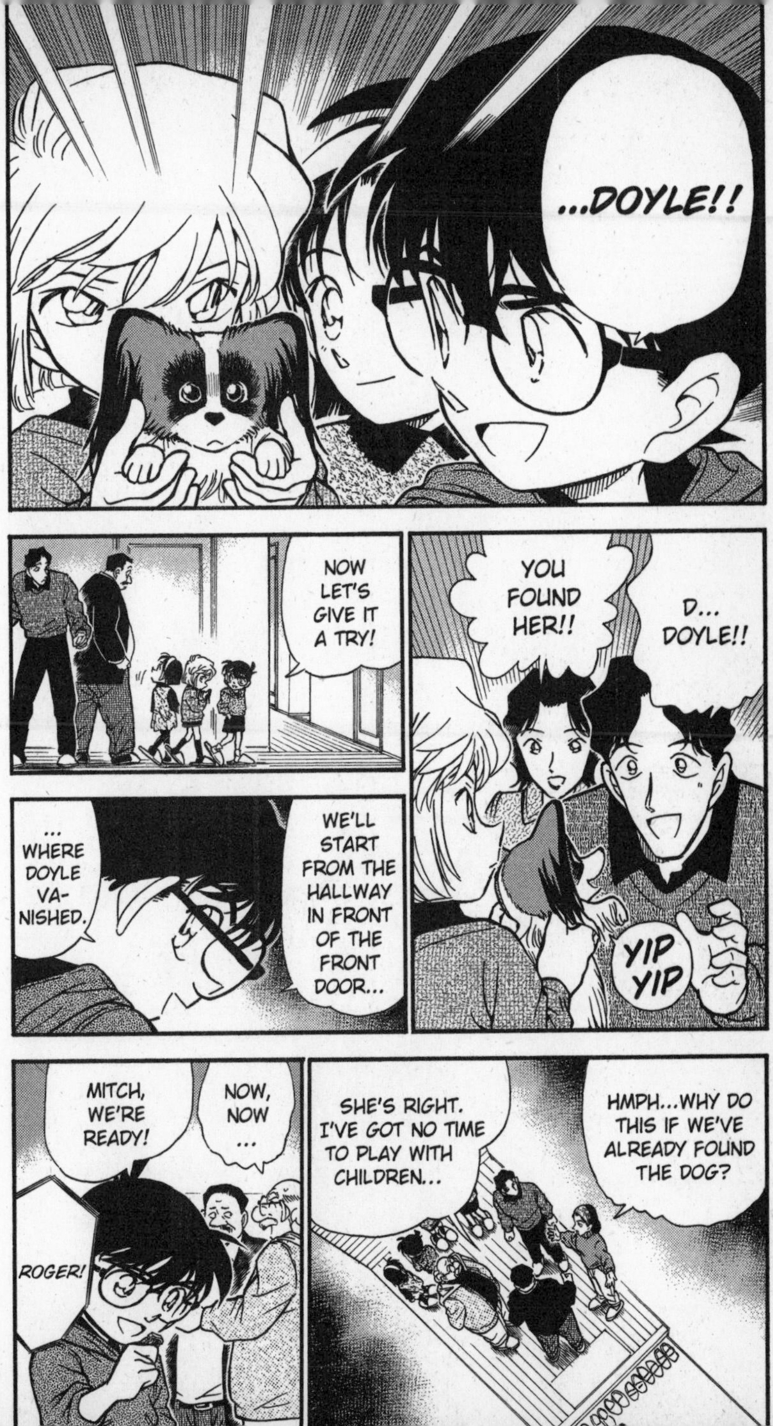
...DOYLE!!
D... DOYLE!!
YOU FOUND HER!!
YIP YIP
NOW LET'S GIVE IT A TRY!
WE'LL START FROM THE HALLWAY IN FRONT OF THE FRONT DOOR...
...WHERE DOYLE VANISHED.
HMPH...WHY DO THIS IF WE'VE ALREADY FOUND THE DOG?
SHE'S RIGHT. I'VE GOT NO TIME TO PLAY WITH CHILDREN...
NOW, NOW ...
MITCH, WE'RE READY!
ROGER!

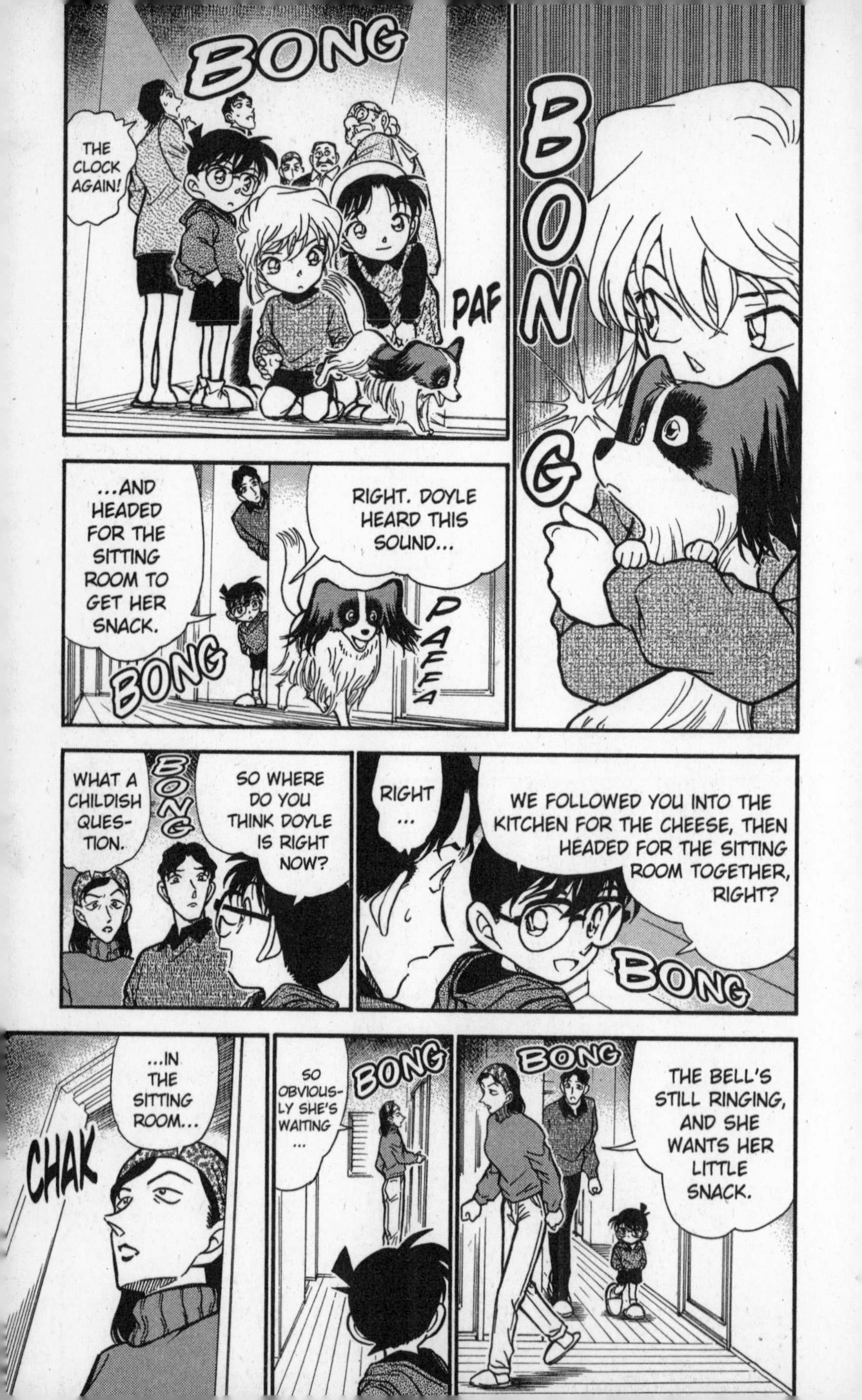
BONG
BONG
THE CLOCK AGAIN!
PAF
RIGHT. DOYLE HEARD THIS SOUND...
...AND HEADED FOR THE SITTING ROOM TO GET HER SNACK.
BONG
PAFFA
WE FOLLOWED YOU INTO THE KITCHEN FOR THE CHEESE, THEN HEADED FOR THE SITTING ROOM TOGETHER, RIGHT?
RIGHT ...
BONG
BONG
SO WHERE DO YOU THINK DOYLE IS RIGHT NOW?
WHAT A CHILDISH QUES-TION.
BONG
THE BELL'S STILL RINGING, AND SHE WANTS HER LITTLE SNACK.
BONG
SO OBVIOUS-LY SHE'S WAITING ...
...IN THE SITTING ROOM...
CHAK

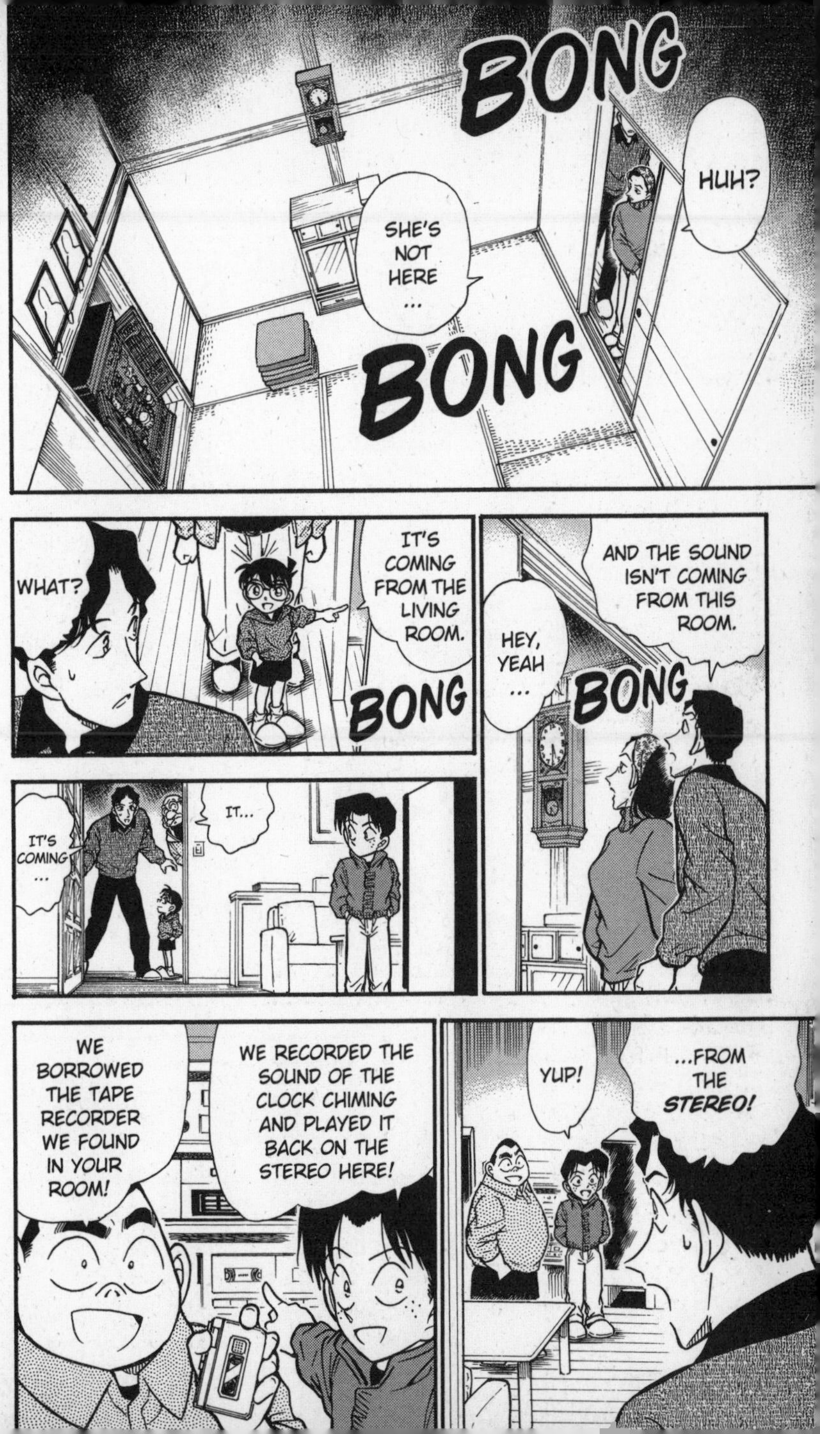
BONG
HUH?
SHE'S NOT HERE ...
BONG
AND THE SOUND ISN'T COMING FROM THIS ROOM.
HEY, YEAH ...
BONG
IT'S COMING FROM THE LIVING ROOM.
BONG
WHAT?
IT...
IT'S COMING ...
...FROM THE STEREO!
YUP!
WE RECORDED THE SOUND OF THE CLOCK CHIMING AND PLAYED IT BACK ON THE STEREO HERE!
WE BORROWED THE TAPE RECORDER WE FOUND IN YOUR ROOM!

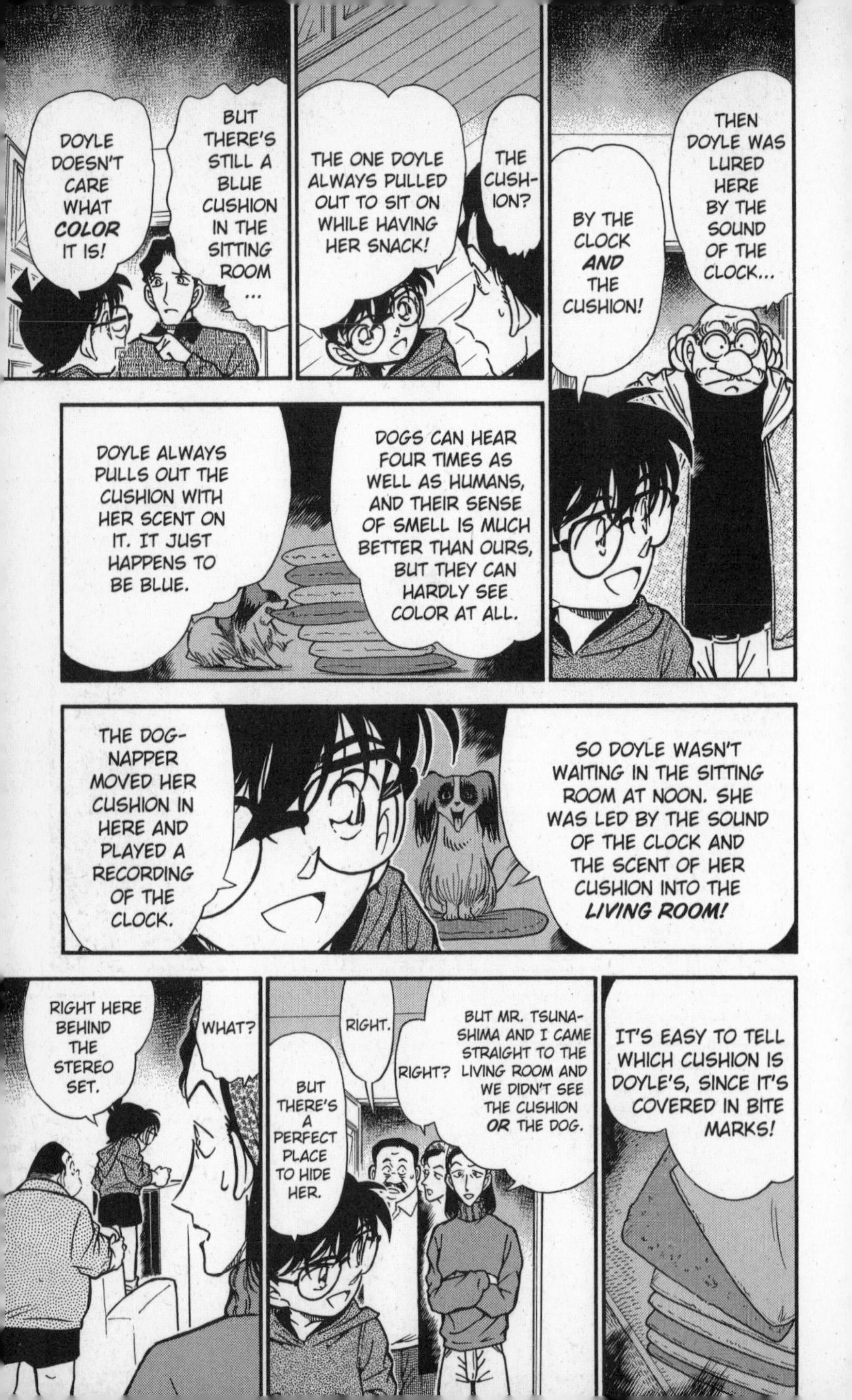
THEN DOYLE WAS LURED HERE BY THE SOUND OF THE CLOCK...
BY THE CLOCK AND THE CUSHION!
THE CUSH-ION?
THE ONE DOYLE ALWAYS PULLED OUT TO SIT ON WHILE HAVING HER SNACK!
BUT THERE'S STILL A BLUE CUSHION IN THE SITTING ROOM ...
DOYLE DOESN'T CARE WHAT COLOR IT IS!
DOGS CAN HEAR FOUR TIMES AS WELL AS HUMANS, AND THEIR SENSE OF SMELL IS MUCH BETTER THAN OURS, BUT THEY CAN HARDLY SEE COLOR AT ALL.
DOYLE ALWAYS PULLS OUT THE CUSHION WITH HER SCENT ON IT. IT JUST HAPPENS TO BE BLUE.
SO DOYLE WASN'T WAITING IN THE SITTING ROOM AT NOON. SHE WAS LED BY THE SOUND OF THE CLOCK AND THE SCENT OF HER CUSHION INTO THE LIVING ROOM!
THE DOG-NAPPER MOVED HER CUSHION IN HERE AND PLAYED A RECORDING OF THE CLOCK.
IT'S EASY TO TELL WHICH CUSHION IS DOYLE'S, SINCE IT'S COVERED IN BITE MARKS!
BUT MR. TSUNA-SHIMA AND I CAME STRAIGHT TO THE LIVING ROOM AND WE DIDN'T SEE THE CUSHION OR THE DOG.
RIGHT?
RIGHT.
BUT THERE'S A PERFECT PLACE TO HIDE HER.
WHAT?
RIGHT HERE BEHIND THE STEREO SET.

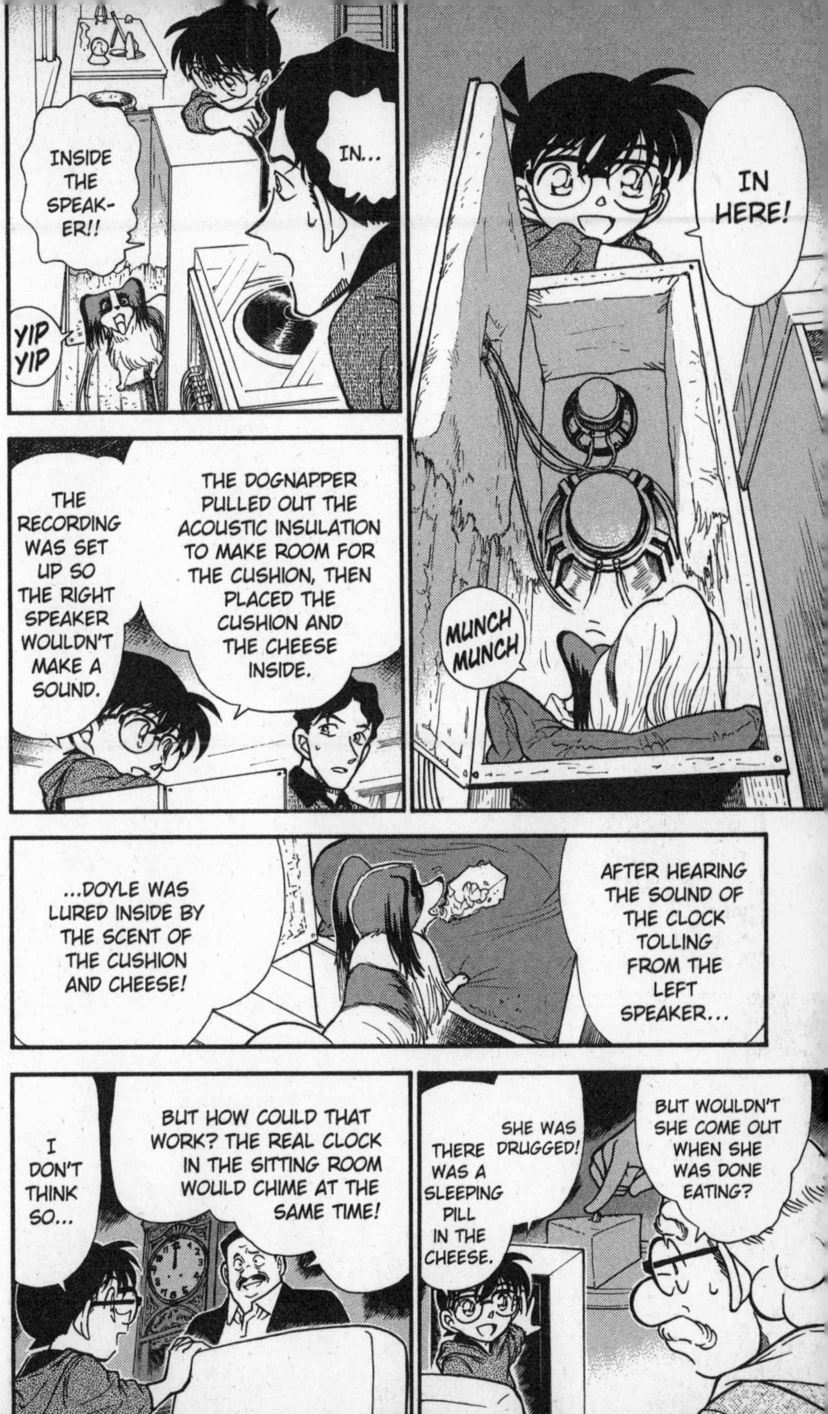
IN HERE!
MUNCH MUNCH
IN...
INSIDE THE SPEAKER!!
YIP YIP
THE DOGNAPPER PULLED OUT THE ACOUSTIC INSULATION TO MAKE ROOM FOR THE CUSHION, THEN PLACED THE CUSHION AND THE CHEESE INSIDE.
THE RECORDING WAS SET UP SO THE RIGHT SPEAKER WOULDN'T MAKE A SOUND.
AFTER HEARING THE SOUND OF THE CLOCK TOLLING FROM THE LEFT SPEAKER...
...DOYLE WAS LURED INSIDE BY THE SCENT OF THE CUSHION AND CHEESE!
BUT WOULDN'T SHE COME OUT WHEN SHE WAS DONE EATING?
SHE WAS DRUGGED!
THERE WAS A SLEEPING PILL IN THE CHEESE.
BUT HOW COULD THAT WORK? THE REAL CLOCK IN THE SITTING ROOM WOULD CHIME AT THE SAME TIME!
I DON'T THINK SO...

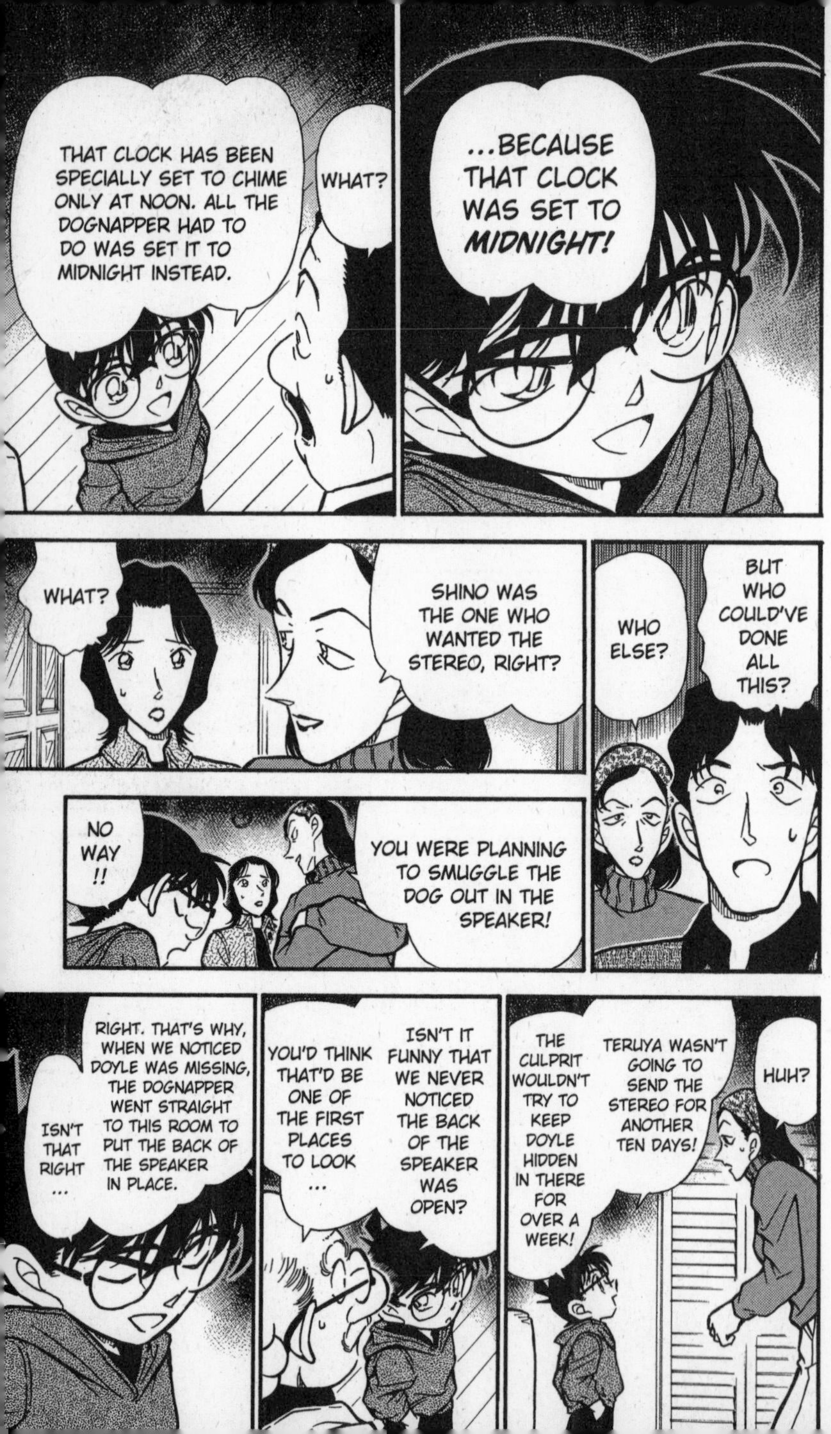
...BECAUSE THAT CLOCK WAS SET TO MIDNIGHT!
WHAT?
THAT CLOCK HAS BEEN SPECIALLY SET TO CHIME ONLY AT NOON. ALL THE DOGNAPPER HAD TO DO WAS SET IT TO MIDNIGHT INSTEAD.
BUT WHO COULD'VE DONE ALL THIS?
WHO ELSE?
SHINO WAS THE ONE WHO WANTED THE STEREO, RIGHT?
WHAT?
YOU WERE PLANNING TO SMUGGLE THE DOG OUT IN THE SPEAKER!
NO WAY !!
HUH?
TERUYA WASN'T GOING TO SEND THE STEREO FOR ANOTHER TEN DAYS!
THE CULPRIT WOULDN'T TRY TO KEEP DOYLE HIDDEN IN THERE FOR OVER A WEEK!
ISN'T IT FUNNY THAT WE NEVER NOTICED THE BACK OF THE SPEAKER WAS OPEN?
YOU'D THINK THAT'D BE ONE OF THE FIRST PLACES TO LOOK ...
RIGHT. THAT'S WHY, WHEN WE NOTICED DOYLE WAS MISSING, THE DOGNAPPER WENT STRAIGHT TO THIS ROOM TO PUT THE BACK OF THE SPEAKER IN PLACE.
ISN'T THAT RIGHT ...

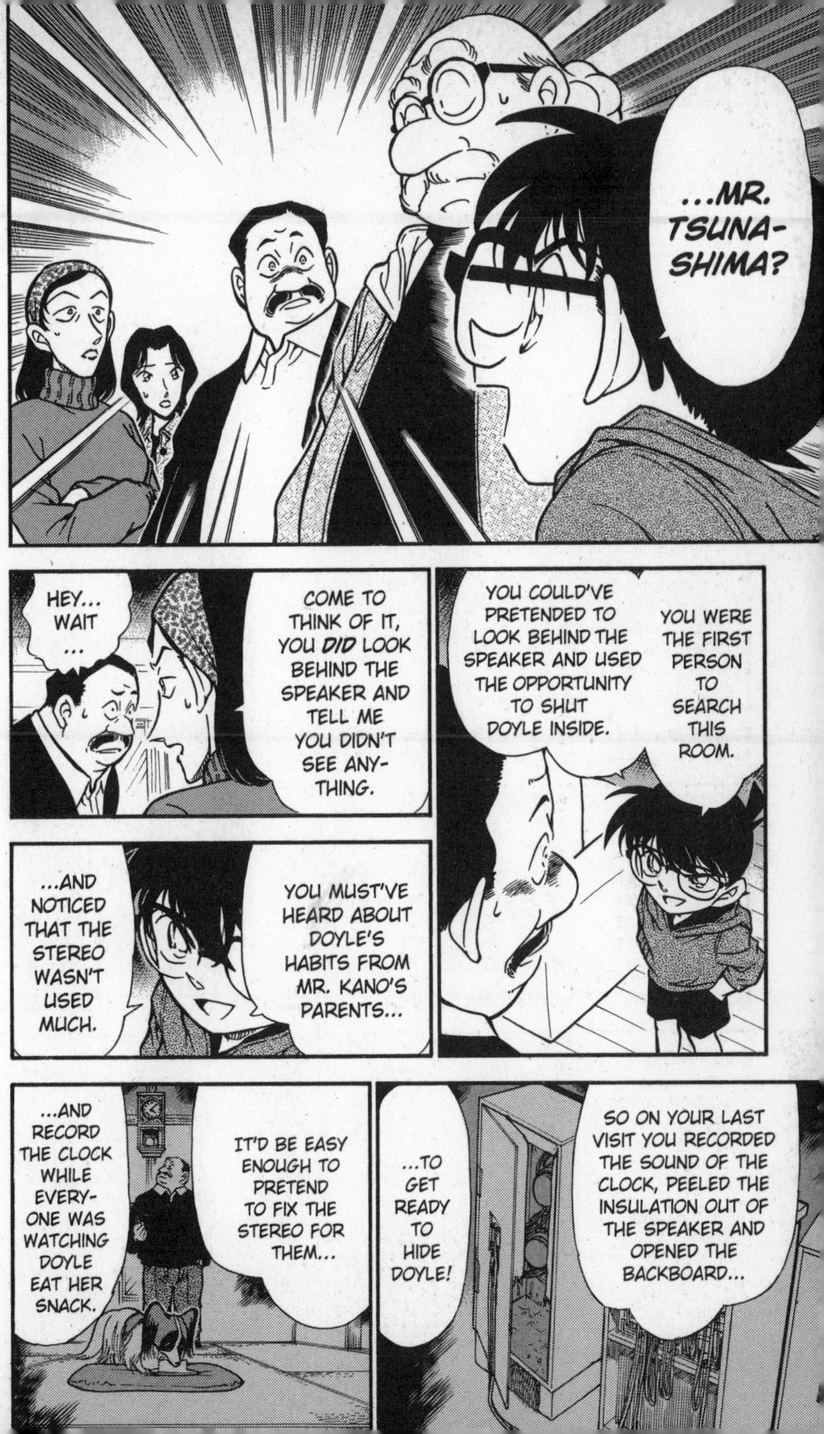
...MR. TSUNA-SHIMA?
YOU WERE THE FIRST PERSON TO SEARCH THIS ROOM.
YOU COULD'VE PRETENDED TO LOOK BEHIND THE SPEAKER AND USED THE OPPORTUNITY TO SHUT DOYLE INSIDE.
COME TO THINK OF IT, YOU *DID* LOOK BEHIND THE SPEAKER AND TELL ME YOU DIDN'T SEE ANY-THING.
HEY... WAIT ...
YOU MUST'VE HEARD ABOUT DOYLE'S HABITS FROM MR. KANO'S PARENTS...
...AND NOTICED THAT THE STEREO WASN'T USED MUCH.
SO ON YOUR LAST VISIT YOU RECORDED THE SOUND OF THE CLOCK, PEELED THE INSULATION OUT OF THE SPEAKER AND OPENED THE BACKBOARD...
...TO GET READY TO HIDE DOYLE!
IT'D BE EASY ENOUGH TO PRETEND TO FIX THE STEREO FOR THEM...
...AND RECORD THE CLOCK WHILE EVERY-ONE WAS WATCHING DOYLE EAT HER SNACK.

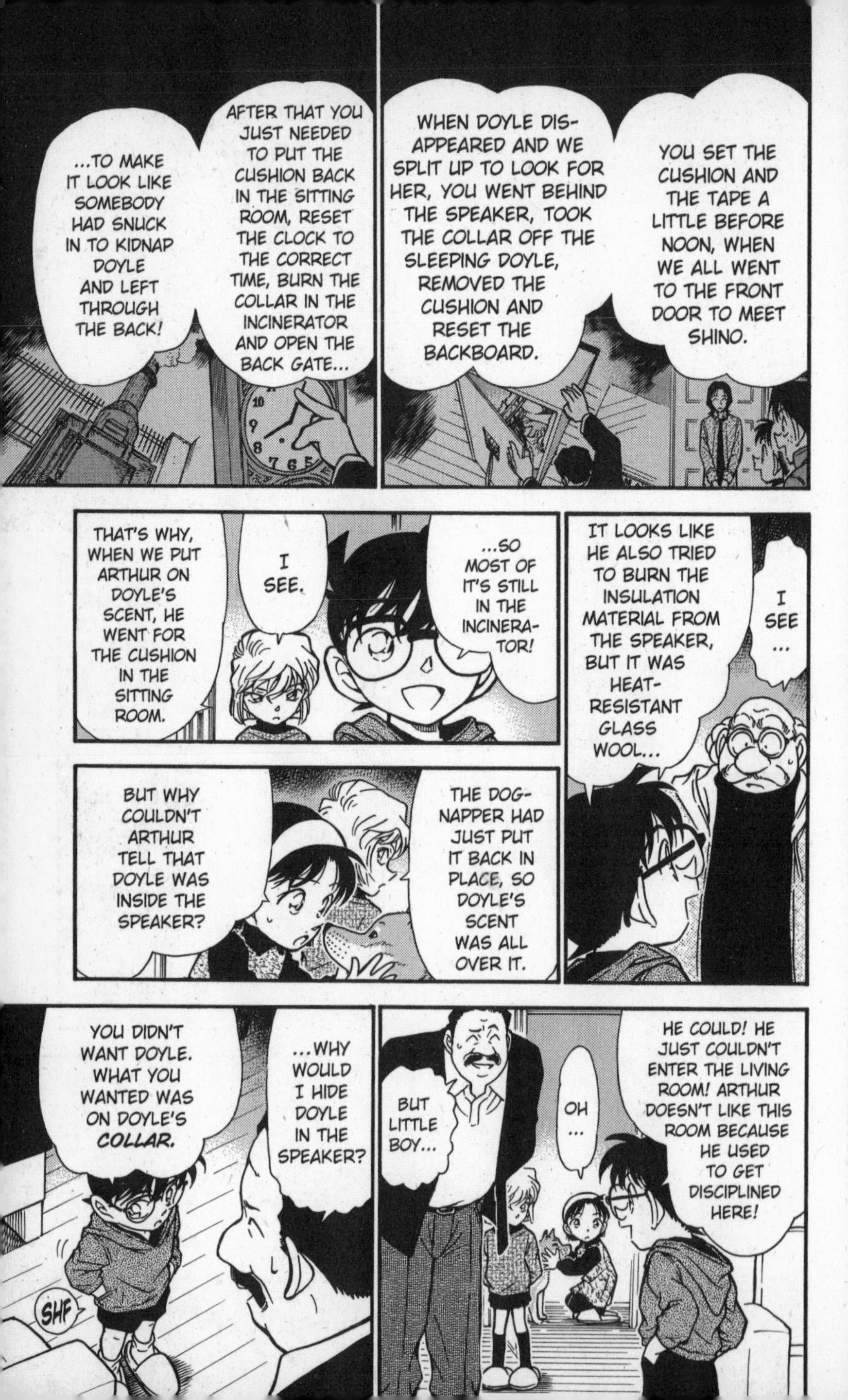
YOU SET THE CUSHION AND THE TAPE A LITTLE BEFORE NOON, WHEN WE ALL WENT TO THE FRONT DOOR TO MEET SHINO.
WHEN DOYLE DIS-APPEARED AND WE SPLIT UP TO LOOK FOR HER, YOU WENT BEHIND THE SPEAKER, TOOK THE COLLAR OFF THE SLEEPING DOYLE, REMOVED THE CUSHION AND RESET THE BACKBOARD.
AFTER THAT YOU JUST NEEDED TO PUT THE CUSHION BACK IN THE SITTING ROOM, RESET THE CLOCK TO THE CORRECT TIME, BURN THE COLLAR IN THE INCINERATOR AND OPEN THE BACK GATE...
...TO MAKE IT LOOK LIKE SOMEBODY HAD SNUCK IN TO KIDNAP DOYLE AND LEFT THROUGH THE BACK!
IT LOOKS LIKE HE ALSO TRIED TO BURN THE INSULATION MATERIAL FROM THE SPEAKER, BUT IT WAS HEAT-RESISTANT GLASS WOOL...
I SEE...
...SO MOST OF IT'S STILL IN THE INCINERA-TOR!
I SEE.
THAT'S WHY, WHEN WE PUT ARTHUR ON DOYLE'S SCENT, HE WENT FOR THE CUSHION IN THE SITTING ROOM.
THE DOG-NAPPER HAD JUST PUT IT BACK IN PLACE, SO DOYLE'S SCENT WAS ALL OVER IT.
BUT WHY COULDN'T ARTHUR TELL THAT DOYLE WAS INSIDE THE SPEAKER?
HE COULD! HE JUST COULDN'T ENTER THE LIVING ROOM! ARTHUR DOESN'T LIKE THIS ROOM BECAUSE HE USED TO GET DISCIPLINED HERE!
OH...
BUT LITTLE BOY...
...WHY WOULD I HIDE DOYLE IN THE SPEAKER?
YOU DIDN'T WANT DOYLE. WHAT YOU WANTED WAS ON DOYLE'S COLLAR.
SHF

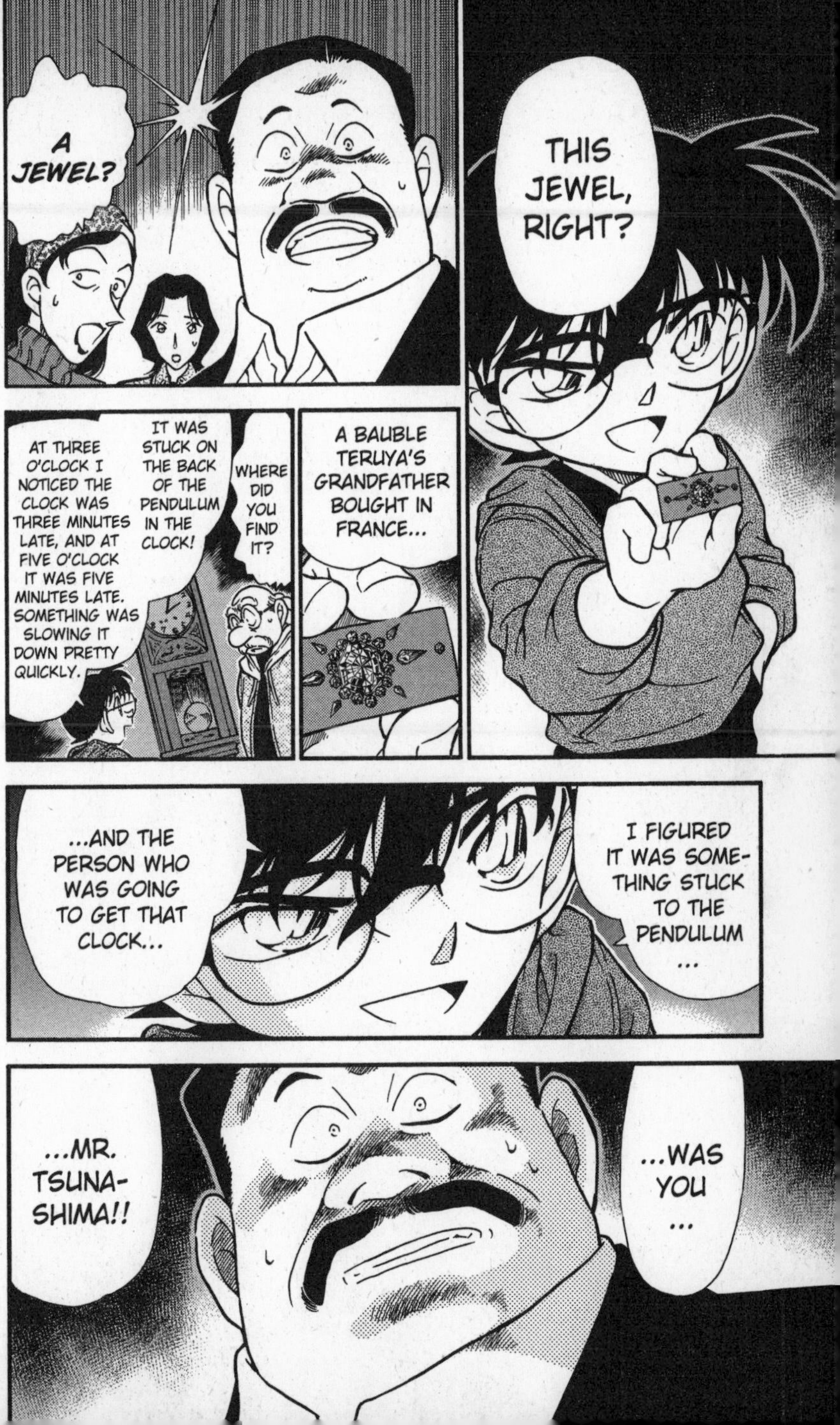
THIS JEWEL, RIGHT?
A JEWEL?
A BAUBLE TERUYA'S GRANDFATHER BOUGHT IN FRANCE...
WHERE DID YOU FIND IT?
IT WAS STUCK ON THE BACK OF THE PENDULUM IN THE CLOCK!
AT THREE O'CLOCK I NOTICED THE CLOCK WAS THREE MINUTES LATE, AND AT FIVE O'CLOCK IT WAS FIVE MINUTES LATE. SOMETHING WAS SLOWING IT DOWN PRETTY QUICKLY.
I FIGURED IT WAS SOME-THING STUCK TO THE PENDULUM ...
...AND THE PERSON WHO WAS GOING TO GET THAT CLOCK...
...WAS YOU ...
...MR. TSUNA-SHIMA!!

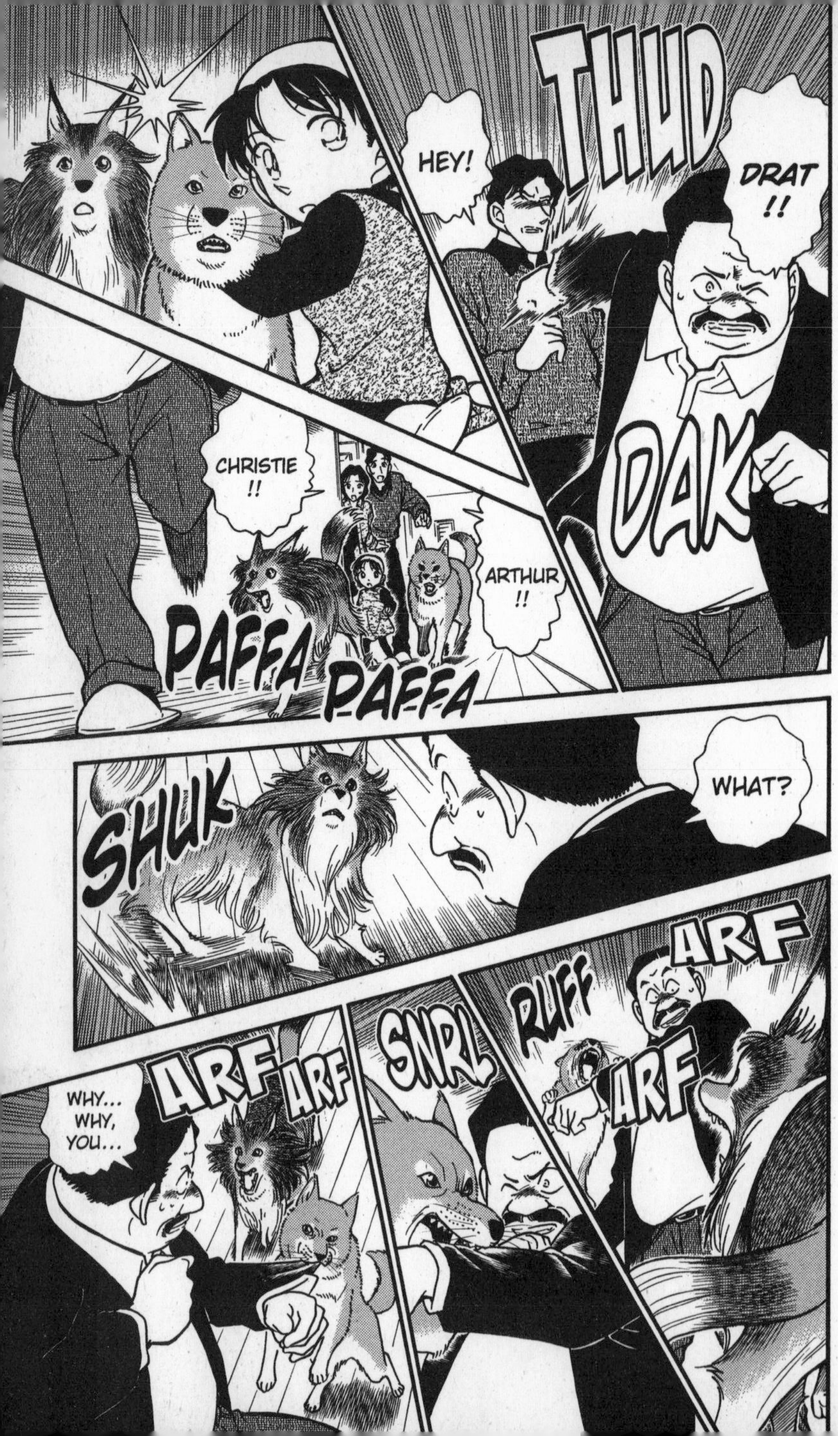
THUD
DRAT !!
HEY!
DAK
ARTHUR !!
CHRISTIE !!
PAFFA
PAFFA
WHAT?
SHUK
ARF
RUFF
ARF
SNRL
ARF ARF
WHY... WHY, YOU...

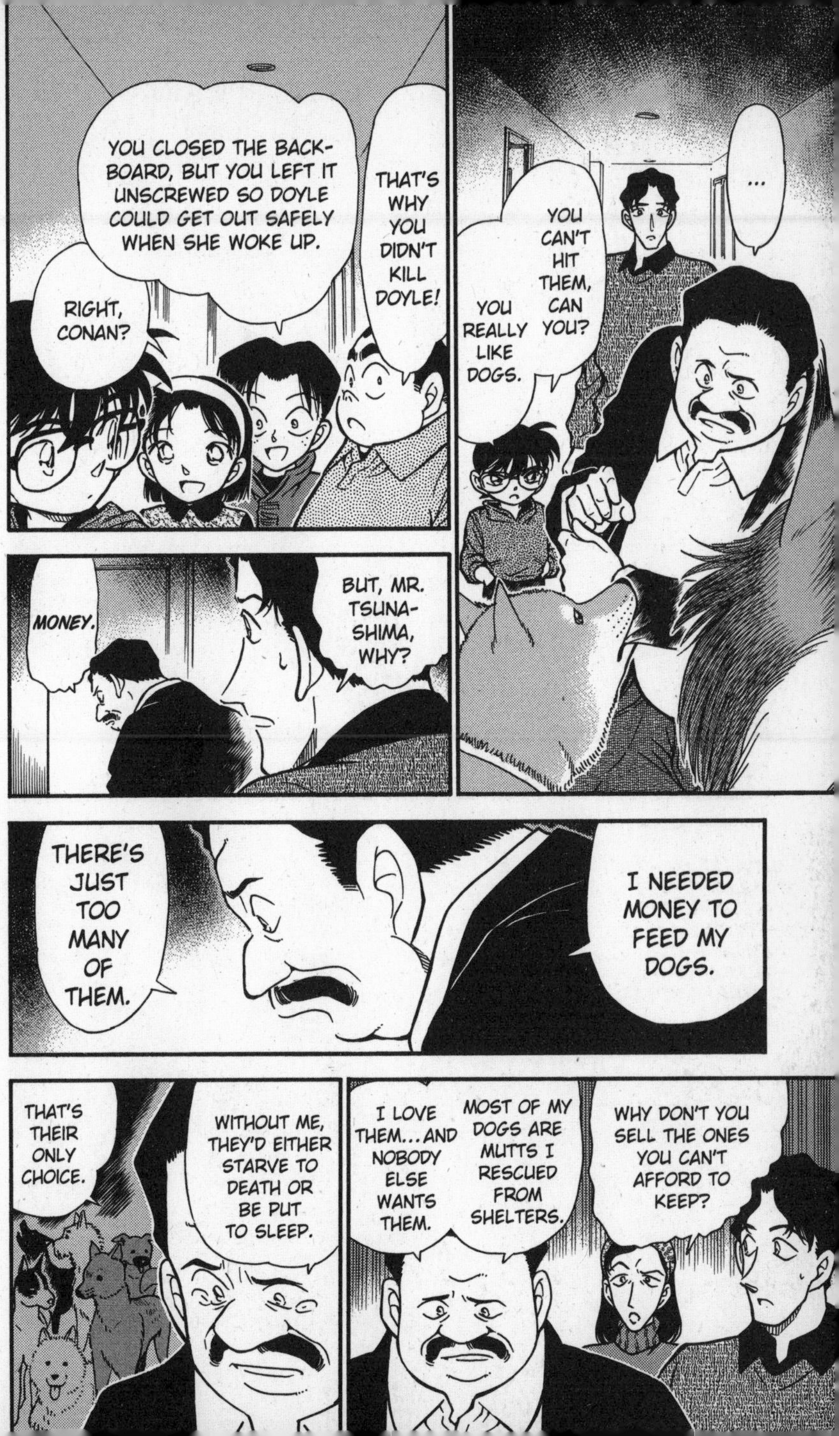
...
YOU CAN'T HIT THEM, CAN YOU?
YOU REALLY LIKE DOGS.
THAT'S WHY YOU DIDN'T KILL DOYLE!
YOU CLOSED THE BACK-BOARD, BUT YOU LEFT IT UNSCREWED SO DOYLE COULD GET OUT SAFELY WHEN SHE WOKE UP.
RIGHT, CONAN?
BUT, MR. TSUNA-SHIMA, WHY?
MONEY.
I NEEDED MONEY TO FEED MY DOGS.
THERE'S JUST TOO MANY OF THEM.
WHY DON'T YOU SELL THE ONES YOU CAN'T AFFORD TO KEEP?
MOST OF MY DOGS ARE MUTTS I RESCUED FROM SHELTERS.
I LOVE THEM...AND NOBODY ELSE WANTS THEM.
WITHOUT ME, THEY'D EITHER STARVE TO DEATH OR BE PUT TO SLEEP.
THAT'S THEIR ONLY CHOICE.

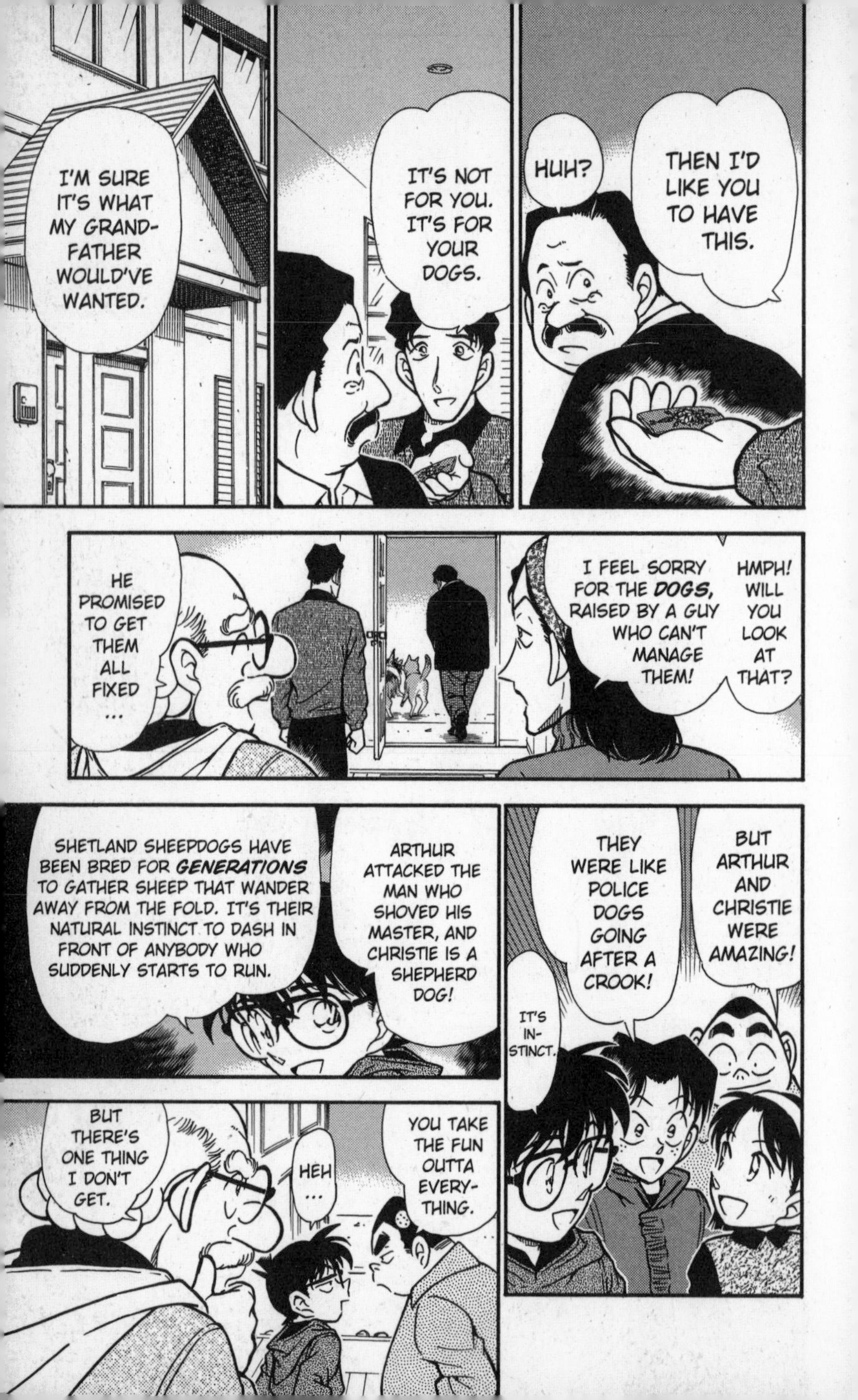
THEN I'D LIKE YOU TO HAVE THIS.
HUH?
IT'S NOT FOR YOU. IT'S FOR YOUR DOGS.
I'M SURE IT'S WHAT MY GRANDFATHER WOULD'VE WANTED.
HMPH! WILL YOU LOOK AT THAT?
I FEEL SORRY FOR THE *DOGS*, RAISED BY A GUY WHO CAN'T MANAGE THEM!
HE PROMISED TO GET THEM ALL FIXED ...
BUT ARTHUR AND CHRISTIE WERE AMAZING!
THEY WERE LIKE POLICE DOGS GOING AFTER A CROOK!
IT'S INSTINCT.
ARTHUR ATTACKED THE MAN WHO SHOVED HIS MASTER, AND CHRISTIE IS A SHEPHERD DOG!
SHETLAND SHEEPDOGS HAVE BEEN BRED FOR *GENERATIONS* TO GATHER SHEEP THAT WANDER AWAY FROM THE FOLD. IT'S THEIR NATURAL INSTINCT TO DASH IN FRONT OF ANYBODY WHO SUDDENLY STARTS TO RUN.
YOU TAKE THE FUN OUTTA EVERYTHING.
HEH ...
BUT THERE'S ONE THING I DON'T GET.

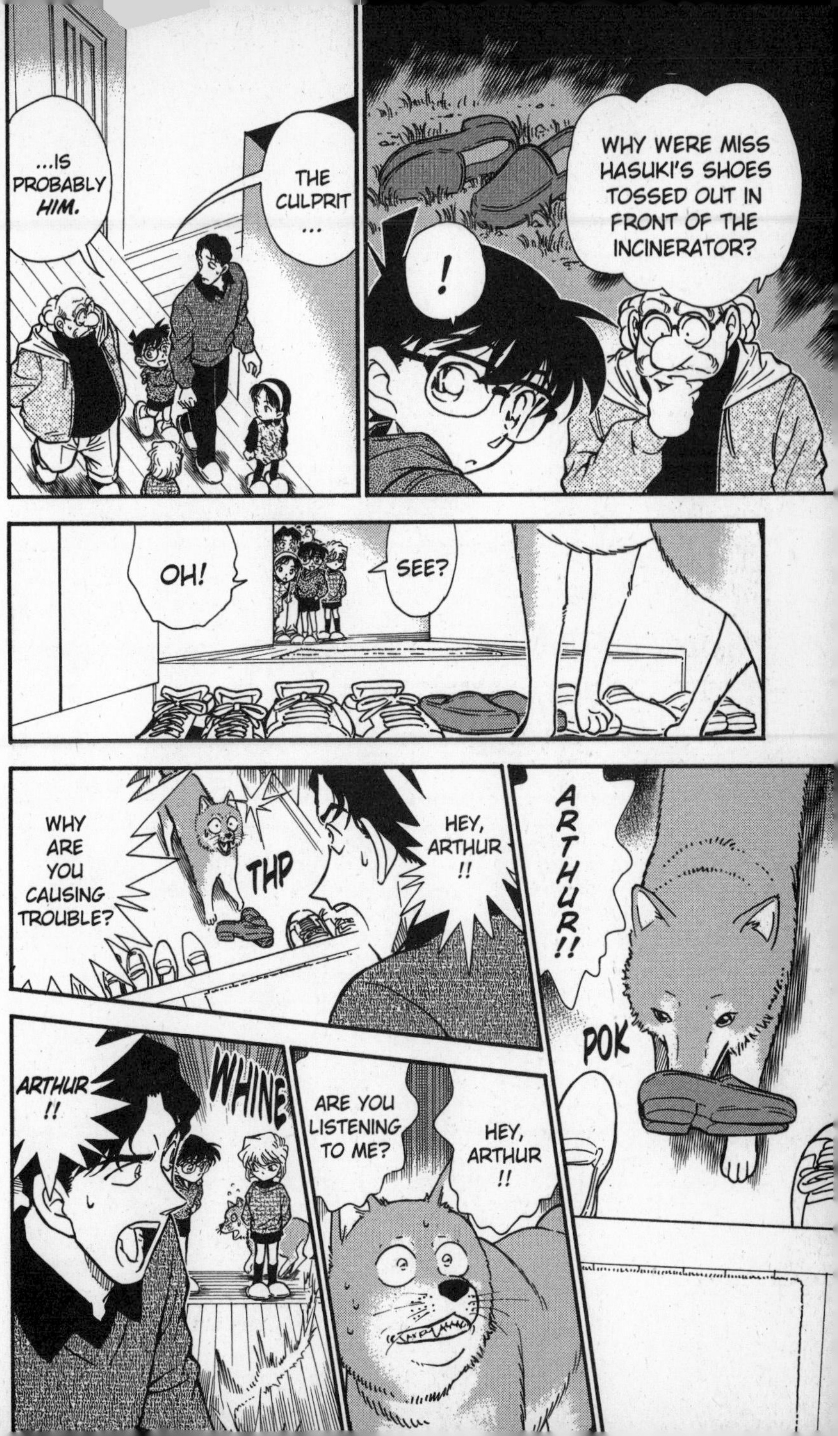
WHY WERE MISS HASUKI'S SHOES TOSSED OUT IN FRONT OF THE INCINERATOR?
!
THE CULPRIT ...
...IS PROBABLY HIM.
SEE?
OH!
ARTHUR!!
POK
HEY, ARTHUR !!
THP
WHY ARE YOU CAUSING TROUBLE?
HEY, ARTHUR !!
ARE YOU LISTENING TO ME?
WHINE
ARTHUR !!

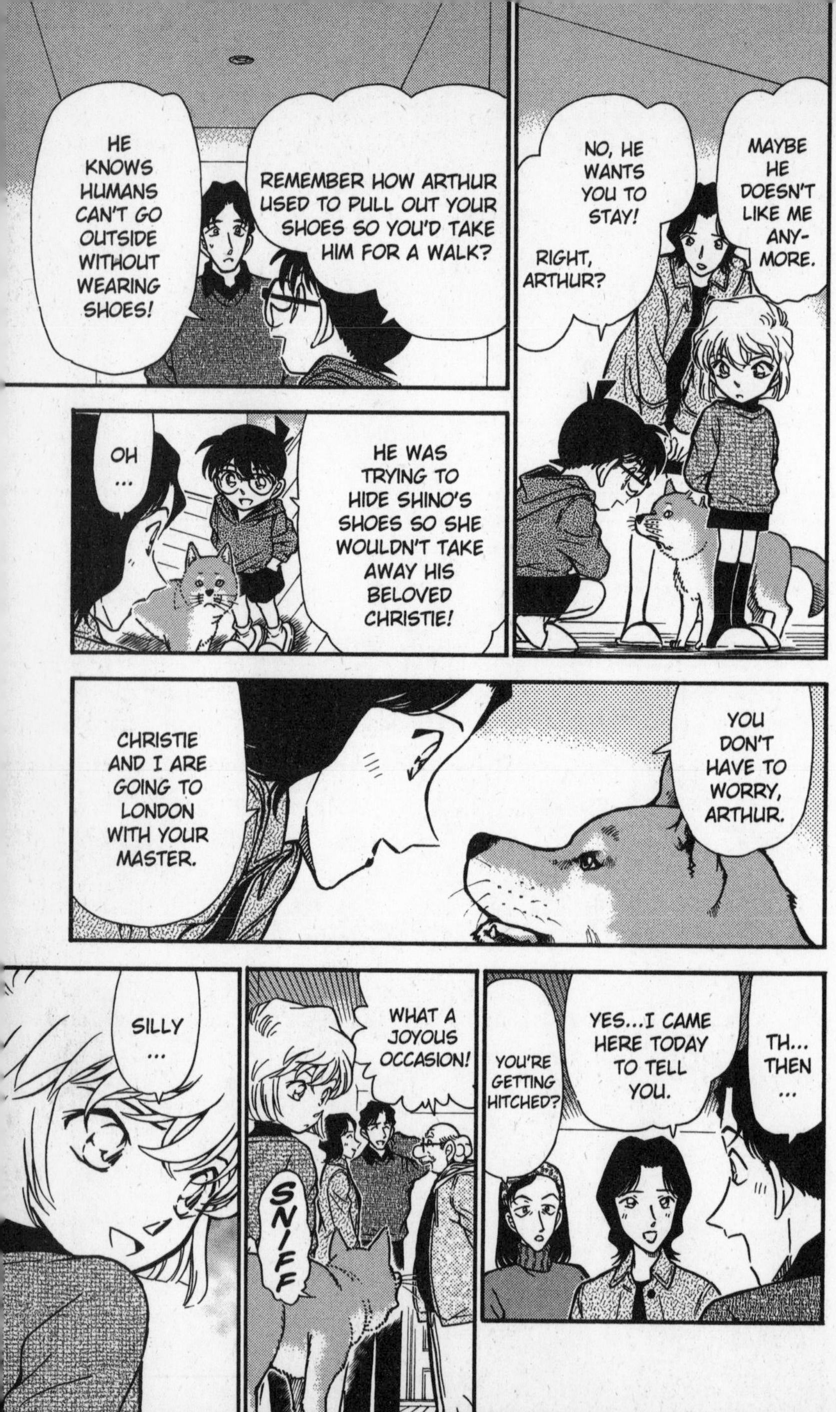
MAYBE HE DOESN'T LIKE ME ANYMORE.
NO, HE WANTS YOU TO STAY!
RIGHT, ARTHUR?
REMEMBER HOW ARTHUR USED TO PULL OUT YOUR SHOES SO YOU'D TAKE HIM FOR A WALK?
HE KNOWS HUMANS CAN'T GO OUTSIDE WITHOUT WEARING SHOES!
HE WAS TRYING TO HIDE SHINO'S SHOES SO SHE WOULDN'T TAKE AWAY HIS BELOVED CHRISTIE!
OH ...
YOU DON'T HAVE TO WORRY, ARTHUR.
CHRISTIE AND I ARE GOING TO LONDON WITH YOUR MASTER.
TH... THEN ...
YES...I CAME HERE TODAY TO TELL YOU.
YOU'RE GETTING HITCHED?
WHAT A JOYOUS OCCASION!
SNIFF
SILLY ...

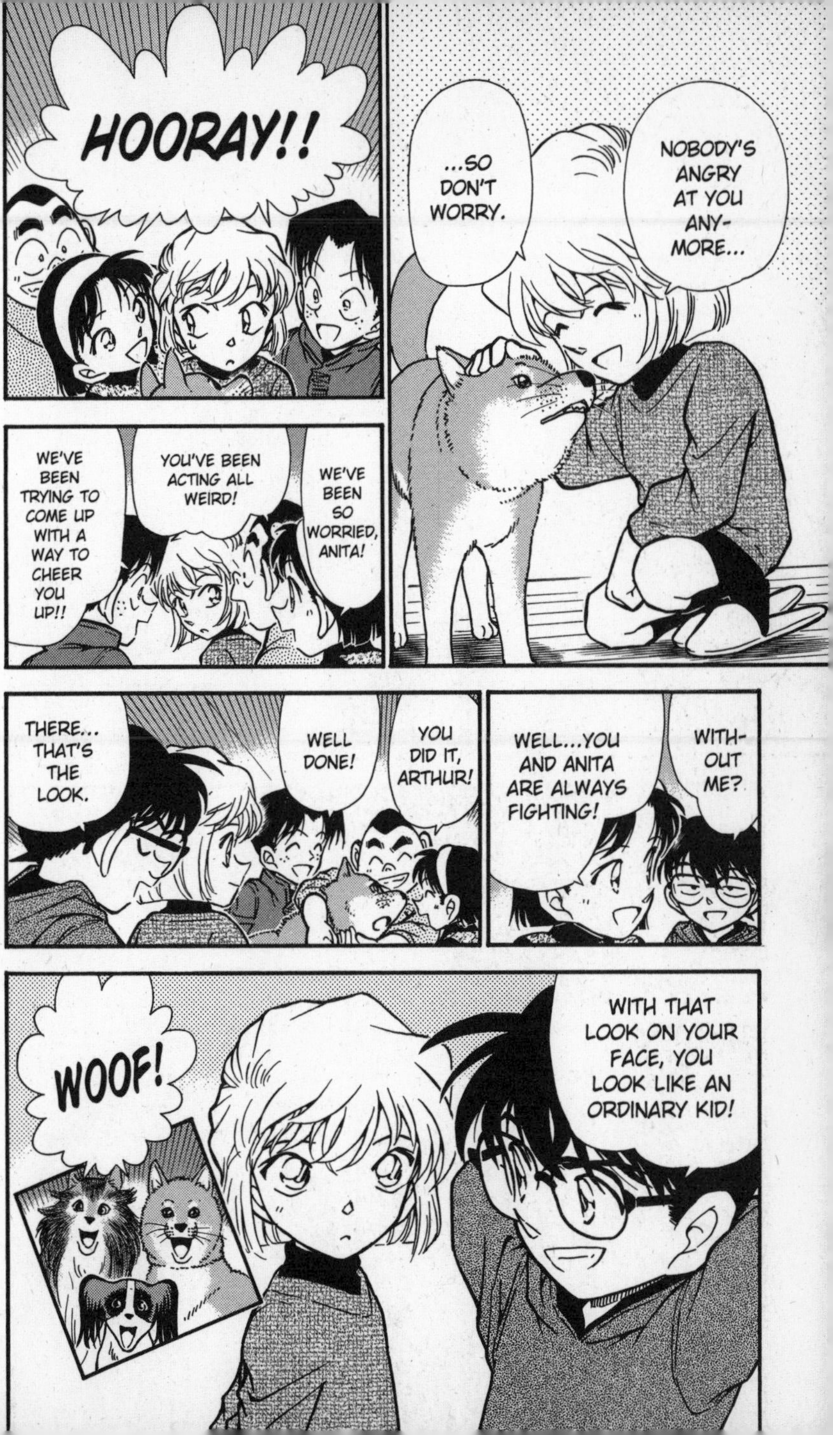
NOBODY'S ANGRY AT YOU ANY-MORE...
...SO DON'T WORRY.
HOORAY!!
WE'VE BEEN SO WORRIED, ANITA!
YOU'VE BEEN ACTING ALL WEIRD!
WE'VE BEEN TRYING TO COME UP WITH A WAY TO CHEER YOU UP!!
WITH-OUT ME?
WELL...YOU AND ANITA ARE ALWAYS FIGHTING!
YOU DID IT, ARTHUR!
WELL DONE!
THERE... THAT'S THE LOOK.
WITH THAT LOOK ON YOUR FACE, YOU LOOK LIKE AN ORDINARY KID!
WOOF!

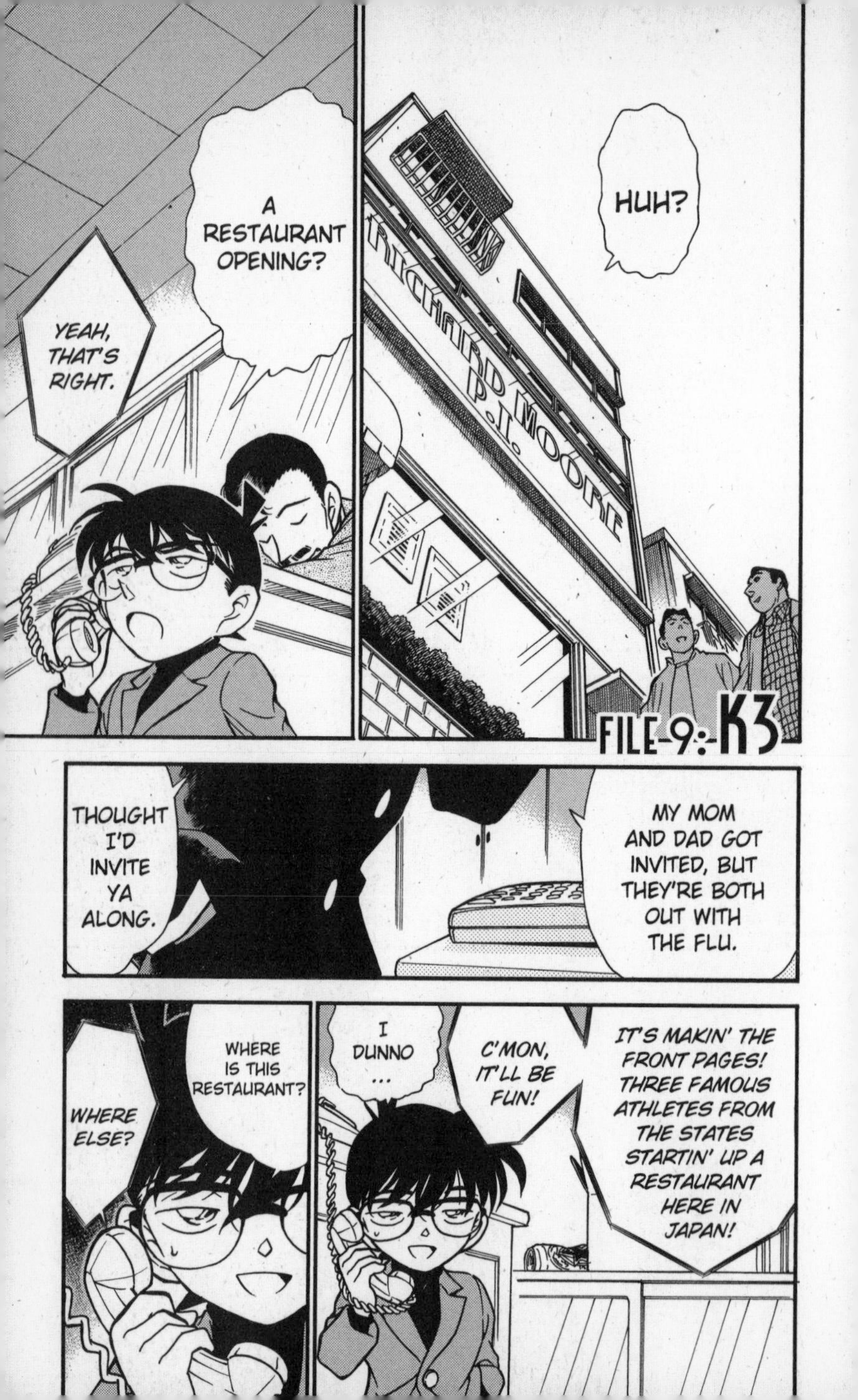
HUH?
RICHARD MOORE P.I.
FILE 9: K3
A RESTAURANT OPENING?
YEAH, THAT'S RIGHT.
MY MOM AND DAD GOT INVITED, BUT THEY'RE BOTH OUT WITH THE FLU.
THOUGHT I'D INVITE YA ALONG.
IT'S MAKIN' THE FRONT PAGES! THREE FAMOUS ATHLETES FROM THE STATES STARTIN' UP A RESTAURANT HERE IN JAPAN!
C'MON, IT'LL BE FUN!
I DUNNO ...
WHERE IS THIS RESTAURANT?
WHERE ELSE?

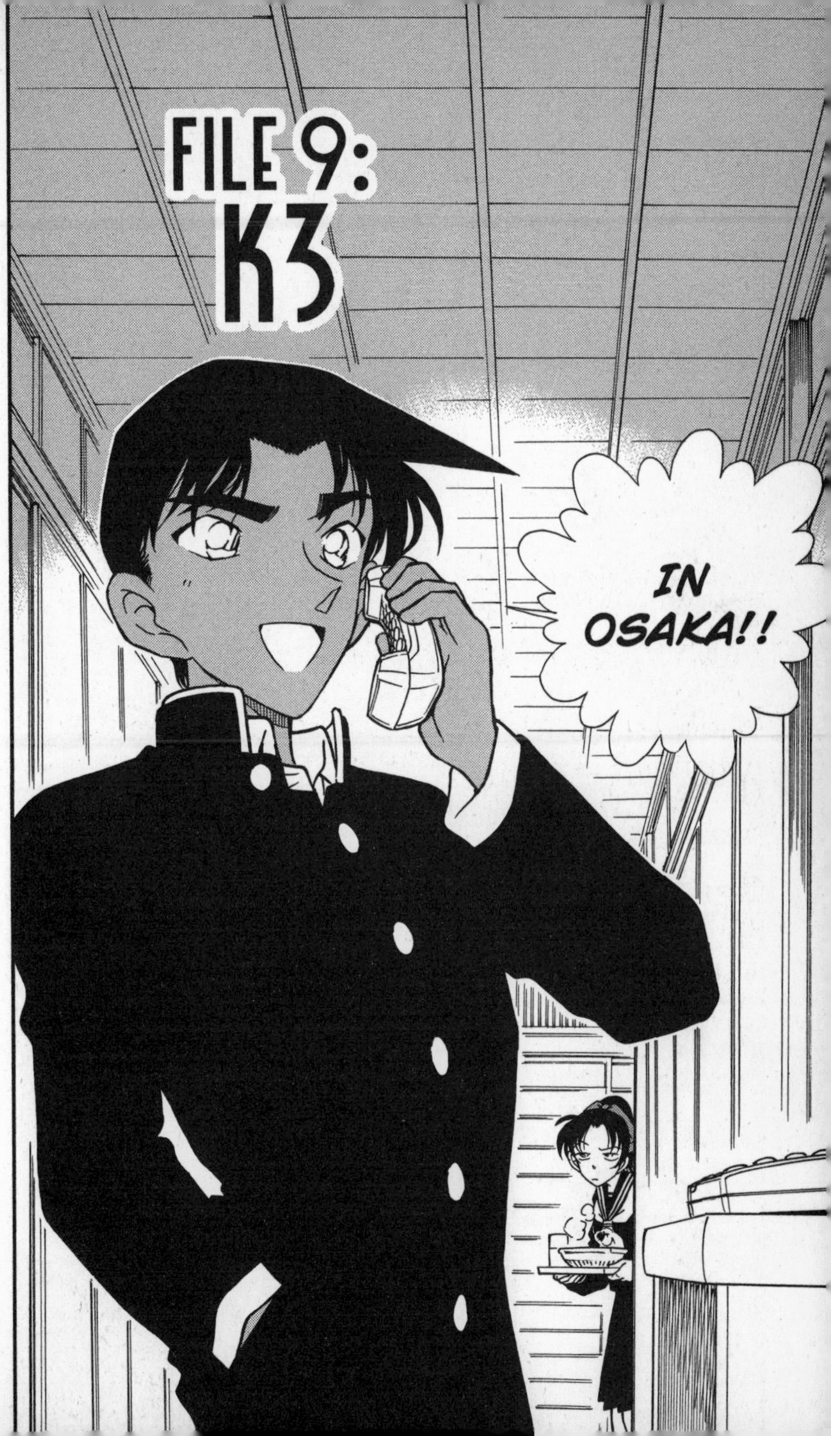
FILE 9:
K3
IN OSAKA!!

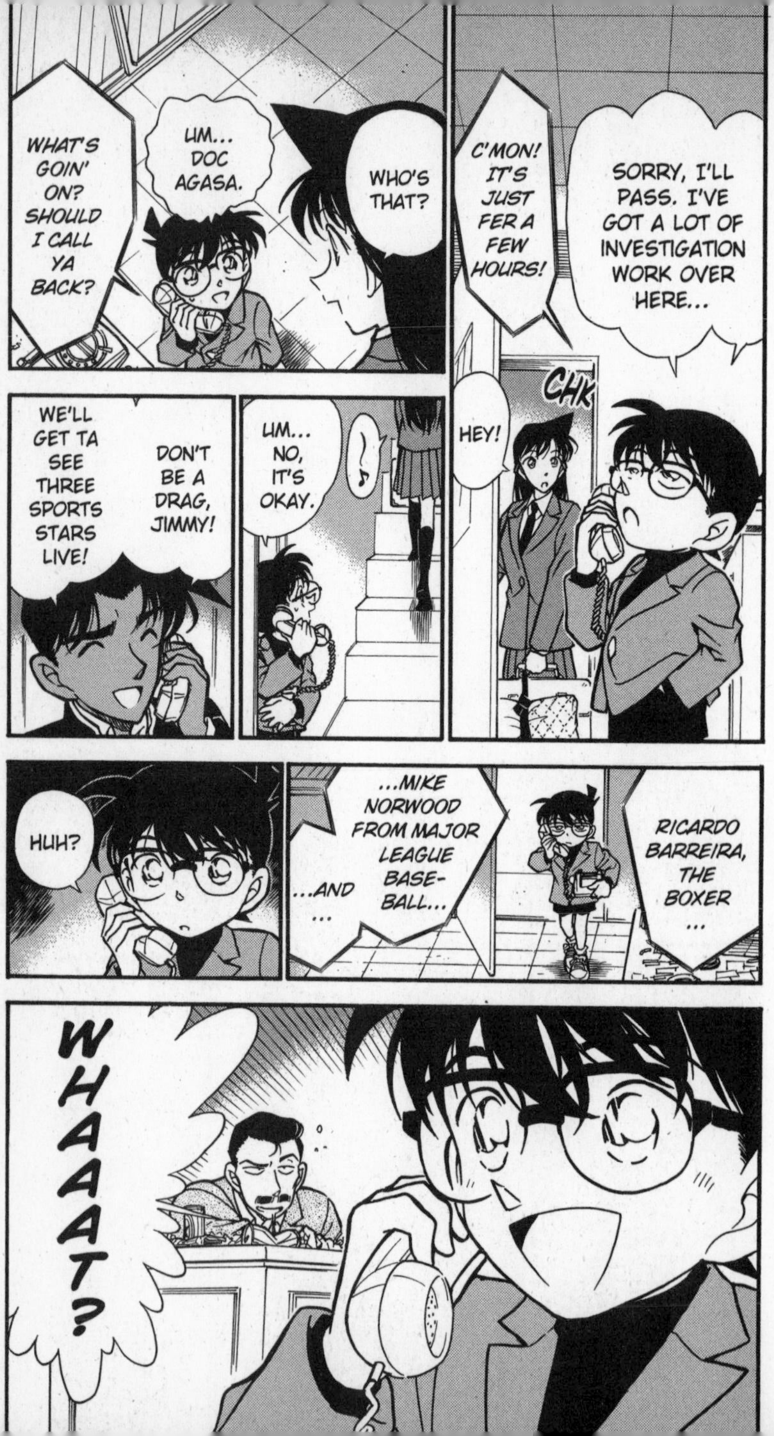
SORRY, I'LL PASS. I'VE GOT A LOT OF INVESTIGATION WORK OVER HERE...
C'MON! IT'S JUST FER A FEW HOURS!
CHK
HEY!
WHO'S THAT?
UM... DOC AGASA.
WHAT'S GOIN' ON? SHOULD I CALL YA BACK?
UM... NO, IT'S OKAY.
DON'T BE A DRAG, JIMMY!
WE'LL GET TA SEE THREE SPORTS STARS LIVE!
RICARDO BARREIRA, THE BOXER ...
...MIKE NORWOOD FROM MAJOR LEAGUE BASE-BALL...
...AND ...
HUH?
WHAAAAT?

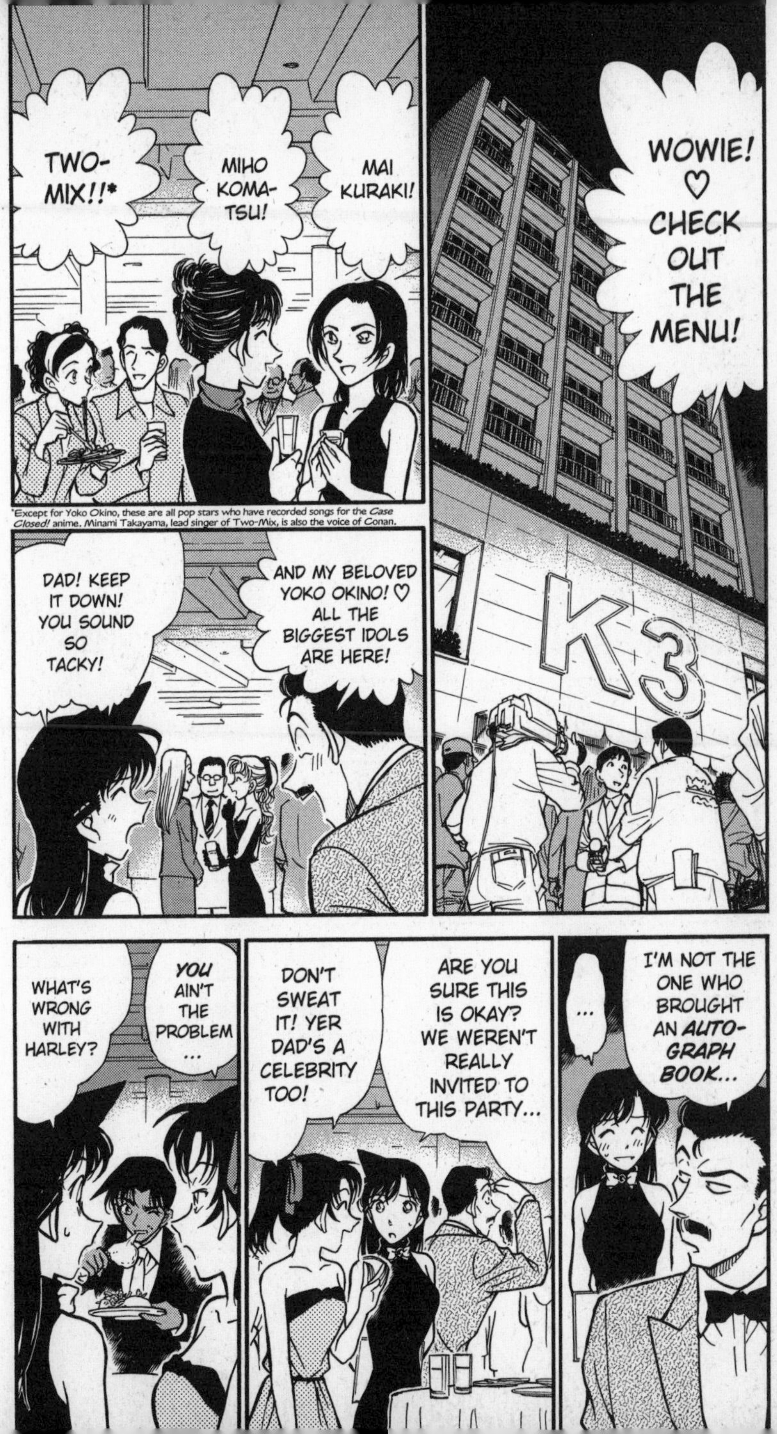
WOWIE! ♡ CHECK OUT THE MENU!
MAI KURAKI!
MIHO KOMATSU!
TWO-MIX!!*
AND MY BELOVED YOKO OKINO! ♡ ALL THE BIGGEST IDOLS ARE HERE!
DAD! KEEP IT DOWN! YOU SOUND SO TACKY!
I'M NOT THE ONE WHO BROUGHT AN *AUTOGRAPH BOOK*...
...
ARE YOU SURE THIS IS OKAY? WE WEREN'T REALLY INVITED TO THIS PARTY...
DON'T SWEAT IT! YER DAD'S A CELEBRITY TOO!
YOU AIN'T THE PROBLEM...
WHAT'S WRONG WITH HARLEY?

*Except for Yoko Okino, these are all pop stars who have recorded songs for the *Case Closed!* anime. Minami Takayama, lead singer of Two-Mix, is also the voice of Conan.

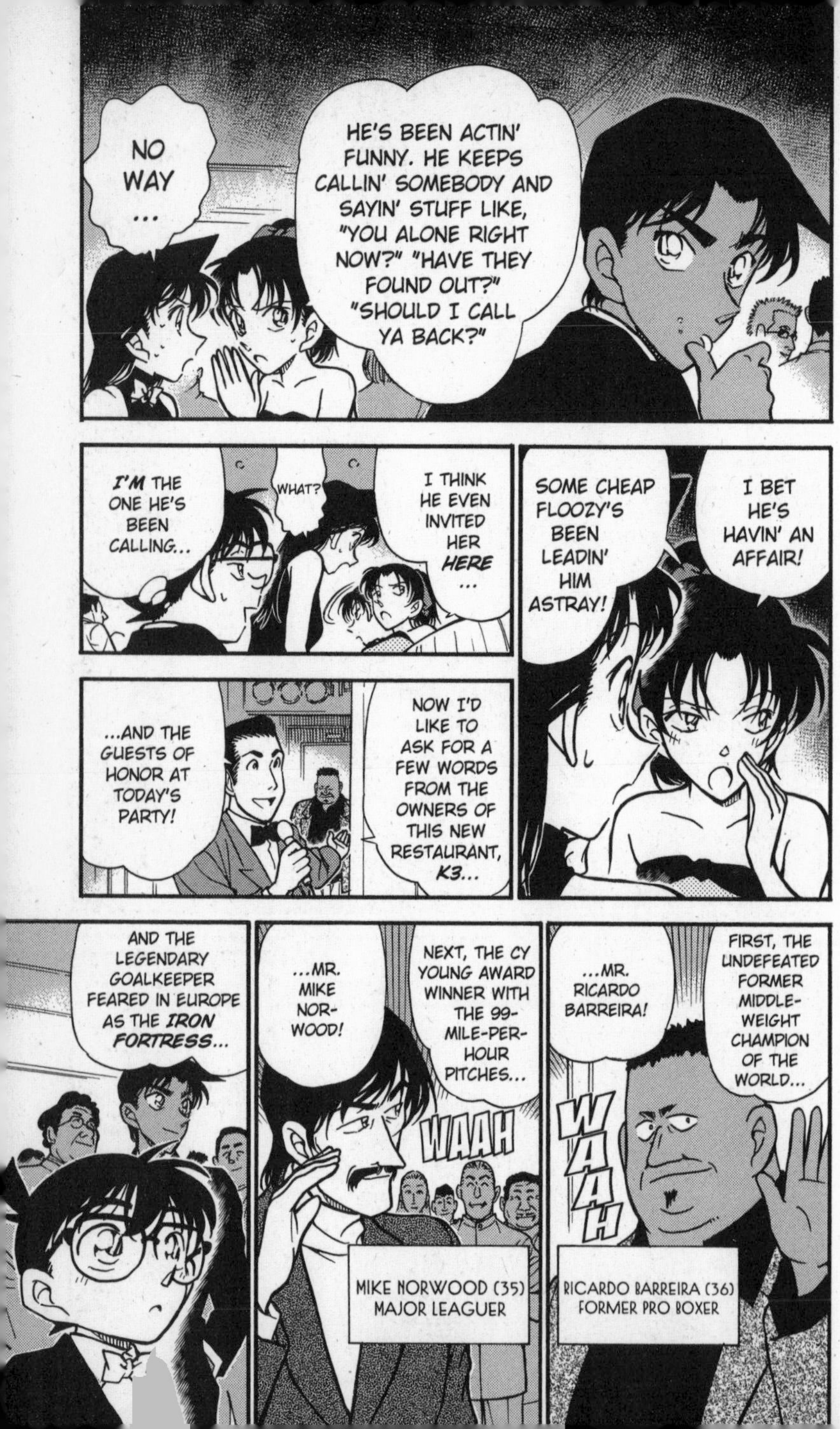
HE'S BEEN ACTIN' FUNNY. HE KEEPS CALLIN' SOMEBODY AND SAYIN' STUFF LIKE, "YOU ALONE RIGHT NOW?" "HAVE THEY FOUND OUT?" "SHOULD I CALL YA BACK?"
NO WAY ...
I BET HE'S HAVIN' AN AFFAIR!
SOME CHEAP FLOOZY'S BEEN LEADIN' HIM ASTRAY!
I THINK HE EVEN INVITED HER *HERE* ...
WHAT?
I'M THE ONE HE'S BEEN CALLING...
NOW I'D LIKE TO ASK FOR A FEW WORDS FROM THE OWNERS OF THIS NEW RESTAURANT, *K3*...
...AND THE GUESTS OF HONOR AT TODAY'S PARTY!
FIRST, THE UNDEFEATED FORMER MIDDLE-WEIGHT CHAMPION OF THE WORLD...
...MR. RICARDO BARREIRA!
WAAH
RICARDO BARREIRA (36)
FORMER PRO BOXER
NEXT, THE CY YOUNG AWARD WINNER WITH THE 99-MILE-PER-HOUR PITCHES...
...MR. MIKE NOR-WOOD!
WAAH
MIKE NORWOOD (35)
MAJOR LEAGUER
AND THE LEGENDARY GOALKEEPER FEARED IN EUROPE AS THE *IRON FORTRESS*...

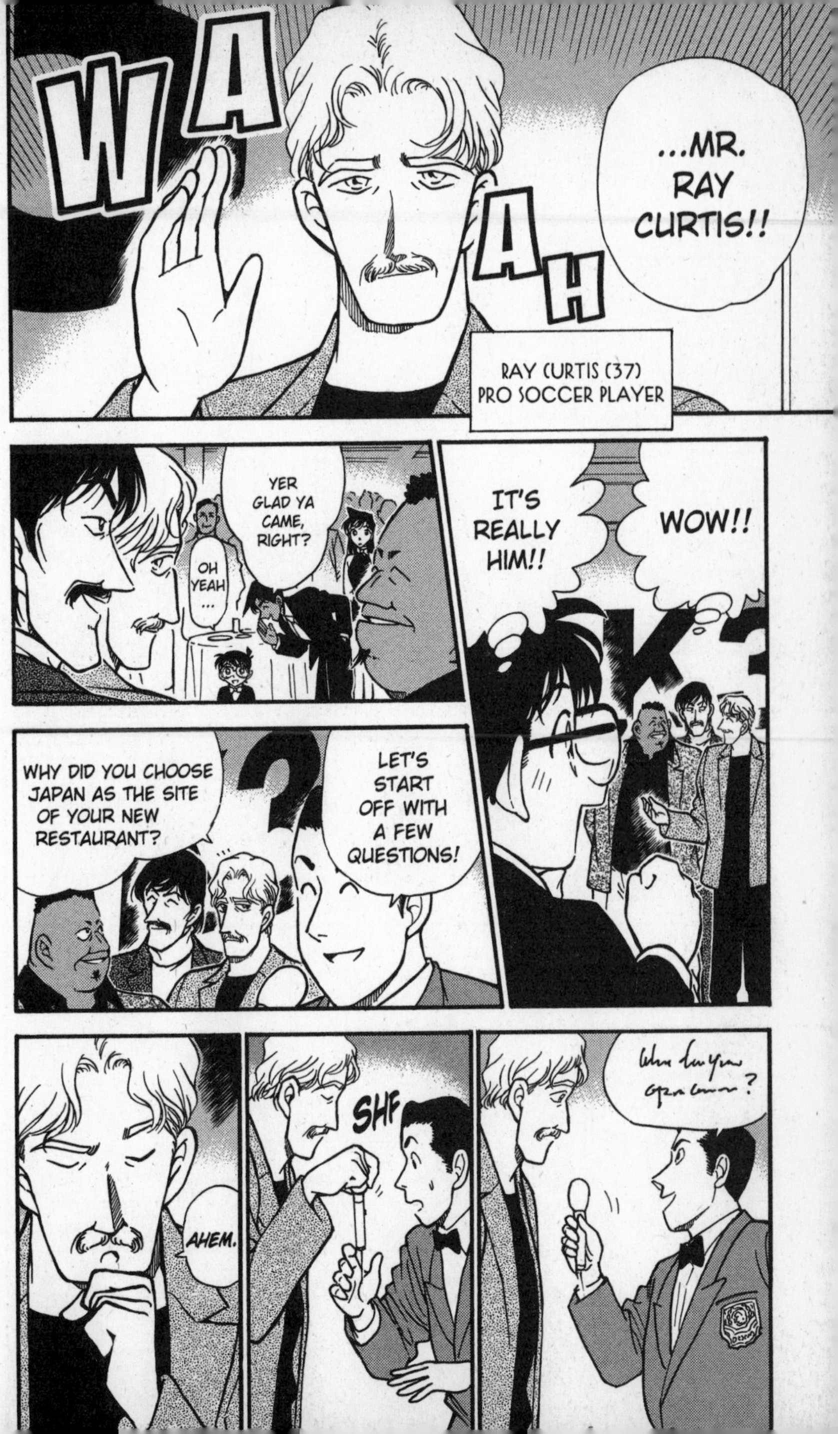
...MR. RAY CURTIS!!
WAAH
RAY CURTIS (37) PRO SOCCER PLAYER
WOW!!
IT'S REALLY HIM!!
YER GLAD YA CAME, RIGHT?
OH YEAH ...
LET'S START OFF WITH A FEW QUESTIONS!
WHY DID YOU CHOOSE JAPAN AS THE SITE OF YOUR NEW RESTAURANT?
SHF
AHEM.

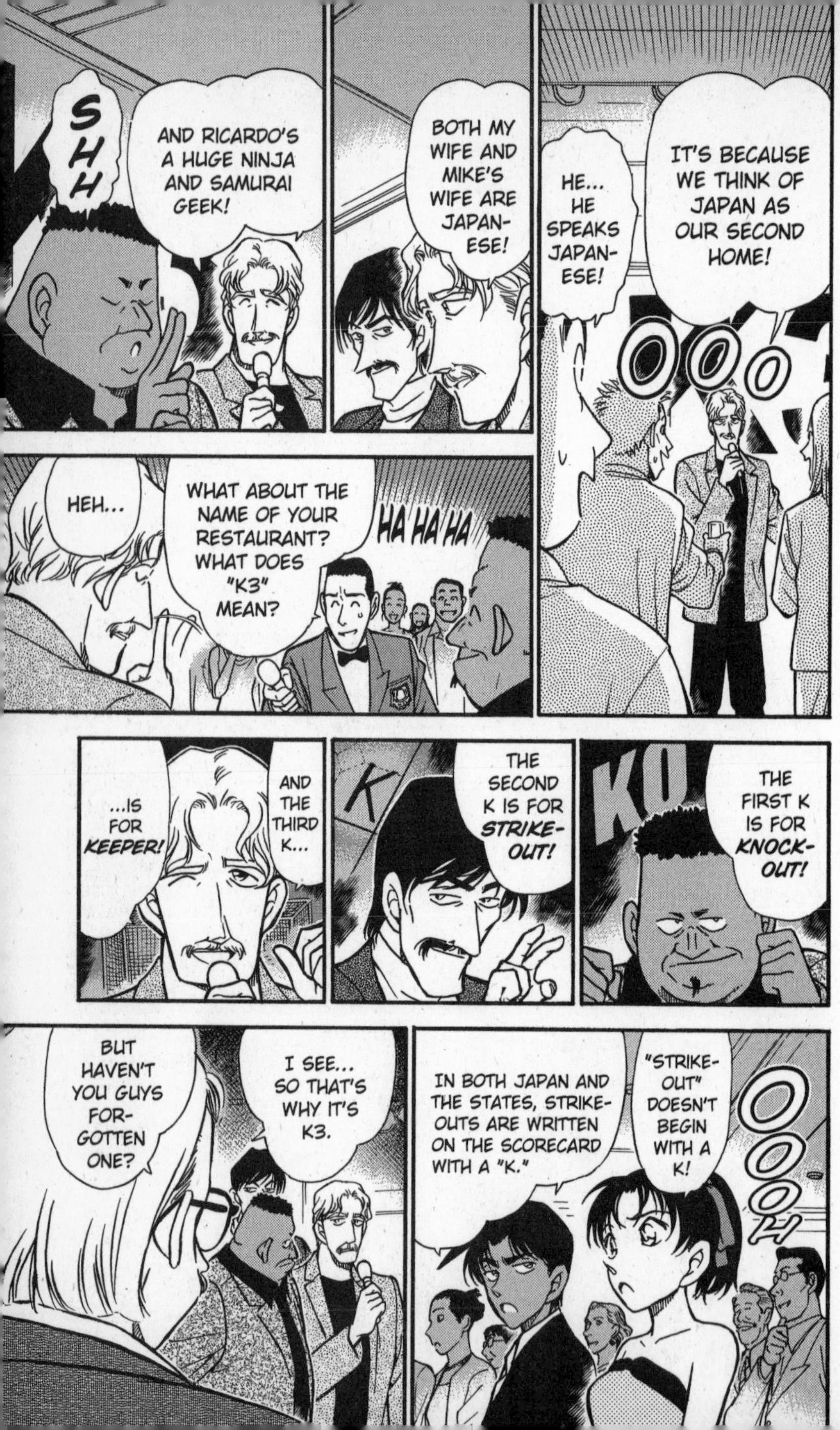

IT'S BECAUSE WE THINK OF JAPAN AS OUR SECOND HOME!
HE... HE SPEAKS JAPAN-ESE!
OOO
BOTH MY WIFE AND MIKE'S WIFE ARE JAPAN-ESE!
AND RICARDO'S A HUGE NINJA AND SAMURAI GEEK!
SHH
HA HA HA
WHAT ABOUT THE NAME OF YOUR RESTAURANT? WHAT DOES "K3" MEAN?
HEH...
KO
THE FIRST K IS FOR KNOCK-OUT!
K
THE SECOND K IS FOR STRIKE-OUT!
AND THE THIRD K...
...IS FOR KEEPER!
OOOH
"STRIKE-OUT" DOESN'T BEGIN WITH A K!
IN BOTH JAPAN AND THE STATES, STRIKE-OUTS ARE WRITTEN ON THE SCORECARD WITH A "K."
I SEE... SO THAT'S WHY IT'S K3.
BUT HAVEN'T YOU GUYS FOR-GOTTEN ONE?

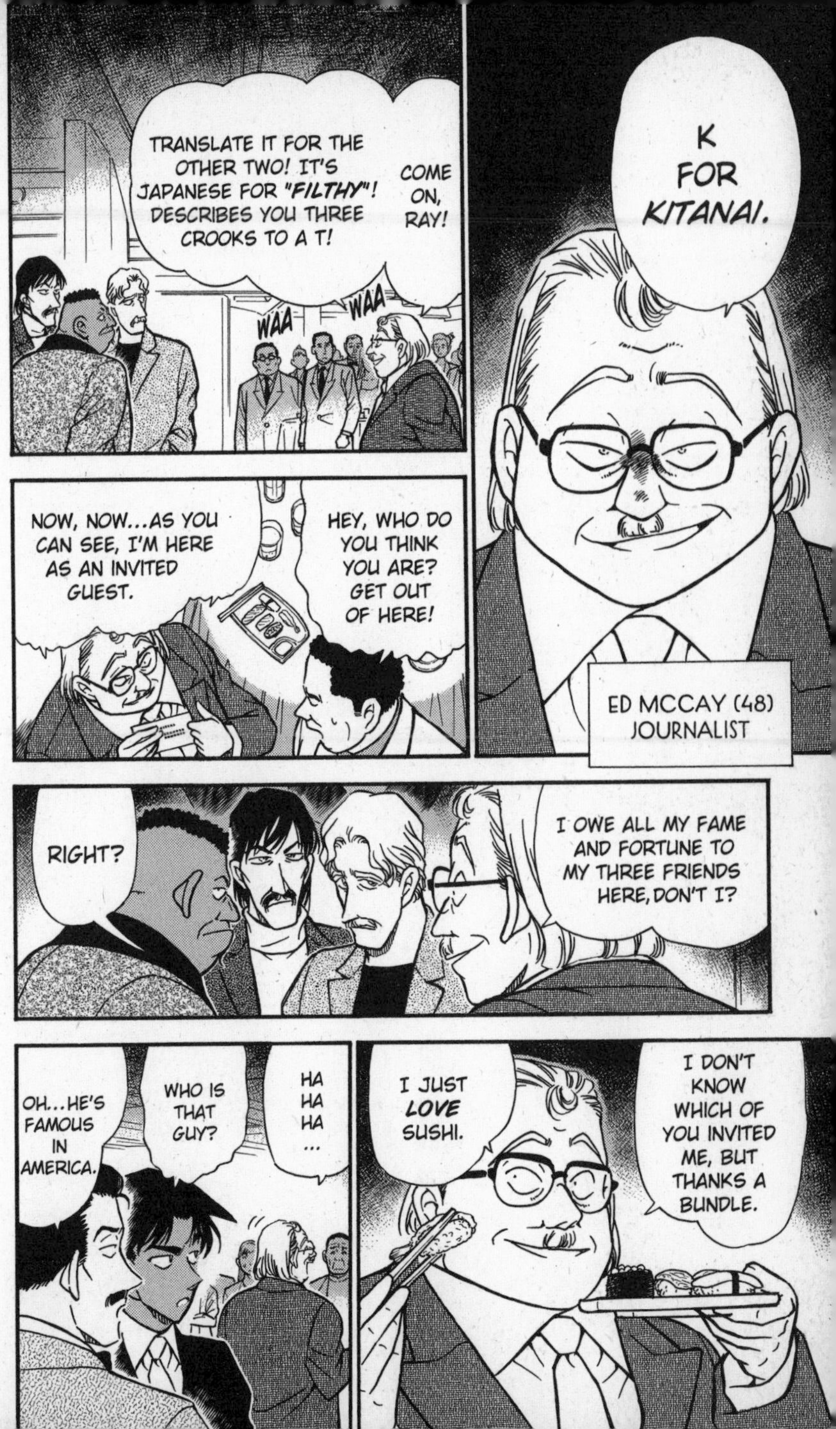
K FOR KITANAI.
ED MCCAY (48) JOURNALIST
COME ON, RAY!
TRANSLATE IT FOR THE OTHER TWO! IT'S JAPANESE FOR "FILTHY"! DESCRIBES YOU THREE CROOKS TO A T!
WAA
WAA
HEY, WHO DO YOU THINK YOU ARE? GET OUT OF HERE!
NOW, NOW...AS YOU CAN SEE, I'M HERE AS AN INVITED GUEST.
I OWE ALL MY FAME AND FORTUNE TO MY THREE FRIENDS HERE, DON'T I?
RIGHT?
I DON'T KNOW WHICH OF YOU INVITED ME, BUT THANKS A BUNDLE.
I JUST LOVE SUSHI.
HA HA HA ...
WHO IS THAT GUY?
OH...HE'S FAMOUS IN AMERICA.

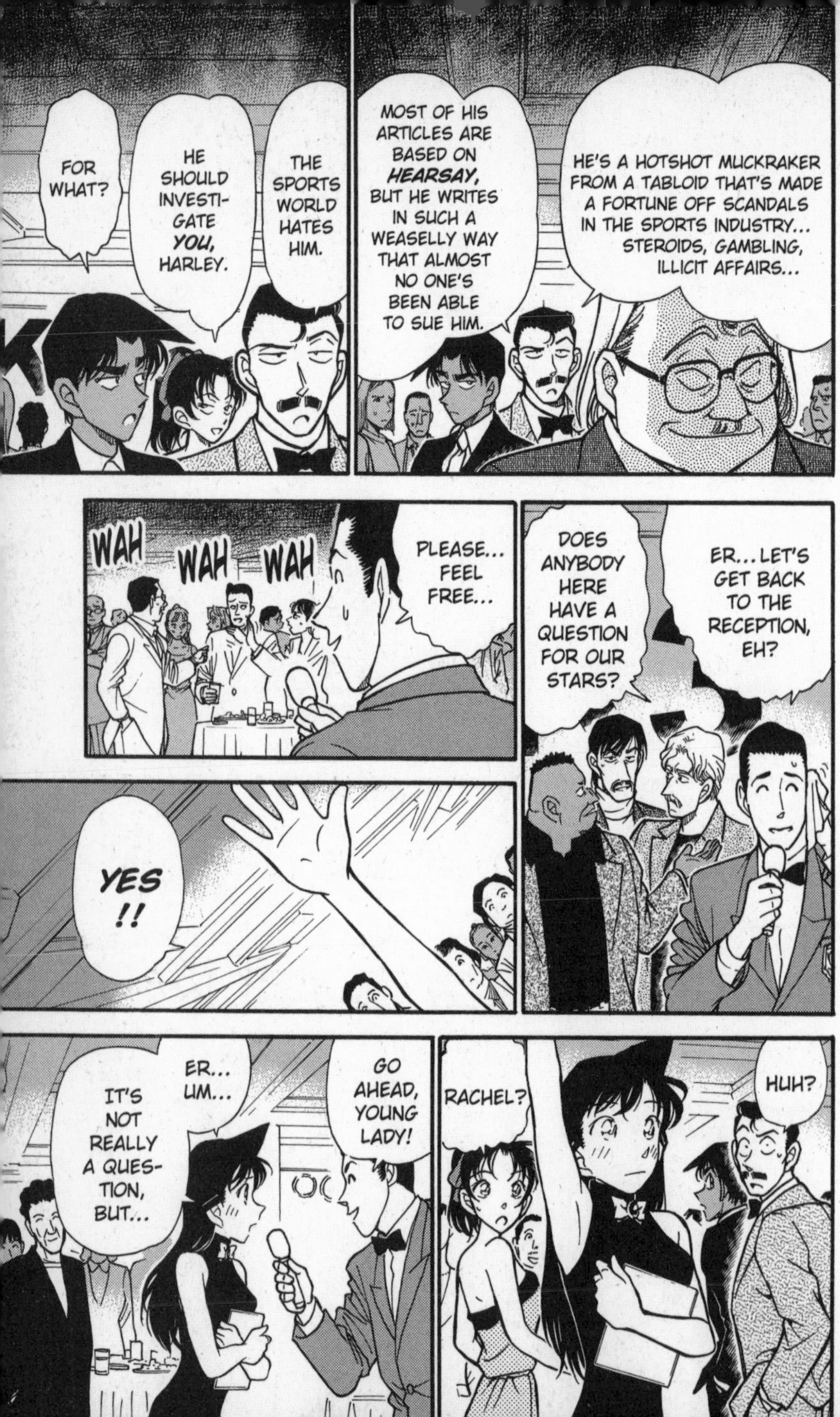
HE'S A HOTSHOT MUCKRAKER FROM A TABLOID THAT'S MADE A FORTUNE OFF SCANDALS IN THE SPORTS INDUSTRY... STEROIDS, GAMBLING, ILLICIT AFFAIRS...
MOST OF HIS ARTICLES ARE BASED ON ***HEARSAY,*** BUT HE WRITES IN SUCH A WEASELLY WAY THAT ALMOST NO ONE'S BEEN ABLE TO SUE HIM.
THE SPORTS WORLD HATES HIM.
HE SHOULD INVESTIGATE ***YOU,*** HARLEY.
FOR WHAT?
ER... LET'S GET BACK TO THE RECEPTION, EH?
DOES ANYBODY HERE HAVE A QUESTION FOR OUR STARS?
PLEASE... FEEL FREE...
WAH
WAH
WAH
YES !!
HUH?
RACHEL?
GO AHEAD, YOUNG LADY!
ER... UM...
IT'S NOT REALLY A QUESTION, BUT...

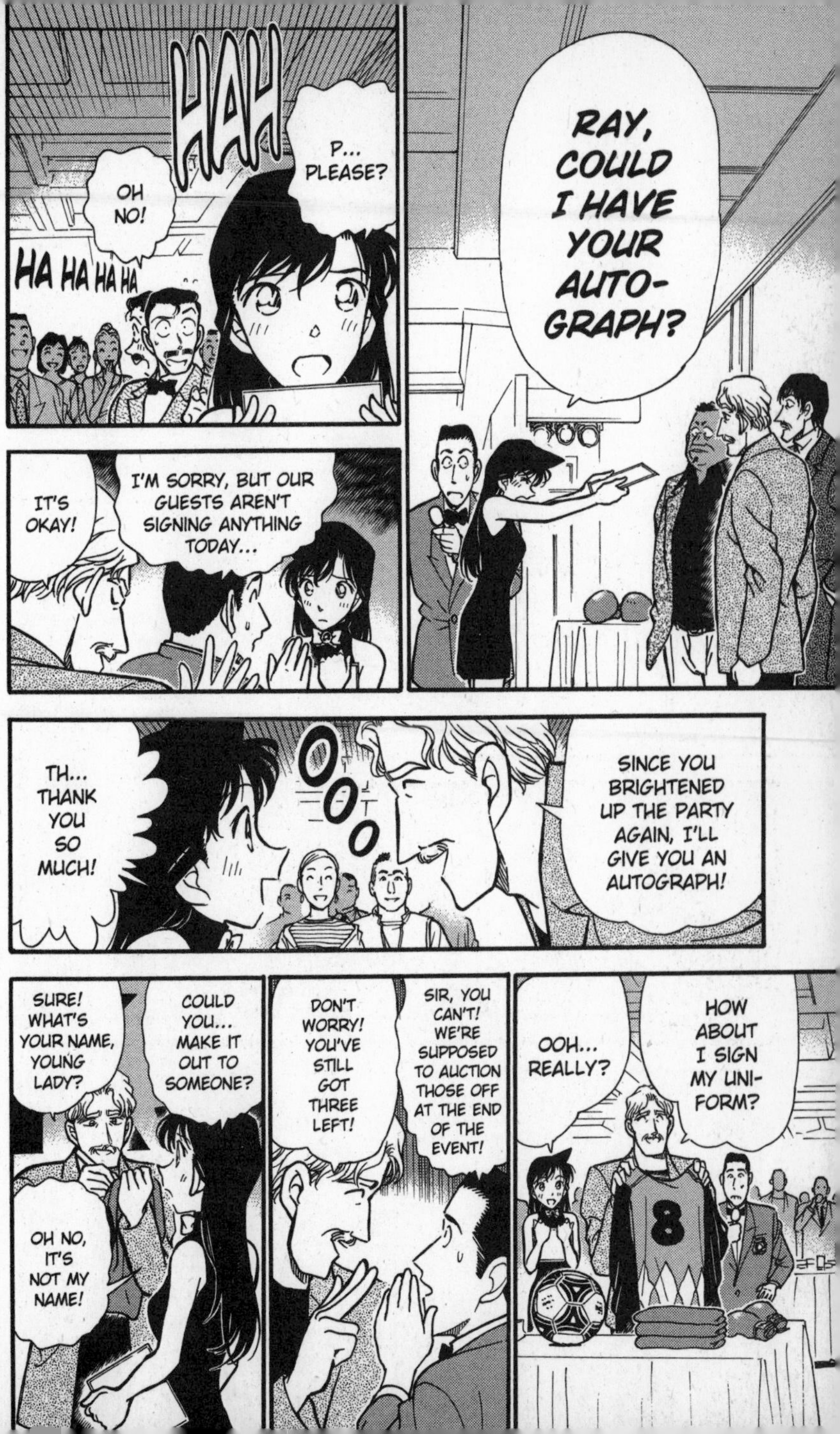
RAY, COULD I HAVE YOUR AUTO-GRAPH?
HAH
P... PLEASE?
OH NO!
HA HA HA HA
I'M SORRY, BUT OUR GUESTS AREN'T SIGNING ANYTHING TODAY...
IT'S OKAY!
SINCE YOU BRIGHTENED UP THE PARTY AGAIN, I'LL GIVE YOU AN AUTOGRAPH!
OOO
TH... THANK YOU SO MUCH!
HOW ABOUT I SIGN MY UNI-FORM?
OOH... REALLY?
SIR, YOU CAN'T! WE'RE SUPPOSED TO AUCTION THOSE OFF AT THE END OF THE EVENT!
DON'T WORRY! YOU'VE STILL GOT THREE LEFT!
COULD YOU... MAKE IT OUT TO SOMEONE?
SURE! WHAT'S YOUR NAME, YOUNG LADY?
OH NO, IT'S NOT MY NAME!

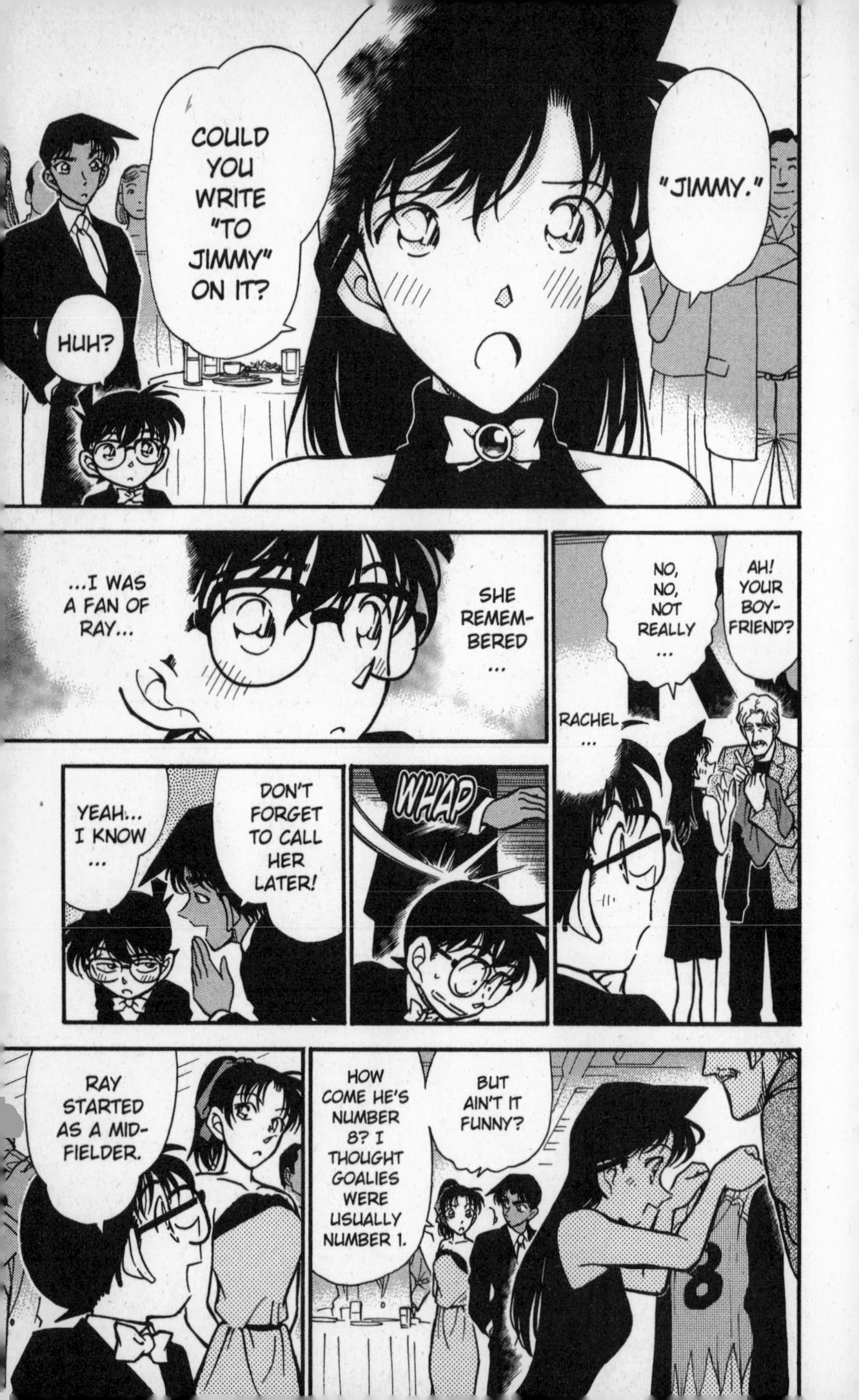
"JIMMY."
COULD YOU WRITE "TO JIMMY" ON IT?
HUH?
AH! YOUR BOY-FRIEND?
NO, NO, NOT REALLY ...
RACHEL ...
SHE REMEMBERED ...
...I WAS A FAN OF RAY...
WHAP
DON'T FORGET TO CALL HER LATER!
YEAH... I KNOW ...
BUT AIN'T IT FUNNY?
HOW COME HE'S NUMBER 8? I THOUGHT GOALIES WERE USUALLY NUMBER 1.
RAY STARTED AS A MID-FIELDER.

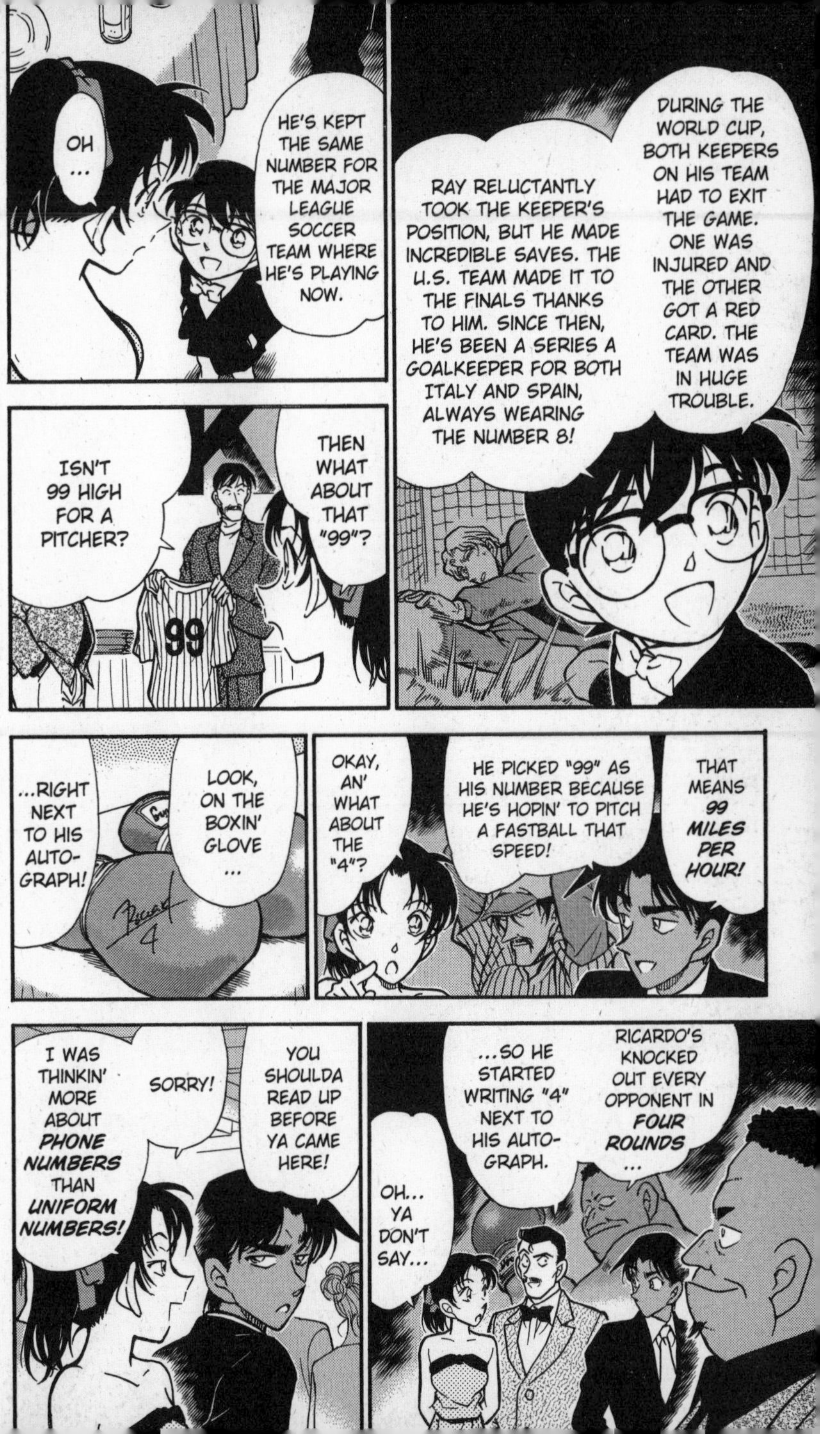
DURING THE WORLD CUP, BOTH KEEPERS ON HIS TEAM HAD TO EXIT THE GAME. ONE WAS INJURED AND THE OTHER GOT A RED CARD. THE TEAM WAS IN HUGE TROUBLE.
RAY RELUCTANTLY TOOK THE KEEPER'S POSITION, BUT HE MADE INCREDIBLE SAVES. THE U.S. TEAM MADE IT TO THE FINALS THANKS TO HIM. SINCE THEN, HE'S BEEN A SERIES A GOALKEEPER FOR BOTH ITALY AND SPAIN, ALWAYS WEARING THE NUMBER 8!
HE'S KEPT THE SAME NUMBER FOR THE MAJOR LEAGUE SOCCER TEAM WHERE HE'S PLAYING NOW.
OH ...
THEN WHAT ABOUT THAT "99"?
ISN'T 99 HIGH FOR A PITCHER?
THAT MEANS *99 MILES PER HOUR!*
HE PICKED "99" AS HIS NUMBER BECAUSE HE'S HOPIN' TO PITCH A FASTBALL THAT SPEED!
OKAY, AN' WHAT ABOUT THE "4"?
LOOK, ON THE BOXIN' GLOVE ...
...RIGHT NEXT TO HIS AUTO-GRAPH!
RICARDO'S KNOCKED OUT EVERY OPPONENT IN *FOUR ROUNDS* ...
...SO HE STARTED WRITING "4" NEXT TO HIS AUTO-GRAPH.
OH... YA DON'T SAY...
YOU SHOULDA READ UP BEFORE YA CAME HERE!
SORRY!
I WAS THINKIN' MORE ABOUT *PHONE NUMBERS* THAN *UNIFORM NUMBERS!*

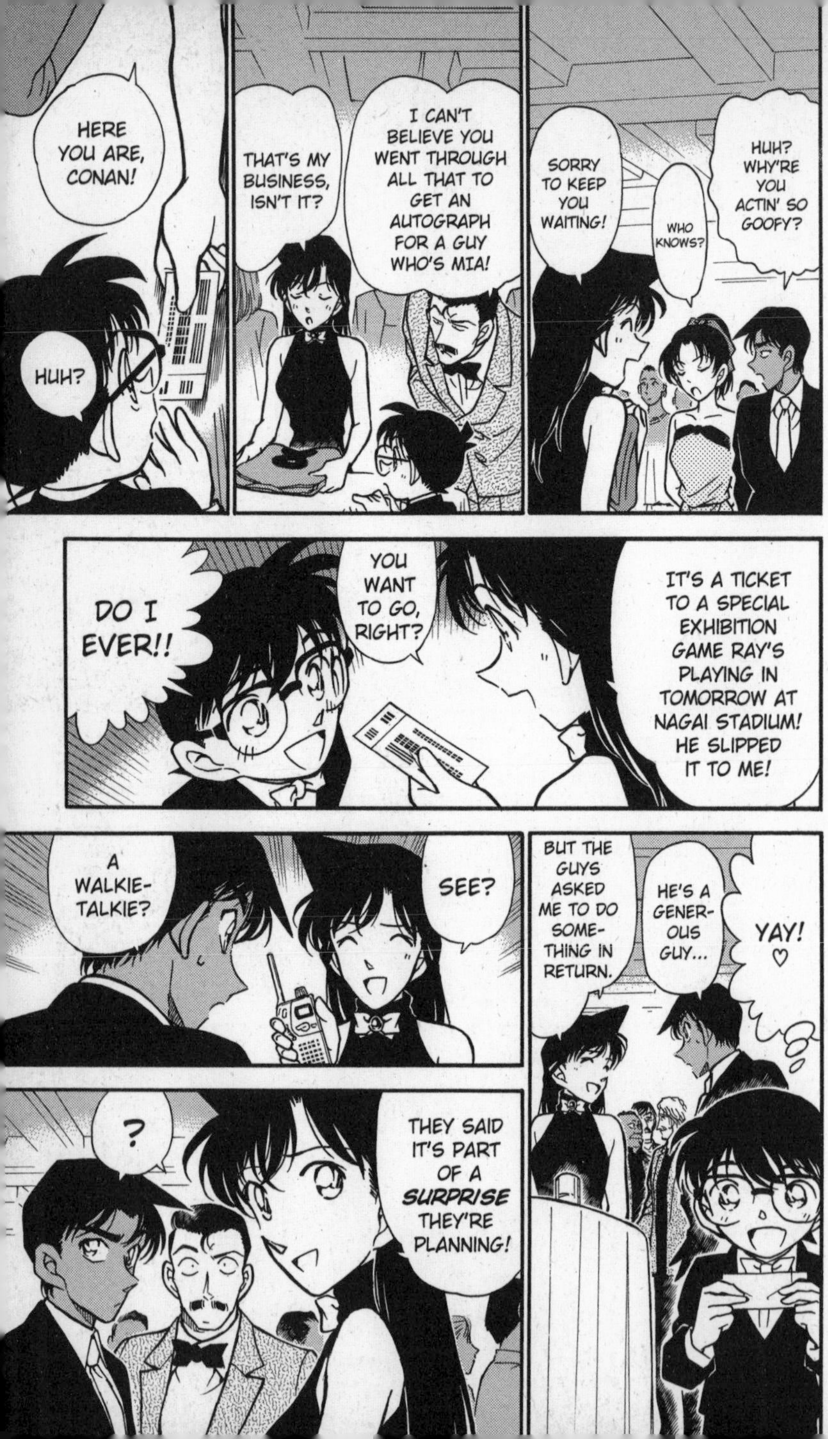
HUH? WHY'RE YOU ACTIN' SO GOOFY?
WHO KNOWS?
SORRY TO KEEP YOU WAITING!
I CAN'T BELIEVE YOU WENT THROUGH ALL THAT TO GET AN AUTOGRAPH FOR A GUY WHO'S MIA!
THAT'S MY BUSINESS, ISN'T IT?
HERE YOU ARE, CONAN!
HUH?
IT'S A TICKET TO A SPECIAL EXHIBITION GAME RAY'S PLAYING IN TOMORROW AT NAGAI STADIUM! HE SLIPPED IT TO ME!
YOU WANT TO GO, RIGHT?
DO I EVER!!
YAY! ♡
HE'S A GENER-OUS GUY...
BUT THE GUYS ASKED ME TO DO SOME-THING IN RETURN.
SEE?
A WALKIE-TALKIE?
THEY SAID IT'S PART OF A SURPRISE THEY'RE PLANNING!
?

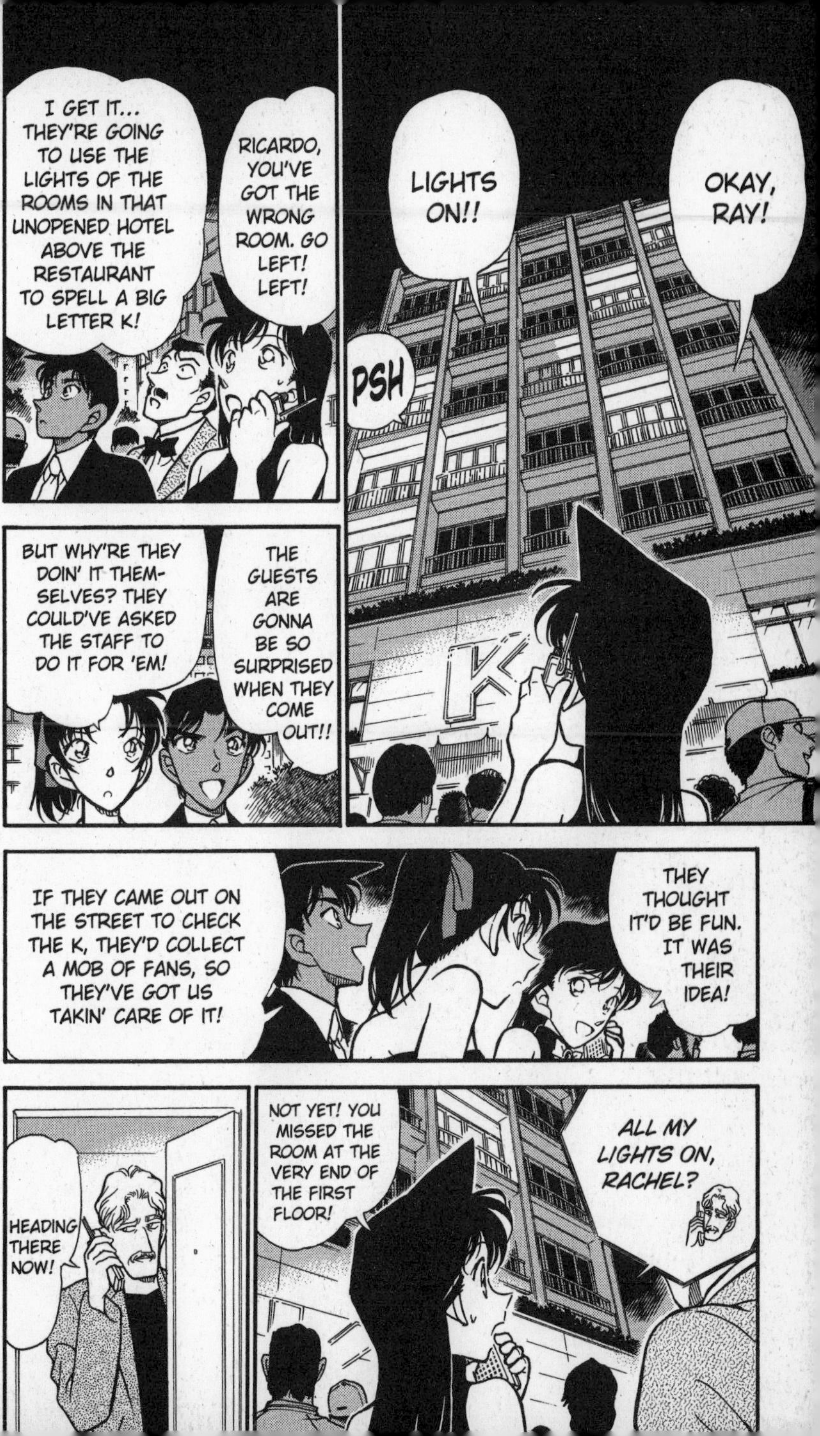
OKAY, RAY!
LIGHTS ON!!
PSH
RICARDO, YOU'VE GOT THE WRONG ROOM. GO LEFT! LEFT!
I GET IT... THEY'RE GOING TO USE THE LIGHTS OF THE ROOMS IN THAT UNOPENED HOTEL ABOVE THE RESTAURANT TO SPELL A BIG LETTER K!
THE GUESTS ARE GONNA BE SO SURPRISED WHEN THEY COME OUT!!
BUT WHY'RE THEY DOIN' IT THEM-SELVES? THEY COULD'VE ASKED THE STAFF TO DO IT FOR 'EM!
THEY THOUGHT IT'D BE FUN. IT WAS THEIR IDEA!
IF THEY CAME OUT ON THE STREET TO CHECK THE K, THEY'D COLLECT A MOB OF FANS, SO THEY'VE GOT US TAKIN' CARE OF IT!
ALL MY LIGHTS ON, RACHEL?
NOT YET! YOU MISSED THE ROOM AT THE VERY END OF THE FIRST FLOOR!
HEADING THERE NOW!

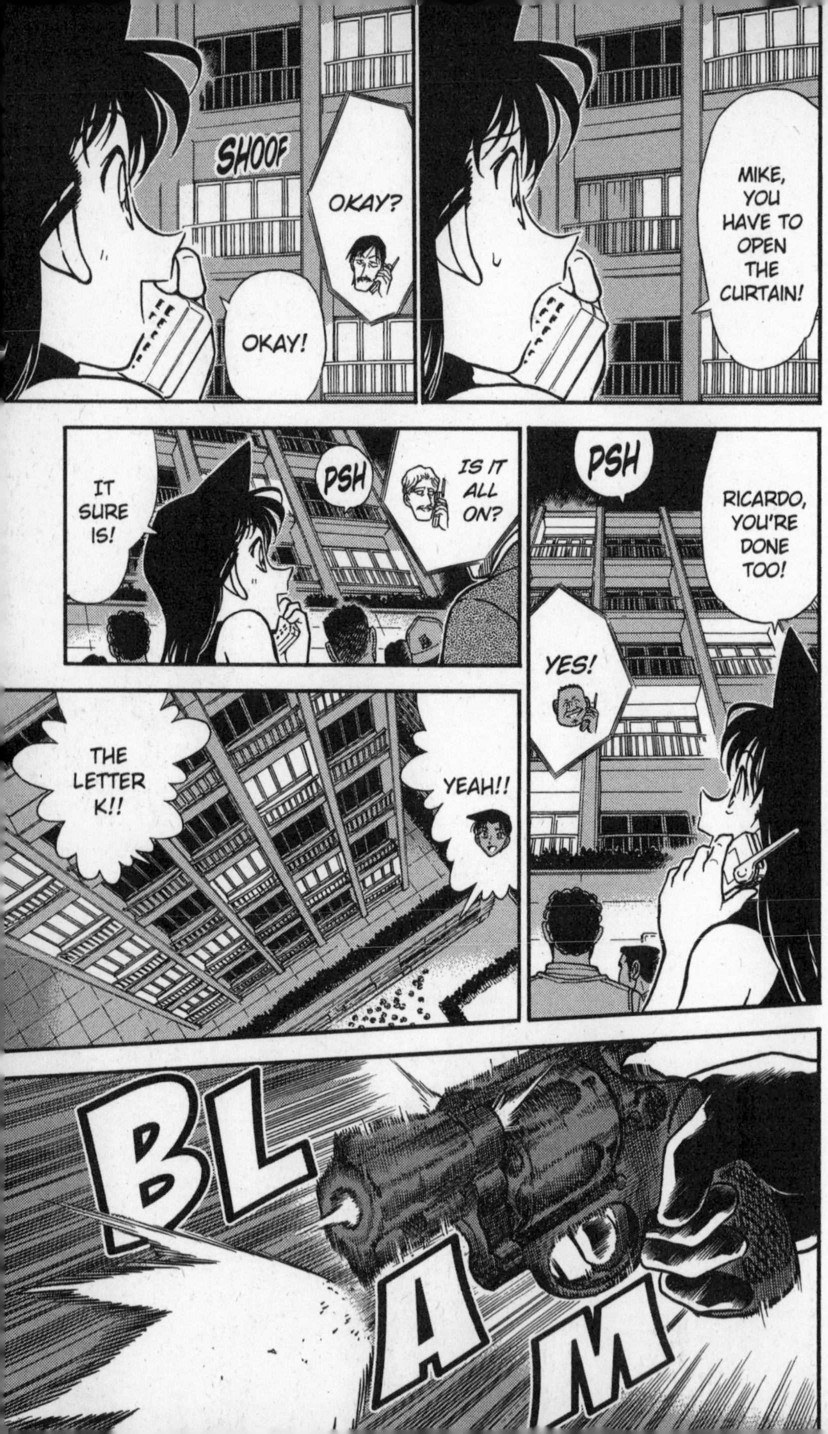
MIKE, YOU HAVE TO OPEN THE CURTAIN!
OKAY?
SHOOF
OKAY!
RICARDO, YOU'RE DONE TOO!
PSH
YES!
IS IT ALL ON?
PSH
IT SURE IS!
YEAH!!
THE LETTER K!!
BLAM

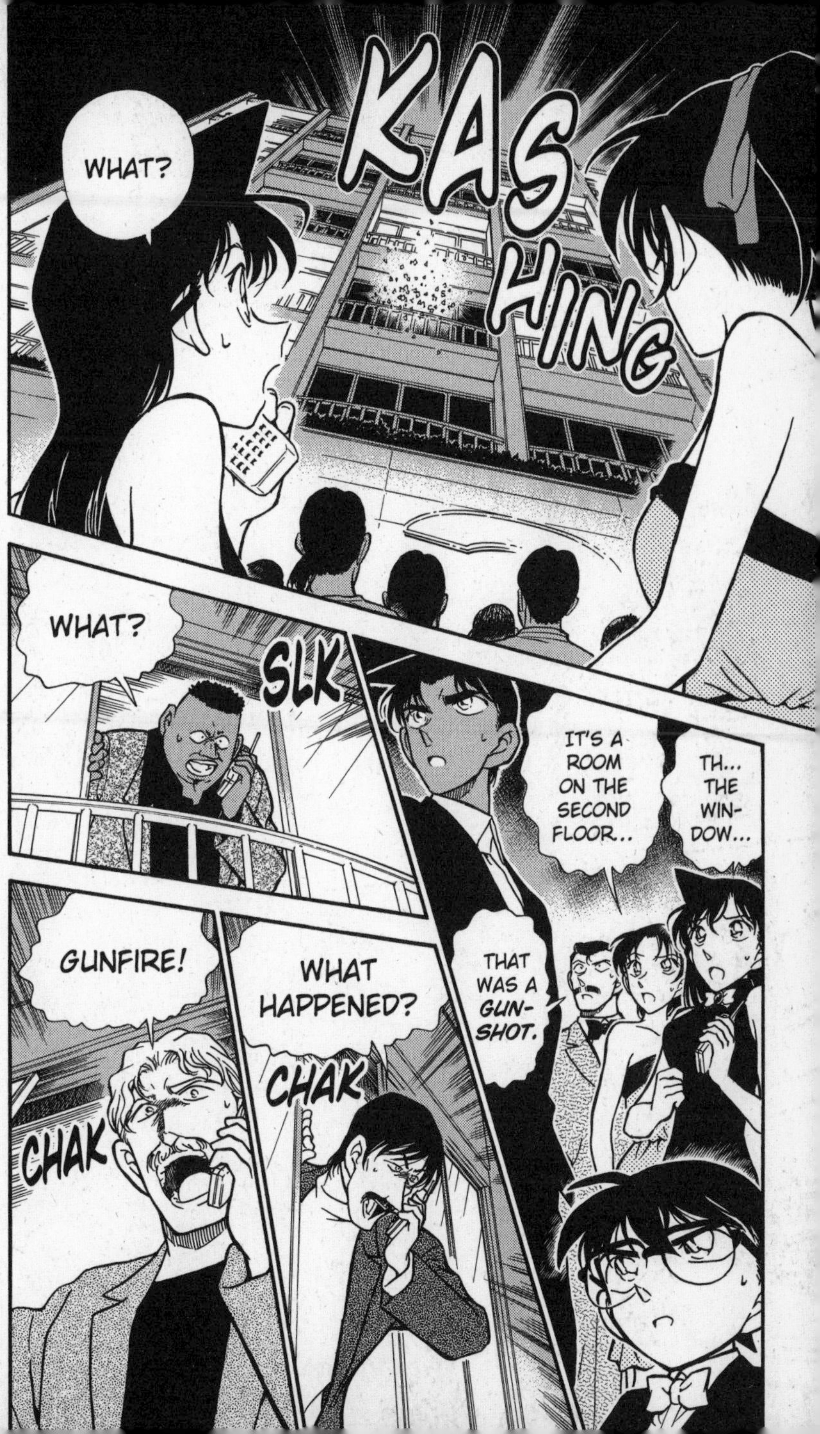
KAS HING
WHAT?
TH... THE WIN-DOW...
IT'S A ROOM ON THE SECOND FLOOR...
THAT WAS A GUN-SHOT.
SLK
WHAT?
WHAT HAPPENED?
CHAK
GUNFIRE!
CHAK

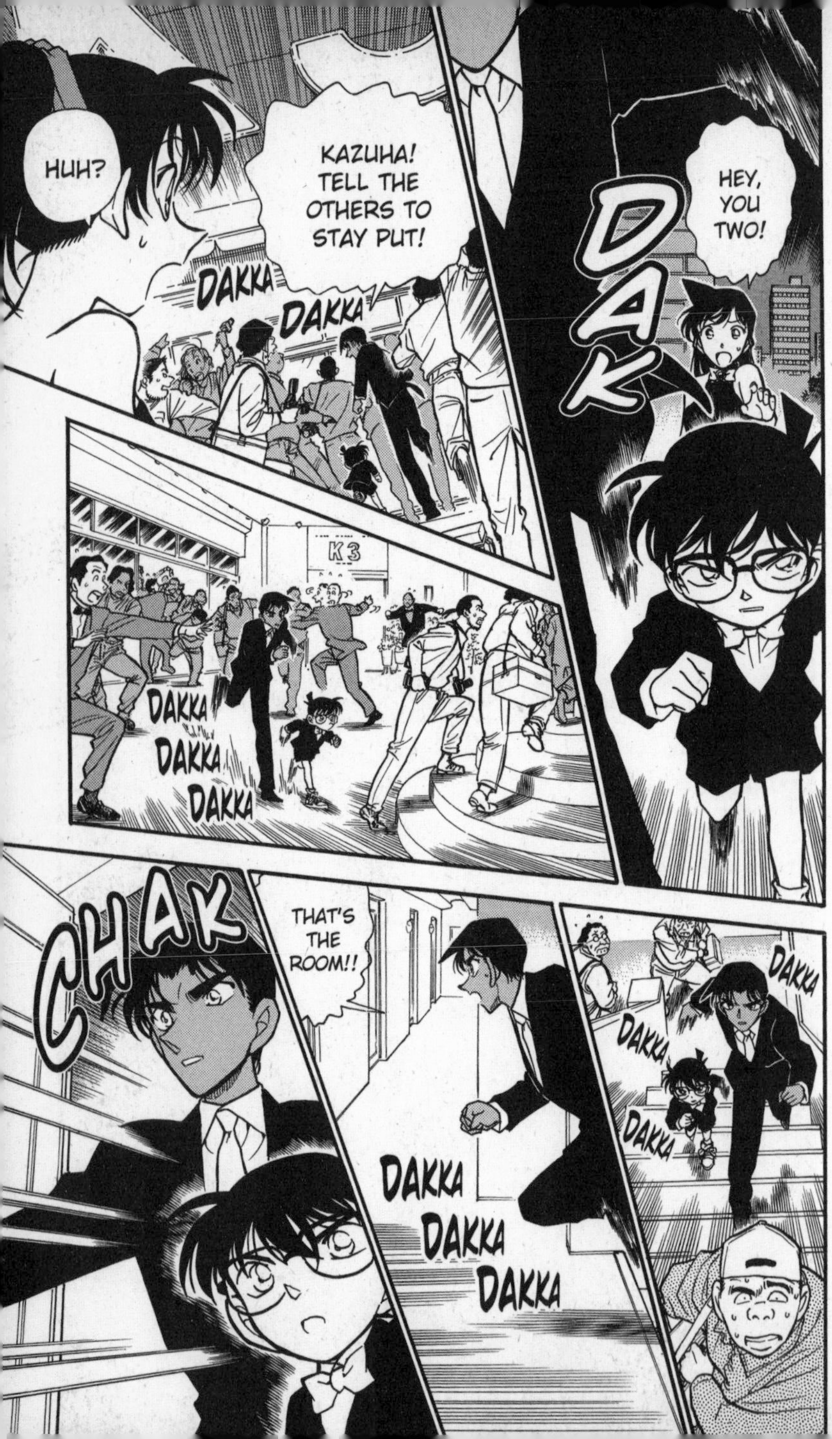
HEY, YOU TWO!
DAK
KAZUHA! TELL THE OTHERS TO STAY PUT!
HUH?
DAKKA
DAKKA
DAKKA
DAKKA
DAKKA
DAKKA
DAKKA
DAKKA
THAT'S THE ROOM!!
DAKKA
DAKKA
DAKKA
CHAK

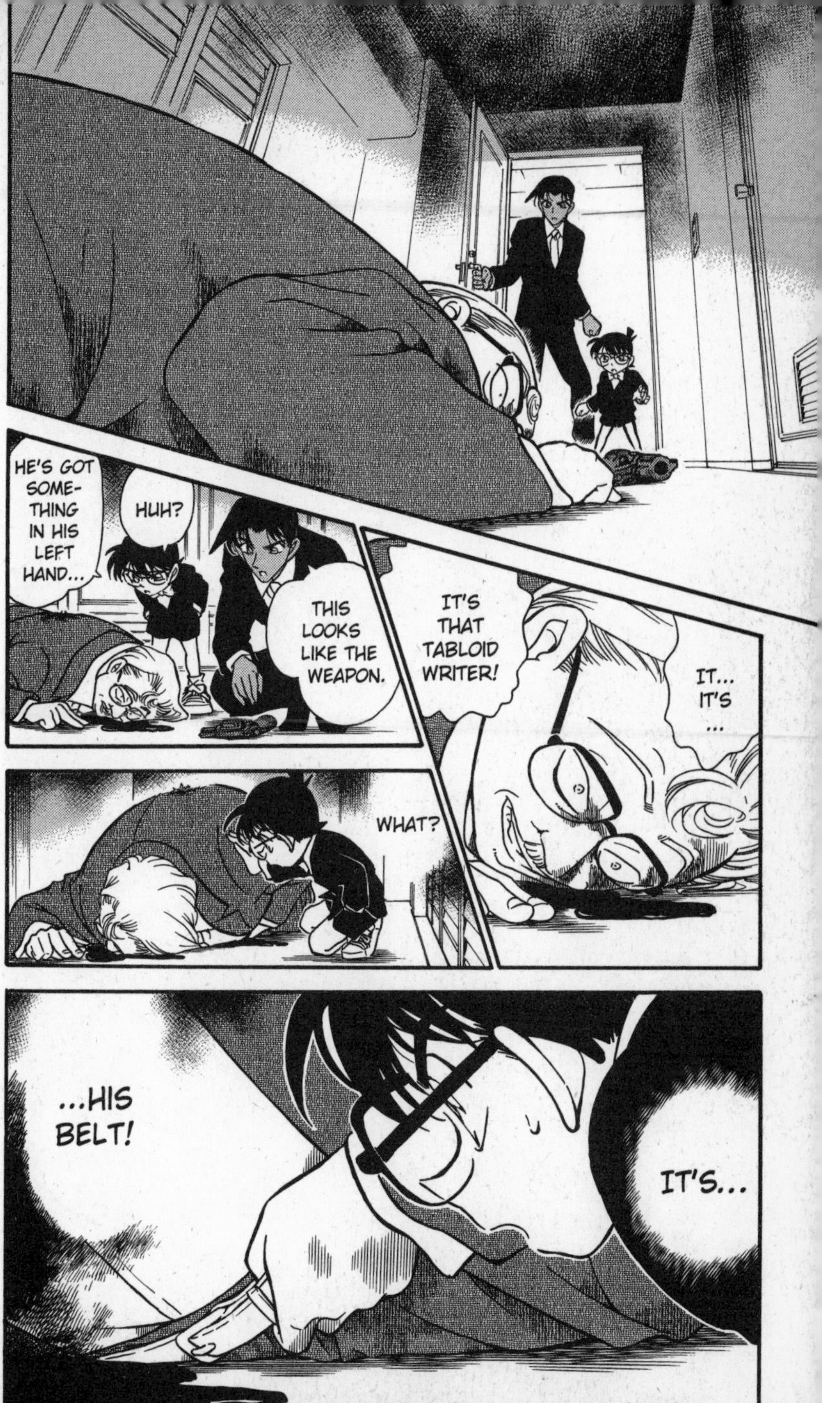
IT... IT'S ...
IT'S THAT TABLOID WRITER!
THIS LOOKS LIKE THE WEAPON.
HUH?
HE'S GOT SOME-THING IN HIS LEFT HAND...
WHAT?
IT'S...
...HIS BELT!

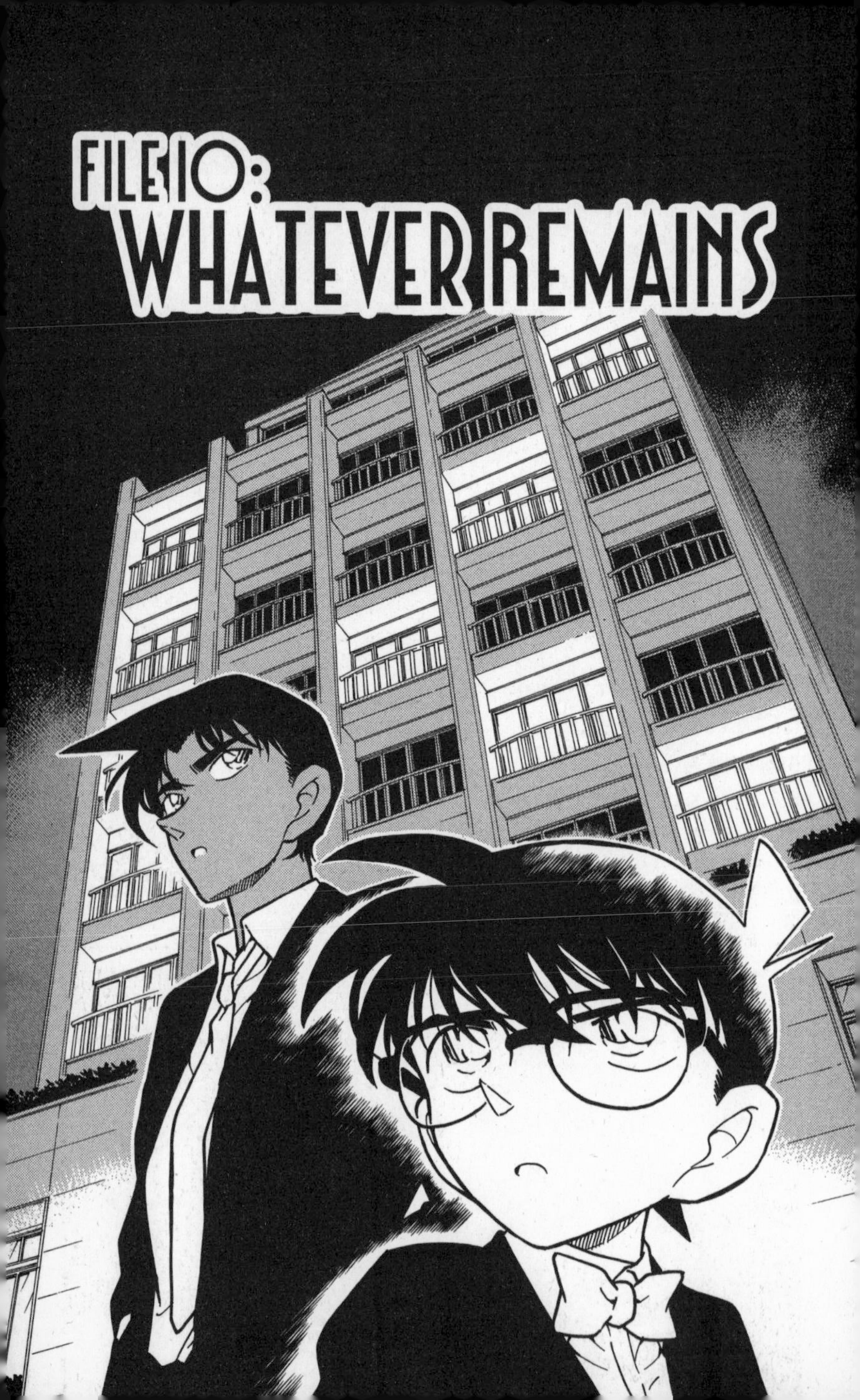
FILE 10:
WHATEVER REMAINS

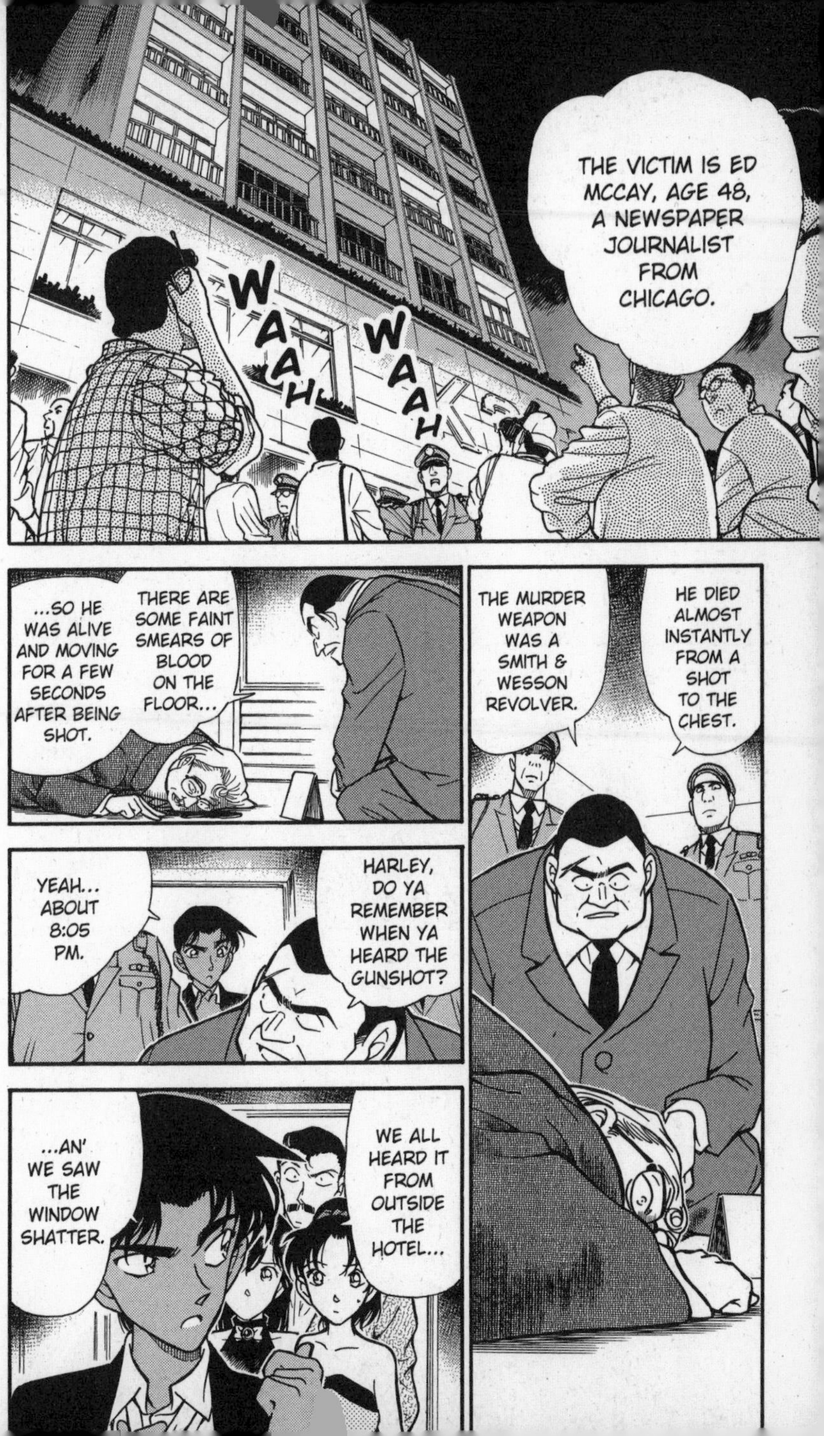
THE VICTIM IS ED MCCAY, AGE 48, A NEWSPAPER JOURNALIST FROM CHICAGO.
WAAH
WAAH
HE DIED ALMOST INSTANTLY FROM A SHOT TO THE CHEST.
THE MURDER WEAPON WAS A SMITH & WESSON REVOLVER.
THERE ARE SOME FAINT SMEARS OF BLOOD ON THE FLOOR...
...SO HE WAS ALIVE AND MOVING FOR A FEW SECONDS AFTER BEING SHOT.
HARLEY, DO YA REMEMBER WHEN YA HEARD THE GUNSHOT?
YEAH... ABOUT 8:05 PM.
WE ALL HEARD IT FROM OUTSIDE THE HOTEL...
...AN' WE SAW THE WINDOW SHATTER.

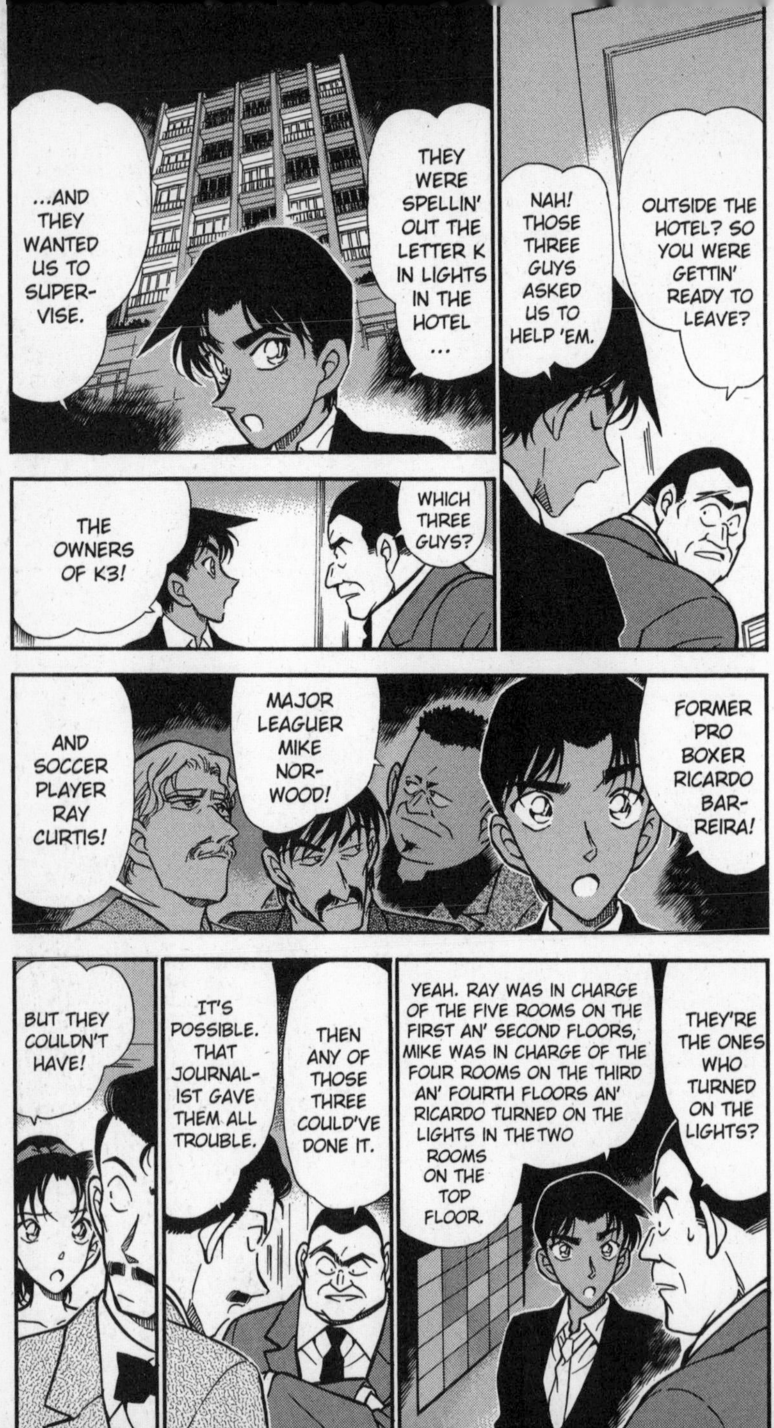
OUTSIDE THE HOTEL? SO YOU WERE GETTIN' READY TO LEAVE?
NAH! THOSE THREE GUYS ASKED US TO HELP 'EM.
THEY WERE SPELLIN' OUT THE LETTER K IN LIGHTS IN THE HOTEL ...
...AND THEY WANTED US TO SUPER-VISE.
WHICH THREE GUYS?
THE OWNERS OF K3!
FORMER PRO BOXER RICARDO BAR-REIRA!
MAJOR LEAGUER MIKE NOR-WOOD!
AND SOCCER PLAYER RAY CURTIS!
THEY'RE THE ONES WHO TURNED ON THE LIGHTS?
YEAH. RAY WAS IN CHARGE OF THE FIVE ROOMS ON THE FIRST AN' SECOND FLOORS, MIKE WAS IN CHARGE OF THE FOUR ROOMS ON THE THIRD AN' FOURTH FLOORS AN' RICARDO TURNED ON THE LIGHTS IN THE TWO ROOMS ON THE TOP FLOOR.
THEN ANY OF THOSE THREE COULD'VE DONE IT.
IT'S POSSIBLE. THAT JOURNAL-IST GAVE THEM ALL TROUBLE.
BUT THEY COULDN'T HAVE!

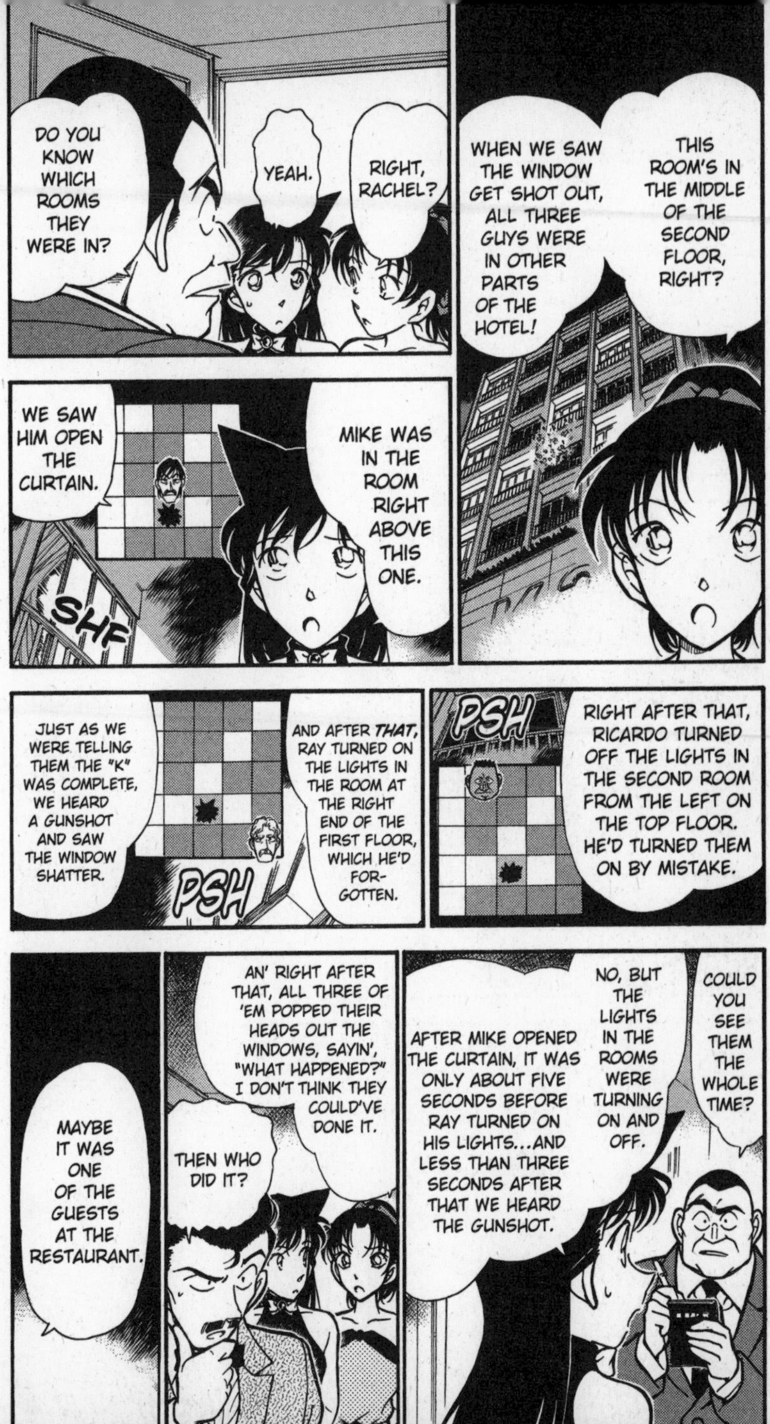
THIS ROOM'S IN THE MIDDLE OF THE SECOND FLOOR, RIGHT?
WHEN WE SAW THE WINDOW GET SHOT OUT, ALL THREE GUYS WERE IN OTHER PARTS OF THE HOTEL!
RIGHT, RACHEL?
YEAH.
DO YOU KNOW WHICH ROOMS THEY WERE IN?
MIKE WAS IN THE ROOM RIGHT ABOVE THIS ONE.
WE SAW HIM OPEN THE CURTAIN.
SHF
PSH
RIGHT AFTER THAT, RICARDO TURNED OFF THE LIGHTS IN THE SECOND ROOM FROM THE LEFT ON THE TOP FLOOR. HE'D TURNED THEM ON BY MISTAKE.
AND AFTER *THAT*, RAY TURNED ON THE LIGHTS IN THE ROOM AT THE RIGHT END OF THE FIRST FLOOR, WHICH HE'D FOR-GOTTEN.
PSH
JUST AS WE WERE TELLING THEM THE "K" WAS COMPLETE, WE HEARD A GUNSHOT AND SAW THE WINDOW SHATTER.
COULD YOU SEE THEM THE WHOLE TIME?
NO, BUT THE LIGHTS IN THE ROOMS WERE TURNING ON AND OFF.
AFTER MIKE OPENED THE CURTAIN, IT WAS ONLY ABOUT FIVE SECONDS BEFORE RAY TURNED ON HIS LIGHTS...AND LESS THAN THREE SECONDS AFTER THAT WE HEARD THE GUNSHOT.
AN' RIGHT AFTER THAT, ALL THREE OF 'EM POPPED THEIR HEADS OUT THE WINDOWS, SAYIN', "WHAT HAPPENED?" I DON'T THINK THEY COULD'VE DONE IT.
THEN WHO DID IT?
MAYBE IT WAS ONE OF THE GUESTS AT THE RESTAURANT.

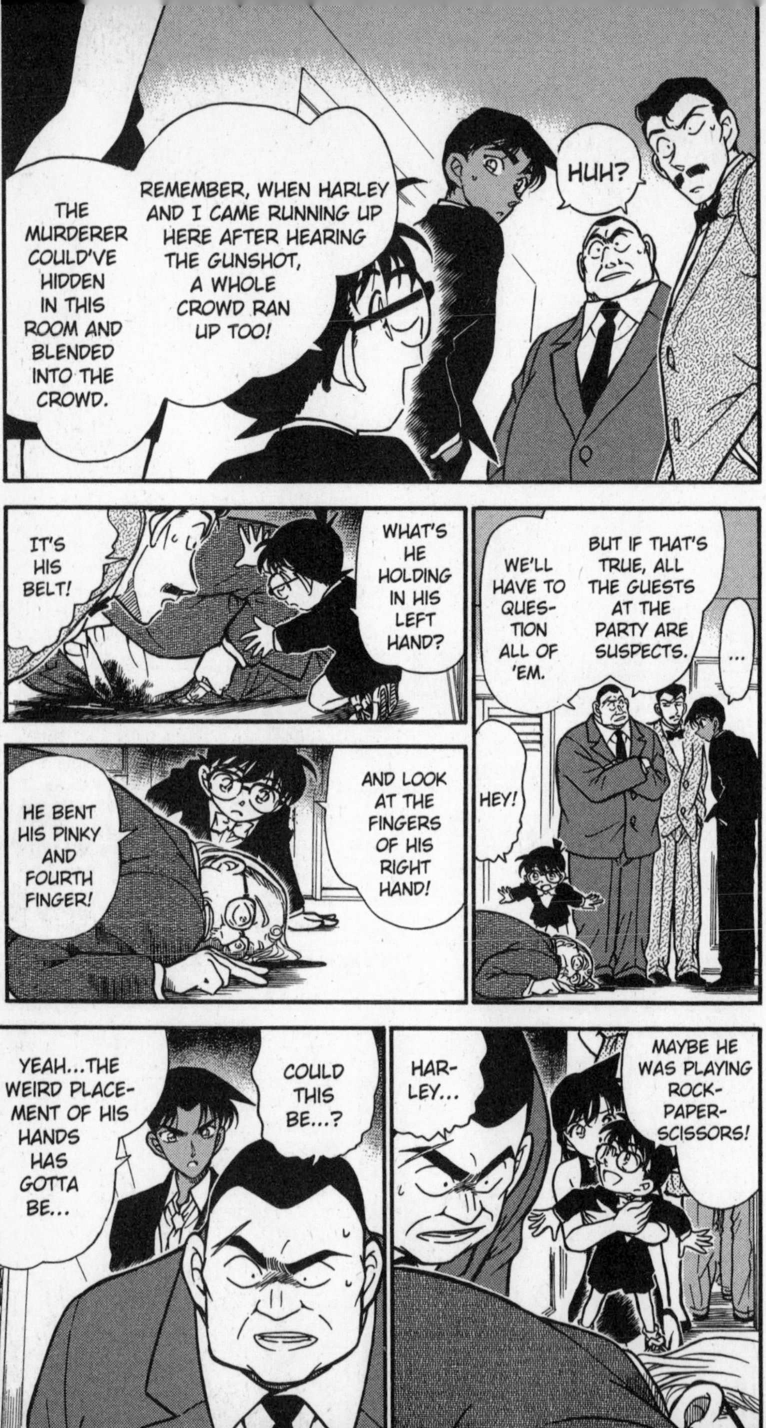
HUH?
REMEMBER, WHEN HARLEY AND I CAME RUNNING UP HERE AFTER HEARING THE GUNSHOT, A WHOLE CROWD RAN UP TOO!
THE MURDERER COULD'VE HIDDEN IN THIS ROOM AND BLENDED INTO THE CROWD.
BUT IF THAT'S TRUE, ALL THE GUESTS AT THE PARTY ARE SUSPECTS.
WE'LL HAVE TO QUES-TION ALL OF 'EM.
...
HEY!
WHAT'S HE HOLDING IN HIS LEFT HAND?
IT'S HIS BELT!
AND LOOK AT THE FINGERS OF HIS RIGHT HAND!
HE BENT HIS PINKY AND FOURTH FINGER!
MAYBE HE WAS PLAYING ROCK-PAPER-SCISSORS!
HAR-LEY...
COULD THIS BE...?
YEAH...THE WEIRD PLACE-MENT OF HIS HANDS HAS GOTTA BE...

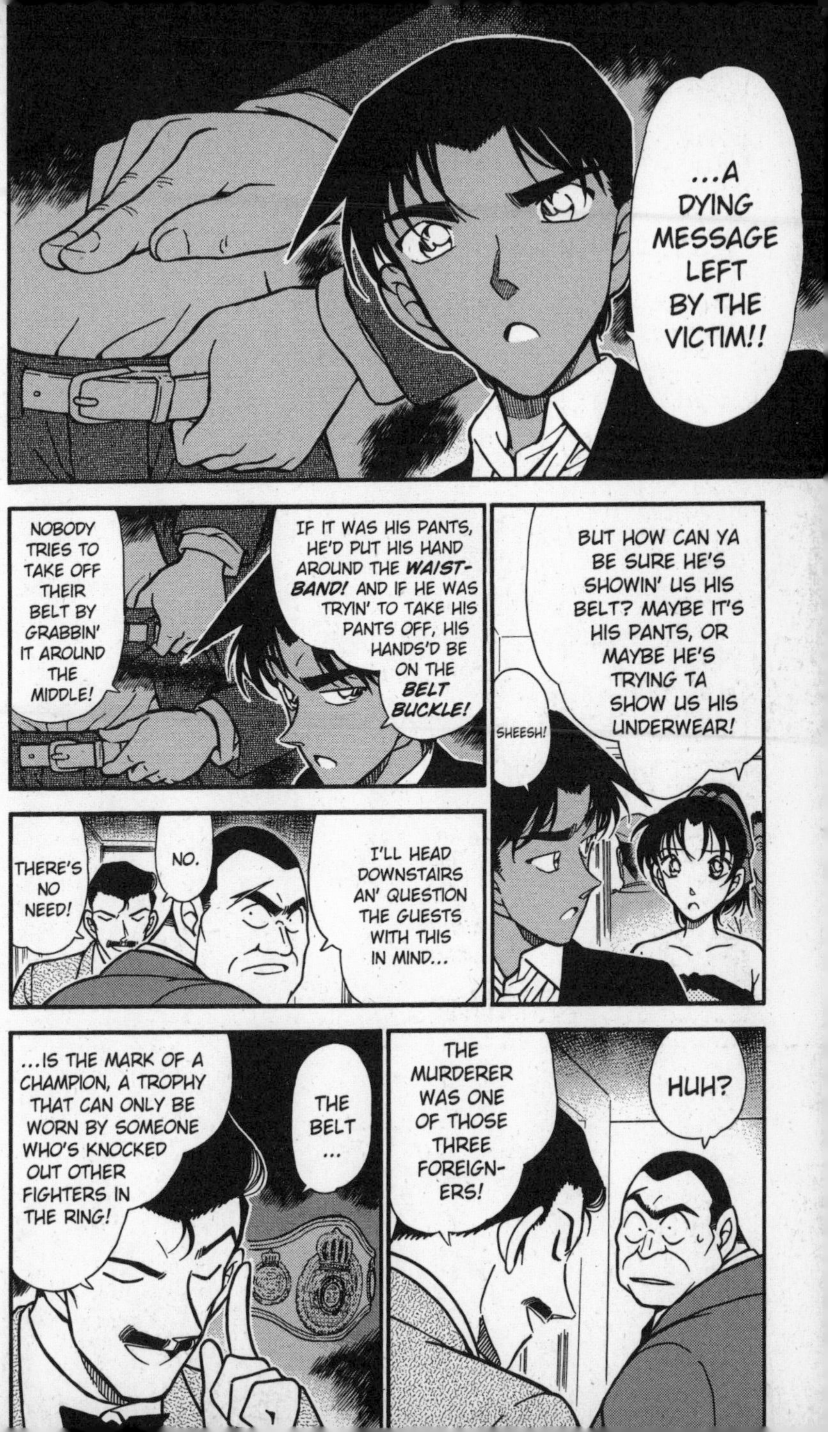
...A DYING MESSAGE LEFT BY THE VICTIM!!
BUT HOW CAN YA BE SURE HE'S SHOWIN' US HIS BELT? MAYBE IT'S HIS PANTS, OR MAYBE HE'S TRYING TA SHOW US HIS UNDERWEAR!
SHEESH!
IF IT WAS HIS PANTS, HE'D PUT HIS HAND AROUND THE WAIST-BAND! AND IF HE WAS TRYIN' TO TAKE HIS PANTS OFF, HIS HANDS'D BE ON THE BELT BUCKLE!
NOBODY TRIES TO TAKE OFF THEIR BELT BY GRABBIN' IT AROUND THE MIDDLE!
I'LL HEAD DOWNSTAIRS AN' QUESTION THE GUESTS WITH THIS IN MIND...
NO.
THERE'S NO NEED!
HUH?
THE MURDERER WAS ONE OF THOSE THREE FOREIGN-ERS!
THE BELT ...
...IS THE MARK OF A CHAMPION, A TROPHY THAT CAN ONLY BE WORN BY SOMEONE WHO'S KNOCKED OUT OTHER FIGHTERS IN THE RING!

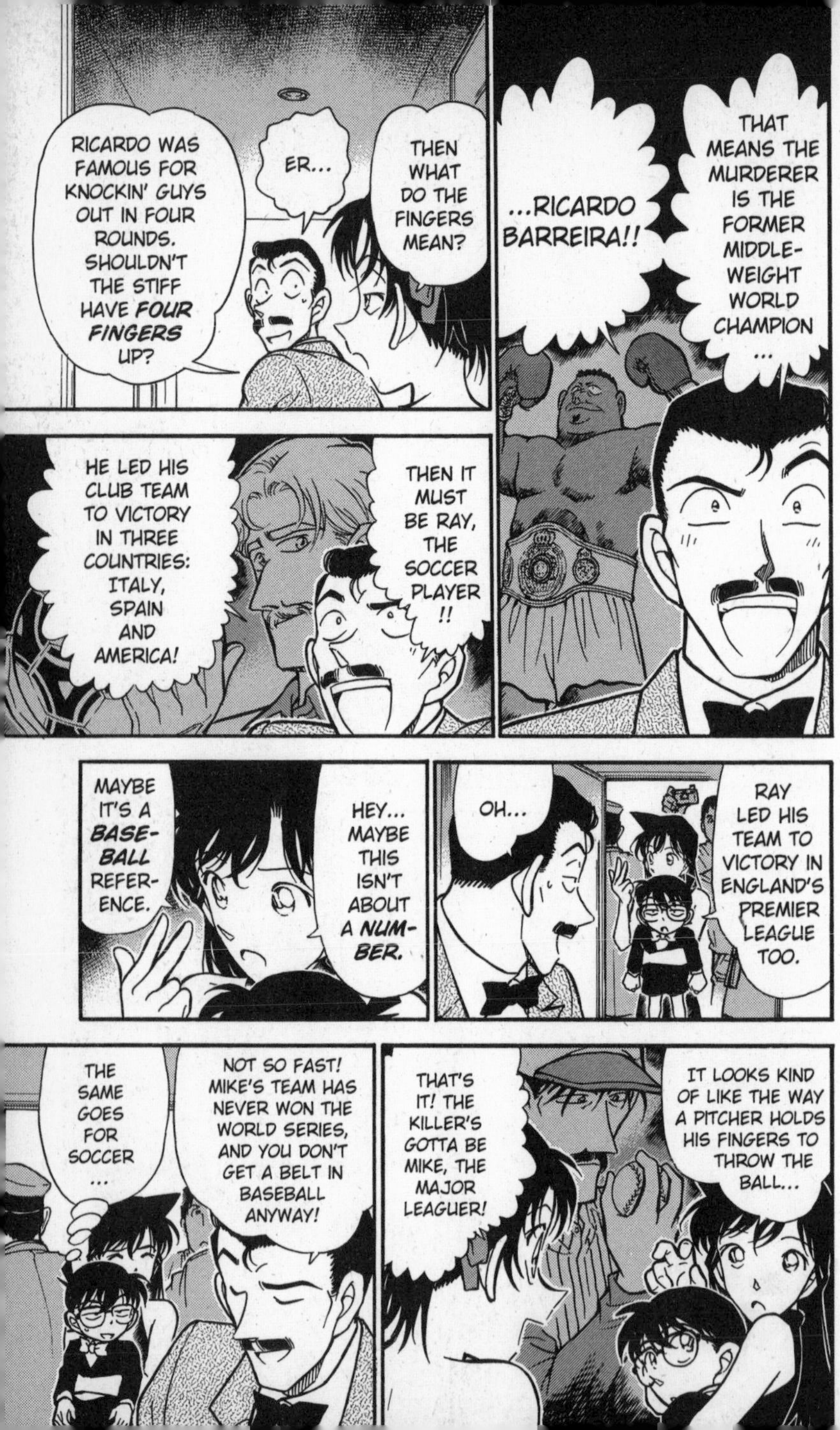
THAT MEANS THE MURDERER IS THE FORMER MIDDLE-WEIGHT WORLD CHAMPION ...
...RICARDO BARREIRA!!
THEN WHAT DO THE FINGERS MEAN?
ER...
RICARDO WAS FAMOUS FOR KNOCKIN' GUYS OUT IN FOUR ROUNDS. SHOULDN'T THE STIFF HAVE FOUR FINGERS UP?
THEN IT MUST BE RAY, THE SOCCER PLAYER !!
HE LED HIS CLUB TEAM TO VICTORY IN THREE COUNTRIES: ITALY, SPAIN AND AMERICA!
RAY LED HIS TEAM TO VICTORY IN ENGLAND'S PREMIER LEAGUE TOO.
OH...
HEY... MAYBE THIS ISN'T ABOUT A NUM-BER.
MAYBE IT'S A BASE-BALL REFER-ENCE.
IT LOOKS KIND OF LIKE THE WAY A PITCHER HOLDS HIS FINGERS TO THROW THE BALL...
THAT'S IT! THE KILLER'S GOTTA BE MIKE, THE MAJOR LEAGUER!
NOT SO FAST! MIKE'S TEAM HAS NEVER WON THE WORLD SERIES, AND YOU DON'T GET A BELT IN BASEBALL ANYWAY!
THE SAME GOES FOR SOCCER ...

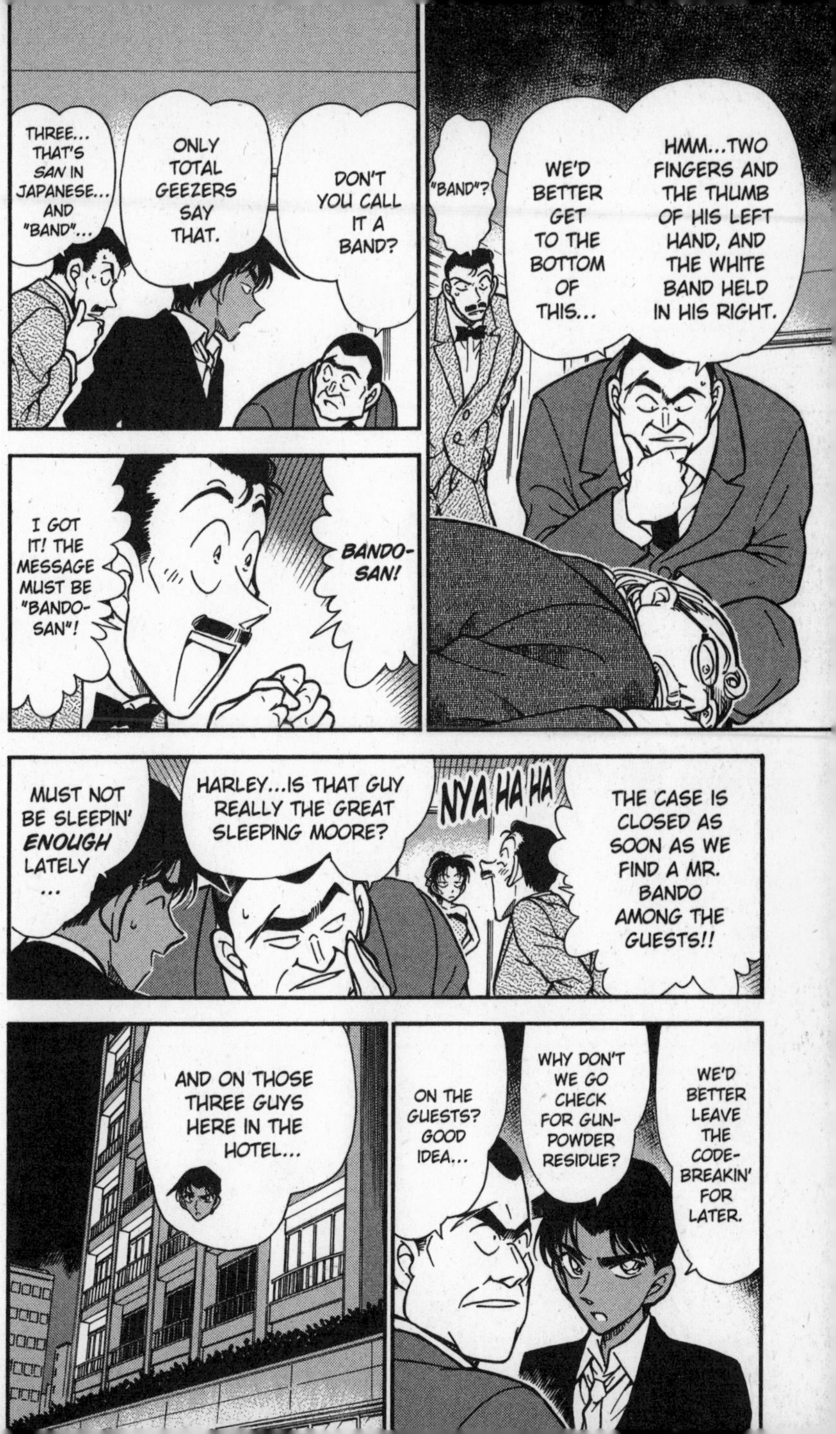
HMM...TWO FINGERS AND THE THUMB OF HIS LEFT HAND, AND THE WHITE BAND HELD IN HIS RIGHT.
WE'D BETTER GET TO THE BOTTOM OF THIS...
"BAND"?
DON'T YOU CALL IT A BAND?
ONLY TOTAL GEEZERS SAY THAT.
THREE... THAT'S *SAN* IN JAPANESE... AND "BAND"...
BANDO-SAN!
I GOT IT! THE MESSAGE MUST BE "BANDO-SAN"!
THE CASE IS CLOSED AS SOON AS WE FIND A MR. BANDO AMONG THE GUESTS!!
NYA HA HA
HARLEY...IS THAT GUY REALLY THE GREAT SLEEPING MOORE?
MUST NOT BE SLEEPIN' **ENOUGH** LATELY ...
WE'D BETTER LEAVE THE CODE-BREAKIN' FOR LATER.
WHY DON'T WE GO CHECK FOR GUN-POWDER RESIDUE?
ON THE GUESTS? GOOD IDEA...
AND ON THOSE THREE GUYS HERE IN THE HOTEL...

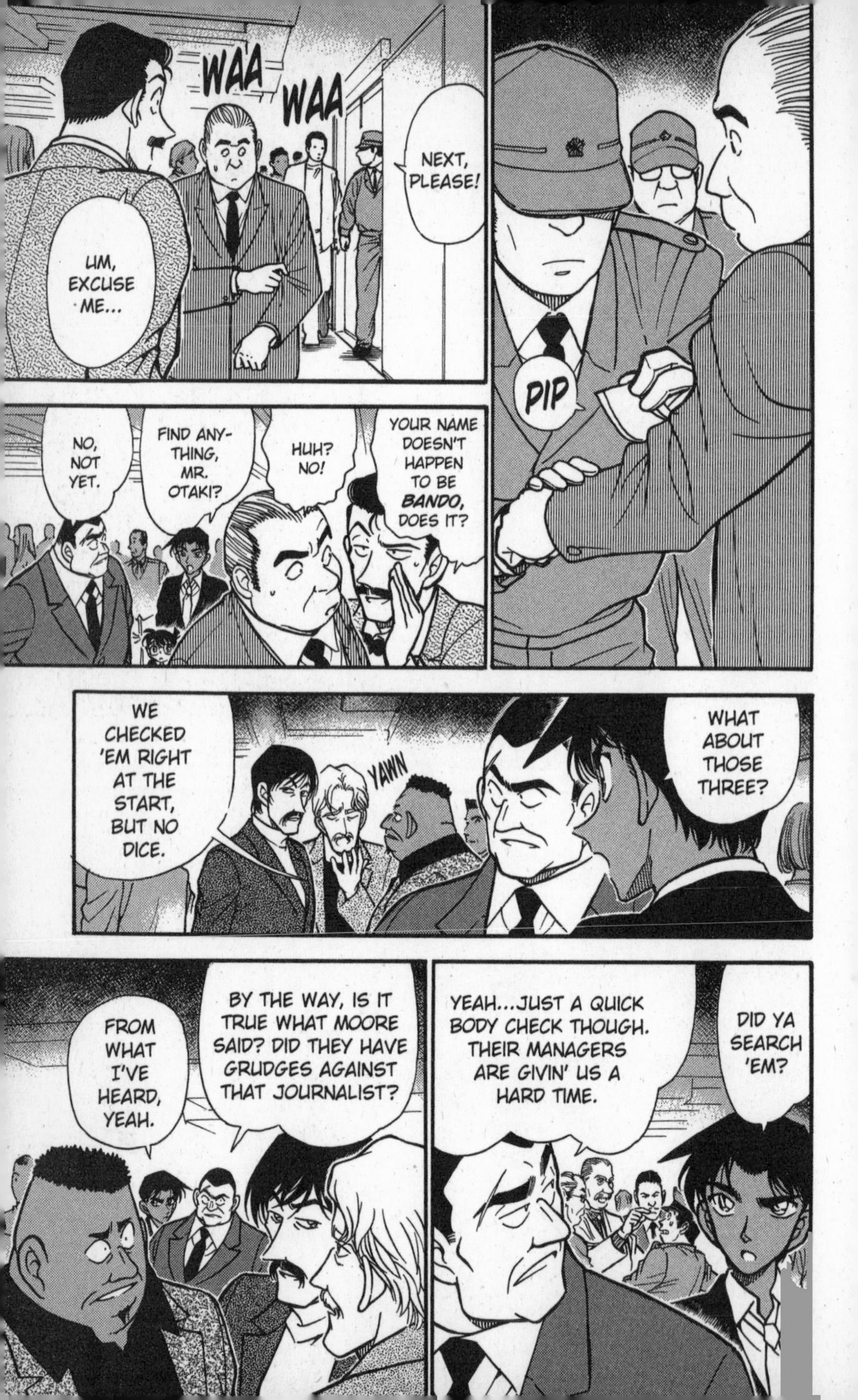
PIP
NEXT, PLEASE!
WAA WAA
UM, EXCUSE ME...
YOUR NAME DOESN'T HAPPEN TO BE *BANDO*, DOES IT?
HUH? NO!
FIND ANY-THING, MR. OTAKI?
NO, NOT YET.
WHAT ABOUT THOSE THREE?
YAWN
WE CHECKED 'EM RIGHT AT THE START, BUT NO DICE.
DID YA SEARCH 'EM?
YEAH...JUST A QUICK BODY CHECK THOUGH. THEIR MANAGERS ARE GIVIN' US A HARD TIME.
BY THE WAY, IS IT TRUE WHAT MOORE SAID? DID THEY HAVE GRUDGES AGAINST THAT JOURNALIST?
FROM WHAT I'VE HEARD, YEAH.

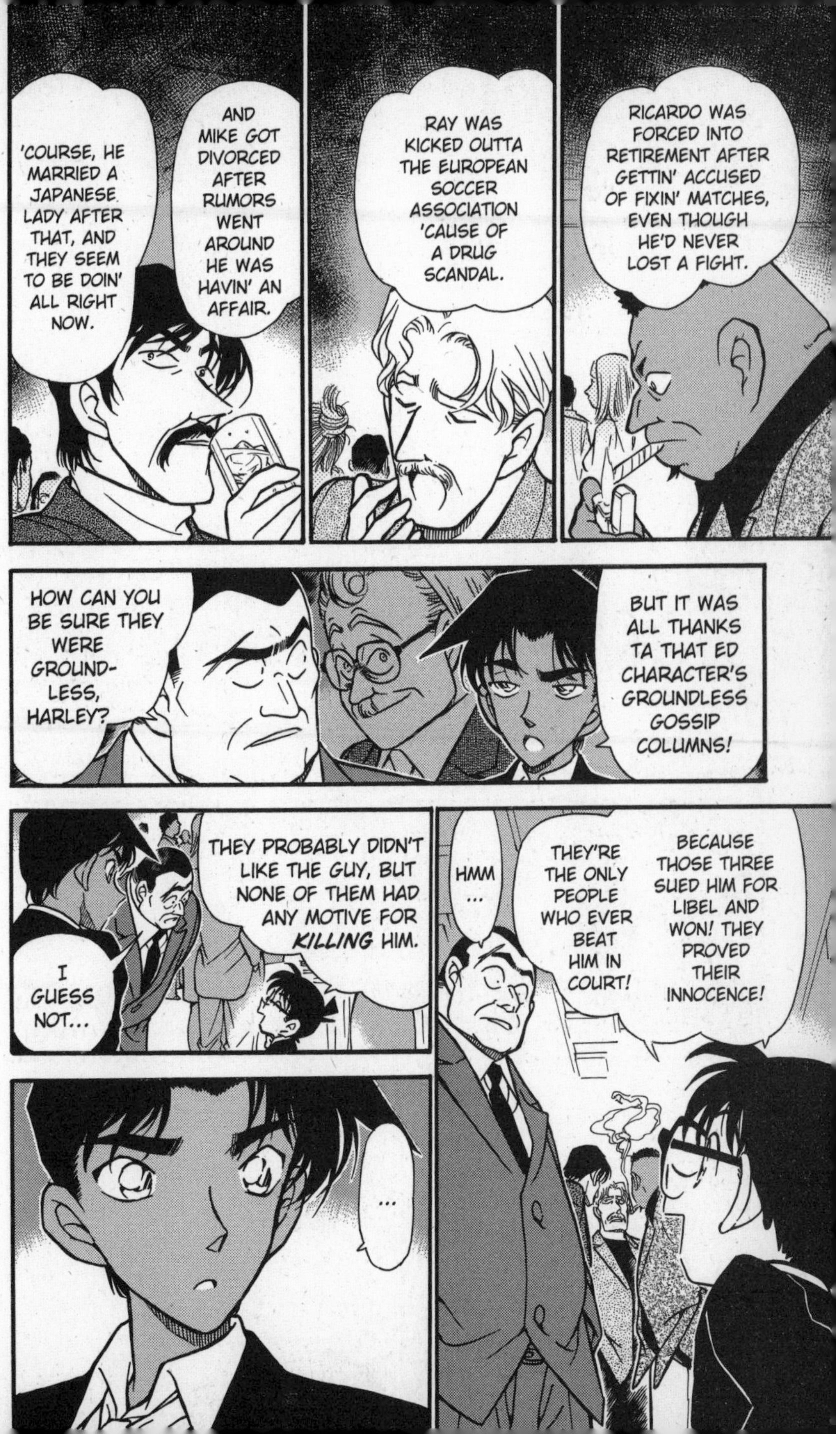
RICARDO WAS FORCED INTO RETIREMENT AFTER GETTIN' ACCUSED OF FIXIN' MATCHES, EVEN THOUGH HE'D NEVER LOST A FIGHT.
RAY WAS KICKED OUTTA THE EUROPEAN SOCCER ASSOCIATION 'CAUSE OF A DRUG SCANDAL.
AND MIKE GOT DIVORCED AFTER RUMORS WENT AROUND HE WAS HAVIN' AN AFFAIR.
'COURSE, HE MARRIED A JAPANESE LADY AFTER THAT, AND THEY SEEM TO BE DOIN' ALL RIGHT NOW.
BUT IT WAS ALL THANKS TA THAT ED CHARACTER'S GROUNDLESS GOSSIP COLUMNS!
HOW CAN YOU BE SURE THEY WERE GROUND-LESS, HARLEY?
BECAUSE THOSE THREE SUED HIM FOR LIBEL AND WON! THEY PROVED THEIR INNOCENCE!
THEY'RE THE ONLY PEOPLE WHO EVER BEAT HIM IN COURT!
HMM ...
THEY PROBABLY DIDN'T LIKE THE GUY, BUT NONE OF THEM HAD ANY MOTIVE FOR *KILLING* HIM.
I GUESS NOT...
...

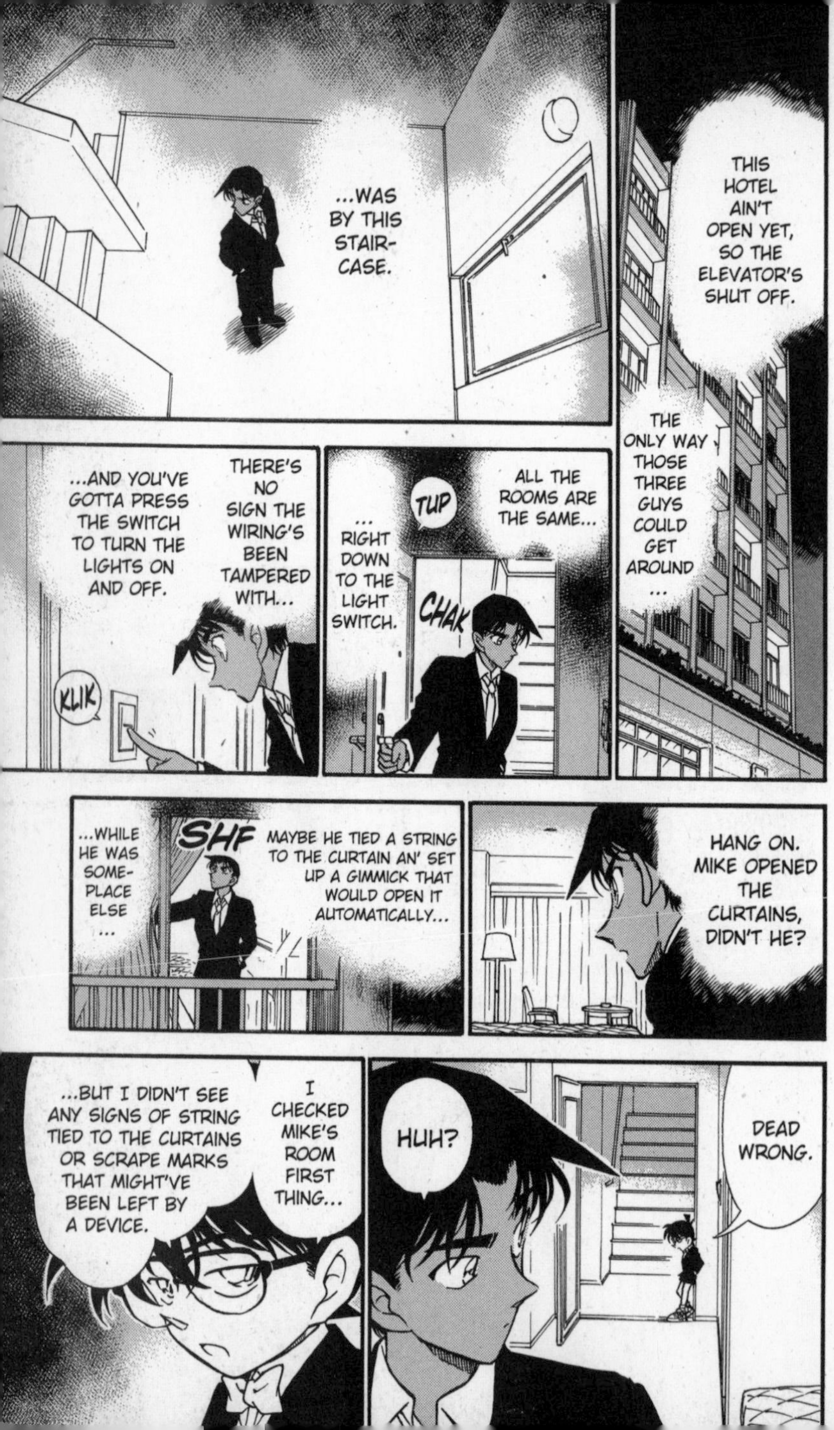
THIS HOTEL AIN'T OPEN YET, SO THE ELEVATOR'S SHUT OFF.
THE ONLY WAY THOSE THREE GUYS COULD GET AROUND...
...WAS BY THIS STAIRCASE.
ALL THE ROOMS ARE THE SAME...
TUP
...RIGHT DOWN TO THE LIGHT SWITCH.
CHAK
THERE'S NO SIGN THE WIRING'S BEEN TAMPERED WITH...
...AND YOU'VE GOTTA PRESS THE SWITCH TO TURN THE LIGHTS ON AND OFF.
KLIK
HANG ON. MIKE OPENED THE CURTAINS, DIDN'T HE?
MAYBE HE TIED A STRING TO THE CURTAIN AN' SET UP A GIMMICK THAT WOULD OPEN IT AUTOMATICALLY...
SHF
...WHILE HE WAS SOMEPLACE ELSE...
DEAD WRONG.
HUH?
I CHECKED MIKE'S ROOM FIRST THING...
...BUT I DIDN'T SEE ANY SIGNS OF STRING TIED TO THE CURTAINS OR SCRAPE MARKS THAT MIGHT'VE BEEN LEFT BY A DEVICE.

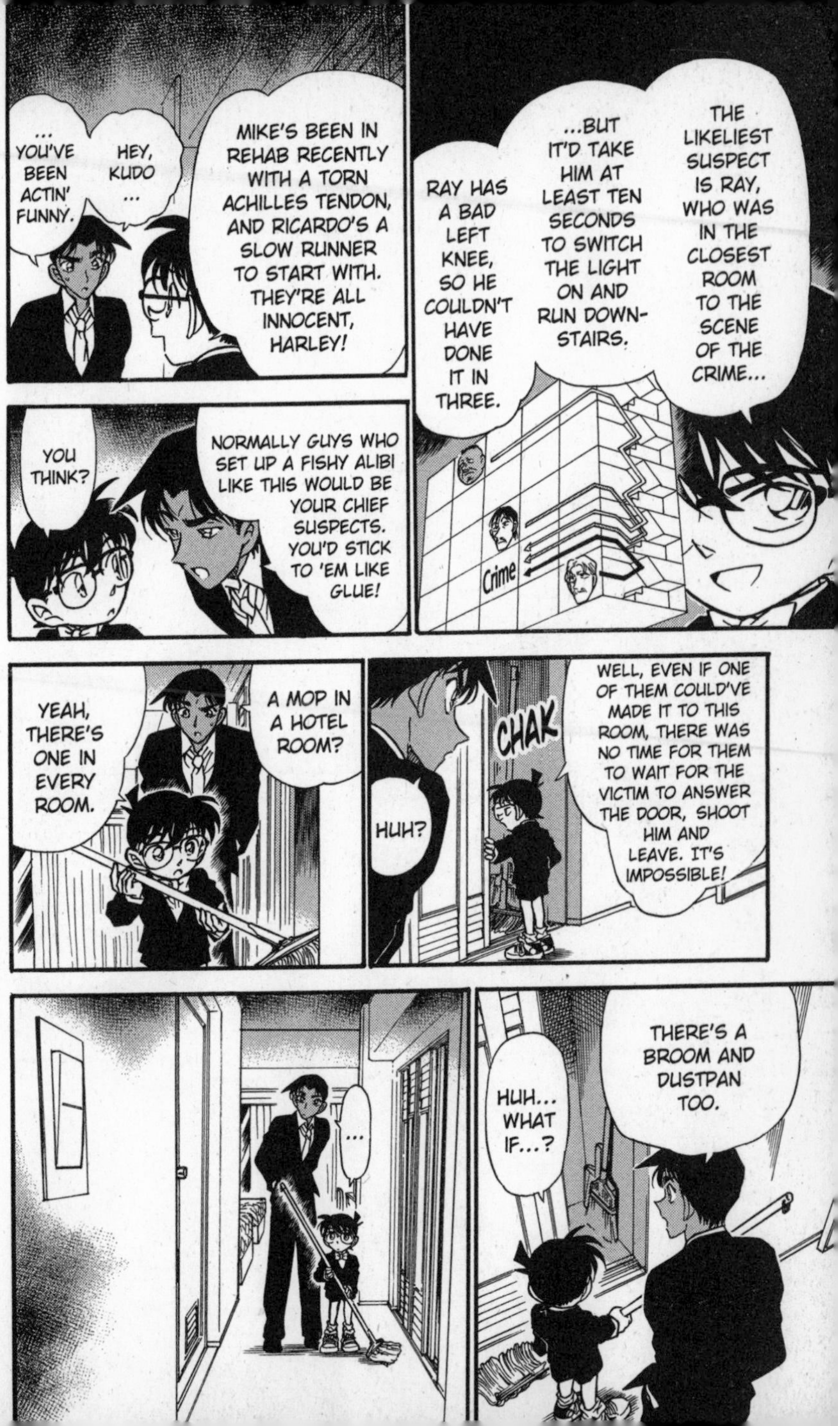
THE LIKELIEST SUSPECT IS RAY, WHO WAS IN THE CLOSEST ROOM TO THE SCENE OF THE CRIME...
...BUT IT'D TAKE HIM AT LEAST TEN SECONDS TO SWITCH THE LIGHT ON AND RUN DOWN-STAIRS.
RAY HAS A BAD LEFT KNEE, SO HE COULDN'T HAVE DONE IT IN THREE.
Crime
MIKE'S BEEN IN REHAB RECENTLY WITH A TORN ACHILLES TENDON, AND RICARDO'S A SLOW RUNNER TO START WITH. THEY'RE ALL INNOCENT, HARLEY!
HEY, KUDO...
...YOU'VE BEEN ACTIN' FUNNY.
NORMALLY GUYS WHO SET UP A FISHY ALIBI LIKE THIS WOULD BE YOUR CHIEF SUSPECTS. YOU'D STICK TO 'EM LIKE GLUE!
YOU THINK?
WELL, EVEN IF ONE OF THEM COULD'VE MADE IT TO THIS ROOM, THERE WAS NO TIME FOR THEM TO WAIT FOR THE VICTIM TO ANSWER THE DOOR, SHOOT HIM AND LEAVE. IT'S IMPOSSIBLE!
CHAK
HUH?
A MOP IN A HOTEL ROOM?
YEAH, THERE'S ONE IN EVERY ROOM.
THERE'S A BROOM AND DUSTPAN TOO.
HUH... WHAT IF...?
...

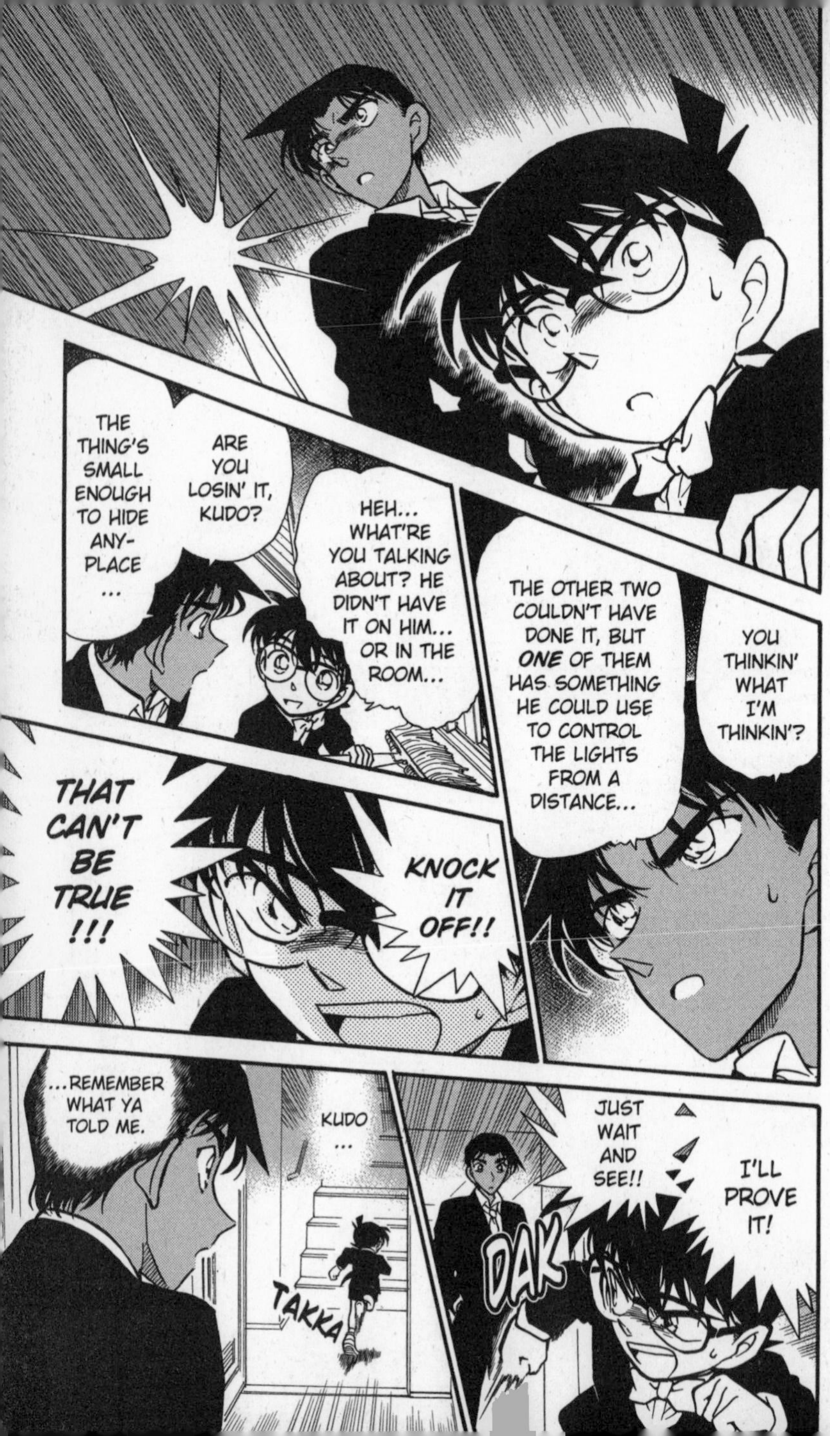
YOU THINKIN' WHAT I'M THINKIN'?
THE OTHER TWO COULDN'T HAVE DONE IT, BUT *ONE* OF THEM HAS SOMETHING HE COULD USE TO CONTROL THE LIGHTS FROM A DISTANCE...
HEH... WHAT'RE YOU TALKING ABOUT? HE DIDN'T HAVE IT ON HIM... OR IN THE ROOM...
ARE YOU LOSIN' IT, KUDO?
THE THING'S SMALL ENOUGH TO HIDE ANY-PLACE...
KNOCK IT OFF!!
THAT CAN'T BE TRUE!!!
I'LL PROVE IT!
JUST WAIT AND SEE!!
DAK
KUDO...
TAKKA
...REMEMBER WHAT YA TOLD ME.

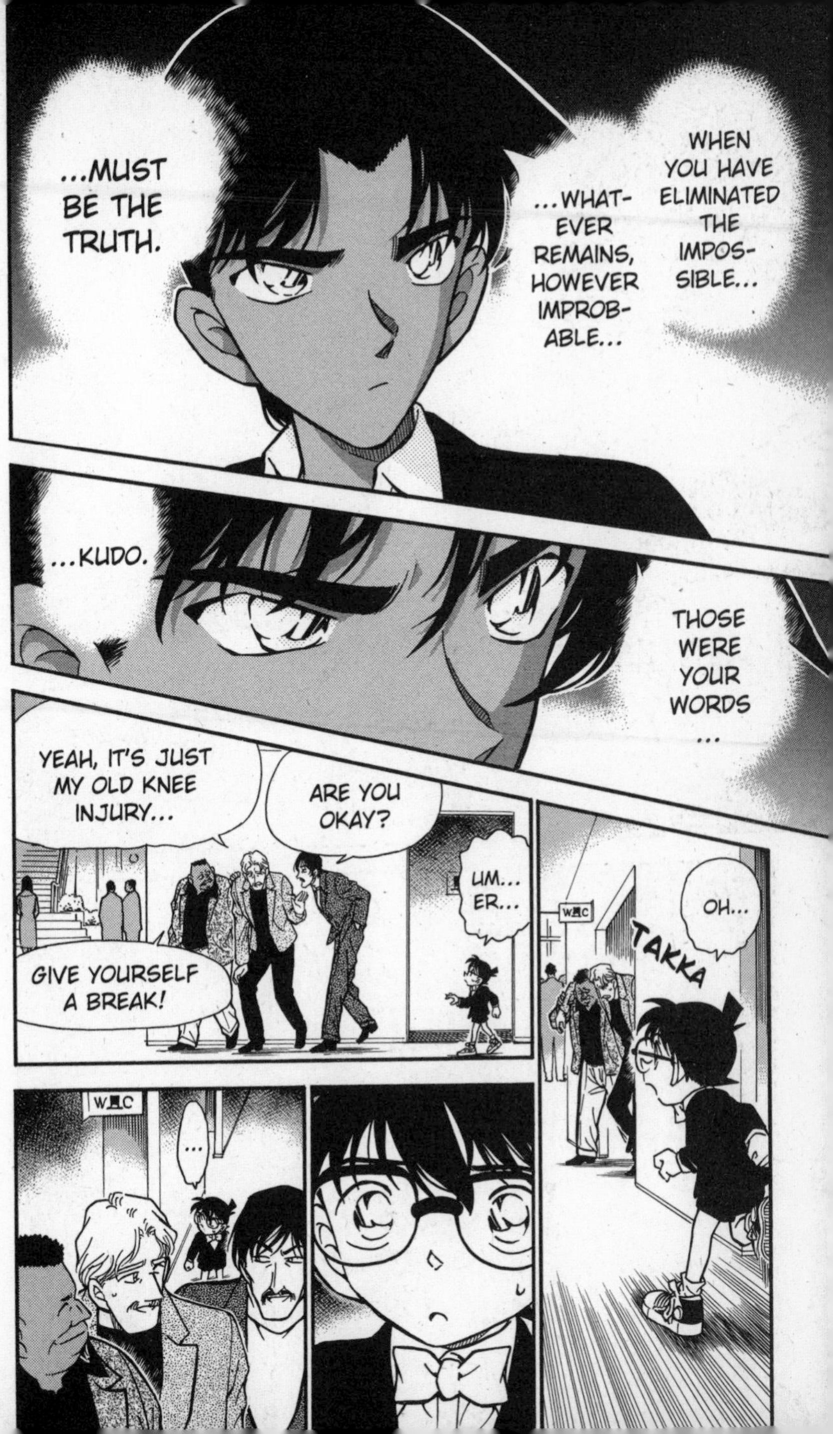
WHEN YOU HAVE ELIMINATED THE IMPOSSIBLE...
...WHATEVER REMAINS, HOWEVER IMPROBABLE...
...MUST BE THE TRUTH.
THOSE WERE YOUR WORDS ...
...KUDO.
OH...
TAKKA
ARE YOU OKAY?
YEAH, IT'S JUST MY OLD KNEE INJURY...
UM... ER...
GIVE YOURSELF A BREAK!
...

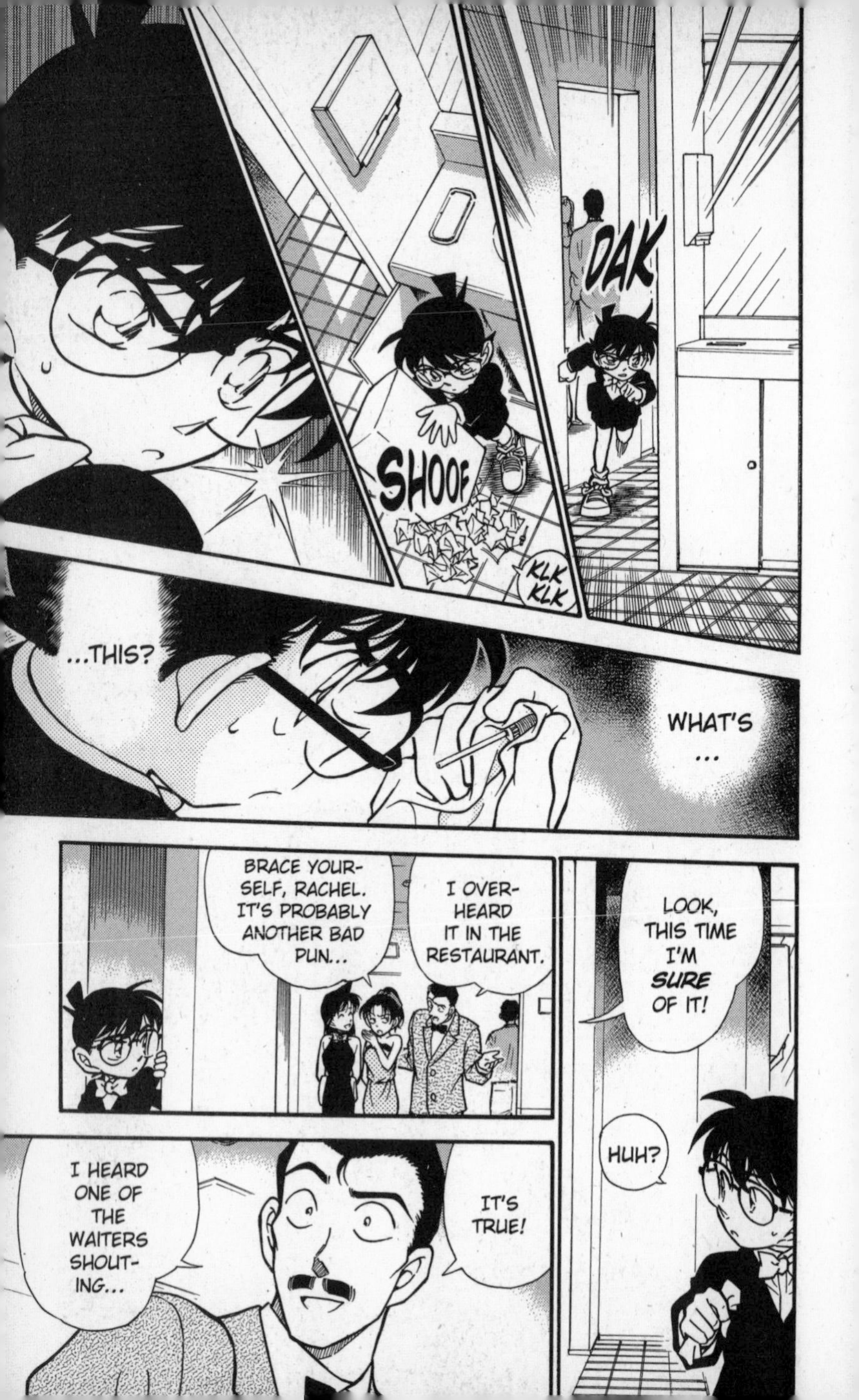
DAK
SHOOF
KLK KLK
WHAT'S ...
...THIS?
LOOK, THIS TIME I'M SURE OF IT!
HUH?
I OVER-HEARD IT IN THE RESTAURANT.
BRACE YOUR-SELF, RACHEL. IT'S PROBABLY ANOTHER BAD PUN...
IT'S TRUE!
I HEARD ONE OF THE WAITERS SHOUT-ING...

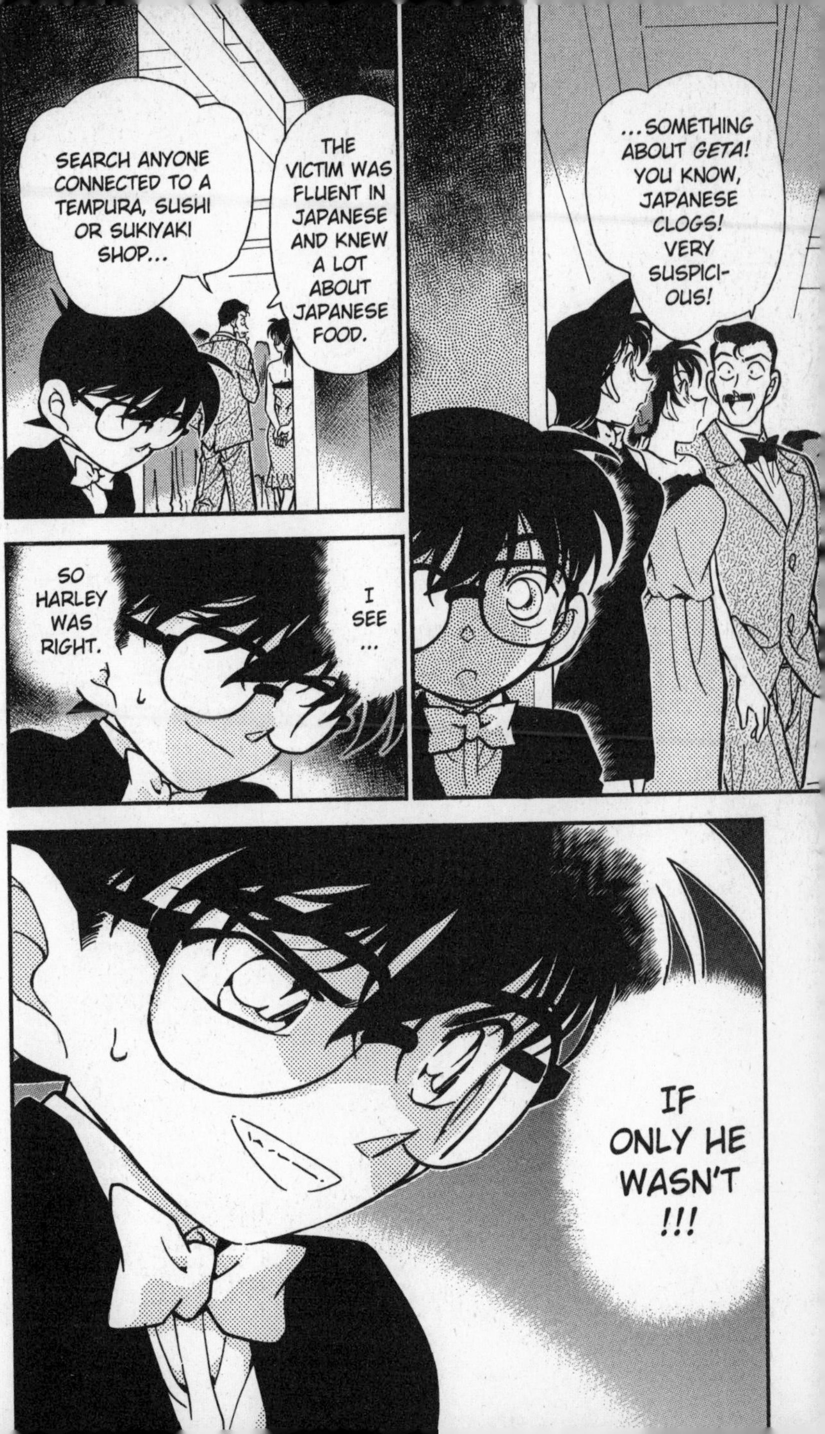
...SOMETHING ABOUT GETA! YOU KNOW, JAPANESE CLOGS! VERY SUSPICIOUS!
THE VICTIM WAS FLUENT IN JAPANESE AND KNEW A LOT ABOUT JAPANESE FOOD.
SEARCH ANYONE CONNECTED TO A TEMPURA, SUSHI OR SUKIYAKI SHOP...
I SEE...
SO HARLEY WAS RIGHT.
IF ONLY HE WASN'T!!!

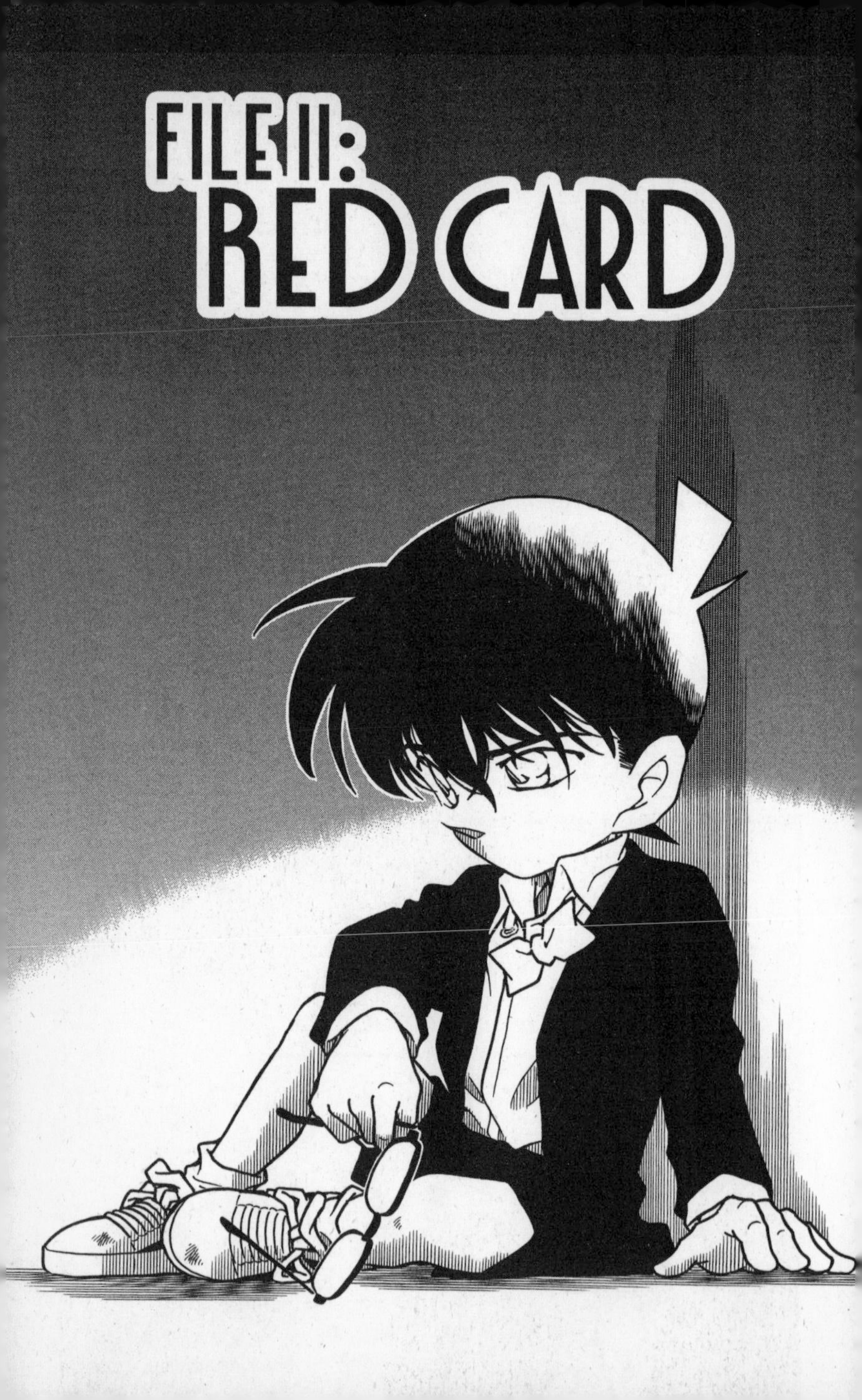
FILE 11:
RED CARD

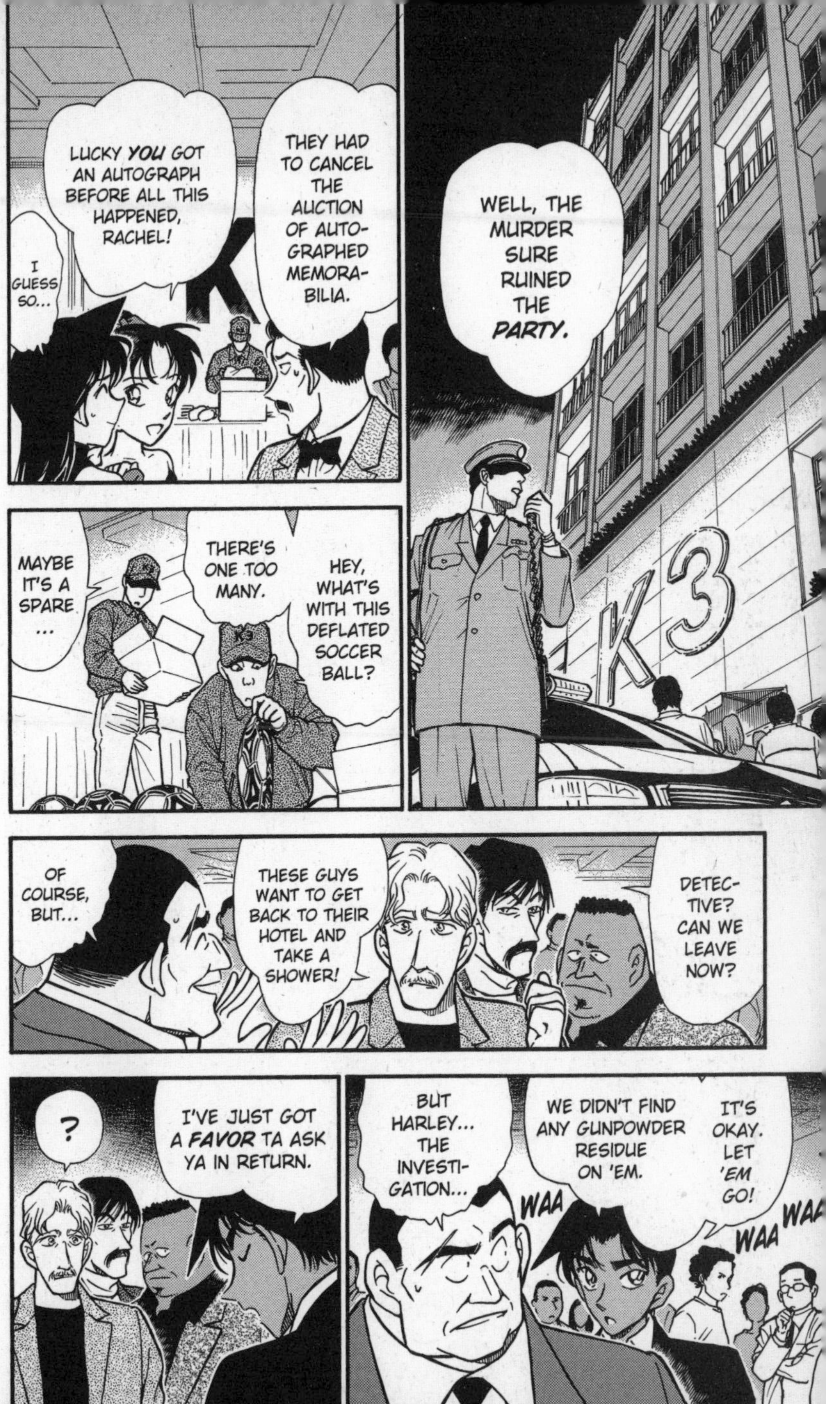
WELL, THE MURDER SURE RUINED THE PARTY.
THEY HAD TO CANCEL THE AUCTION OF AUTOGRAPHED MEMORABILIA.
LUCKY YOU GOT AN AUTOGRAPH BEFORE ALL THIS HAPPENED, RACHEL!
I GUESS SO...
HEY, WHAT'S WITH THIS DEFLATED SOCCER BALL?
THERE'S ONE TOO MANY.
MAYBE IT'S A SPARE...
DETECTIVE? CAN WE LEAVE NOW?
THESE GUYS WANT TO GET BACK TO THEIR HOTEL AND TAKE A SHOWER!
OF COURSE, BUT...
IT'S OKAY. LET 'EM GO!
WAA WAA WAA
WE DIDN'T FIND ANY GUNPOWDER RESIDUE ON 'EM.
BUT HARLEY... THE INVESTIGATION...
I'VE JUST GOT A FAVOR TA ASK YA IN RETURN.
?

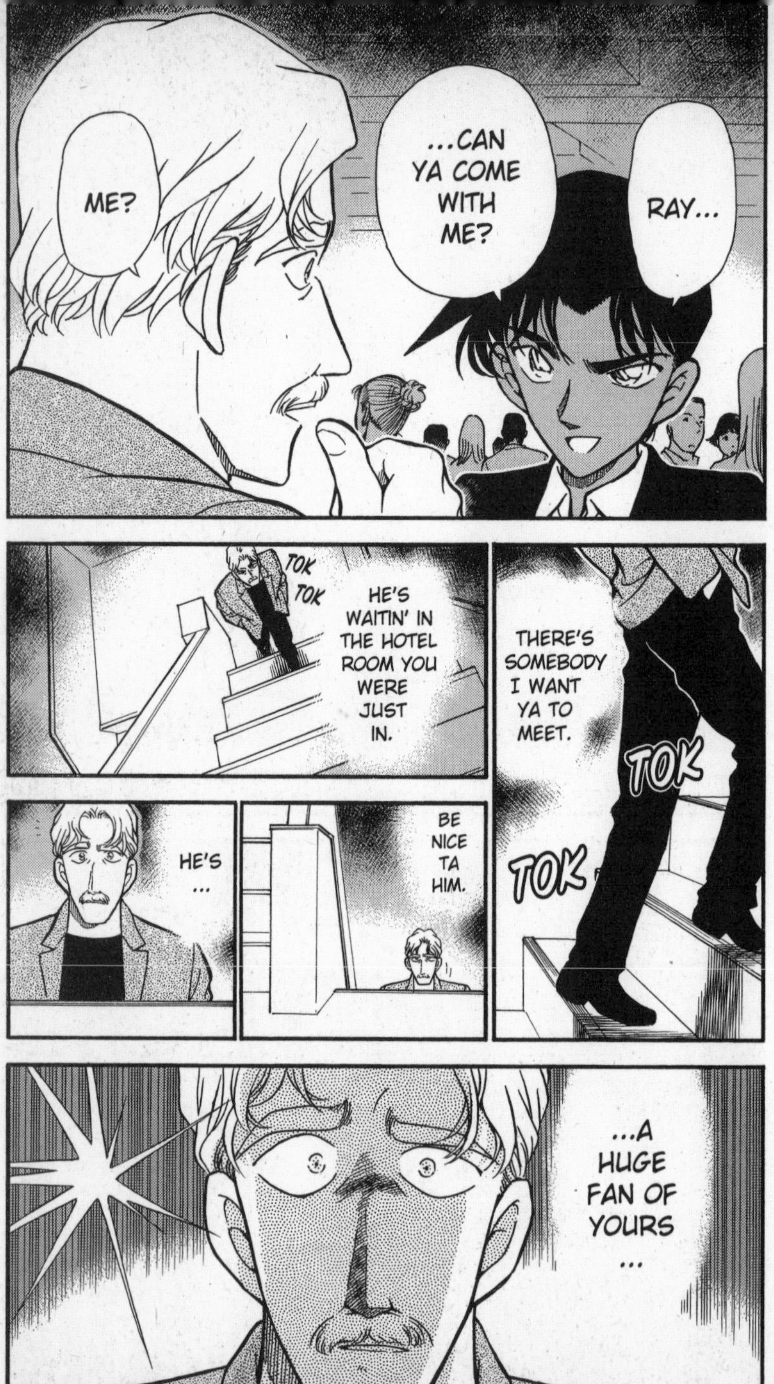
RAY...
...CAN YA COME WITH ME?
ME?
THERE'S SOMEBODY I WANT YA TO MEET.
TOK
TOK
HE'S WAITIN' IN THE HOTEL ROOM YOU WERE JUST IN.
TOK TOK
BE NICE TA HIM.
HE'S ...
...A HUGE FAN OF YOURS ...

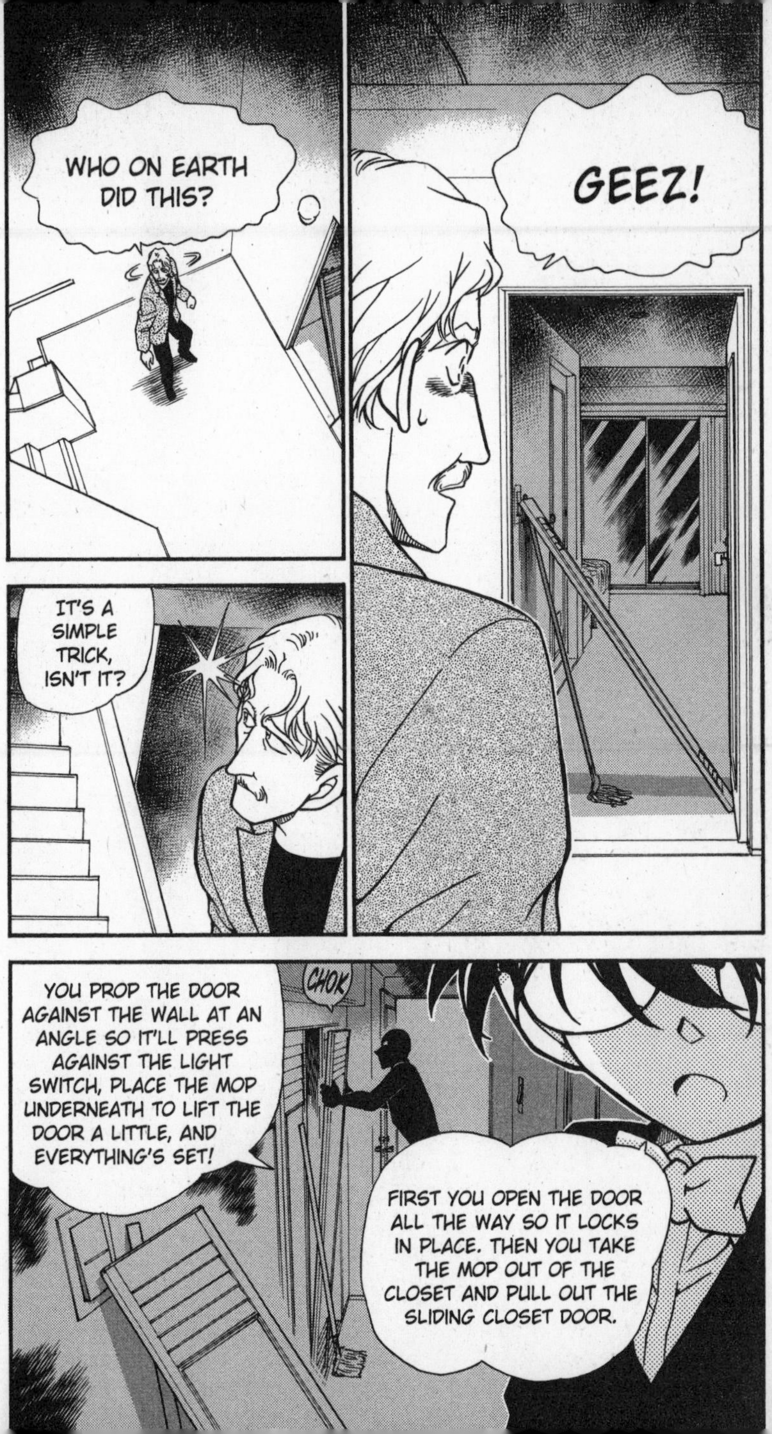
GEEZ!
WHO ON EARTH DID THIS?
IT'S A SIMPLE TRICK, ISN'T IT?
CHOK
FIRST YOU OPEN THE DOOR ALL THE WAY SO IT LOCKS IN PLACE. THEN YOU TAKE THE MOP OUT OF THE CLOSET AND PULL OUT THE SLIDING CLOSET DOOR.
YOU PROP THE DOOR AGAINST THE WALL AT AN ANGLE SO IT'LL PRESS AGAINST THE LIGHT SWITCH, PLACE THE MOP UNDERNEATH TO LIFT THE DOOR A LITTLE, AND EVERYTHING'S SET!

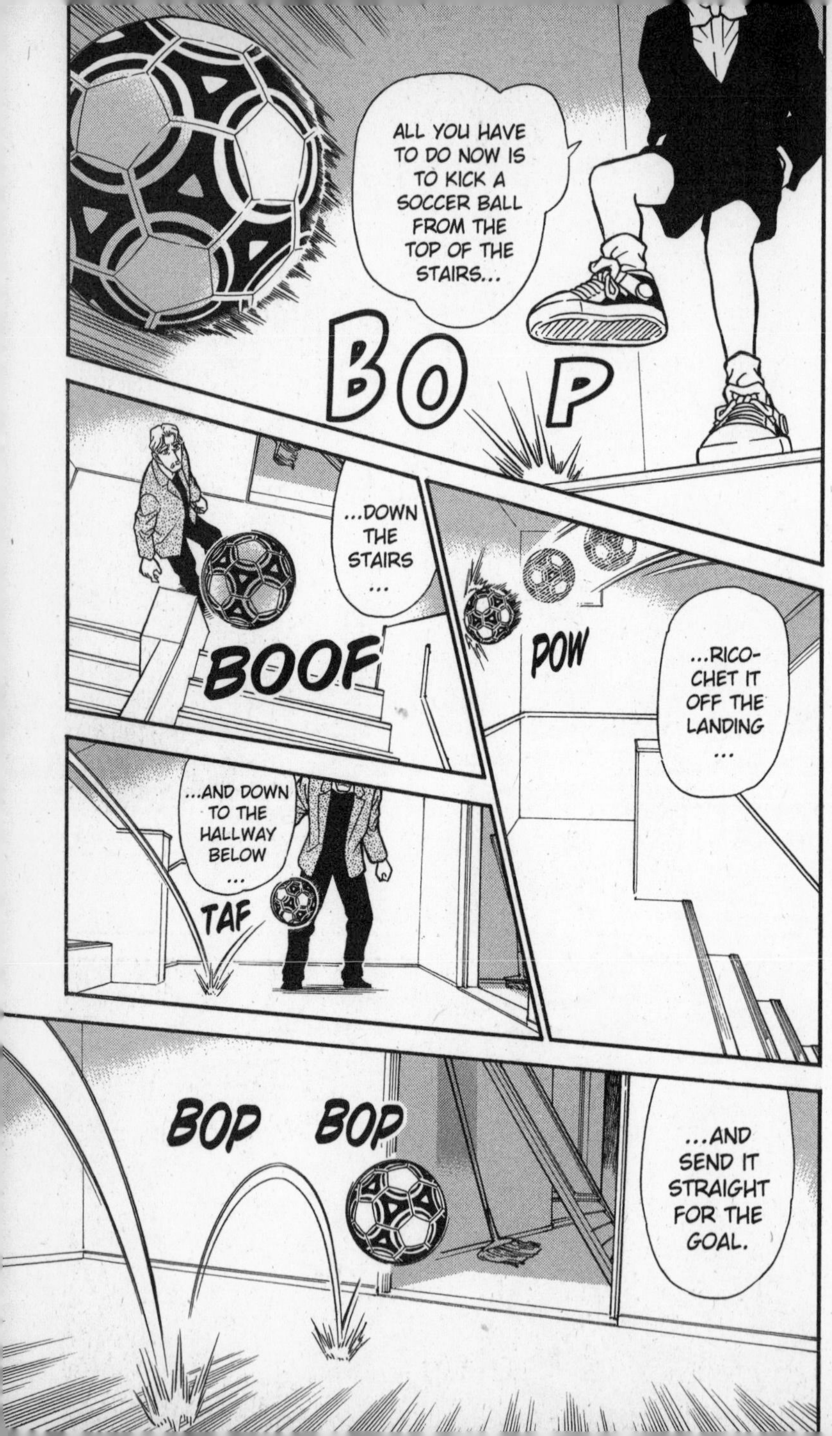
ALL YOU HAVE TO DO NOW IS TO KICK A SOCCER BALL FROM THE TOP OF THE STAIRS...
BOP
...DOWN THE STAIRS ...
BOOF
POW
...RICO-CHET IT OFF THE LANDING ...
...AND DOWN TO THE HALLWAY BELOW ...
TAF
...AND SEND IT STRAIGHT FOR THE GOAL.
BOP BOP

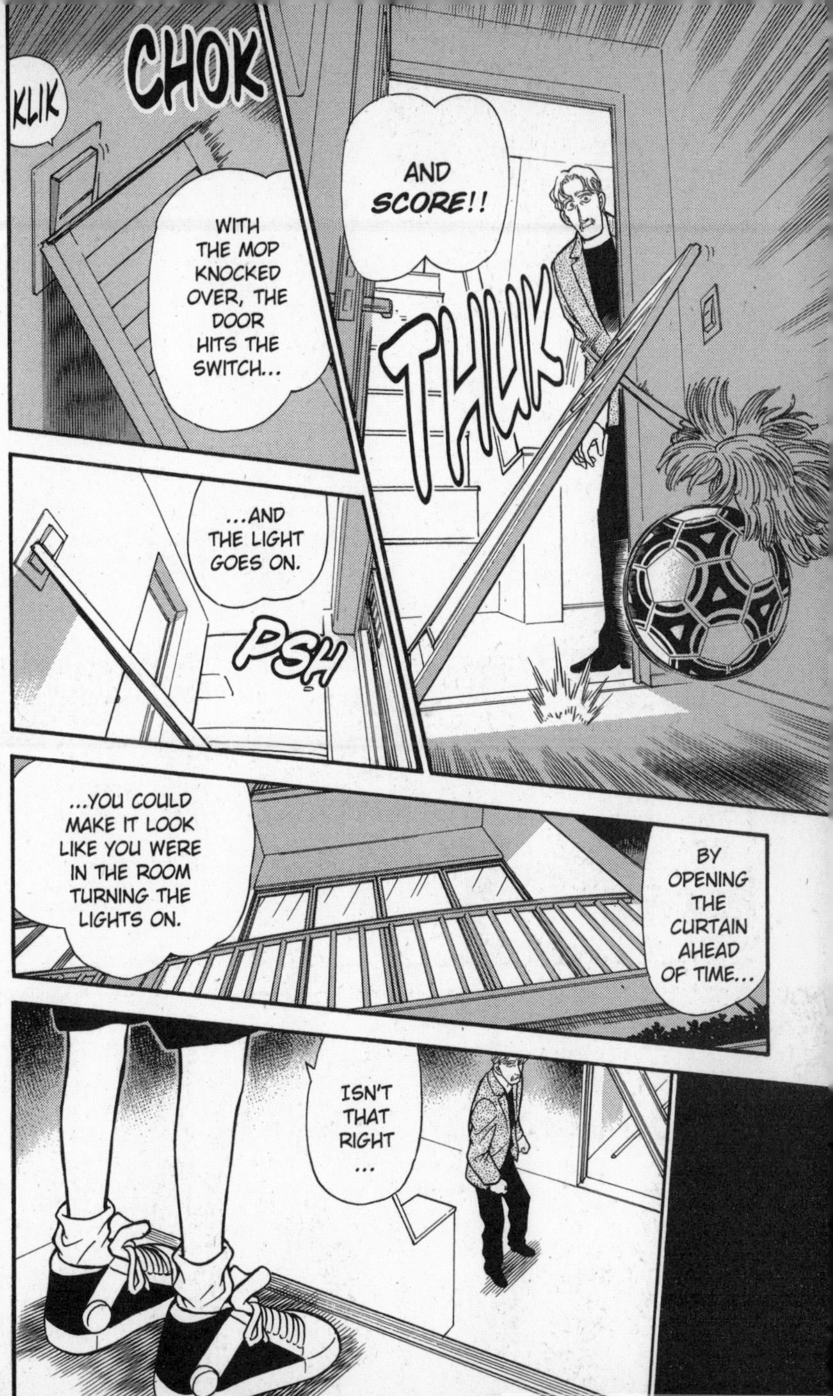
AND SCORE!!
THUK
CHOK
KLIK
WITH THE MOP KNOCKED OVER, THE DOOR HITS THE SWITCH...
...AND THE LIGHT GOES ON.
PSH
BY OPENING THE CURTAIN AHEAD OF TIME...
...YOU COULD MAKE IT LOOK LIKE YOU WERE IN THE ROOM TURNING THE LIGHTS ON.
ISN'T THAT RIGHT ...

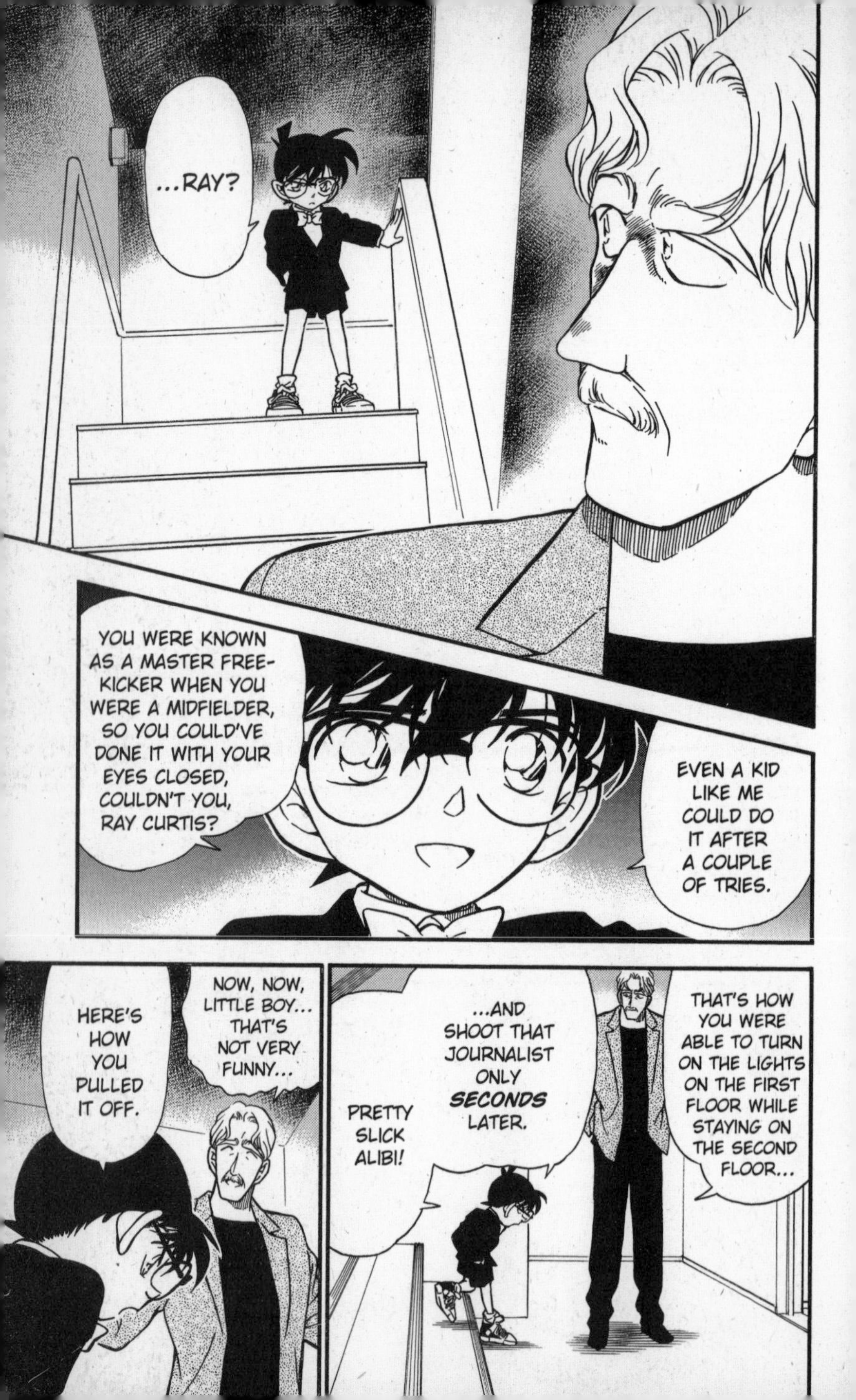
...RAY?
EVEN A KID LIKE ME COULD DO IT AFTER A COUPLE OF TRIES.
YOU WERE KNOWN AS A MASTER FREE-KICKER WHEN YOU WERE A MIDFIELDER, SO YOU COULD'VE DONE IT WITH YOUR EYES CLOSED, COULDN'T YOU, RAY CURTIS?
THAT'S HOW YOU WERE ABLE TO TURN ON THE LIGHTS ON THE FIRST FLOOR WHILE STAYING ON THE SECOND FLOOR...
...AND SHOOT THAT JOURNALIST ONLY ***SECONDS*** LATER.
PRETTY SLICK ALIBI!
NOW, NOW, LITTLE BOY... THAT'S NOT VERY FUNNY...
HERE'S HOW YOU PULLED IT OFF.

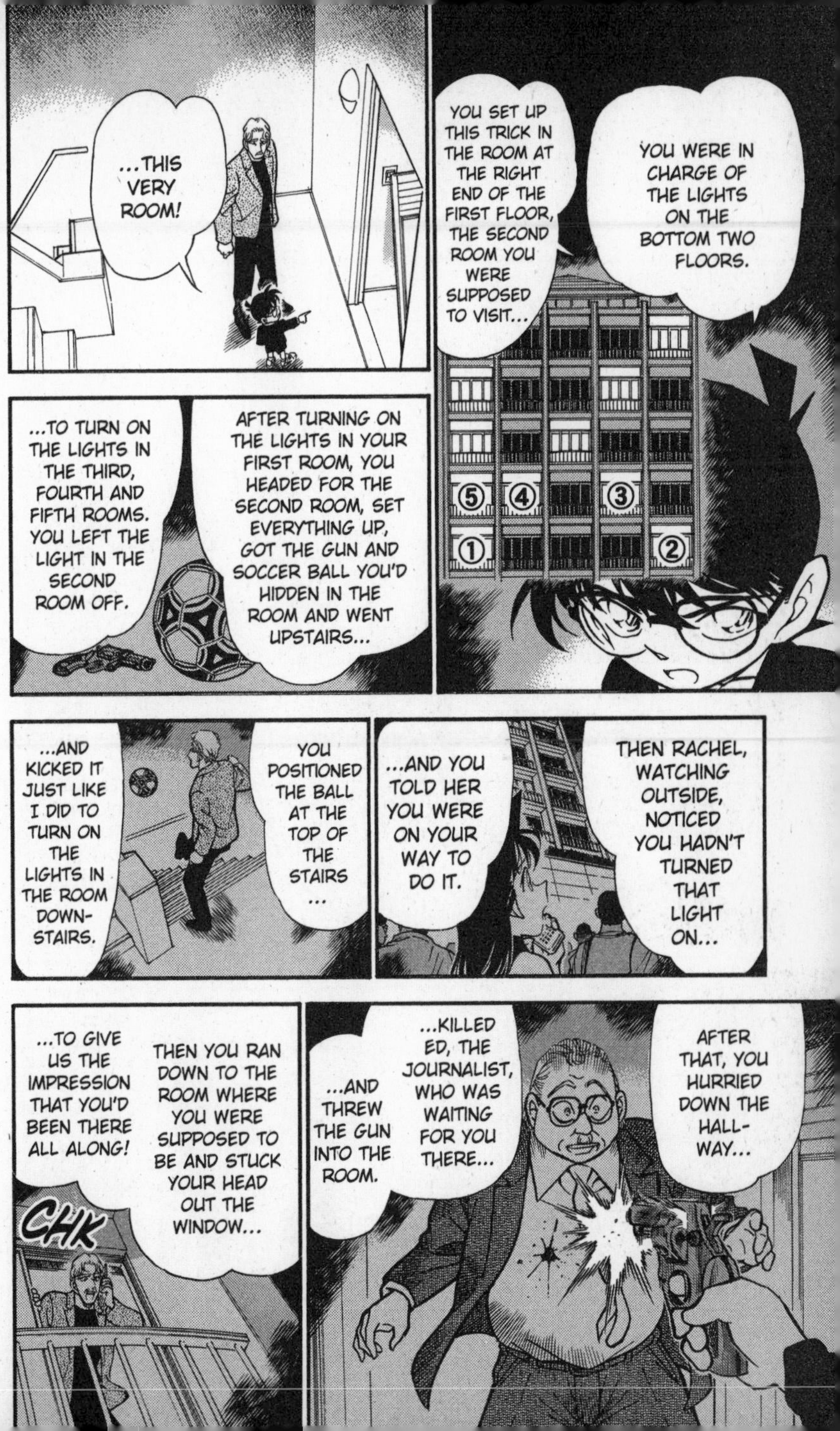
...THIS VERY ROOM!
YOU WERE IN CHARGE OF THE LIGHTS ON THE BOTTOM TWO FLOORS.
YOU SET UP THIS TRICK IN THE ROOM AT THE RIGHT END OF THE FIRST FLOOR, THE SECOND ROOM YOU WERE SUPPOSED TO VISIT...
⑤ ④ ③
① ②
AFTER TURNING ON THE LIGHTS IN YOUR FIRST ROOM, YOU HEADED FOR THE SECOND ROOM, SET EVERYTHING UP, GOT THE GUN AND SOCCER BALL YOU'D HIDDEN IN THE ROOM AND WENT UPSTAIRS...
...TO TURN ON THE LIGHTS IN THE THIRD, FOURTH AND FIFTH ROOMS. YOU LEFT THE LIGHT IN THE SECOND ROOM OFF.
THEN RACHEL, WATCHING OUTSIDE, NOTICED YOU HADN'T TURNED THAT LIGHT ON...
...AND YOU TOLD HER YOU WERE ON YOUR WAY TO DO IT.
YOU POSITIONED THE BALL AT THE TOP OF THE STAIRS...
...AND KICKED IT JUST LIKE I DID TO TURN ON THE LIGHTS IN THE ROOM DOWNSTAIRS.
AFTER THAT, YOU HURRIED DOWN THE HALLWAY...
...KILLED ED, THE JOURNALIST, WHO WAS WAITING FOR YOU THERE...
...AND THREW THE GUN INTO THE ROOM.
THEN YOU RAN DOWN TO THE ROOM WHERE YOU WERE SUPPOSED TO BE AND STUCK YOUR HEAD OUT THE WINDOW...
...TO GIVE US THE IMPRESSION THAT YOU'D BEEN THERE ALL ALONG!
CHK

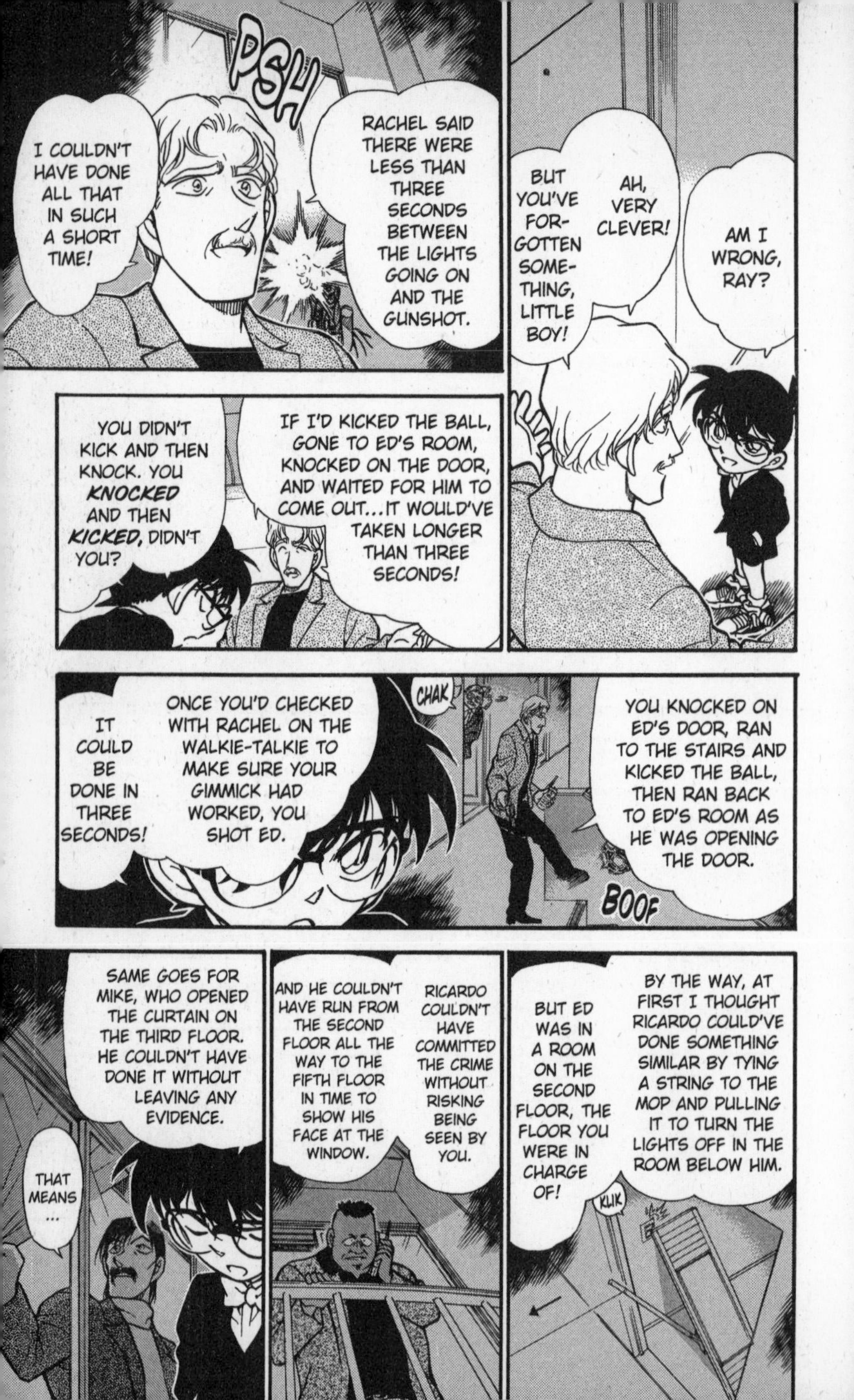

AM I WRONG, RAY?
AH, VERY CLEVER!
BUT YOU'VE FORGOTTEN SOMETHING, LITTLE BOY!
PSH
RACHEL SAID THERE WERE LESS THAN THREE SECONDS BETWEEN THE LIGHTS GOING ON AND THE GUNSHOT.
I COULDN'T HAVE DONE ALL THAT IN SUCH A SHORT TIME!
IF I'D KICKED THE BALL, GONE TO ED'S ROOM, KNOCKED ON THE DOOR, AND WAITED FOR HIM TO COME OUT…IT WOULD'VE TAKEN LONGER THAN THREE SECONDS!
YOU DIDN'T KICK AND THEN KNOCK. YOU *KNOCKED* AND THEN *KICKED*, DIDN'T YOU?
YOU KNOCKED ON ED'S DOOR, RAN TO THE STAIRS AND KICKED THE BALL, THEN RAN BACK TO ED'S ROOM AS HE WAS OPENING THE DOOR.
BOOF
CHAK
ONCE YOU'D CHECKED WITH RACHEL ON THE WALKIE-TALKIE TO MAKE SURE YOUR GIMMICK HAD WORKED, YOU SHOT ED.
IT COULD BE DONE IN THREE SECONDS!
BY THE WAY, AT FIRST I THOUGHT RICARDO COULD'VE DONE SOMETHING SIMILAR BY TYING A STRING TO THE MOP AND PULLING IT TO TURN THE LIGHTS OFF IN THE ROOM BELOW HIM.
BUT ED WAS IN A ROOM ON THE SECOND FLOOR, THE FLOOR YOU WERE IN CHARGE OF!
KLIK
RICARDO COULDN'T HAVE COMMITTED THE CRIME WITHOUT RISKING BEING SEEN BY YOU.
AND HE COULDN'T HAVE RUN FROM THE SECOND FLOOR ALL THE WAY TO THE FIFTH FLOOR IN TIME TO SHOW HIS FACE AT THE WINDOW.
SAME GOES FOR MIKE, WHO OPENED THE CURTAIN ON THE THIRD FLOOR. HE COULDN'T HAVE DONE IT WITHOUT LEAVING ANY EVIDENCE.
THAT MEANS …

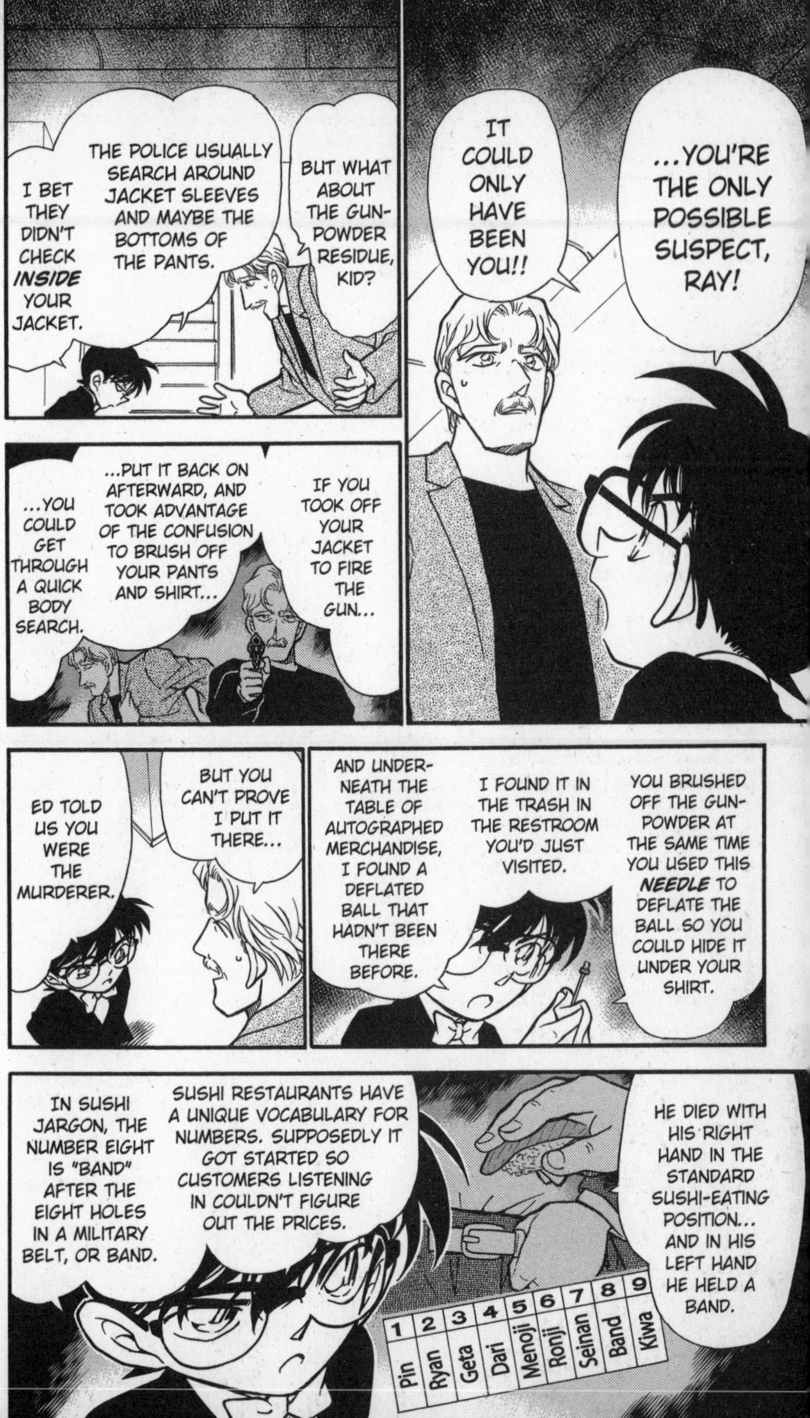
...YOU'RE THE ONLY POSSIBLE SUSPECT, RAY!
IT COULD ONLY HAVE BEEN YOU!!
BUT WHAT ABOUT THE GUN-POWDER RESIDUE, KID?
THE POLICE USUALLY SEARCH AROUND JACKET SLEEVES AND MAYBE THE BOTTOMS OF THE PANTS.
I BET THEY DIDN'T CHECK *INSIDE* YOUR JACKET.
IF YOU TOOK OFF YOUR JACKET TO FIRE THE GUN...
...PUT IT BACK ON AFTERWARD, AND TOOK ADVANTAGE OF THE CONFUSION TO BRUSH OFF YOUR PANTS AND SHIRT...
...YOU COULD GET THROUGH A QUICK BODY SEARCH.
YOU BRUSHED OFF THE GUN-POWDER AT THE SAME TIME YOU USED THIS ***NEEDLE*** TO DEFLATE THE BALL SO YOU COULD HIDE IT UNDER YOUR SHIRT.
I FOUND IT IN THE TRASH IN THE RESTROOM YOU'D JUST VISITED.
AND UNDER-NEATH THE TABLE OF AUTOGRAPHED MERCHANDISE, I FOUND A DEFLATED BALL THAT HADN'T BEEN THERE BEFORE.
BUT YOU CAN'T PROVE I PUT IT THERE...
ED TOLD US YOU WERE THE MURDERER.
HE DIED WITH HIS RIGHT HAND IN THE STANDARD SUSHI-EATING POSITION... AND IN HIS LEFT HAND HE HELD A BAND.
1 Pin
2 Ryan
3 Geta
4 Dari
5 Menoji
6 Ronji
7 Seinan
8 Band
9 Kiwa
SUSHI RESTAURANTS HAVE A UNIQUE VOCABULARY FOR NUMBERS. SUPPOSEDLY IT GOT STARTED SO CUSTOMERS LISTENING IN COULDN'T FIGURE OUT THE PRICES.
IN SUSHI JARGON, THE NUMBER EIGHT IS "BAND" AFTER THE EIGHT HOLES IN A MILITARY BELT, OR BAND.

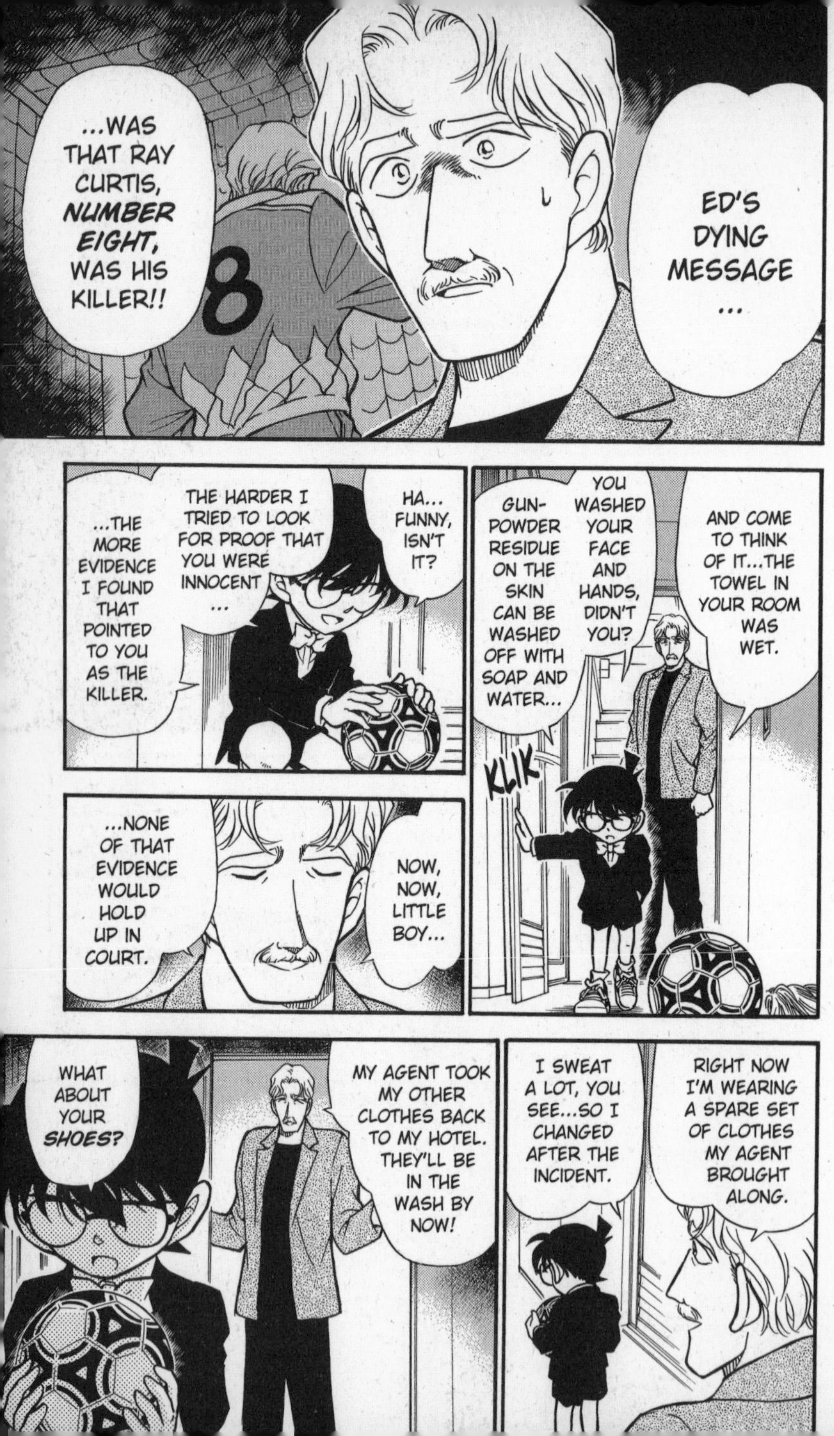
ED'S DYING MESSAGE ...
...WAS THAT RAY CURTIS, **NUMBER EIGHT**, WAS HIS KILLER!!
AND COME TO THINK OF IT...THE TOWEL IN YOUR ROOM WAS WET.
YOU WASHED YOUR FACE AND HANDS, DIDN'T YOU?
GUN-POWDER RESIDUE ON THE SKIN CAN BE WASHED OFF WITH SOAP AND WATER...
KLIK
HA... FUNNY, ISN'T IT?
THE HARDER I TRIED TO LOOK FOR PROOF THAT YOU WERE INNOCENT ...
...THE MORE EVIDENCE I FOUND THAT POINTED TO YOU AS THE KILLER.
NOW, NOW, LITTLE BOY...
...NONE OF THAT EVIDENCE WOULD HOLD UP IN COURT.
RIGHT NOW I'M WEARING A SPARE SET OF CLOTHES MY AGENT BROUGHT ALONG.
I SWEAT A LOT, YOU SEE...SO I CHANGED AFTER THE INCIDENT.
MY AGENT TOOK MY OTHER CLOTHES BACK TO MY HOTEL. THEY'LL BE IN THE WASH BY NOW!
WHAT ABOUT YOUR *SHOES?*

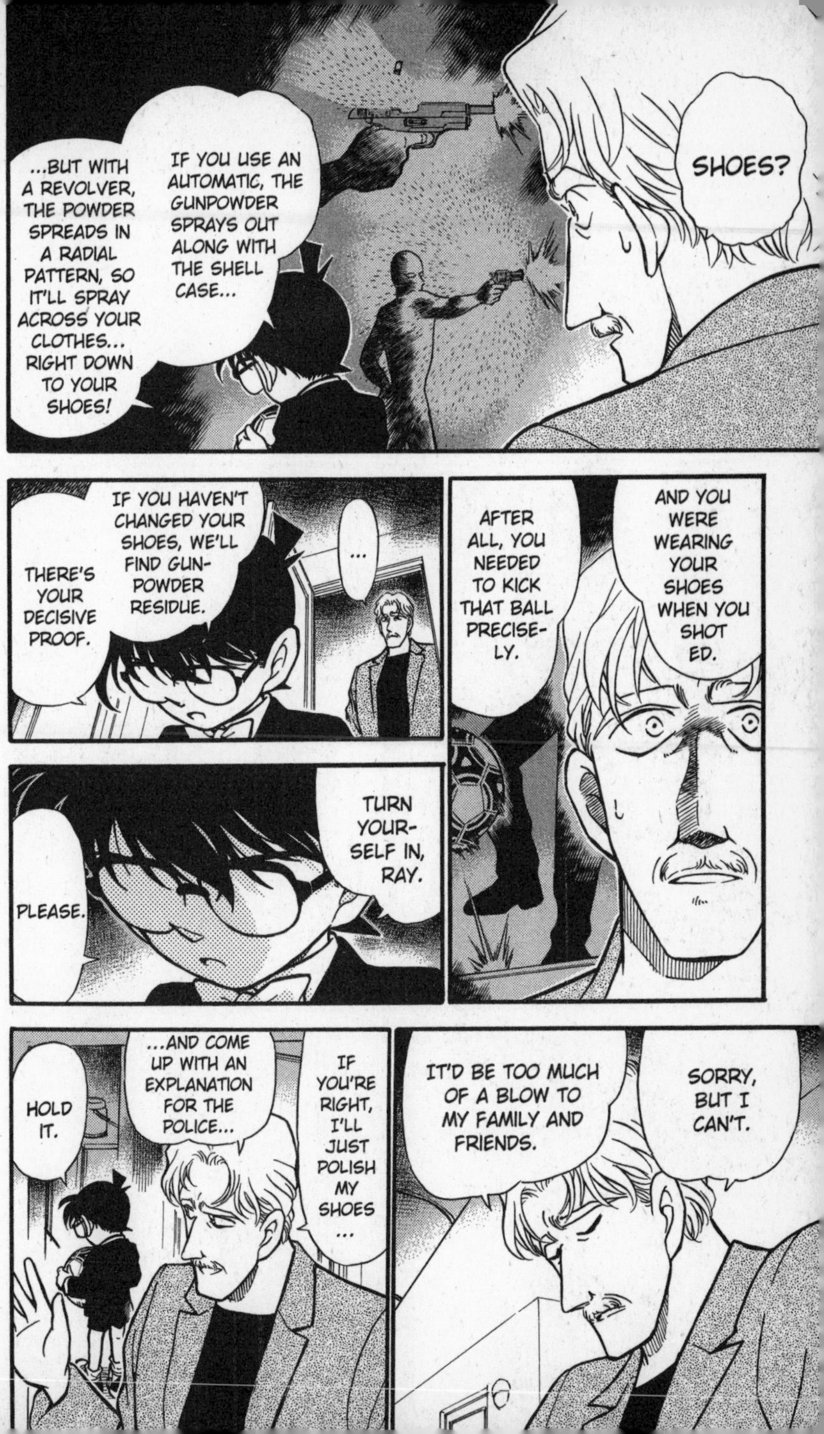
SHOES?
IF YOU USE AN AUTOMATIC, THE GUNPOWDER SPRAYS OUT ALONG WITH THE SHELL CASE...
...BUT WITH A REVOLVER, THE POWDER SPREADS IN A RADIAL PATTERN, SO IT'LL SPRAY ACROSS YOUR CLOTHES... RIGHT DOWN TO YOUR SHOES!
AND YOU WERE WEARING YOUR SHOES WHEN YOU SHOT ED.
AFTER ALL, YOU NEEDED TO KICK THAT BALL PRECISE-LY.
...
IF YOU HAVEN'T CHANGED YOUR SHOES, WE'LL FIND GUN-POWDER RESIDUE.
THERE'S YOUR DECISIVE PROOF.
TURN YOUR-SELF IN, RAY.
PLEASE.
SORRY, BUT I CAN'T.
IT'D BE TOO MUCH OF A BLOW TO MY FAMILY AND FRIENDS.
IF YOU'RE RIGHT, I'LL JUST POLISH MY SHOES...
...AND COME UP WITH AN EXPLANATION FOR THE POLICE...
HOLD IT.

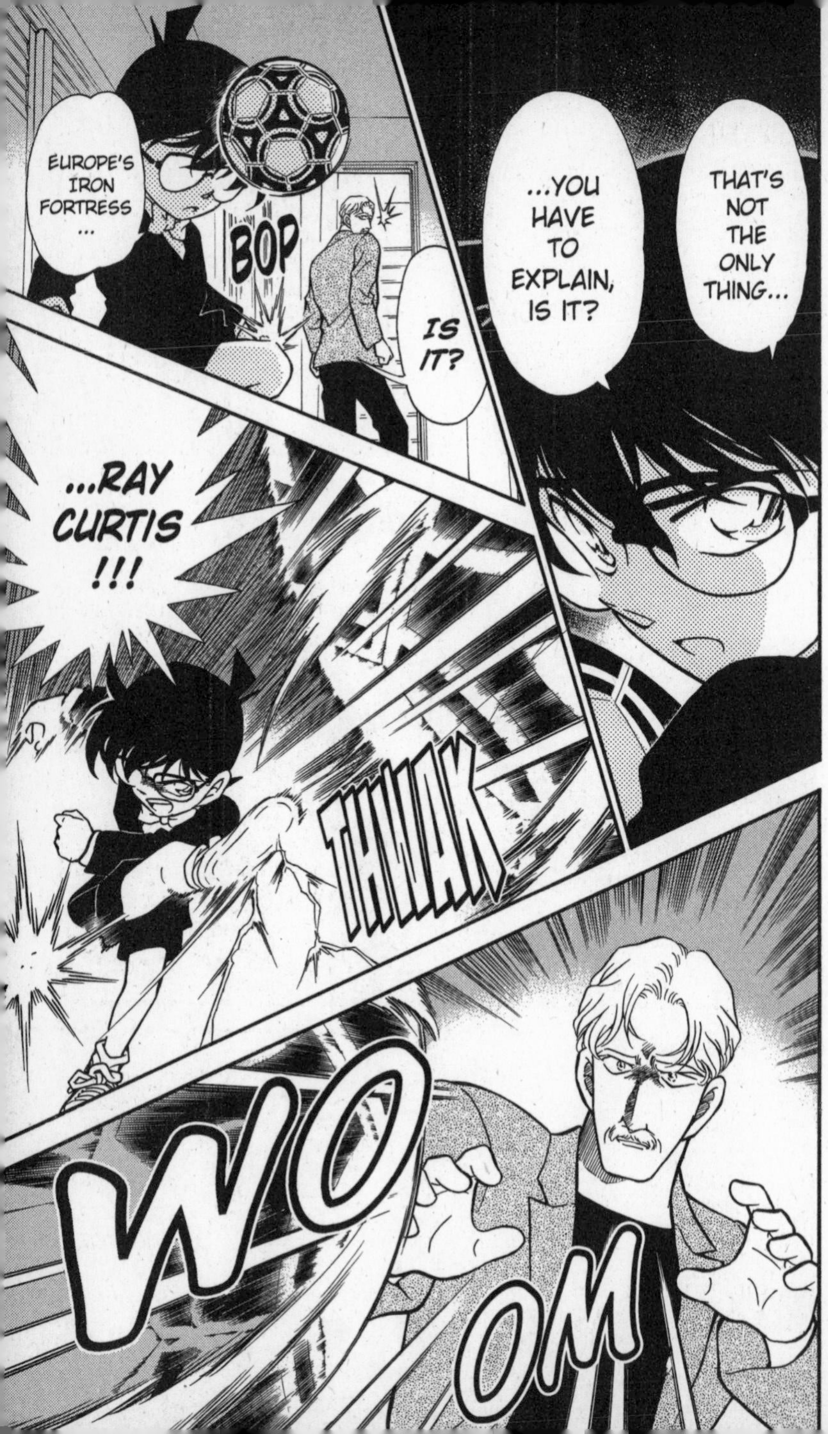
THAT'S NOT THE ONLY THING...
...YOU HAVE TO EXPLAIN, IS IT?
IS IT?
BOP
EUROPE'S IRON FORTRESS ...
...RAY CURTIS !!!
THWAK
WO
OM

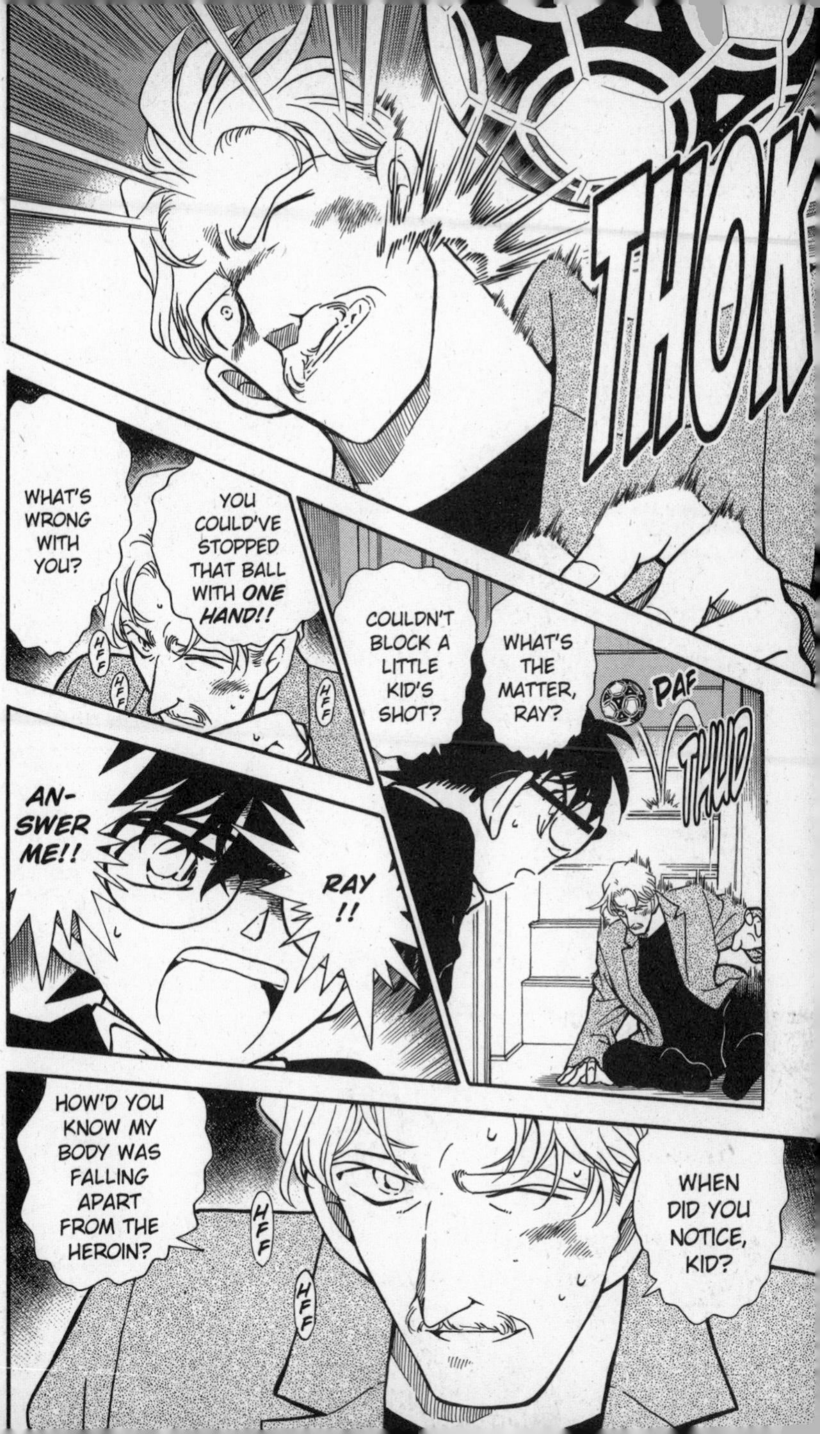
THONK
WHAT'S THE MATTER, RAY?
COULDN'T BLOCK A LITTLE KID'S SHOT?
PAF
THUD
YOU COULD'VE STOPPED THAT BALL WITH *ONE HAND!!*
WHAT'S WRONG WITH YOU?
HFF
HFF
HFF
RAY !!
AN-SWER ME!!
WHEN DID YOU NOTICE, KID?
HOW'D YOU KNOW MY BODY WAS FALLING APART FROM THE HEROIN?
HFF
HFF

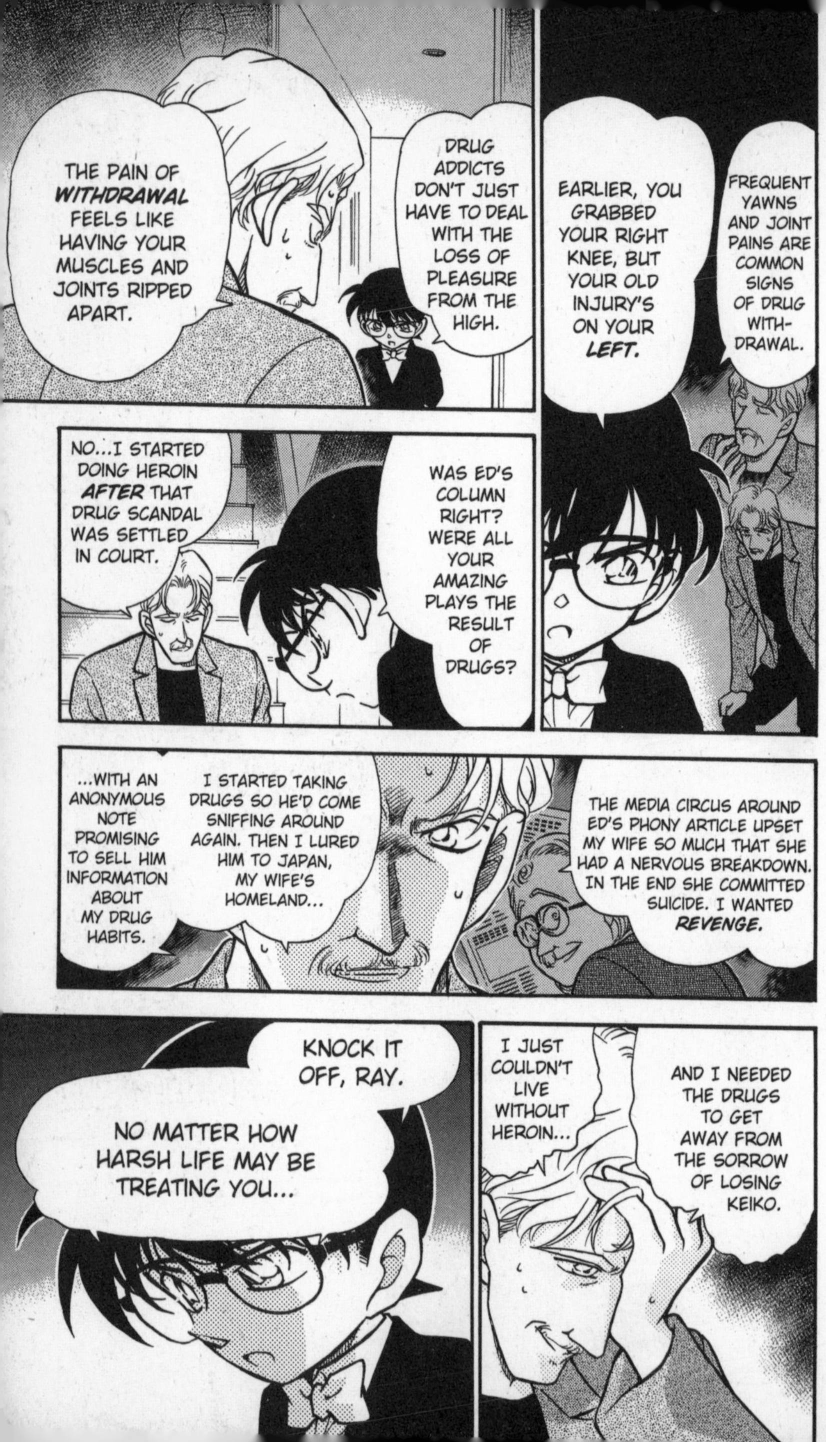
FREQUENT YAWNS AND JOINT PAINS ARE COMMON SIGNS OF DRUG WITH-DRAWAL.
EARLIER, YOU GRABBED YOUR RIGHT KNEE, BUT YOUR OLD INJURY'S ON YOUR LEFT.
DRUG ADDICTS DON'T JUST HAVE TO DEAL WITH THE LOSS OF PLEASURE FROM THE HIGH.
THE PAIN OF WITHDRAWAL FEELS LIKE HAVING YOUR MUSCLES AND JOINTS RIPPED APART.
WAS ED'S COLUMN RIGHT? WERE ALL YOUR AMAZING PLAYS THE RESULT OF DRUGS?
NO...I STARTED DOING HEROIN AFTER THAT DRUG SCANDAL WAS SETTLED IN COURT.
THE MEDIA CIRCUS AROUND ED'S PHONY ARTICLE UPSET MY WIFE SO MUCH THAT SHE HAD A NERVOUS BREAKDOWN. IN THE END SHE COMMITTED SUICIDE. I WANTED REVENGE.
I STARTED TAKING DRUGS SO HE'D COME SNIFFING AROUND AGAIN. THEN I LURED HIM TO JAPAN, MY WIFE'S HOMELAND...
...WITH AN ANONYMOUS NOTE PROMISING TO SELL HIM INFORMATION ABOUT MY DRUG HABITS.
I JUST COULDN'T LIVE WITHOUT HEROIN...
AND I NEEDED THE DRUGS TO GET AWAY FROM THE SORROW OF LOSING KEIKO.
KNOCK IT OFF, RAY.
NO MATTER HOW HARSH LIFE MAY BE TREATING YOU...

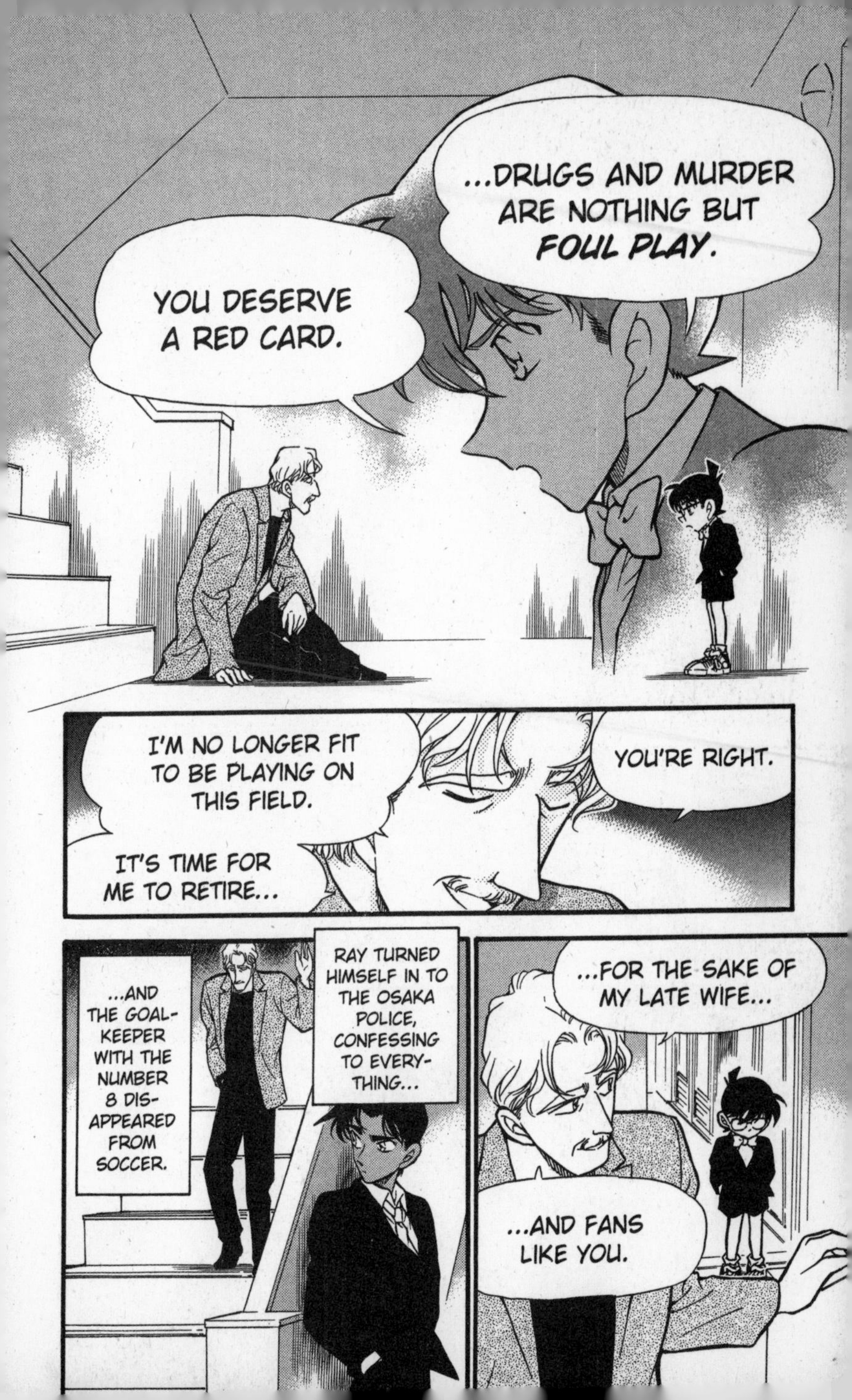
...DRUGS AND MURDER ARE NOTHING BUT FOUL PLAY.
YOU DESERVE A RED CARD.
YOU'RE RIGHT.
I'M NO LONGER FIT TO BE PLAYING ON THIS FIELD.
IT'S TIME FOR ME TO RETIRE...
...FOR THE SAKE OF MY LATE WIFE...
...AND FANS LIKE YOU.
RAY TURNED HIMSELF IN TO THE OSAKA POLICE, CONFESSING TO EVERY-THING...
...AND THE GOAL-KEEPER WITH THE NUMBER 8 DIS-APPEARED FROM SOCCER.

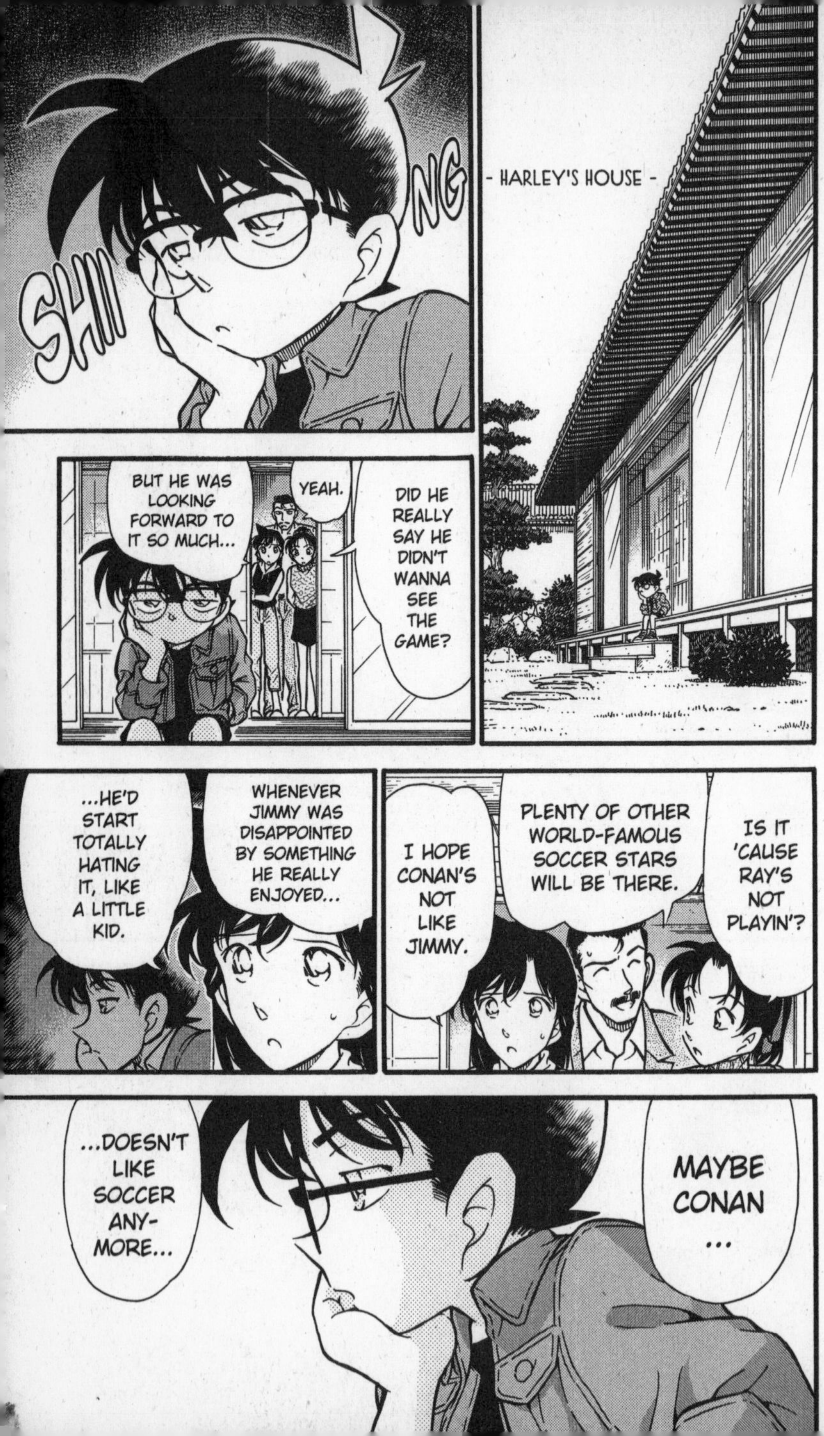
- HARLEY'S HOUSE -
SHIIING
DID HE REALLY SAY HE DIDN'T WANNA SEE THE GAME?
YEAH.
BUT HE WAS LOOKING FORWARD TO IT SO MUCH...
IS IT 'CAUSE RAY'S NOT PLAYIN'?
PLENTY OF OTHER WORLD-FAMOUS SOCCER STARS WILL BE THERE.
I HOPE CONAN'S NOT LIKE JIMMY.
WHENEVER JIMMY WAS DISAPPOINTED BY SOMETHING HE REALLY ENJOYED...
...HE'D START TOTALLY HATING IT, LIKE A LITTLE KID.
MAYBE CONAN ...
...DOESN'T LIKE SOCCER ANY-MORE...

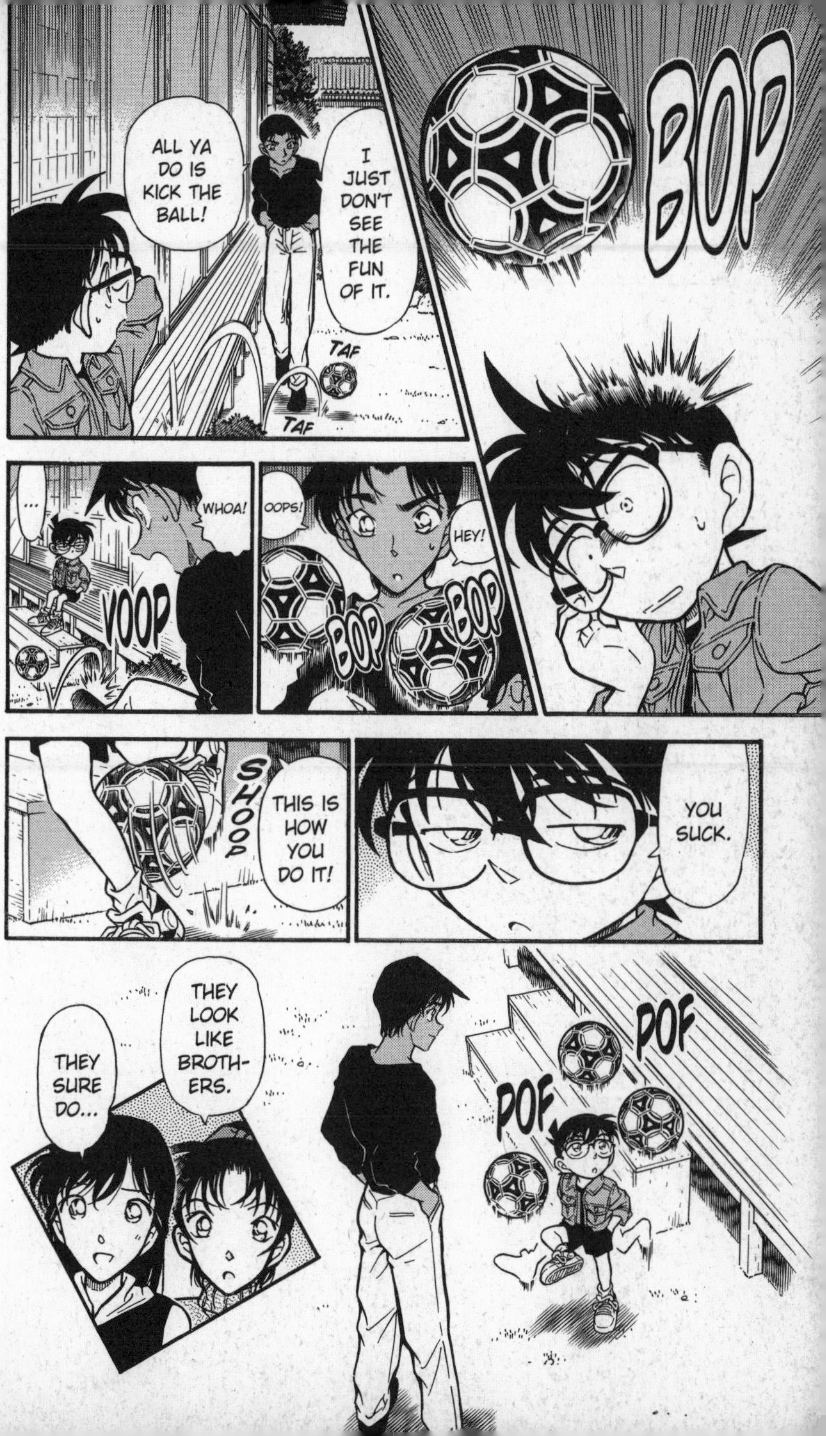
BOP
I JUST DON'T SEE THE FUN OF IT.
ALL YA DO IS KICK THE BALL!
TAF
TAF
HEY!
OOPS!
BOP
BOP
WHOA!
...
VOOP
YOU SUCK.
THIS IS HOW YOU DO IT!
SHOOOP
POF
POF
THEY LOOK LIKE BROTH-ERS.
THEY SURE DO...

Hello, Aoyama here.

My high school, Yuraikuei High, made it to the final preliminaries for Koshien! They were defeated in a very close match, but it was a great game! Wow!

If you guys ever make it all the way to Koshien, I'm definitely going down to cheer you on! Good luck in the future, Yura High!

*Editor's Note: Koshien, so called because it's held at Hanshin Koshien Stadium, is a nationwide high school baseball tournament. The Summer Koshien is the biggest amateur sports event in Japan.

Gosho Aoyama's
Mystery Library

29

CHARLIE CHAN

The image of a master sleuth tends to be a lonely, unmarried man, but Detective Charlie Chan, created by Earl Derr Biggers, has 14 children! The Chief Investigator of Hawaii's Honolulu Police Department, he lives with most of his family on Punchbowl Hill–his oldest daughter is studying abroad. He is not too tall, on the heavy side, and very modest and unassuming, often quoting Chinese idioms and aphorisms. At first glance he seems like an ordinary middle-aged man, but his sleepy eyes catch even the tiniest detail, and his discreet and patient investigations gradually drive the criminal into a corner. He's a great detective who deserves his nickname, "The Wisdom of the East." But he never fails to be modest, claiming, "He who is arrogant today will have nothing to be proud of tomorrow." I wish my Richard could learn a bit of his modesty...

I recommend *Charlie Chan Carries On*.